WORLDVIEW AND PHILOSOPHY
THROUGH THE LENS OF ECCLESIASTES

2nd Edition

Life Beyond the Sun: Worldview and Philosophy Through the Lens of Ecclesiastes, 2nd Edition
©2016 Christopher Cone
Exegetica Publishing, Ft. Worth, TX

ISBN – 978-0-9982805-0-9

All rights reserved. No part of this publication may be reproduced, stored in a retrieval system, or transmitted in any form or by any means – electronic, mechanical, photocopy, recording, or any other – except for brief quotation in printed reviews, without the prior permission of the publisher.

All Scripture quotations not from the King James Version are taken from the New American Standard Bible®, Copyright © 1960, 1962, 1963, 1968, 1971, 1972, 1973, 1975, 1977, 1995 by The Lockman Foundation. Used by permission. (www.Lockman.org)

Thank you my Precious Lord for your mercy to me. Thank you for allowing me to enjoy the richness of life with you. I pray this work is pleasing to You. May You use it for your glory.

Thank you my dearest Cat for your amazing love, selflessness, support...thank you for you....I rejoice in you, dear bride of my youth, and I love you forever.

Thank you my beloved daughters Christiana and Cara for your patience with me. I love you both dearly. I pray that the words herein may be of encouragement to you.

To the staff and faculty of Calvary University, Southern California Seminary, and Tyndale Theological Seminary: I thank you for your support, your inspiration, your diligence, and your love. I have been truly blessed to serve with each of you.

"Philosophy and science start with the bold confession of faith that not caprice but an inherent orderliness underlies the phenomena, and the explanation of nature is to be sought within nature itself…"

-W.K.C Guthrie, *History of Philosophy,* Vol I

"It is not that the methods and institutions of science somehow compel us to accept a material explanation of the phenomenological world, but on the contrary, that we are forced by our a priori adherence to material causes to create an apparatus of investigation and a set of concepts that produce material explanations, no matter how counter-intuitive, no matter how mystifying to the uninitiated. Moreover, that materialism is absolute, for we cannot allow a divine foot in the door."

-Richard Lewontin, *Billions and Billions of Demons*

"Remember also your Creator in the days of your youth, before the evil days come and the years draw near when you will say, 'I have no delight in them'"

-Qoheleth 12:1

Preface

This is perhaps a very odd sort of book. It is part introduction to Ecclesiastes and part introduction to philosophy – and perhaps a clumsy handling of the two at that. I beg the reader to grant me a charitable reading, as the intention here is not a detailed exegesis of the Book of Ecclesiastes, nor is it a thorough introduction to philosophy. The goal here is very simply to examine the Biblical worldview as broadly stated by Solomon. Consideration for the longstanding truth of his analysis will be given as I have taken some pains to address certain historical parallels to aspects of vain endeavor that Solomon decries. It is as if Solomon anticipates the worldly philosophies that would come after him. Certainly their seeds were planted long before his day, but I find it quite remarkable how directly his criticisms of godless endeavor can be applied to many great and historical pursuits. Thus I have sought to connect some of the ancient as well as more recent philosophical systems to those elements that Solomon condemns as without value.

While there must certainly be exegetical elements here, the text is handled here in a rather introductory manner – if the commentary here stood alone perhaps it could serve as a worthy introduction and overview of the book, like as one might expect from an Old Testament survey or introduction. Likewise, while there is some degree of systematic handling of the philosophical issues, I expect if these writings (the philosophical parts: the introductions, the essays, and the primary source excerpts) stood alone, they might only scratch the surface of what a worthy introduction to philosophy would attempt. But it is my hope that these two elements brought together will provide for the reader the following results:

(1) a very clear understanding of the universal vanity of any and all endeavor pursued outside of a right relationship to and perspective of God. The philosophical bits of this present work are intended to illustrate this quite distinctly.
(2) A very clear understanding of the tremendous value even in the most ordinary tasks of life (eating, drinking, labor, etc.) when they are pursued within the context of a right relationship to and perspective of God.

In short, I want to demonstrate Solomon's project by historical, if only very limited, example. Such a demonstration is intended as an aid for studying Ecclesiastes and as introduction to significant concepts of philosophy and worldview.

Also, I felt it appropriate that the entire text of Ecclesiastes be represented here, and for copyright reasons I have chosen to use the KJV primarily with complementary references to the NASB along with my own occasional translation. But I must also exhort the reader that study in the original languages is a must. Biblical exegesis can scarcely be accomplished in the English text alone, so the reader will observe an emphasis on key Hebrew words, syntax, and grammar from time to time. I hope that emphasis helps to increase your appreciation for Biblical Hebrew and might perhaps provide some impetus for your further study in this regard. I pray you enjoy the journey.

To God be the glory.

Table of Contents

Introduction..1

1:1-11 Vanity: Life Under the Sun..............................5
– Philosophical Parallel: Empiricism and Moral Sentiment
– Primary Source Excerpt: Hume: Enquiry on Human Understanding
– Primary Source Excerpt: Hume: A Treatise of Human Nature
– Philosophical Parallel: Existentialism
– Primary Source Excerpt: Nietzsche: The Madman

1:12-18 Vanity: The "Under the Sun" Quest for Wisdom.....29
– Excursus: The Rise of Philosophy and Conflict with Theology
– Philosophical Parallel: Basic Elements of Philosophy
– Primary Source Excerpt: Plato: The Euthyphro

2:1-11 Vanity: Good and Enjoyment Under the Sun..........70
– Philosophical Parallel: Virtue Ethics
– Primary Source Excerpt: Aristotle: Nicomachean Ethics

2:12-17 Vanity: Wisdom, Madness, and Folly Under the Sun..117
– Philosophical Parallel: Epistemological Grounding
  (Platonic Dualism, Cartesian Rationalism, Kantian Structuralism)
– Primary Source Excerpt: Plato: Allegory of the Cave
– Excursus: On Descartes' Discourse on the Method
– Primary Source Excerpt: Descartes: Meditation II
– Primary Source Excerpt: Kant: Critique of Pure Reason

2:18-23 Vanity: Labor and Consequence Under the Sun...161
– Philosophical Parallel: Utilitarianism
– Primary Source Excerpt: Bentham: An Introduction to the Principles of Morals and Legislation

2:24-26 Conclusion: God Is..171
– Philosophical Parallel: The Existence of God
  (culminating with Presuppositional Epistemology)
– Primary Source Excerpt: Anselm: Proslogion
– Primary Source Excerpt: Aquinas: The Five Ways
– Primary Source Excerpt: Russell: Why I Am Not a Christian

3:1-10 Conclusion: God Has Ordered the Universe................203
– Excursus: The Philosophical and Theological Compatibility of Mechanistic Evolution and an Ordered Universe

3:11-22 Conclusion: God Has a "Beyond the Sun" Program For Man..219
– Excursus: Environmental Ethics: The Spirit of Man and Intrinsic Value

4:1-3 Vanity: Life and Oppression Under the Sun..................237
– Philosophical Parallel: Marxism
– Primary Source Excerpt: Marx and Engels: A Communist Manifesto
– Excursus: Introductory Survey of the Problem of Evil

4:4-6 Vanity: Survival and Rivalry Under the Sun..............287
– Philosophical Parallel: Social Contract
– Primary Source Excerpt: Hobbes: The Leviathan

4:7-12 Vanity: Egocentrism and Aloneness Under the Sun...299
– Philosophical Parallel: Ethical Egoism

4:13-16 Vanity: Foolishness Under the Sun...........................301
– Philosophical Parallel: Will to Power
– Excursus: On the Will to Power: Nietzsche's Pedigree

5:1-20 Conclusion: Fear God and Enjoy His Gifts..................315
– Philosophical Parallel: Consensual Democracy
– Primary Source Excerpt: Locke: The Second Treatise on Civil Government

6:1-12 Vanity: Riches, Wealth, and Honor Under the Sun....329
– Excursus: Postmodernism and Globalism

7:1-8:17 Conclusion: Well-Being Comes Through "Beyond the Sun" Perspective...347
– Philosophical Parallel: Piety and Moral Theory of Obligation
– Primary Source Excerpt: Kant: Fundamental Principles of the Metaphysics of Morals

9:1-10 Conclusion: The Urgency of Life Under the Sun........379

9:11-10:19 Conclusion: The Apparatus for Life Under the Sun: Wisdom >Strength..383
– Philosophical Parallel: Platonic Aristocracy

10:20-11:8 Conclusion: Apply Wisdom Under the Sun.........391

11:9-10 Conclusion: Enjoy Life with A "Beyond the Sun" Perspective...395
– Excursus: Lucretian Atomism

12:1-7 Conclusion: Remember Your Creator.....................399
– Excursus: Contrasting Hume's Naturalistic Viewpoint with Calvin's Innate Awareness of Deity

12:8-14 Conclusion: Life with God Is Not Vanity................415
– Excursus: The Commandments Of Jesus: The Ethics of the Gospels

Notes and Bibliography..443

Introduction[1]

The Hebrew title is *Qoheleth*, for the preacher who identifies himself as the author in 1:1, saying:

> The words of the preacher, the son of David, king in Jerusalem.

The English title Ecclesiastes comes from the Greek word *ekklesia* meaning to assemble, and referring to the preacher's function which Solomon performed in I Kings 8:1 (for example).

While the statement of authorship seems quite self-explanatory, it is not without difficulty.

Due to the presence of Aramaic and even Persian linguistic characteristics within Qoheleth, some suggest a very late date of writing, and consequently challenge Solomonic authorship. These criticisms do not seem, however, to consider the possibility that the manuscripts we now possess today could have been copied and even translated to and from Aramaic back into Hebrew during the Exilic or Post-Exilic periods. In any case, the claim for authorship requires the author to have been a king in Jerusalem, which, if not referring directly to Solomon, then it would have been referring to a descendant of David who ruled in Jerusalem, and could have been no later than 586 BC, a date which would not have allowed for the Persian or Aramaic influences.

It is suggested here, in agreement with Jewish tradition, that Solomon indeed did author the book during the latter part of his life, no later than around 950-935 BC.

Content

Probably the single most important textual factor is the repeating of the phrase *under the sun*, which occurs nearly thirty times within the book. The phrase emphasizes an earth-centered perspective, and provides the scope for his blistering critique of all things considered apart from a proper perspective of and relationship to God: "Vanity of vanities! All is vanity." (1:2) Solomon takes his readers (his son, in particular, see 12:1) on a journey of his earlier investigations (note his use of the Hebrew perfect denoting completed action, i.e., the past tense) in which he discovered and verified the emptiness of every pursuit in life under the sun and that without eternal perspective, life is meaningless (note his use of the Hebrew imperfect denoting incomplete action, i.e., the present tense).

His thesis is twofold: (1) the hopelessness and emptiness of life without God (under the sun), and (2) the meaningfulness of even the most ordinary acts (eating, drinking, labor, etc.) when one enjoys the proper perspective of and relationship to God (a particular kind of *beyond the sun* worldview):

> The conclusion, when all has been heard, is: fear God and keep His commandments, because this applies to every person. For God will bring every act to judgment, everything which is hidden, whether it is good or evil. (12:13-14)

Historically man has sought to be free of accountability and responsibility by avoiding acknowledgment of his Creator – and has used many devices to do so. Solomon exposes these devices, demonstrating their ineptitude at answering the major question of meaning in life. The ways of humanity without God are empty, foolish, and fruitless. The wisest man who ever lived would have us understand our role in the Creator's wondrous plan – we are to possess the proper perspective of Him and we are to relate rightly to Him. Only in doing so can we truly appreciate the blessings He has prepared for us. Only then can we understand His design and provision for our rich and meaningful lives. So the journey begins...

1:1-11 Vanity: Life Under the Sun

[1] The words of the Preacher, the son of David, king in Jerusalem.

The authorship claim is quite clear. Also note 1:12 – the author was King of Israel (all Israel, while it was still united) in Jerusalem – as only three men were: Saul, David, and Solomon and only one of them could be described as son of David.

Qoheleth - preacher. The writer is preaching a message of right perspective of and relationship to God.

[2] Vanity of vanities, saith the Preacher, vanity of vanities; all is vanity.

Vanity – *hebel* – is an oft repeated term in the book (37 times) and references a breath or vapor and denotes primarily emptiness and meaninglessness. He paints with a broad and comprehensive brush – nothing escapes his criticism here, thus it is critical to understand the scope of his claim (all done under the sun is vanity). Here it is *hebel hebelim,* an emphatic repetition – vanity of vanities. All, literally the whole, is vanities. Five appearances of a term in one verse is indicative of a very important role for the word.

[3] What profit hath a man of all his labour which he taketh

under the sun?

Profit – *yithron* – gain, profit, excellence, or advantage (NASB).

Under the Sun – *tachath hashemesh* – below or at the bottom of the brilliance of the sun. This is a crucial phrase as it provides the scope of Solomon's indictment: everything under the sun will be shown to be vanity. Thus if there is any profit or advantage for man, he must go beyond the sun. He must not operate from a naturalistic perspective.

[4] One generation passeth away, and another generation cometh: but the earth abideth forever.

The cycle of life continues but yet the earth remains. Thus significance is not to be found in an individual's life – it is fleeting, passing quickly. And another springs up in his place. Yet the earth remains. The term *olam* is translated forever by both the KJV and NASB, yet it can also have the meaning of always or continually. Solomon is not asserting here an eternal cosmos, but rather emphasizing that if there is to be found any lasting meaning it cannot be anthropocentric.

[5] The sun also ariseth, and the sun goeth down, and hasteth to his place where he arose.

Again, the cycle of life and seasons continues. Note the earthly perspective of sunrise and sunset. Also, lest anyone mistake this as a flawed attempt at a scientific statement, representing an earth-centered cosmos, let the reader take note of the present day usage of sunrise and sunset. We speak in this manner due to perspective not precision.

[6] The wind goeth toward the south, and turneth about unto the north; it whirleth about continually, and the wind returneth again according to his circuits.

Yet another element of cyclical motion. The winds operate as if programmed – as if designed. This would not be emblematic of meaninglessness, yet all is vanity nonetheless. In Solomon's description of these natural cycles he is giving hints of what is to come: there is a Designer who gives meaning. Apart from Him, there can be found none.

[7] All the rivers run into the sea; yet the sea is not full; unto the place from whence the rivers come, thither they return again.

More cycles...more systematic process of the earth with no consideration for the brevity of human life. The rivers and the seas don't care. They continue on as designed.

The precision of these cycles is notable. Randomness is certainly not in play here. Such cycles cannot arise accidentally.

[8] All things are full of labour; man cannot utter it: the eye is not satisfied with seeing, nor the ear filled with hearing.

Labour – *yagea* – tired or tiresome. Not the same word used in v. 3 (*amal* – work in the NASB). All things are tiresome. Man can't even communicate (*davar*) it. He is not filled (*saba*) with seeing or filled (*mala*) with hearing. Sensory experience leaves much to be desired.

Hume's brand of empiricism (that certain knowledge can be gained only through experience) is undermined here. Solomon asserts that experience is necessarily limited and the senses can fail.

Philosophical Parallel: Empiricism and Moral Sentiment

Epistemology is the study of knowledge and asks the question "how can we know?" An epistemology is the first basic element in philosophy that must be encountered. Before one can begin inquiry he must first accept a set of ground rules. He must adopt a system whereby he can accept certain propositions and reject others. He must accept first principles upon which he will build. On what grounds does the interlocutor accept the ground rules? The "F" word: faith. Whether atheistic or theistic, all must begin with faith. David Hume is no exception.

David Hume (1711-1776) is noted for his radical skepticism and contempt for religion. He developed strong (although not strong enough) arguments against the existence of God and existence of the metaphysical in general. His metaphysical presupposition (that there is no God and nothing beyond the natural) led quite naturally to his particular brand of empiricism. He argued against dualism of knowledge (higher and lower) and held to two basic forms of perceptions: (1) impressions – having the greatest force, and (2) thoughts or ideas – having lesser force (including recollection, as a lesser copy of the original impression). In order to do away with a priori knowledge (knowledge from before, which if it exists implies that someone had to put it there – this is a premise Hume cannot accept) he de-emphasized originality, saying that the creative power of the mind is simply manipulating materials via sense and experience. His starting point was a metaphysical presupposition against the existence of God. His conclusion? God cannot be experienced or empirically justified. His existence must then be dismissed. (Note how Hume is drawing his conclusion from his first principles.)

Hume, seeking to scientify philosophy, developed laws of association:

1. resemblance – ideas similar tend to be associated with one another
2. contiguity – ideas that appear closely together in time and space are oftentimes connected (e.g., Hume's apartment building)
3. cause and effect – when one event follows another in regular fashion, three elements of causality are implied:
   a. contiguity (see previous)
   b. priority in time – cause happens first
   c. necessary connection – it is here that Hume is most critical, suggesting that such connection cannot be experienced, and while there is connection, there is only feelings of compulsion, not true cause and effect outside of the imagination.

He argues these come from imagination not reason, and that there is no necessary connection, and thus Hume criticizes causality, thus diminishing cause and effect as a reality. The ramifications of this turn are significant: if cause and effect is established, then one must deal with the necessity of a first efficient cause. By eliminating cause and effect and characterizing it as simply relational, this necessity vanishes.

While Hume is adamant in his opposition to the existence of God and in his reliance on sensory experience as the means to certain knowledge, he is at times very troubled at the outcome of his pursuits:

> The *intense* view of these manifold contradictions and imperfections in human reason has so wrought upon me, and heated my brain, that I am ready to reject all belief and reasoning, and can look upon no opinion even as more probable or likely than another. Where am I, or what?

> From what causes do I derive my existence, and to what condition shall I return? Whose favour shall I court, and whose anger must I dread? What beings surround me? and on whom have I any influence, or who have any influence on me? I am confounded with all these questions, and begin to fancy myself in the most deplorable condition imaginable, invironed with the deepest darkness, and utterly deprived of the use of every member and faculty.[2]

This statement seems to reflect exactly the kind of attitude Solomon might expect from his observations in 1:8.

This is not to say that empiricism as an epistemology is adopted strictly in an atheistic worldview, as empiricists John Locke (1632-1704) and George Berkeley (1685-1753) both held to theistic ideas.

Locke pondered the source of ideas, asserting that children were born with a *tabula rasa* (Latin, blank tablet) – a blank mind with no a priori ideas. Locke understood there to be two kinds of experience: (1) sensation – ideas of the external world (color, heat, taste, etc.) and (2) reflection – ideas of the mind (perception, thinking, doubting, etc.). Emerging from this was his view of two kinds of ideas: (1) simple ideas – from simple sensations, and (2) complex ideas – can be broken down into simple ones. Locke rejected innate ideas, consistent with his *tabula rasa* concept, and identified two qualities whereby sensations are experienced: (1) primary qualities – figure, solidity, extension, motion, number – qualities inherent in objects, and (2) secondary qualities – taste, color, smell, texture – qualities that belong to the perceiver.

George Berkeley rejected the idea of primary qualities, asserting that all qualities belong to the perceiver (*Esse est Percipe* - to be is to be perceived). Experience therefore identifies reality. Interestingly, he held that God was the perpetual perceiver, and thus all things are relative to the Absolute.

Locke's and Berkeley's brands of empiricism, while not atheistic, still do not square with Solomon's epistemology put forth in Proverbs 1:7 and 9:10 and which begins *with* God and builds a framework of knowledge *from* Him rather than arguing to Him. Recall David's introduction to Psalm 14 – "The fool has said in his heart, there is no God." Beginning with the non-existence of God and working toward His existence is, according to the Psalmist and his son, foolishness. Not exactly a desired moniker for epistemological pursuit.

From Hume's epistemological grounding emerges his ethical construct of moral sentiments (Adam Smith was also very influential on this topic). Observing the challenging *is / ought problem* (whether prescriptive statements can come from descriptive statements) he concluded that reason does not enable action, but rather sentiment does. Sentiment governs reason, yet is reasonable in that sentiment only conflicts with reason under two conditions: (1) if sentiment is based on belief in something that is nonexistent (God), or (2) if from sentiment the wrong instrument is chosen to achieve the ends.

As it can be said that beauty is in the eye of the beholder, so, for Hume, is morality. He distinguishes between three parties involved in a moral perception: (1) the agent – who does the action, (2) the receiver – the one acted upon, and (3) the spectator – the one who makes the moral discernment based upon the sentiment the action creates in him.

Hume concludes that there are four irreducible categories of qualities that constitute moral virtue: (1) qualities useful to others, which include benevolence, meekness, charity, justice, fidelity and veracity; (2) qualities useful to oneself, which include industry, perseverance, and patience; (3) qualities immediately agreeable to others, which include wit, eloquence and cleanliness; and (4) qualities immediately agreeable to oneself, which include good humor, self-esteem and pride. Thus for Hume, key moral values are societal inventions.

Primary Source Excerpt: Hume: An Enquiry Concerning Human Understanding (1748)

Section II: Of the Origin of Ideas
Everyone will readily allow, that there is a considerable difference between the perceptions of the mind, when a man feels the pain of excessive heat, or the pleasure of moderate warmth, and when he afterwards recalls to his memory this sensation, or anticipates it by his imagination. These faculties may mimic or copy the perceptions of the senses; but they never can entirely reach the force and vivacity of the original sentiment. The utmost we say of them, even when they operate with greatest vigour, is, that they represent their object in so lively a manner, that we could almost say we feel or see it: But, except the mind be disordered by disease or madness, they never can arrive at such a pitch of vivacity, as to render these perceptions altogether undistinguishable. All the colours of poetry, however splendid, can never paint natural objects in such a manner as to make the description be taken for a real landskip. The most lively thought is still inferior to the dullest sensation.

We may observe a like distinction to run through all the other perceptions of the mind. A man in a fit of anger, is actuated in a very different manner from one who only thinks of that emotion. If you tell me, that any person is in love, I easily understand your meaning, and from a just conception of his situation; but never can mistake that conception for the real disorders and agitations of the passion. When we reflect on our past sentiments and affections, our thought is a faithful mirror, and copies its objects truly; but the colours which it employs are faint and dull, in comparison of those in which our original perceptions were clothed. It requires no nice discernment or metaphysical head to mark the distinction between them.

Here therefore we may divide all the perceptions of the mind into two classes or species, which are distinguished by their different degrees of force and vivacity. The less forcible and lively are commonly denominated Thoughts or Ideas. The other species want a name in our language, and in most others; I suppose, because it was not requisite for any, but philosophical purposes, to rank them under a general term or appellation. Let us, therefore, use a little freedom, and call them Impressions; employing that word in a sense somewhat different from the usual. By the term impression, then, I mean all our more lively perceptions, when we hear, or see, or feel, or love, or hate, or desire, or will. And impressions are distinguished from ideas, which are the less lively perceptions, of which we are conscious, when we reflect on any of those sensations or movements above mentioned.

Nothing, at first view, may seem more unbounded than the thought of man, which not only escapes all human power and authority, but is not even restrained within the limits of nature and reality. To form monsters, and join incongruous shapes and appearances, costs the imagination no more trouble than to conceive the most natural and familiar objects. And while the body is confined to one planet, along which it creeps with pain and difficulty; the thought can in an instant transport us into the most distant regions of the universe; or even beyond the universe, into the unbounded chaos, where nature is supposed to lie in total confusion. What never was seen, or heard of, may yet be conceived; nor is anything beyond the power of thought, except what implies an absolute contradiction.

But though our thought seems to possess this unbounded

liberty, we shall find, upon a nearer examination, that it is really confined within very narrow limits, and that all this creative power of the mind amounts to no more than the faculty of compounding, transposing, augmenting, or diminishing the materials afforded us by the senses and experience. When we think of a golden mountain, we only join two consistent ideas, gold, and mountain, with which we were formerly acquainted. A virtuous horse we can conceive; because, from our own feeling, we can conceive virtue; and this we may unite to the figure and shape of a horse, which is an animal familiar to us. In short, all the materials of thinking are derived either from our outward or inward sentiment: the mixture and composition of these belongs alone to the mind and will. Or, to express myself in philosophical language, all our ideas or more feeble perceptions are copies of our impressions or more lively ones.

To prove this, the two following arguments will, I hope, be sufficient. First, when we analyze our thoughts or ideas, however compounded or sublime, we always find that they resolve themselves into such simple ideas as were copied from a precedent feeling or sentiment. Even those ideas, which, at first view, seem the most wide of this origin, are found, upon a nearer scrutiny, to be derived from it. The idea of God, as meaning an infinitely intelligent, wise, and good Being, arises from reflecting on the operations of our own mind, and augmenting, without limit, those qualities of goodness and wisdom. We may prosecute this enquiry to what length we please; where we shall always find, that every idea which we examine is copied from a similar impression. Those who would assert that this position is not universally true nor without exception, have only one, and that an easy method of refuting it; by producing that idea, which, in their opinion, is not derived from this source. It will then be incumbent on us, if we would maintain our doctrine, to produce the impression, or lively perception, which corresponds to it.

Secondly. If it happen, from a defect of the organ, that a man is not susceptible of any species of sensation, we always find that he is as little susceptible of the correspondent ideas. A blind man can form no notion of colours; a deaf man of sounds. Restore either of them that sense in which he is deficient; by opening this new inlet for his sensations, you also open an inlet for the ideas; and he finds no difficulty in conceiving these objects. The case is the same, if the object, proper for exciting any sensation, has never been applied to the organ. A Laplander or Negro has no notion of the relish of wine. And though there are few or no instances of a like deficiency in the mind, where a person has never felt or is wholly incapable of a sentiment or passion that belongs to his species; yet we find the same observation to take place in a less degree. A man of mild manners can form no idea of inveterate revenge or cruelty; nor can a selfish heart easily conceive the heights of friendship and generosity. It is readily allowed, that other beings may possess many senses of which we can have no conception; because the ideas of them have never been introduced to us in the only manner by which an idea can have access to the mind, to wit, by the actual feeling and sensation.

There is, however, one contradictory phenomenon, which may prove that it is not absolutely impossible for ideas to arise, independent of their correspondent impressions. I believe it will readily be allowed, that the several distinct ideas of colour, which enter by the eye, or those of sound, which are conveyed by the ear, are really different from each other; though, at the same time, resembling. Now if this be true of different colours, it must be no less so of the different shades of the same colour; and each shade produces a distinct idea, independent of the rest. For if this should be denied, it is possible, by the continual gradation of shades, to run a colour insensibly into what is most remote from it; and if you will not allow any of the means to be different, you cannot, without absurdity, deny the extremes to be the same. Suppose, therefore, a person to have enjoyed his sight for thirty years, and to have become perfectly acquainted with colours of all kinds except one particular shade of blue, for instance, which it never has been his fortune to meet with. Let all the different shades of that colour, except that single one, be placed before him, descending gradually from the deepest to the lightest; it is plain that he will perceive a blank, where that shade is wanting, and will be sensible that there is a greater distance in that place between the contiguous colour than in any other. Now I ask, whether it be possible for him, from his own imagination, to supply this deficiency, and raise up to himself the idea of that particular shade, though it had never been conveyed to him by his senses? I believe there are few but will be of opinion that he can: and this may serve as a proof that the simple ideas are not always, in every instance, derived from the correspondent impressions; though this instance is so singular, that it is scarcely worth our observing, and does not merit that for it alone we should alter our general maxim.

Here, therefore, is a proposition, which not only seems, in itself, simple and intelligible; but, if a proper use were made of it, might render every dispute equally intelligible, and banish all that jargon, which has so long taken possession of metaphysical reasonings, and drawn disgrace upon them. All ideas, especially abstract ones, are naturally faint and obscure: the mind has but a slender hold of them: they are apt to be confounded with other resembling ideas; and when we have often employed any term, though without a distinct meaning, we are apt to imagine it has a determinate idea annexed to it. On the contrary, all impressions, that is, all sensations, either outward or inward, are strong and vivid: the limits between them are more exactly determined: nor is it easy to fall into any error or mistake with regard to them. When we entertain, therefore, any suspicion that a philosophical term is employed without any meaning or idea (as is but too frequent), we need but enquire, from what impression is that supposed idea derived? And if it be impossible to assign any, this will serve to confirm our suspicion. By bringing ideas into so clear a light we may reasonably hope to remove all dispute, which may arise, concerning their nature and reality.

Section X: On Miracles
...A miracle is a violation of the laws of nature; and as a firm and unalterable experience has established these laws, the proof against a miracle, from the very nature of the fact, is as entire as any argument from experience can possibly be imagined. Why is it more than probable, that all men must die; that lead cannot, of itself, remain suspended in the air; that fire consumes wood, and is extinguished by water; unless it be, that these events are found agreeable to the laws of nature, and there is required a violation of these laws, or in other words, a miracle to prevent them? Nothing is esteemed a miracle, if it ever happen in the common course of nature. It is no miracle that a man, seemingly in good health, should die on a sudden: because such a kind of death, though more unusual than any other, has yet been frequently observed to happen. But it is a miracle, that a dead man should come to life; because that has never been observed in any age or country. There must, therefore, be a uniform experience against every miraculous event, otherwise the event would not merit that appellation. And as a uniform experience amounts to a proof, there is here a direct and full proof, from the nature of the fact, against the existence of any miracle; nor can such a proof be destroyed, or the miracle rendered credible, but by an opposite proof, which is superior.

The plain consequence is (and it is a general maxim

worthy of our attention), 'that no testimony is sufficient to establish a miracle, unless the testimony be of such a kind, that its falsehood would be more miraculous, than the fact, which it endeavors to establish; and even in that case there is a mutual destruction of arguments, and the superior only gives us an assurance suitable to that degree of force, which remains, after deducting the inferior.' When anyone tells me, that he saw a dead man restored to life, I immediately consider with myself, whether it be more probable, that this person should either deceive or be deceived, or that the fact, which he relates, should really have happened. I weigh the one miracle against the other; and according to the superiority, which I discover, I pronounce my decision, and always reject the greater miracle. If the falsehood of his testimony would be more miraculous, than the event which he relates; then, and not till then, can he pretend to command my belief or opinion.

Primary Source Excerpt: Hume: A Treatise of Human Nature (1739-1740)

Book III, Part I, Sect. II

Moral distinctions deriv'd from a moral sense
Thus the course of the argument leads us to conclude, that since vice and virtue are not discoverable merely by reason, or the comparison of ideas, it must be by means of some impression or sentiment they occasion, that we are able to mark the difference betwixt them. Our decisions concerning moral rectitude and depravity are evidently perceptions; and as all perceptions are either impressions or ideas, the exclusion of the one is a convincing argument for the other. Morality, therefore, is more properly felt than judg'd of; tho' this feeling or sentiment is commonly so soft and gentle, that we are apt to confound it with

an idea, according to our common custom of taking all things for the same, which have any near resemblance to each other.

The next question is, Of what nature are these impressions, and after what manner do they operate upon us? Here we cannot remain long in suspense, but must pronounce the impression arising from virtue, to be agreeable, and that proceeding from vice to be uneasy. Every moments experience must convince us of this. There is no spectacle so fair and beautiful as a noble and generous action; nor any which gives us more abhorrence than one that is cruel and treacherous. No enjoyment. equals the satisfaction we receive from the company of those we love and esteem; as the greatest of all punishments is to be oblig'd to pass our lives with those we hate or contemn. A very play or romance may afford us instances of this pleasure, which virtue conveys to us; and pain, which arises from vice.

Now since the distinguishing impressions, by which moral good or evil is known, are nothing but particular pains or pleasures; it follows, that in all enquiries concerning these moral distinctions, it will be sufficient to shew the principles, which make us feel a satisfaction or uneasiness from the survey of any character, in order to satisfy us why the character is laudable or blameable. An action, or sentiment, or character is virtuous or vicious; why? because its view causes a pleasure or uneasiness of a particular kind. In giving a reason, therefore, for the pleasure or uneasiness, we sufficiently explain the vice or virtue. To have the sense of virtue, is nothing but to feel a satisfaction of a particular kind from the contemplation of a character. The very feeling constitutes our praise or admiration. We go no farther; nor do we enquire into the cause of the satisfaction. We do not infer a character to be virtuous, because it pleases: But in feeling that it pleases after such a particular manner, we in effect feel that it is virtuous. The case is the same as in our judgments concerning all kinds of beauty, and tastes, and sensations. Our approbation is imply'd in the immediate pleasure they convey to us.

I have objected to the system, which establishes eternal rational measures of right and wrong, that 'tis impossible to shew, in the actions of reasonable creatures, any relations, which are not found in external objects; and therefore, if morality always attended these relations, 'twere possible for inanimate matter to become virtuous or vicious. Now it may, in like manner, be objected to the present system, that if virtue and vice be determin'd by pleasure and pain, these qualities must, in every case, arise from the sensations; and consequently any object, whether animate or inanimate, rational or irrational, might become morally good or evil, provided it can excite a satisfaction or uneasiness. But tho' this objection seems to be the very same, it has by no means the same force, in the one case as in the other. For, first, 'tis evident, that under the term pleasure, we comprehend sensations, which are very different from each other, and which have only such a distant resemblance, as is requisite to make them be express'd by the same abstract term. A good composition of music and a bottle of good wine equally produce pleasure; and what is more, their goodness is determin'd merely by the pleasure. But shall we say upon that account, that the wine is harmonious, or the music of a good flavour? In like manner an inanimate object, and the character or sentiments of any person may, both of them, give satisfaction; but as the satisfaction is different, this keeps our sentiments concerning them from being confounded, and makes us ascribe virtue to the one, and not to the other. Nor is every sentiment of pleasure or pain, which arises from characters and actions, of that peculiar kind, which makes us praise or condemn. The good qualities of an enemy are hurtful to us; but may still command our esteem and respect. 'Tis only when a character is considered in general, without reference to our particular interest, that it causes such a feeling or sentiment, as denominates it morally good or evil. 'Tis true, those sentiments, from interest and morals, are apt to be confounded, and naturally run into one another. It seldom happens, that we do not think an enemy vicious, and can distinguish betwixt his opposition to our interest and real villainy or baseness. But this hinders not, but that the sentiments are, in themselves, distinct; and a man of temper and judgment may preserve himself from these illusions. In like manner, tho' 'tis certain a musical voice is nothing but one that naturally gives a particular kind of pleasure; yet 'tis difficult for a man to be sensible, that the voice of an enemy is agreeable, or to allow it to be musical. But a person of a fine ear, who has the command of himself, can separate these feelings, and give praise to what deserves it.

Secondly, We may call to remembrance the preceding system of the passions, in order to remark a still more considerable difference among our pains and pleasures. Pride and humility, love and hatred are excited, when there is anything presented to us, that both bears a relation to the object of the passion, and produces a separate sensation related to the sensation of the passion. Now virtue and vice are attended with these circumstances. They must necessarily be plac'd either in ourselves or others, and excite either pleasure or uneasiness; and therefore must give rise to one of these four passions; which clearly distinguishes them from the pleasure and pain arising from inanimate objects, that often bear no relation to us: And this is, perhaps, the most considerable effect that virtue and vice have upon the human mind.

It may now be ask'd in general, concerning this pain or pleasure, that distinguishes moral good and evil, *From what principles is it derived, and whence does it arise in the human mind?* To this I reply, first, that 'tis absurd to imagine, that in every particular instance, these sentiments are produc'd by an original quality and primary constitution. For as the number of our duties is, in a manner, infinite, 'tis impossible that our original instincts should extend to each of them, and from our very first infancy impress on the human mind all that multitude of precepts, which are contain'd in the compleatest system of ethics. Such a method of proceeding is not conformable to the usual maxims, by which nature is conducted, where a few principles produce all that variety we observe in the universe, and everything is carry'd on in the easiest and most simple manner. 'Tis necessary, therefore, to abridge these primary impulses, and find some more general principles, upon which all our notions of morals are founded.

But in the second place, should it be ask'd, Whether we ought to search for these principles in nature, or whether we must look for them in some other origin? I wou'd reply, that our answer to this question depends upon the definition of the word, Nature, than which there is none more ambiguous and equivocal. If nature be oppos'd to miracles, not only the distinction betwixt vice and virtue is natural, but also every event, which has ever happen'd in the world, *excepting those miracles, on which our religion is founded.* In saying, then, that the sentiments of vice and virtue are natural in this sense, we make no very extraordinary discovery.

But nature may also be opposed to rare and unusual; and in this sense of the word, which is the common one, there may often arise disputes concerning what is natural or unnatural; and one may in general affirm, that we are not possess'd of any very precise standard, by which these disputes can be decided. Frequent and rare depend upon the number of examples we have observ'd; and as this number may gradually encrease or diminish, 'twill be impossible to fix any exact boundaries betwixt them. We may only affirm on this head, that if ever there was anything, which cou'd be call'd natural in this sense, the sentiments of morality certainly may; since there never was any nation of the world, nor any single person in any nation, who was utterly depriv'd of them, and who never, in any instance, shew'd the least approbation or dislike of manners. These sentiments are so rooted in our constitution and temper, that without entirely confounding the human mind by disease or madness, 'tis impossible to extirpate and destroy them.

But nature may also be opposed to artifice, as well as to what is rare and unusual; and in this sense it may be disputed, whether the notions of virtue be natural or not. We readily forget, that the designs, and projects, and views of men are principles as necessary in their operation as heat and cold, moist and dry: But taking them to be free and entirely our own, 'tis usual for us to set them in opposition to the other principles of nature. Shou'd it, therefore, be demanded, whether the sense of virtue be natural or artificial, I am of opinion, that 'tis impossible for me at present to give any precise answer to this question. Perhaps it will appear afterwards, that our sense of some virtues is artificial, and that of others natural. The discussion of this question will be more proper, when we enter upon an exact detail of each particular vice and virtue.

Meanwhile it may not be amiss to observe from these definitions of natural and unnatural, that nothing can be more unphilosophical than those systems, which assert, that virtue is the same with what is natural, and vice with what is unnatural. For in the first sense of the word, Nature, as opposed to miracles, both vice and virtue are equally natural; and in the second sense, as oppos'd to what is unusual, perhaps virtue will be found to be the most unnatural. At least it must be own'd, that heroic virtue, being as unusual, is as little natural as the most brutal barbarity. As to the third sense of the word, 'tis certain, that both vice and virtue are equally artificial, and out of nature. For however it may be disputed, whether the notion of a merit or demerit in certain actions be natural or artificial, 'tis evident, that the actions themselves are artificial, and are perform'd with a certain design and intention; otherwise they cou'd never be rank'd under any of these denominations. 'Tis impossible, therefore, that the character of natural and unnatural can ever, in any sense, mark the boundaries of vice and virtue.

Thus we are still brought back to our first position, that virtue is distinguished by the pleasure, and vice by the pain, that any action, sentiment or character gives us by the mere view and contemplation. This decision is very commodious; because it reduces us to this simple question, *Why any action or sentiment upon the general view or survey, gives a certain satisfaction or uneasiness,* in order to shew the origin of its moral rectitude or depravity, without looking for any incomprehensible relations and qualities, which never did exist in nature, nor even in our imagination, by any clear and distinct conception. I flatter myself I have executed a great part of my present design by a state of the question, which appears to me so free from ambiguity and obscurity.

1:1-11 Vanity: Life Under the Sun (cont.)

[9] *The thing that hath been, it is that which shall be; and that which is done is that which shall be done: and there is no new thing under the sun.*

Even beyond the cycles nothing new emerges. Life is repetitive and empty. While there is order, there seems no apparent meaning.

[10] *Is there anything whereof it may be said, See, this is new? it hath been already of old time, which was before us.*

Solomon challenges the reader to prove wrong his assertion that there is nothing new. All under the sun functions are cyclical and repetitive.

[11] There is no remembrance of former things; neither shall there be any remembrance of things that are to come with those that shall come after.

Despite the persistence of natural cycles (the solar day, the water cycle, etc.) each generation learns anew - even in the present day when information is more readily available than at any other time in world history.

Solomon identifies two levels of forgetfulness: (1) regarding former things and (2) regarding the future things when they have become former things. Thus along with other natural cycles, there is the passing of one generation to the next and the forgetfulness due to insignificance of that which is past and that which will become past. Thus all under the sun is meaningless and empty.

Philosophical Parallel: Existentialism

Solomon's initial assertion (all is vanity) has been borne out in existentialism. First an epistemology, existentialism asserts that there is no absolute meaning or that if there is, it cannot be identified and is thus irrelevant.

Friederich Nietzsche (1844-1900) held to the latter idea. He didn't deny ultimate meaning, but was certain (as a first principle) that it could not be identified, so he deemed it irrelevant at best. He saw an insurmountable chasm between noumenal reality (noumena – essential reality) and phenomenal reality (the noumena experienced or perceived) and concluded that there was no way the two could interact. While his was not an outright denial of noumenal reality, since it was not in any way approachable (since the phenomena taints the noumena) in its pure form, he viewed it as irrelevant, and thus nonexistent for any practical purposes. Naturally, this would preclude any theistic belief, and he is a strong critic of theism and its followers (particularly Christians and Jews), considering them to be representative of the slave morality (not a good thing...in contrast to the master morality, which he considers good).

Existentialist epistemology prescribes two alternate worldviews: (1) pessimism or suicidal nihilism – since there is no meaning, there is no reason to continue meaningless existence; (2) optimism – since there is no discernable ultimate meaning one must create his own meaning. For Nietzsche the second is manifest in his will to power concept (to be discussed later). He is also noted for his assertion that "God is dead."

Primary Source Excerpt: Nietzsche: The Madman (1882)[3]

Have you not heard of that madman who lit a lantern in the bright morning hours, ran to the market place, and cried incessantly: "I seek God! I seek God!" As many of those who did not believe in God were standing around just then, he provoked much laughter. Has he got lost? asked one. Did he lose his way like a child? asked another. Or is he hiding? Is he afraid of us? Has he gone on a voyage? emigrated? Thus they yelled and laughed.

The madman jumped into their midst and pierced them with his eyes. "Whither is God?" he cried; "I will tell you. *We have killed him* – you and I. All of us are his murderers. But how did we do this? How could we drink up the sea? Who gave us the sponge to wipe away the entire horizon? What were we doing when we unchained this earth from its sun? Whither is it moving now? Whither are we moving? Away from all suns? Are we not plunging continually? Backward, sideward, forward, in all directions? Is there still any up or down? Are we not straying, as through an infinite nothing? Do we not feel the breath of empty space? Has it not become colder? Is not night continually closing in on us? Do we not need to light lanterns in the morning? Do we hear nothing as yet of the noise of the gravediggers who are burying God? Do we smell nothing as yet of the divine decomposition? Gods, too, decompose. God is dead. God remains dead. And we have killed him.

"How shall we comfort ourselves, the murderers of all murderers? What was holiest and mightiest of all that the world has yet owned has bled to death under our knives: who will wipe this blood off us? What water is there for us to clean ourselves? What festivals of atonement, what sacred games shall we have to invent? Is not the greatness of this deed too great for us? Must we ourselves not become gods simply to appear worthy of it? There has never been a greater deed; and whoever is born after us — for the sake of this deed he will belong to a higher history than all history hitherto."

Here the madman fell silent and looked again at his listeners; and they, too, were silent and stared at him in astonishment. At last he threw his lantern on the ground, and it broke into pieces and went out. "I have come too early," he said then; "my time is not yet. This tremendous event is still on its way, still wandering; it has not yet reached the ears of men. Lightning and thunder require time; the light of the stars requires time; deeds, though done, still require time to be seen and heard. This deed is still more distant from them than most distant stars -- *and yet they have done it themselves.*

It has been related further that on the same day the madman forced his way into several churches and there struck up his *requiem aeternam deo*. Led out and called to account, he is said always to have replied nothing but: "What after all are these churches now if they are not the tombs and sepulchers of God?"

1:12-18 Vanity:
The Under the Sun Quest for Wisdom

[12] I the Preacher was king over Israel in Jerusalem.

Qoheleth's identity reiterated: undoubtedly Solomon. It is noteworthy that Solomon was king when his investigations began. As such he had the resources to conduct a thorough investigation.

[13] And I gave my heart to seek and search out by wisdom concerning all things that are done under heaven: this sore travail hath God given to the sons of man to be exercised therewith.

The recounting of his investigation begins in earnest.

Gave – Qal perfect of *nathan* – the use of the perfect throughout Solomon's narrative is not insignificant. He is not presently working through the issues, rather he investigated it and has drawn his conclusion. Solomon should not be understood to be struggling with frustration, despair, or any other issue at this point. He has clear resolution and he passes that on to the reader.

The mode of inquiry is an exploration by wisdom (*chokmah*) (*sophia* in the LXX). Note the qualification here: this is not heavenly wisdom, but rather wisdom concerning the things under the heavens (*ha shamim*). It is the seeking out, from a naturalistic perspective the true nature of things. This is precisely the stated aim of ancient Greek philosophy, for example.

The inquiry itself is grievous (perhaps evil is a better rendering of *ra'a*) and yet is a gift (*nathan*) given by God to afflict (or even depress) man with. Perhaps in similar fashion to the Law, which serves as a tutor to lead interlocutors to Christ by demonstrating man's inability to achieve independently the holiness of God, such an inquiry can point one to their need for a right perspective of and relationship to God. It seems at the surface not to be a good gift, yet allowing an observer the opportunity observe the futility of life without God would seemingly be of great benefit, even motivating one to seek God. Sadly, though, there are none who seek after God. Solomon will deal this troubling issue as well.

[14] I have seen all the works that are done under the sun; and, behold, all is vanity and vexation of spirit.

Works – *ma'aseh* – better, actions or activities. They are observed through the lens of naturalistic wisdom and found to be emptiness (*hebel*) and (KJV translates best here) vexation or gasping (*reuth*) of spirit (*ruach*, best translated spirit rather than wind). The metaphor of wind is unnecessary, and not the most natural or simple usage, thus I take the KJV's rendering to be more literal in this case. This denotes an extreme inner strife.

The investigation, from a non-metaphysical presupposition, of activities done under the sun shows all to be meaningless.

Existentialism seems a natural conclusion here.

[15] That which is crooked cannot be made straight: and that which is wanting cannot be numbered.

Man by his own efforts has no real impact. He cannot improve or alter the situation.

[16] I communed with mine own heart, saying, Lo, I am come to great estate, and have gotten more wisdom than all they that have been before me in Jerusalem: yea, my heart had great experience of wisdom and knowledge.

I said to myself (NASB) – more literal rendering: spoke to my own heart.

Lo – *hineh* – an emphatic, behold or see. What follows is of importance.

Great experience in wisdom and knowledge – chokmah and da'ath. Again, the scope is important – this is under the sun wisdom and knowledge in contrast to wisdom and knowledge from God (Prov. 1:7, 9:10, etc.).

[17] And I gave my heart to know wisdom, and to know madness and folly: I perceived that this also is vexation of spirit.

Adding to the pursuit of worldly wisdom, Solomon sought after madness and folly, or folly and silliness. His conclusion regarding worldly wisdom is the same as that of madness and folly: vexation of spirit

[18] For in much wisdom is much grief: and he that increaseth

knowledge increaseth sorrow.

Grief – *kahas* – even sorrow or wrath. The ancient philosophers developed speculative philosophy: knowledge for the sake of knowledge, while at the same time extolling happiness as the chief good. The contradiction is obvious.

Excursus: The Rise of Philosophy and Conflict With Theology

Despite assertions that "any conflict between philosophy and theology must be apparent rather than real, the result of a misunderstanding,"[4] conflict endures nonetheless. Paul Tillich asks if there is a necessary conflict between the two and if there is a possible synthesis between them.[5] He answers both questions negatively on grounds that the two stand on disparate bases. There is no necessary conflict as there is no common ground, at least methodologically between the two. For the same reason no synthesis can be had. They are decidedly distinct in that manner.

Whether or not one would accept *en toto* Tillich's diagnosis is not a matter of import here, but rather the characterization of difference is significant. How can this variance in grounding be explained? Most assuredly it would seem that the answer lies in the origins and elementary components of both pursuits. The foundations of theology will not be expressed here but only to say that they must extend by definition beyond the purely material, lest the matter at hand become entirely superfluous and be of necessity relegated to discussions of human imagination possessing only aesthetic value as fiction or perhaps some therapeutic value. The effort here will be, on the other hand, given to discussion of causative factors in the rise of philosophy – and specifically that of pre-Socratic thinking. Once accomplished this can be elsewhere expanded to the end that roots of divergence between philosophy and theology are readily apparent. Yet in order to discuss in a comparative sense we must first have the sense of definition, and as Guthrie says by way of Aristotle, "the only complete definition is one which includes a statement of the cause."[6] Hence the centrality of the question: what caused philosophy?

As Guthrie suggests in his *History of Greek Philosophy*, the emergence of philosophy was not sudden, but rather was a gradual shift from pre-rational, mythic, and anthropomorphic perspectives to a more rational and scientific perception.[7] This plodding yet measured development has been attributed to a number of influences including (1) the move itself from feudal society to urbanization, (2) the resultant increase in leisure of the citizenry, which allowed for more time for inquiry and intellectual pursuit, (3) increase in trade, which promoted heightened cultural interaction and impacted modes of thought, (4) the rise in literacy as result of directed use of leisure, and (5) a naturalistic drive which becomes more evident as the field develops. Each will be considered briefly here in an attempt to underscore the magnitude of their influence and perhaps understand that while a plurality of influences is likely a reality, there seems to be an underlying motivation which is not to be ignored.

From Feudal to Urban
As to how the shift from the rural to the urban occurred, there are divergent suggestions – e.g., Hanson understood the polis to be based in an egalitarian agricultural society,[8] while Snodgrass attributed the rise of the polis to the development of the military[9] - yet despite uncertainty in primary causation, it is clear that the shift occurred nonetheless between the 7th-5th centuries B.C, and the result of the evolution can perhaps be summed up best by Morris' characterization of the polis as "a

complex hierarchical society built around the notion of citizenship."[10]

The provision for shared duties and responsibilities among citizens helped to establish the conditions for centralization, and centralization provided fertile ground for shared ideas. A sort of micro-globalization took place as commonality in resources, responsibilities, and ideas carried the citizenry toward new modes of thought, and these were influenced by naturalism, as these shared ideas brought a broader questioning of previous mythical bases. Guthrie points out that during these early days the materialism of the Greek polis offered a contrast to the foundations of other burgeoning civilizations in relation to attitudes toward the mythical:

> ...once the moment for this abandonment of mythological and theological modes of thought seemed to have come, its development was facilitated by the fact that neither here nor in any other Greek state was freedom of thought inhibited by the demands of a theocratic form of society such as existed in the neighbouring Oriental countries.[11]

It is apparent that with a heightened degree of centralization in Greek society came an increase in naturalistic thinking, whereas the same cultural developments of centralization and shared ideas that were seemingly present in other (nearby) countries did not produce the same inclination toward naturalism. Thus, while the urban transfer provided the conditions for naturalistic philosophy, the result here was rather unique, albeit gradual in its arrival. Perhaps the result could be attributed primarily to something other than the simple reallocation of persons, resources, and ideas.

Appeal of Leisure

Aristotle had much to say on *schole* (leisure), indicating that he reckoned it to be prerequisite in setting the conditions for philosophical pursuit. He asserts that it is the primary principle, saying,

> ...nature herself, as has been often said, requires that we should be able, not only to work well, but to use leisure well; for, as I must repeat once again, *the first principle of all action is leisure* [emphasis mine]. Both are required, but leisure is better than occupation and is its end[12]

> ... leisure of itself gives pleasure and happiness and enjoyment of life, which are experienced, not by the busy man, but by those who have leisure.[13]

And ultimately he views it as prerequisite to, at least certain aspects of literacy:

> ...there are branches of learning and education which we must study merely with a view to leisure spent in intellectual activity, and these are to be valued for their own sake....[14]

Seneca echoes the Aristotelian sentiment, even asserting that

> Of all men they alone are at leisure who take time for philosophy, they alone really live; for they are not content to be good guardians of their own lifetime only.[15]

The preeminence of *schole* in Aristotle seems an appropriate diagnosis of his time, and Guthrie suggests Aristotle is correct in his assertion that disinterested intellectual activity (the work of philosophy) is indeed a product of leisure.[16] Guthrie further offers the words of both Aristotle and Hobbes in support of this conclusion:

> Philosophy did not arise from a demand for the necessities or amenities of human life. Rather was the satisfaction of those demands a precondition of its existence. We may agree with Aristotle, who, after making his point that philosophy has its origin in wonder, adds: "History supports this conclusion, for it was after the provision of the chief necessities not only for life but for an easy life that the search for this intellectual satisfaction began"; as also in this matter with Hobbes, who said much the same thing: "Leisure is the mother of Philosophy; and Common-wealth, the mother of Peace and Leisure: Where first were great and flourishing Cities, there was first the study of Philosophy."[17]

Note in particular Hobbes' description of the Commonwealth as mother of peace and leisure. If it be so, then such events as the feudal-to-polis shift would have been prerequisite to the promulgation of leisure and of more import than the leisure itself inasmuch as that transfer provided the societal conditions under which leisure could exist. Leisure was most assuredly contributive, but perhaps not entirely causative, as that leisure could have been used for other pursuits. Still, the question of "why philosophy?" remains unanswered.

Trade in Ideas

With trade evident earlier in the Phoenician culture, and if trade was indeed so impactful in providing opportunity for philosophy, then how to explain the blossoming of philosophy in the later arriving Greek culture? The answer to this question provides yet another indicator that cultural evolutions which provided the prerequisite conditions for the rise of philosophy must not be of necessity considered as causative to philosophy's genesis. Nonetheless, trade is a key factor, and specifically here – trade in ideas.

Ancient Greek philosophy reflects an awareness of key ideas from other cultures. Guthrie describes the acquisition of this familiarity:

> Milesians like all Ionians must have had plenty of opportunity of getting to know the Oriental mind. On the active side, these enterprising Greeks made journeys by land to Mesopotamia and by sea to Egypt; and the evidence all suggests that the first philosophers were no recluses, who shut themselves off from this ferment of their times....[18]

Thales, for example, had been to Egypt,[19] and also seemed to rely on Babylonian understandings of astronomy.[20] In Greek mathematical thinking Egyptian and Babylonian influences were recognized.[21] Notably this evidence of early trade in ideas shows some distinction, however, between the Greeks' utilization of the ideas and that of the Egyptians and Babylonians, for example, in that the Greeks' scope of inquiry reached new levels (as will be further discussed later, see *Literacy alters the Dialogue*).

The Greeks recognized, for example, that Egypt had much to offer – holding Egyptian culture and wisdom in higher regard than that of other cultures. Plato records in the Timaeus an illustrative encounter between Solon and an Egyptian priest:

> A very old priest said to him, "Oh Solon, Solon, you Greeks are all children, and there's no such thing as an

old Greek...you are all young in mind...you have no belief rooted in old tradition and no knowledge hoary with age....with you and others, writing and the other necessities of civilization have only just been developed...."[22]

The dialogue at this point indicates (1) the Greek respect for Egyptian ideas and culture, and (2) the interchange of (cosmogonical) ideas between the Egyptians and Greeks. But the conversation recorded here also gives rise to an appropriate question: if interchange of ideas was a reality, then can trade in ideas really be seen as causative for the development of philosophy? Perhaps a prerequisite observation would be that Egypt had opportunity to profit equally from idea sharing, and yet philosophy did not rise first in Egypt. For the Greeks, however, as trade increased so did their exposure to diverse and contrary accounts of cosmogony, for example. The Greek response was reasoned inquiry: questioning not only the imported accounts but those of their own traditions as well.

Literacy Alters the Dialogue
As mythos provided a vehicle for the proliferation of traditional narrative, it generally did so in poetic form. Interpreted thus as a mnemonic instrument, mythos was often in possession of a number of characteristics which granted it import and provided a profoundness as a mode of communication, and specifically a means of preserving tradition orally. Even as political thought developed in early Greek culture orality was still preeminent, as politics was in itself a type of oral tradition.

Although development of the Greek alphabet is traced from the eighth century BC, schooling in written texts does not appear until the sixth century BC in Ionia, but once it appeared it gained prominence, as Ford says,

> Schooling in letters is first attested for Ionia in the later sixth century, but there has been a good deal of debate about how rapidly it spread and when *paideia* came to involve not only the traditional lyre teacher (*kitharistēs*) but the letter teacher (*grammatistēs*) as well. Havelock's intellectual history led him to posit that elementary education in reading and writing became normalized in Athens somewhere between the childhood of Socrates and that of Plato (i.e., the 460s and 420s, respectively). But many point to the 480s, when Athenian vases begin to represent school scenes complete with tablets, styluses, and book rolls....[23]

Ford's comments indicate two important elements: (1) While the date of formalized education is perhaps a bit unclear (anywhere from the 480's-420's BC), it nonetheless coincided with the rise of philosophy, and (2) that while initially emphasized in music, literacy, i.e., the written text, and more, formalized systems of education are evidenced by a number of archaeological sources. So we see the rise in literacy confirmed and coinciding with the rise of philosophy, but what of its impact?

There are two recent perspectives on the impact of literacy in ancient Greece: (1) the autonomous model (Havelock, Goody, Ong, etc.) which asserts literacy to be a tool causative of dramatic cultural impact in areas such as democracy and analytic thinking; and the opposing perspective, (2) the ideological model (Street, Stock, Carruthers), which sees literacy as being shaped by culture rather than offering shape to it.[24] The autonomous model would offer more support (seemingly) for literacy as causative, but the ideological model introduces doubt regarding literacy's role as grounds for the birth of philosophy.

There is another pertinent variable in the discussion on literacy, and that is the Greeks' inimitable use of it. While other cultures were also progressing in their own pursuits of literacy, the Greek's use of literacy was not perhaps as utilitarian as that of other cultures, as Guthrie compares the Egyptian knowledge of fire as a useful tool with the Greeks inquiry as to the very substance of fire and why it functions as it does, noting that a significant step in literacy was taken by the Greek mode of thought.[25] More complex questions give rise to more complex answers, and thus require perhaps an unparalleled utilization of literacy which could only (as perhaps Guthrie might argue) have begun here. In order to maintain a certain philosophical spirit a certain aptitude for abstraction is required.[26]

While it is inarguable that literacy provided very favorable conditions for engagement in philosophic inquiry (though such inquiry would not have been impossible previously), there is debate (notably autonomous vs. ideological) regarding its causative impact on philosophy.

Naturalistic Drive

To what did the earliest philosophical inquiries attend? Notably, causation was an immediate focus. How could the cosmos be explained? To what did the cosmos owe its existence, its function, its order? Could the eruption of lightning be attributed to the anger of Zeus? Or was there a different wizard behind the curtain?[27] Guthrie also sees causation as relevant to the early discussion:

> The gradual emergence into consciousness of the problem of the first cause of motion, bound up as it is with that of the relation between matter and life, is one of the main threads to be followed in an exposition of Presocratic thought.[28]

Guthrie describes even more directly the birthing moment of Greek philosophy as that moment when

> The conviction began to take shape in men's minds that the apparent chaos of events must conceal an underlying order, and that this order is the product of impersonal forces.[29]

Although he does admit that while philosophy began with the pronouncement of the teleological, it did not fully abandon mythical conceptions – and has not done so even to this day.[30] It can be ascertained that while, especially at the earliest moments, Greek philosophy maintained a degree of connection with the mythical framework of mainstream Greek theology[31] the prevailing intellectual motivation appeared to be the search for impersonal forces as causative. Sahakian describes the efforts of the early Greek thinkers:

> The Ionian philosophers set for themselves the task of ascertaining the nature of substance, of cosmic matter, of the very stuff out of which the entire universe is composed.[32]

Initial inquiry was directed toward providing explanation for the appearance of reality, and indeed, even seeking the reality behind the appearance. Wells discusses Platonic thought as emblematic of the times and type of inquiry, characterizing ancient Greek thought as challenging traditional interpretations and thus impacting how mankind was to live. This kind of thinking was

> ...a landmark in this history; it is a new thing in the development of mankind, this appearance of the idea of willfully and completely recasting human conditions. So far mankind has been living by traditions under the fear of the gods. Here is a man [Plato] who says boldly to our race, and as if it were a quite reasonable and natural thing to say, "Take hold of your lives. Most of the things that distress you, you can avoid; most of these things that dominate you, you can overthrow. You can do as you will with them."[33]

As evidenced by the curious univocality (in regard to the content of inquiry not the results) of the early Greek thinkers, demonstrable by their commitment to natural philosophy – at least until Socrates, it seems as though the most definitive characteristic of ancient Greek thought was the pursuit and emergence of a *naturalistic* world view whereby the cosmos could be explained in terms of both (to differing degrees) the rational and the empirical, to the exclusion of the mystical. This represented a colossal redirect in Greek culture as the mythological record and the pantheon became less and less relevant, giving way to an increasingly secular approach.

Philosophy vs. Theology?
While each of these perspectives offers somewhat convincing explanations prima facie, it is perhaps most likely that the justification for the rise in philosophy is not an either/or proposition *exclusively*, but that instead each of the elements discussed worked cooperatively in providing a context in which philosophic inquiry could thrive uniquely as it had not had opportunity to do in previous cultures and eras. It does however seem that if there is to be a primary causation that *it should be linked to a naturalistic drive*, as this seems a most internal

element of motive, implying greater force in causation over the other factors which must be reckoned as external – albeit no less than magnificently important to setting the conditions - to the pursuit itself. In short, the naturalistic drive seems a moral principle whereas the others are in greater part descriptive.

If this be an accurate assessment, then what of interconnectedness? Jean Grandin speaks of a "new proximity between theology and philosophy," appealing to the previous desirability of interactions between the two as a model for future sharing of inquiry.[34]

Tillich's view on the possibility of synthesis seems to counter Grandin's hopeful assessment, causing one to wonder if indeed naturalistic drive as primary cause of philosophic origin eliminates the possibility of a theological impact on philosophy. Yet this writer is not willing to concede that the initial (and in many senses, ongoing) motivating factors which contributed in large part to the genesis of a particular class of thought (philosophy) also require a grounding of methodology untouchable by theology and theological perspective. Naturalistic drive has inarguably given impetus in the development (or to some, the debasement) of inquiry, yet it needs not necessarily find within itself the resolution. In short, despite divergence in origin and motivation, there is an interconnectedness to be seen between philosophy and theology, as can be illustrated by question and answer. Questions may be provided in one context and may be answered in yet another. If the conflict between philosophy and theology then arises from disparate foundations, is interaction between the two impossible? Is that which is philosophical non-theological, and is that which is theological non-philosophical? No, on all counts.

First, it seems there should be sharp distinction between causation and content – between motivation and result. If indeed the motivation for philosophy historically is grounded purely in the naturalistic, the content of philosophic inquiry need not necessarily be. Second, both philosophical and theological can be enhanced by the process of testing at the hands of the other. Both pursuits ought to avoid prejudice and fear of interaction. As philosophy's naturalism – chance and necessity, resultant cosmogonies and ethical systems – should be unafraid in the face of theological critiques, so theology's metaphysical groundings should fear no challenge from philosophy's sometimes rationalistic and sometimes empirical critiques. Theology can learn much from critiques offered from philosophy. Perhaps much error is maintained on both sides by an unwillingness to suffer such criticism. Third, too many intersections have historically been unearthed than can be ignored. It is not coincidence that most philosophy compendiums and readers will consider theological texts, and that epistemology, metaphysics, and ethics, at least, inextricably connect the two disciplines. This interconnectedness has historically been so strong that to some degree it is difficult to calculate where theology ends and philosophy begins and where, if at all, each discipline restricts the other.

Finally, it seems that philosophy and theology are of the same kind – not in presupposition or conclusion, but rather in that the legitimacy of both are tied to previous faith commitments, as is evidenced by the respective handling of that which seems (at least) beyond human capacity for understanding – either by the rational or the empirical. Thomas Aquinas, illustrates from a theological perspective this kind of presuppositional commitment, saying,

> ...although things which are beyond human knowledge are not to be sought by man through reason, such things are revealed by God, and are to be accepted by faith.[35]

1:12-18 Vanity: The Under the Sun Quest for Wisdom 45

Harvard Research Professor Richard Lewontin, from perhaps an extreme naturalistic perspective illustrates the same kind of commitment, yet with a dramatically different conclusion:

> Our willingness to accept scientific claims that are against common sense is the key to an understanding of the real struggle between science and the supernatural. We take the side of science in spite of the patent absurdity of some of its constructs, in spite of its failure to fulfill many of its extravagant promises of health and life, in spite of the tolerance of the scientific community for unsubstantiated just-so stories, because we have a prior commitment, a commitment to materialism. It is not that the methods and institutions of science somehow compel us to accept a material explanation of the phenomenological world, but on the contrary, that we are forced by our a priori adherence to material causes to create an apparatus of investigation and a set of concepts that produce material explanations, no matter how counterintuitive, no matter how mystifying to the uninitiated. Moreover, that materialism is absolute, for we cannot allow a divine foot in the door.[36]

Lewontin's commentary here brings to mind the pre-Socratic attempts at explaining the cosmos. Initially they were grounded at least to some degree in mythos, and swiftly became almost exclusively naturalistic. Assuming the commitment is based on an appropriate grounding it would be expected that progress resultant from increased abilities in the science (and art) of inquiry would draw us closer to better understanding not just the world around us but also existence itself. However, if that condition of prior commitment (materialism) is not reliable, then interpretations not shared by philosophy, science, *and* theology can be called into question, and hence arrives the importance of the interconnectedness between philosophy and theology. The debate perhaps should not be primarily about method, but rather about the legitimacy of prior commitments and presuppositions.

Philosophical Parallel: Basic Elements of Philosophy (Outlines)

Basic Challenges in the Study of Philosophy:
1. What views among the many diverse views are valid?
2. What sources have authority?
3. If human reason/experience is flawed, can it arrive at truth?
4. Exaltation of human reason/experience
5. What is truth?

Basic Fields of Philosophy:
1. Epistemology – How is knowledge possible? What constitutes truth? Five basic epistemological approaches:
    a. Platonic dualism – divided line theory of knowledge: visible world of becoming, intelligible world of being (Gnosticism a late result).
    b. Cartesian rationalism – reason the ultimate sense of truth, all things can and must be rationalized, cogito ergo sum (I think therefore I am).
    c. Humean Empiricism – sensory experience the ultimate sense of truth.
    d. Kantian structuralism – knowledge a result of experience translated by reason
    e. Presuppositionalism – recognition that all epistemologies must begin by faith, but what are the correct first principles?

2. Metaphysics – does reality extend beyond the material? What are some major metaphysical issues?
   a. the existence of God
   b. freedom of the will
   c. meaning in life
3. Logic – science of reasoning, primary instrument of philosophy.
4. Ethics – morality and human conduct.
   a. axiology – inquiry on non-moral values (e.g., aesthetics – objective or subjective standards).
5. Social/political philosophy – morality extended beyond the individual to society as a whole.
   a. issues of a free and well-ordered society
   b. relation of individuals to the state
   c. environmental philosophy

Chronological Periods of Western Philosophy:
1. Ancient (6th – 3rd centuries BC) – Thales, Pythagoras, Parmenides, Zeno, Socrates, Plato, Aristotle
2. Medieval (AD 4th -16th centuries) – mystical, theological (faith vs. reason) – Augustine, Anselm, Aquinas
3. Modern (16th-19th centuries) – Rousseau, Newton, Kant, Hume, Descartes
   a. Age of Enlightenment 1650-1770's
4. Contemporary (early 20th century)
   a. Analytic philosophers– conceptual analysis – Chalmers, Chomsky, Plantinga, Rawls
   b. Continental philosophers – (existentialists, phenomenologists) – Sartre
5. Postmodernist (20th century- present) – Beudrillard, Foucault, Derrida, Lyotard

Basic Aspects of Logic
Two kinds of logical argument, both utilizing premises leading to a conclusion:

1. Inductive – yields probable conclusions (examples: (a) appealing to previous experience: one has stolen three times in the past and is thus likely to steal again; (b) by analogy - A, B, and C have X and Y, A and B have Z, therefore, C probably has Z also; (c) inductive generalization – statement on all based on observation of some).
2. Deductive – yields necessary conclusions (example: if A then B, not A, therefore not B); if premises are true the conclusion will be as well; either valid or invalid (dealing with proper structure), sound or unsound (dealing with truth value); no invalid argument will produce a sound conclusion.

Basic Logical Fallacies:
Ad Hominem (argument to the person).
Straw Man (misrepresentation of an opposing argument)
Circular Reasoning (begging the question)
Two Wrongs (defending one wrong by citing another)
Slippery Slope (creating an inappropriate chain)
Appealing to Authority (so and so says it is so, therefore it is so)
Red Herring (hounds chase fox, red herring dragged across path and away from fox to divert...going on the offensive rather than dealing with the issue)

Primary Source Excerpt: Plato: The Euthyphro (399BC) (trans. Benjamin Jowett)

Euthyphro. Why have you left the Lyceum, Socrates? and what are you doing in the Porch of the King Archon? Surely you cannot be concerned in a suit before the King, like myself?
Socrates. Not in a suit, Euthyphro; impeachment is the word which the Athenians use.
Euthyphro. What! I suppose that some one has been prosecuting you, for I cannot believe that you are the prosecutor of another.
Socrates. Certainly not.
Euthyphro. Then some one else has been prosecuting you?
Socrates. Yes.
Euthyphro. And who is he?
Socrates. A young man who is little known, Euthyphro; and I hardly know him: his name is Meletus, and he is of the deme of Pitthis. Perhaps you may remember his appearance; he has a beak, and long straight hair, and a beard which is ill grown.
Euthyphro. No, I do not remember him, Socrates. But what is the charge which he brings against you?
Socrates. What is the charge? Well, a very serious charge, which shows a good deal of character in the young man, and for which he is certainly not to be despised. He says he knows how the youth are corrupted and who are their corruptors. I fancy that he must be a wise man, and seeing that I am the reverse of a wise man, he has found me out, and is going to accuse me of corrupting his young friends. And of this our mother the state is to be the judge. Of all our political men he is the only one who seems to me to begin in the right way, with the cultivation of virtue in youth; like a good husbandman, he makes the young shoots his first care, and clears away us who are the destroyers of them. This is only the first step; he will afterwards attend to

the elder branches; and if he goes on as he has begun, he will be a very great public benefactor.

Euthyphro. I hope that he may; but I rather fear, Socrates, that the opposite will turn out to be the truth. My opinion is that in attacking you he is simply aiming a blow at the foundation of the state. But in what way does he say that you corrupt the young?

Socrates. He brings a wonderful accusation against me, which at first hearing excites surprise: he says that I am a poet or maker of gods, and that I invent new gods and deny the existence of old ones; this is the ground of his indictment.

Euthyphro. I understand, Socrates; he means to attack you about the familiar sign which occasionally, as you say, comes to you. He thinks that you are a neologian, and he is going to have you up before the court for this. He knows that such a charge is readily received by the world, as I myself know too well; for when I speak in the assembly about divine things, and foretell the future to them, they laugh at me and think me a madman. Yet every word that I say is true. But they are jealous of us all; and we must be brave and go at them.

Socrates. Their laughter, friend Euthyphro, is not a matter of much consequence. For a man may be thought wise; but the Athenians, I suspect, do not much trouble themselves about him until he begins to impart his wisdom to others, and then for some reason or other, perhaps, as you say, from jealousy, they are angry.

Euthyphro. I am never likely to try their temper in this way.

Socrates. I dare say not, for you are reserved in your behaviour, and seldom impart your wisdom. But I have a benevolent habit of pouring out myself to everybody, and would even pay for a listener, and I am afraid that the Athenians may think me too talkative. Now if, as I was saying, they would only laugh at me, as you say that they laugh at you, the time might pass gaily enough in the court; but perhaps they may be in earnest, and then what the end will be you soothsayers only can predict.

Euthyphro. I dare say that the affair will end in nothing, Socrates, and that you will win your cause; and I think that I shall win my own.

Socrates. And what is your suit, Euthyphro? are you the pursuer or the defendant?

Euthyphro. I am the pursuer.

Socrates. Of whom?

Euthyphro. You will think me mad when I tell you.

Socrates. Why, has the fugitive wings?

Euthyphro. Nay, he is not very volatile at his time of life.

Socrates. Who is he?

Euthyphro. My father.

Socrates. Your father! my good man?

Euthyphro. Yes.

Socrates. And of what is he accused?

Euthyphro. Of murder, Socrates.

Socrates. By the powers, Euthyphro! how little does the common herd know of the nature of right and truth. A man must be an extraordinary man, and have made great strides in wisdom, before he could have seen his way to bring such an action.

Euthyphro. Indeed, Socrates, he must.

Socrates. I suppose that the man whom your father murdered was one of your relatives -- clearly he was; for if he had been a stranger you would never have thought of prosecuting him.

Euthyphro. I am amused, Socrates, at your making a distinction between one who is a relation and one who is not a relation; for surely the pollution is the same in either case, if you knowingly associate with the murderer when you ought to clear yourself and him by proceeding against him. The real question is whether the murdered man has been justly slain. If justly, then your duty is to let the matter alone; but if unjustly, then even if the murderer lives under the same roof with you and eats at the same table, proceed against him. Now the man who is dead was a poor dependent of mine who worked for us as a field labourer on our farm in Naxos, and one day in a fit of drunken passion he got into a quarrel with one of our domestic servants and slew him. My father bound him hand and foot and threw him into a ditch, and then sent to Athens to ask of a diviner what he should do with him. Meanwhile he never attended to him and took no care about him, for he regarded him as a murderer; and thought that no great harm would be done even if he did die. Now this was just what happened. For such was the effect of cold and hunger and chains upon him, that before the messenger returned from the diviner, he was dead. And my father and family are angry with me for taking the part of the murderer and prosecuting my father. They say that he did not kill him, and that if he did, the dead man was but a murderer, and I ought not to take any notice, for that a son is impious who prosecutes a father. Which shows, Socrates, how little they know what the gods think about piety and impiety.

Socrates. Good heavens, Euthyphro! and is your knowledge of religion and of things pious and impious so very exact, that, supposing the circumstances to be as you state them, you are not afraid lest you too may be doing an impious thing in bringing an action against your father?

Euthyphro. The best of Euthyphro, and that which distinguishes him, Socrates, from other men, is his exact knowledge of all such matters. What should I be good for without it?

Socrates. Rare friend! I think that I cannot do better than be your disciple. Then before the trial with Meletus comes on I shall challenge him, and say that I have always had a great interest in religious questions, and now, as he charges me with rash imaginations and innovations in religion, I have become your disciple. You, Meletus, as I shall say to him, acknowledge

Euthyphro to be a great theologian, and sound in his opinions; and if you approve of him you ought to approve of me, and not have me into court; but if you disapprove, you should begin by indicting him who is my teacher, and who will be the ruin, not of the young, but of the old; that is to say, of myself whom he instructs, and of his old father whom he admonishes and chastises. And if Meletus refuses to listen to me, but will go on, and will not shift the indictment from me to you, I cannot do better than repeat this challenge in the court.

Euthyphro. Yes, indeed, Socrates; and if he attempts to indict me I am mistaken if I do not find a flaw in him; the court shall have a great deal more to say to him than to me.

Socrates. And I, my dear friend, knowing this, am desirous of becoming your disciple. For I observe that no one appears to notice you -- not even this Meletus; but his sharp eyes have found me out at once, and he has indicted me for impiety. And therefore, I adjure you to tell me the nature of piety and impiety, which you said that you knew so well, and of murder, and of other offences against the gods. What are they? Is not piety in every action always the same? and impiety, again- is it not always the opposite of piety, and also the same with itself, having, as impiety, one notion which includes whatever is impious?

Euthyphro. To be sure, Socrates.

Socrates. And what is piety, and what is impiety?

Euthyphro. Piety is doing as I am doing; that is to say, prosecuting anyone who is guilty of murder, sacrilege, or of any similar crime -- whether he be your father or mother, or whoever he may be -- that makes no difference; and not to prosecute them is impiety. And please to consider, Socrates, what a notable proof I will give you of the truth of my words, a proof which I have already given to others: -- of the principle, I mean, that the impious, whoever he may be, ought not to go unpunished. For do not men regard Zeus as the best and most righteous of the gods?- and yet they admit that he bound his father (Cronos) because he wickedly devoured his sons, and that he too had punished his own father (Uranus) for a similar reason, in a nameless manner. And yet when I proceed against my father, they are angry with me. So inconsistent are they in their way of talking when the gods are concerned, and when I am concerned.

Socrates. May not this be the reason, Euthyphro, why I am charged with impiety -- that I cannot away with these stories about the gods? and therefore I suppose that people think me wrong. But, as you who are well informed about them approve of them, I cannot do better than assent to your superior wisdom. What else can I say, confessing as I do, that I know nothing about them? Tell me, for the love of Zeus, whether you really believe that they are true.

Euthyphro. Yes, Socrates; and things more wonderful still, of which the world is in ignorance.

Socrates. And do you really believe that the gods, fought with one another, and had dire quarrels, battles, and the like, as the poets say, and as you may see represented in the works of great artists? The temples are full of them; and notably the robe of Athene, which is carried up to the Acropolis at the great Panathenaea, is embroidered with them. Are all these tales of the gods true, Euthyphro?

Euthyphro. Yes, Socrates; and, as I was saying, I can tell you, if you would like to hear them, many other things about the gods which would quite amaze you.

Socrates. I dare say; and you shall tell me them at some other time when I have leisure. But just at present I would rather hear from you a more precise answer, which you have not as yet given, my friend, to the question, What is "piety"? When asked, you only replied, Doing as you do, charging your father with murder.

Euthyphro. And what I said was true, Socrates.

Socrates. No doubt, Euthyphro; but you would admit that there are many other pious acts?

Euthyphro. There are.

Socrates. Remember that I did not ask you to give me two or three examples of piety, but to explain the general idea which makes all pious things to be pious. Do you not recollect that there was one idea which made the impious impious, and the pious pious?

Euthyphro. I remember.

Socrates. Tell me what is the nature of this idea, and then I shall have a standard to which I may look, and by which I may measure actions, whether yours or those of any one else, and then I shall be able to say that such and such an action is pious, such another impious.

Euthyphro. I will tell you, if you like.

Socrates. I should very much like.

Euthyphro. Piety, then, is that which is dear to the gods, and impiety is that which is not dear to them.

Socrates. Very good, Euthyphro; you have now given me the sort of answer which I wanted. But whether what you say is true or not I cannot as yet tell, although I make no doubt that you will prove the truth of your words.

Euthyphro. Of course.

Socrates. Come, then, and let us examine what we are saying. That thing or person which is dear to the gods is pious, and that thing or person which is hateful to the gods is impious, these two being the extreme opposites of one another. Was not that said?

Euthyphro. It was.

Socrates. And well said?

Euthyphro. Yes, Socrates, I thought so; it was certainly said.

Socrates. And further, Euthyphro, the gods were admitted to have enmities and hatreds and differences?

Euthyphro. Yes, that was also said.

Socrates. And what sort of difference creates enmity and anger? Suppose for example that you and I, my good friend, differ about a number; do differences of this sort make us enemies and set us at variance with one another? Do we not go at once to arithmetic, and put an end to them by a sum?
Euthyphro. True.
Socrates. Or suppose that we differ about magnitudes, do we not quickly end the differences by measuring?
Euthyphro. Very true.
Socrates. And we end a controversy about heavy and light by resorting to a weighing machine?
Euthyphro. To be sure.
Socrates. But what differences are there which cannot be thus decided, and which therefore make us angry and set us at enmity with one another? I dare say the answer does not occur to you at the moment, and therefore I will suggest that these enmities arise when the matters of difference are the just and unjust, good and evil, honourable and dishonourable. Are not these the points about which men differ, and about which when we are unable satisfactorily to decide our differences, you and I and all of us quarrel, when we do quarrel?
Euthyphro. Yes, Socrates, the nature of the differences about which we quarrel is such as you describe.
Socrates. And the quarrels of the gods, noble Euthyphro, when they occur, are of a like nature?
Euthyphro. Certainly they are.
Socrates. They have differences of opinion, as you say, about good and evil, just and unjust, honourable and dishonourable: there would have been no quarrels among them, if there had been no such differences -- would there now?
Euthyphro. You are quite right.
Socrates. Does not every man love that which he deems noble and just and good, and hate the opposite of them?

Euthyphro. Very true.
Socrates. But, as you say, people regard the same things, some as just and others as unjust, -- about these they dispute; and so there arise wars and fightings among them.
Euthyphro. Very true.
Socrates. Then the same things are hated by the gods and loved by the gods, and are both hateful and dear to them?
Euthyphro. True.
Socrates. And upon this view the same things, Euthyphro, will be pious and also impious?
Euthyphro. So I should suppose.
Socrates. Then, my friend, I remark with surprise that you have not answered the question which I asked. For I certainly did not ask you to tell me what action is both pious and impious: but now it would seem that what is loved by the gods is also hated by them. And therefore, Euthyphro, in thus chastising your father you may very likely be doing what is agreeable to Zeus but disagreeable to Cronos or Uranus, and what is acceptable to Hephaestus but unacceptable to Here, and there may be other gods who have similar differences of opinion.
Euthyphro. But I believe, Socrates, that all the gods would be agreed as to the propriety of punishing a murderer: there would be no difference of opinion about that.
Socrates. Well, but speaking of men, Euthyphro, did you ever hear any one arguing that a murderer or any sort of evil-doer ought to be let off?
Euthyphro. I should rather say that these are the questions which they are always arguing, especially in courts of law: they commit all sorts of crimes, and there is nothing which they will not do or say in their own defence.
Socrates. But do they admit their guilt, Euthyphro, and yet say that they ought not to be punished?
Euthyphro. No; they do not.

Socrates. Then there are some things which they do not venture to say and do: for they do not venture to argue that the guilty are to be unpunished, but they deny their guilt, do they not?
Euthyphro. Yes.
Socrates. Then they do not argue that the evil-doer should not be punished, but they argue about the fact of who the evil-doer is, and what he did and when?
Euthyphro. True.
Socrates. And the gods are in the same case, if as you assert they quarrel about just and unjust, and some of them say while others deny that injustice is done among them. For surely neither God nor man will ever venture to say that the doer of injustice is not to be punished?
Euthyphro. That is true, Socrates, in the main.
Socrates. But they join issue about the particulars -- gods and men alike; and, if they dispute at all, they dispute about some act which is called in question, and which by some is affirmed to be just, by others to be unjust. Is not that true?
Euthyphro. Quite true.
Socrates. Well then, my dear friend Euthyphro, do tell me, for my better instruction and information, what proof have you that in the opinion of all the gods a servant who is guilty of murder, and is put in chains by the master of the dead man, and dies because he is put in chains before he who bound him can learn from the interpreters of the gods what he ought to do with him, dies unjustly; and that on behalf of such an one a son ought to proceed against his father and accuse him of murder. How would you show that all the gods absolutely agree in approving of his act? Prove to me that they do, and I will applaud your wisdom as long as I live.
Euthyphro. It will be a difficult task; but I could make the matter very dear indeed to you.

Socrates. I understand; you mean to say that I am not so quick of apprehension as the judges: for to them you will be sure to prove that the act is unjust, and hateful to the gods.

Euthyphro. Yes indeed, Socrates; at least if they will listen to me.

Socrates. But they will be sure to listen if they find that you are a good speaker. There was a notion that came into my mind while you were speaking; I said to myself: "Well, and what if Euthyphro does prove to me that all the gods regarded the death of the serf as unjust, how do I know anything more of the nature of piety and impiety? for granting that this action may be hateful to the gods, still piety and impiety are not adequately defined by these distinctions, for that which is hateful to the gods has been shown to be also pleasing and dear to them." And therefore, Euthyphro, I do not ask you to prove this; I will suppose, if you like, that all the gods condemn and abominate such an action. But I will amend the definition so far as to say that what all the gods hate is impious, and what they love pious or holy; and what some of them love and others hate is both or neither. Shall this be our definition of piety and impiety?

Euthyphro. Why not, Socrates?

Socrates. Why not! certainly, as far as I am concerned, Euthyphro, there is no reason why not. But whether this admission will greatly assist you in the task of instructing me as you promised, is a matter for you to consider.

Euthyphro. Yes, I should say that what all the gods love is pious and holy, and the opposite which they all hate, impious.

Socrates. Ought we to enquire into the truth of this, Euthyphro, or simply to accept the mere statement on our own authority and that of others? What do you say?

Euthyphro. We should enquire; and I believe that the statement will stand the test of enquiry.

Socrates. We shall know better, my good friend, in a little while. The point which I should first wish to understand is whether the pious or holy is beloved by the gods because it is holy, or holy because it is beloved of the gods.

Euthyphro. I do not understand your meaning, Socrates.

Socrates. I will endeavour to explain: we, speak of carrying and we speak of being carried, of leading and being led, seeing and being seen. You know that in all such cases there is a difference, and you know also in what the difference lies?

Euthyphro. I think that I understand.

Socrates. And is not that which is beloved distinct from that which loves?

Euthyphro. Certainly.

Socrates. Well; and now tell me, is that which is carried in this state of carrying because it is carried, or for some other reason?

Euthyphro. No; that is the reason.

Socrates. And the same is true of what is led and of what is seen?

Euthyphro. True.

Socrates. And a thing is not seen because it is visible, but conversely, visible because it is seen; nor is a thing led because it is in the state of being led, or carried because it is in the state of being carried, but the converse of this. And now I think, Euthyphro, that my meaning will be intelligible; and my meaning is, that any state of action or passion implies previous action or passion. It does not become because it is becoming, but it is in a state of becoming because it becomes; neither does it suffer because it is in a state of suffering, but it is in a state of suffering because it suffers. Do you not agree?

Euthyphro. Yes.

Socrates. Is not that which is loved in some state either of becoming or suffering?

Euthyphro. Yes.

Socrates. And the same holds as in the previous instances; the state of being loved follows the act of being loved, and not the act the state.
Euthyphro. Certainly.
Socrates. And what do you say of piety, Euthyphro: is not piety, according to your definition, loved by all the gods?
Euthyphro. Yes.
Socrates. Because it is pious or holy, or for some other reason?
Euthyphro. No, that is the reason.
Socrates. It is loved because it is holy, not holy because it is loved?
Euthyphro. Yes.
Socrates. And that which is dear to the gods is loved by them, and is in a state to be loved of them because it is loved of them?
Euthyphro. Certainly.
Socrates. Then that which is dear to the gods, Euthyphro, is not holy, nor is that which is holy loved of God, as you affirm; but they are two different things.
Euthyphro. How do you mean, Socrates?
Socrates. I mean to say that the holy has been acknowledge by us to be loved of God because it is holy, not to be holy because it is loved.
Euthyphro. Yes.
Socrates. But that which is dear to the gods is dear to them because it is loved by them, not loved by them because it is dear to them.
Euthyphro. True.
Socrates. But, friend Euthyphro, if that which is holy is the same with that which is dear to God, and is loved because it is holy, then that which is dear to God would have been loved as being dear to God; but if that which is dear to God is dear to him because loved by him, then that which is holy would have been holy because loved by him. But now you see that the reverse is

the case, and that they are quite different from one another. For one (*theophiles*) is of a kind to be loved cause it is loved, and the other (*osion*) is loved because it is of a kind to be loved. Thus you appear to me, Euthyphro, when I ask you what is the essence of holiness, to offer an attribute only, and not the essence -- the attribute of being loved by all the gods. But you still refuse to explain to me the nature of holiness. And therefore, if you please, I will ask you not to hide your treasure, but to tell me once more what holiness or piety really is, whether dear to the gods or not (for that is a matter about which we will not quarrel) and what is impiety?

Euthyphro. I really do not know, Socrates, how to express what I mean. For somehow or other our arguments, on whatever ground we rest them, seem to turn round and walk away from us.

Socrates. Your words, Euthyphro, are like the handiwork of my ancestor Daedalus; and if I were the sayer or propounder of them, you might say that my arguments walk away and will not remain fixed where they are placed because I am a descendant of his. But now, since these notions are your own, you must find some other gibe, for they certainly, as you yourself allow, show an inclination to be on the move.

Euthyphro. Nay, Socrates, I shall still say that you are the Daedalus who sets arguments in motion; not I, certainly, but you make them move or go round, for they would never have stirred, as far as I am concerned.

Socrates. Then I must be a greater than Daedalus: for whereas he only made his own inventions to move, I move those of other people as well. And the beauty of it is, that I would rather not. For I would give the wisdom of Daedalus, and the wealth of Tantalus, to be able to detain them and keep them fixed. But enough of this. As I perceive that you are lazy, I will myself endeavor to show you how you might instruct me in the nature

of piety; and I hope that you will not grudge your labour. Tell me, then -- Is not that which is pious necessarily just?
Euthyphro. Yes.
Socrates. And is, then, all which is just pious? or, is that which is pious all just, but that which is just, only in part and not all, pious?
Euthyphro. I do not understand you, Socrates.
Socrates. And yet I know that you are as much wiser than I am, as you are younger. But, as I was saying, revered friend, the abundance of your wisdom makes you lazy. Please to exert yourself, for there is no real difficulty in understanding me. What I mean I may explain by an illustration of what I do not mean. The poet (Stasinus) sings -- "Of Zeus, the author and creator of all these things, You will not tell: for where there is fear there is also reverence." Now I disagree with this poet. Shall I tell you in what respect?
Euthyphro. By all means.
Socrates. I should not say that where there is fear there is also reverence; for I am sure that many persons fear poverty and disease, and the like evils, but I do not perceive that they reverence the objects of their fear.
Euthyphro. Very true.
Socrates. But where reverence is, there is fear; for he who has a feeling of reverence and shame about the commission of any action, fears and is afraid of an ill reputation.
Euthyphro. No doubt.
Socrates. Then we are wrong in saying that where there is fear there is also reverence; and we should say, where there is reverence there is also fear. But there is not always reverence where there is fear; for fear is a more extended notion, and reverence is a part of fear, just as the odd is a part of number, and number is a more extended notion than the odd. I suppose that you follow me now?

Euthyphro. Quite well.
Socrates. That was the sort of question which I meant to raise when I asked whether the just is always the pious, or the pious always the just; and whether there may not be justice where there is not piety; for justice is the more extended notion of which piety is only a part. Do you dissent?
Euthyphro. No, I think that you are quite right.
Socrates. Then, if piety is a part of justice, I suppose that we should enquire what part? If you had pursued the enquiry in the previous cases; for instance, if you had asked me what is an even number, and what part of number the even is, I should have had no difficulty in replying, a number which represents a figure having two equal sides. Do you not agree?
Euthyphro. Yes, I quite agree.
Socrates. In like manner, I want you to tell me what part of justice is piety or holiness, that I may be able to tell Meletus not to do me injustice, or indict me for impiety, as I am now adequately instructed by you in the nature of piety or holiness, and their opposites.
Euthyphro. Piety or holiness, Socrates, appears to me to be that part of justice which attends to the gods, as there is the other part of justice which attends to men.
Socrates. That is good, Euthyphro; yet still there is a little point about which I should like to have further information, What is the meaning of "attention"? For attention can hardly be used in the same sense when applied to the gods as when applied to other things. For instance, horses are said to require attention, and not every person is able to attend to them, but only a person skilled in horsemanship. Is it not so?
Euthyphro. Certainly.
Socrates. I should suppose that the art of horsemanship is the art of attending to horses?
Euthyphro. Yes.

Socrates. Nor is every one qualified to attend to dogs, but only the huntsman?
Euthyphro. True.
Socrates. And I should also conceive that the art of the huntsman is the art of attending to dogs?
Euthyphro. Yes.
Socrates. As the art of the ox herd is the art of attending to oxen?
Euthyphro. Very true.
Socrates. In like manner holiness or piety is the art of attending to the gods? -- that would be your meaning, Euthyphro?
Euthyphro. Yes.
Socrates. And is not attention always designed for the good or benefit of that to which the attention is given? As in the case of horses, you may observe that when attended to by the horseman's art they are benefited and improved, are they not?
Euthyphro. True.
Socrates. As the dogs are benefited by the huntsman's art, and the oxen by the art of the ox herd, and all other things are tended or attended for their good and not for their hurt?
Euthyphro. Certainly, not for their hurt.
Socrates. But for their good?
Euthyphro. Of course.
Socrates. And does piety or holiness, which has been defined to be the art of attending to the gods, benefit or improve them? Would you say that when you do a holy act you make any of the gods better?
Euthyphro. No, no; that was certainly not what I meant.
Socrates. And I, Euthyphro, never supposed that you did. I asked you the question about the nature of the attention, because I thought that you did not.
Euthyphro. You do me justice, Socrates; that is not the sort of attention which I mean.

Socrates. Good: but I must still ask what is this attention to the gods which is called piety?

Euthyphro. It is such, Socrates, as servants show to their masters.

Socrates. I understand -- a sort of ministration to the gods.

Euthyphro. Exactly.

Socrates. Medicine is also a sort of ministration or service, having in view the attainment of some object -- would you not say of health?

Euthyphro. I should.

Socrates. Again, there is an art which ministers to the shipbuilder with a view to the attainment of some result?

Euthyphro. Yes, Socrates, with a view to the building of a ship.

Socrates. As there is an art which ministers to the housebuilder with a view to the building of a house?

Euthyphro. Yes.

Socrates. And now tell me, my good friend, about the art which ministers to the gods: what work does that help to accomplish? For you must surely know if, as you say, you are of all men living the one who is best instructed in religion.

Euthyphro. And I speak the truth, Socrates.

Socrates. Tell me then, oh tell me -- what is that fair work which the gods do by the help of our ministrations?

Euthyphro. Many and fair, Socrates, are the works which they do.

Socrates. Why, my friend, and so are those of a general. But the chief of them is easily told. Would you not say that victory in war is the chief of them?

Euthyphro. Certainly.

Socrates. Many and fair, too, are the works of the husbandman, if I am not mistaken; but his chief work is the production of food from the earth?

Euthyphro. Exactly.

Socrates. And of the many and fair things done by the gods, which is the chief or principal one?

Euthyphro. I have told you already, Socrates, that to learn all these things accurately will be very tiresome. Let me simply say that piety or holiness is learning, how to please the gods in word and deed, by prayers and sacrifices. Such piety, is the salvation of families and states, just as the impious, which is unpleasing to the gods, is their ruin and destruction.

Socrates. I think that you could have answered in much fewer words the chief question which I asked, Euthyphro, if you had chosen. But I see plainly that you are not disposed to instruct me -- dearly not: else why, when we reached the point, did you turn, aside? Had you only answered me I should have truly learned of you by this time the nature of piety. Now, as the asker of a question is necessarily dependent on the answerer, whither he leads -- I must follow; and can only ask again, what is the pious, and what is piety? Do you mean that they are a, sort of science of praying and sacrificing?

Euthyphro. Yes, I do.

Socrates. And sacrificing is giving to the gods, and prayer is asking of the gods?

Euthyphro. Yes, Socrates.

Socrates. Upon this view, then piety is a science of asking and giving?

Euthyphro. You understand me capitally, Socrates.

Socrates. Yes, my friend; the reason is that I am a votary of your science, and give my mind to it, and therefore nothing which you say will be thrown away upon me. Please then to tell me, what is the nature of this service to the gods? Do you mean that we prefer requests and give gifts to them?

Euthyphro. Yes, I do.

Socrates. Is not the right way of asking to ask of them what we want?

Euthyphro. Certainly.

Socrates. And the right way of giving is to give to them in return what they want of us. There would be no meaning in an art which gives to any one that which he does not want.

Euthyphro. Very true, Socrates.

Socrates. Then piety, Euthyphro, is an art which gods and men have of doing business with one another?

Euthyphro. That is an expression which you may use, if you like.

Socrates. But I have no particular liking for anything but the truth. I wish, however, that you would tell me what benefit accrues to the gods from our gifts. There is no doubt about what they give to us; for there is no good thing which they do not give; but how we can give any good thing to them in return is far from being equally clear. If they give everything and we give nothing, that must be an affair of business in which we have very greatly the advantage of them.

Euthyphro. And do you imagine, Socrates, that any benefit accrues to the gods from our gifts?

Socrates. But if not, Euthyphro, what is the meaning of gifts which are conferred by us upon the gods?

Euthyphro. What else, but tributes of honour; and, as I was just now saying, what pleases them?

Socrates. Piety, then, is pleasing to the gods, but not beneficial or dear to them?

Euthyphro. I should say that nothing could be dearer.

Socrates. Then once more the assertion is repeated that piety is dear to the gods?

Euthyphro. Certainly.

Socrates. And when you say this, can you wonder at your words not standing firm, but walking away? Will you accuse me of being the Daedalus who makes them walk away, not perceiving that there is another and far greater artist than Daedalus who makes them go round in a circle, and he is yourself; for the

argument, as you will perceive, comes round to the same point. Were we not saying that the holy or pious was not the same with that which is loved of the gods? Have you forgotten?
Euthyphro. I quite remember.
Socrates. And are you not saying that what is loved of the gods is holy; and is not this the same as what is dear to them -- do you see?
Euthyphro. True.
Socrates. Then either we were wrong in former assertion; or, if we were right then, we are wrong now.
Euthyphro. One of the two must be true.
Socrates. Then we must begin again and ask, What is piety? That is an enquiry which I shall never be weary of pursuing as far as in me lies; and I entreat you not to scorn me, but to apply your mind to the utmost, and tell me the truth. For, if any man knows, you are he; and therefore I must detain you, like Proteus, until you tell. If you had not certainly known the nature of piety and impiety, I am confident that you would never, on behalf of a serf, have charged your aged father with murder. You would not have run such a risk of doing wrong in the sight of the gods, and you would have had too much respect for the opinions of men. I am sure, therefore, that you know the nature of piety and impiety. Speak out then, my dear Euthyphro, and do not hide your knowledge.
Euthyphro. Another time, Socrates; for I am in a hurry, and must go now.
Socrates. Alas! my companion, and will you leave me in despair? I was hoping that you would instruct me in the nature of piety and impiety; and then I might have cleared myself of Meletus and his indictment. I would have told him that I had been enlightened by Euthyphro, and had given up rash innovations and speculations, in which I indulged only through ignorance, and that now I am about to lead a better life.

2:1-11 Vanity: Good and Enjoyment Under the Sun

[1] I said in mine heart, Go to now, I will prove thee with mirth, therefore enjoy pleasure: and, behold, this also is vanity.

Prove – or test (*nasah*) – Solomon will set out to confirm the results of life conducted with mirth (KJV) or pleasure (NASB).

Mirth (*simchah*) - better translated as good or rejoicing. Not pleasure, as in hedonism (the LXX translates as *euphrosune*, joyfulness or gladness).

Therefore enjoy pleasure, lit. good (*tov*). Solomon is not simply testing the meaningfulness of pleasure, but rather goodness in general. The outcome? *Hebel*. Meaninglessness.

[2] I said of laughter, It is mad: and of mirth, What doeth it?

Lit., I said to laughter (*l'shachuq*)...and to joyfulness (*simchah*). Solomon personifies both. He finds laughter to be as raging foolishness (*m'holal*). Joyfulness is pointless (To what end? To make what? *Ma zo asah*).

[3] I sought in mine heart to give myself unto wine, yet acquainting mine heart with wisdom; and to lay hold on folly, till I might see what was that good for the sons of men, which

they should do under the heaven all the days of their life.

Give myself – to dwell on or prolong my body in wine (*b'yayin*). He does this both while seeking wisdom and while seeking folly to see if he can discover good (*tov*) under heaven.

[4] I made me great works; I built me houses; I planted me vineyards:
[5] I made me gardens and orchards, and I planted trees in them of all kind of fruits:
[6] I made me pools of water, to water therewith the wood that bringeth forth trees:

His inquiry regarding good and enjoyment extends beyond the use of wine. He constructs great works (in general): houses, vineyards, gardens, well stocked orchards, and irrigation to be most efficient (in particular).

[7] I got me servants and maidens, and had servants born in my house; also I had great possessions of great and small cattle above all that were in Jerusalem before me:

In addition to the projects of architecture and biotechnology, Solomon acquired a great many men, women, and cattle. He had an overstock of living and non-living resources.

[8] I gathered me also silver and gold, and the peculiar treasure of kings and of the provinces: I gat me men singers and women singers, and the delights of the sons of men, as musical instruments, and that of all sorts.

He gathered silver and gold. Recalling that he was king in Israel for the duration of this investigation, there were many aspects

2:1-11 Vanity: Good and Enjoyment Under the Sun   73

of the investigation which were in direct conflict with the Law's requirements for the king in Israel:

> Moreover, he shall not multiply horses for himself, nor shall he cause the people to return to Egypt to multiply horses, since the LORD has said to you, 'You shall never again return that way.' He shall not multiply wives for himself or else his heart will turn away; nor shall he greatly increase silver and gold for himself. Now it shall come about when he sits on the throne of his kingdom, he shall write for himself a copy of this law on a scroll in the presence of the Levitical priests. It shall be with him and he shall read it all the days of his life, that he may learn to fear the LORD his God, by carefully observing all the words of this law and these statutes, that his heart may not be lifted above his countrymen and that he may not turn aside from the commandment, to the right or the left, so that he and his sons may continue long in his kingdom in the midst of Israel. (Deut. 17:16-20, NASB)

Rather than obey these various commands, and learn to fear God through special revelation, Solomon learned by experience the meaninglessness and worthlessness of empirical investigation apart from special revelation.

[9] So I was great, and increased more than all that were before me in Jerusalem: also my wisdom remained with me.

He became great (*gadal*), and greater still, increasing (*yasaph*) all the while with his wisdom standing by. He gave up neither wisdom nor success, maintaining both – a rare combination of greatness, and the most anyone under the sun can hope to achieve. His forthcoming assessment will not give much comfort

[10] And whatsoever mine eyes desired I kept not from them, I withheld not my heart from any joy; for my heart rejoiced in all my labour: and this was my portion of all my labour.
His investigation was thorough. He sought to satisfy his eyes (*ayin*) and his heart (*leb*) with joy (*simchah*).

[11] Then I looked on all the works that my hands had wrought, and on the labour that I had laboured to do: and, behold, all was vanity and vexation of spirit, and there was no profit under the sun.

What was his assessment of the outcome of this stage of his investigation — the pursuit of joyfulness? Meaninglessness and inner strife. Furthermore, there was no gain (*yithron*) in any of it. The pursuit of happiness or joyfulness as the final end proved to be pointless.

Philosophical Parallel: Virtue Ethics

Virtue ethics reckons happiness as the highest end, achievable by means of virtue. Happiness is the highest end because all else is done for the sake of itself and for the sake of something else, while happiness is supposed to be pursued only for its own sake. This system represents man's natural pursuit of goodness or piety. The desired destination is happiness under the sun rather than goodness in the sight of God.

Aristotle's brand of virtue ethics is presented in the *Nicomachean Ethics*, which five Books contain the following highlights:

Book 1: Happiness is the highest good; three classes of good: external, of the soul, of the body.

Book 2: Two kinds of virtue: intellectual (or excellence, from teaching, and moral – from habit or *ethos*), moral excellence concerned with pleasure and pain (pleasure makes us do bad, pain keeps us from doing noble); three aspects of the soul (emotions, capacities, characteristics – virtues are characteristics), *moral virtue a mean, between two vices*, the median is worthy of praise. The median is the point of excellence.

Book 3: Voluntary and involuntary actions: ignorance does not equate to involuntary, choice voluntary, but not all voluntary is of choice; deliberation: we cannot deliberate about ends, but about the means by which ends are attained. Wish: end is object of wish, man is responsible, man can choose good and make proper judgments. Courage: a mean between fear and confidence (a thing is defined by its end). Courage keeps to the median. Five assumed types of courage: (1) citizen soldier (2) experience in facing certain dangers (3) a spirited temper (4) optimists (5) acting in ignorance of danger.

Book 4: Extravagance, magnificence, highmindedness. Ambition and lack of ambition – extremes of nameless virtue; gentleness, friendliness, truthfulness, wittiness – all means.

Book 5: Different kinds of justice – complete (justice, the whole of virtue) and partial – distribution and rectification, reciprocity. Justice in political sense, justice by nature vs. justice by convention.

Plato and Aristotle are critical of social contract as an equalization of the law of nature (brutal strong vs. the weak).

The weak create law to equalize, thus social contract represents the failure of the strong to act in accordance with nature. Virtue ethics, on the other hand, they view to be in accordance with rather than a violation of nature.

Plato emphasized 3 parts of the soul (1) rational (2) spirited element (3) appetites. Aristotle made slight adjustments: (1) rational – uniquely human (2) appetitive – shared with animals (3) nutritive – shared with plants – man lives an animal life governed by the rational. To Aristotle, a morally good being is a functional being. Functionality is estimable by the golden mean: the balance between defect and excess.

Primary Source Excerpt: Aristotle: The Nicomachean Ethics (350 BC) (trans. W.D. Ross)

Book I

1   Every art and every inquiry, and similarly every action and pursuit, is thought to aim at some good; and for this reason the good has rightly been declared to be that at which all things aim. But a certain difference is found among ends; some are activities, others are products apart from the activities that produce them. Where there are ends apart from the actions, it is the nature of the products to be better than the activities. Now, as there are many actions, arts, and sciences, their ends also are many; the end of the medical art is health, that of shipbuilding a vessel, that of strategy victory, that of economics wealth. But where such arts fall under a single capacity- as bridle-making and the other arts concerned with the equipment of horses fall under the art of riding, and this and every military action under strategy, in the same way other arts fall under yet others- in all of these the ends of the master arts are to be preferred to all the subordinate ends; for it is for the sake of the former that the

latter are pursued. It makes no difference whether the activities themselves are the ends of the actions, or something else apart from the activities, as in the case of the sciences just mentioned.

2   If, then, there is some end of the things we do, which we desire for its own sake (everything else being desired for the sake of this), and if we do not choose everything for the sake of something else (for at that rate the process would go on to infinity, so that our desire would be empty and vain), clearly this must be the good and the chief good. Will not the knowledge of it, then, have a great influence on life? Shall we not, like archers who have a mark to aim at, be more likely to hit upon what is right? If so, we must try, in outline at least, to determine what it is, and of which of the sciences or capacities it is the object. It would seem to belong to the most authoritative art and that which is most truly the master art. And politics appears to be of this nature; for it is this that ordains which of the sciences should be studied in a state, and which each class of citizens should learn and up to what point they should learn them; and we see even the most highly esteemed of capacities to fall under this, e.g. strategy, economics, rhetoric; now, since politics uses the rest of the sciences, and since, again, it legislates as to what we are to do and what we are to abstain from, the end of this science must include those of the others, so that this end must be the good for man. For even if the end is the same for a single man and for a state, that of the state seems at all events something greater and more complete whether to attain or to preserve; though it is worth while to attain the end merely for one man, it is finer and more godlike to attain it for a nation or for city-states. These, then, are the ends at which our inquiry aims, since it is political science, in one sense of that term.

3   Our discussion will be adequate if it has as much clearness as the subject-matter admits of, for precision is not to be sought for alike in all discussions, any more than in all the products of the crafts. Now fine and just actions, which political science investigates, admit of much variety and fluctuation of opinion, so that they may be thought to exist only by convention, and not by nature. And goods also give rise to a similar fluctuation because they bring harm to many people; for before now men have been undone by reason of their wealth, and others by reason of their courage. We must be content, then, in speaking of such subjects and with such premises to indicate the truth roughly and in outline, and in speaking about things which are only for the most part true and with premisses of the same kind to reach conclusions that are no better. In the same spirit, therefore, should each type of statement be received; for it is the mark of an educated man to look for precision in each class of things just so far as the nature of the subject admits; it is evidently equally foolish to accept probable reasoning from a mathematician and to demand from a rhetorician scientific proofs.

Now each man judges well the things he knows, and of these he is a good judge. And so the man who has been educated in a subject is a good judge of that subject, and the man who has received an all-round education is a good judge in general. Hence a young man is not a proper hearer of lectures on political science; for he is inexperienced in the actions that occur in life, but its discussions start from these and are about these; and, further, since he tends to follow his passions, his study will be vain and unprofitable, because the end aimed at is not knowledge but action. And it makes no difference whether he is young in years or youthful in character; the defect does not depend on time, but on his living, and pursuing each successive object, as passion directs. For to such persons, as to the incontinent, knowledge brings no profit; but to those who desire and act in accordance with a rational principle knowledge about such matters will be of great benefit.

These remarks about the student, the sort of treatment to be expected, and the purpose of the inquiry, may be taken as our preface.

4   Let us resume our inquiry and state, in view of the fact that all knowledge and every pursuit aims at some good, what it is that we say political science aims at and what is the highest of all goods achievable by action. Verbally there is very general agreement; for both the general run of men and people of superior refinement say that it is happiness, and identify living well and doing well with being happy; but with regard to what happiness is they differ, and the many do not give the same account as the wise. For the former think it is some plain and obvious thing, like pleasure, wealth, or honour; they differ, however, from one another- and often even the same man identifies it with different things, with health when he is ill, with wealth when he is poor; but, conscious of their ignorance, they admire those who proclaim some great ideal that is above their comprehension. Now some thought that apart from these many goods there is another which is self-subsistent and causes the goodness of all these as well. To examine all the opinions that have been held were perhaps somewhat fruitless; enough to examine those that are most prevalent or that seem to be arguable.

Let us not fail to notice, however, that there is a difference between arguments from and those to the first principles. For Plato, too, was right in raising this question and asking, as he used to do, "are we on the way from or to the first principles?" There is a difference, as there is in a race-course between the course from the judges to the turning-point and the way back. For, while we must begin with what is known, things are objects of knowledge in two senses- some to us, some without qualification. Presumably, then, we must begin with things known to us. Hence anyone who is to listen intelligently to lectures about what is noble and just, and generally, about the subjects of political science must have been brought up in good habits. For the fact is the starting-point, and if this is sufficiently plain to him, he will not at the start need the reason as well; and the man who has been well brought up has or can easily get starting points. And as for him who neither has nor can get them, let him hear the words of Hesiod:

Far best is he who knows all things himself;
Good, he that hearkens when men counsel right;
But he who neither knows, nor lays to heart
Another's wisdom, is a useless wight.

5   Let us, however, resume our discussion from the point at which we digressed. To judge from the lives that men lead, most men, and men of the most vulgar type, seem (not without some ground) to identify the good, or happiness, with pleasure; which is the reason why they love the life of enjoyment. For there are, we may say, three prominent types of life- that just mentioned, the political, and thirdly the contemplative life. Now the mass of mankind are evidently quite slavish in their tastes, preferring a life suitable to beasts, but they get some ground for their view from the fact that many of those in high places share the tastes of Sardanapallus. A consideration of the prominent types of life shows that people of superior refinement and of active disposition identify happiness with honour; for this is, roughly speaking, the end of the political life. But it seems too superficial to be what we are looking for, since it is thought to depend on

those who bestow honour rather than on him who receives it, but the good we divine to be something proper to a man and not easily taken from him. Further, men seem to pursue honour in order that they may be assured of their goodness; at least it is by men of practical wisdom that they seek to be honoured, and among those who know them, and on the ground of their virtue; clearly, then, according to them, at any rate, virtue is better. And perhaps one might even suppose this to be, rather than honour, the end of the political life. But even this appears somewhat incomplete; for possession of virtue seems actually compatible with being asleep, or with lifelong inactivity, and, further, with the greatest sufferings and misfortunes; but a man who was living so no one would call happy, unless he were maintaining a thesis at all costs. But enough of this; for the subject has been sufficiently treated even in the current discussions. Third comes the contemplative life, which we shall consider later.

The life of money-making is one undertaken under compulsion, and wealth is evidently not the good we are seeking; for it is merely useful and for the sake of something else. And so one might rather take the aforenamed objects to be ends; for they are loved for themselves. But it is evident that not even these are ends; yet many arguments have been thrown away in support of them. Let us leave this subject, then.

6 We had perhaps better consider the universal good and discuss thoroughly what is meant by it, although such an inquiry is made an uphill one by the fact that the Forms have been introduced by friends of our own. Yet it would perhaps be thought to be better, indeed to be our duty, for the sake of maintaining the truth even to destroy what touches us closely, especially as we are philosophers or lovers of wisdom; for, while both are dear, piety requires us to honour truth above our friends.

The men who introduced this doctrine did not posit Ideas of classes within which they recognized priority and posteriority (which is the reason why they did not maintain the existence of an Idea embracing all numbers); but the term "good" is used both in the category of substance and in that of quality and in that of relation, and that which is per se, i.e. substance, is prior in nature to the relative (for the latter is like an off shoot and accident of being); so that there could not be a common Idea set over all these goods. Further, since "good" has as many senses as "being" (for it is predicated both in the category of substance, as of God and of reason, and in quality, i.e. of the virtues, and in quantity, i.e. of that which is moderate, and in relation, i.e. of the useful, and in time, i.e. of the right opportunity, and in place, i.e. of the right locality and the like), clearly it cannot be something universally present in all cases and single; for then it could not have been predicated in all the categories but in one only. Further, since of the things answering to one Idea there is one science, there would have been one science of all the goods; but as it is there are many sciences even of the things that fall under one category, e.g. of opportunity, for opportunity in war is studied by strategics and in disease by medicine, and the moderate in food is studied by medicine and in exercise by the science of gymnastics. And one might ask the question, what in the world they mean by "a thing itself," is (as is the case) in "man himself" and in a particular man the account of man is one and the same. For in so far as they are man, they will in no respect differ; and if this is so, neither will "good itself" and particular goods, in so far as they are good. But again it will not be good any the more for being eternal, since that which lasts long is no whiter than that which perishes in a day. The Pythagoreans seem to give a more plausible account of the good, when they place the one in the column of goods; and it is they that Speusippus seems to have followed.

But let us discuss these matters elsewhere; an objection to what we have said, however, may be discerned in the fact that the Platonists have not been speaking about all goods, and that the goods that are pursued and loved for themselves are called good by reference to a single Form, while those which tend to produce or to preserve these somehow or to prevent their contraries are called so by reference to these, and in a secondary sense. Clearly, then, goods must be spoken of in two ways, and some must be good in themselves, the others by reason of these. Let us separate, then, things good in themselves from things useful, and consider whether the former are called good by reference to a single Idea. What sort of goods would one call good in themselves? Is it those that are pursued even when isolated from others, such as intelligence, sight, and certain pleasures and honours? Certainly, if we pursue these also for the sake of something else, yet one would place them among things good in themselves. Or is nothing other than the Idea of good good in itself? In that case the Form will be empty. But if the things we have named are also things good in themselves, the account of the good will have to appear as something identical in them all, as that of whiteness is identical in snow and in white lead. But of honour, wisdom, and pleasure, just in respect of their goodness, the accounts are distinct and diverse. The good, therefore, is not some common element answering to one Idea.

But what then do we mean by the good? It is surely not like the things that only chance to have the same name. Are goods one, then, by being derived from one good or by all contributing to one good, or are they rather one by analogy? Certainly as sight is in the body, so is reason in the soul, and so on in other cases. But perhaps these subjects had better be dismissed for the present; for perfect precision about them would be more appropriate to another branch of philosophy. And similarly with regard to the Idea; even if there is some one good which is universally predicable of goods or is capable of separate and independent existence, clearly it could not be achieved or attained by man; but we are now seeking something attainable. Perhaps, however, some one might think it worthwhile to recognize this with a view to the goods that are attainable and achievable; for having this as a sort of pattern we shall know better the goods that are good for us, and if we know them shall attain them. This argument has some plausibility, but seems to clash with the procedure of the sciences; for all of these, though they aim at some good and seek to supply the deficiency of it, leave on one side the knowledge of the good. Yet that all the exponents of the arts should be ignorant of, and should not even seek, so great an aid is not probable. It is hard, too, to see how a weaver or a carpenter will be benefited in regard to his own craft by knowing this "good itself," or how the man who has viewed the Idea itself will be a better doctor or general thereby. For a doctor seems not even to study health in this way, but the health of man, or perhaps rather the health of a particular man; it is individuals that he is healing. But enough of these topics.

7   Let us again return to the good we are seeking, and ask what it can be. It seems different in different actions and arts; it is different in medicine, in strategy, and in the other arts likewise. What then is the good of each? Surely that for whose sake everything else is done. In medicine this is health, in strategy victory, in architecture a house, in any other sphere something else, and in every action and pursuit the end; for it is for the sake of this that all men do whatever else they do. Therefore, if there is an end for all that we do, this will be the good achievable by action, and if there are more than one, these will be the goods achievable by action.

So the argument has by a different course reached the same point; but we must try to state this even more clearly.

Since there are evidently more than one end, and we choose some of these (e.g. wealth, flutes, and in general instruments) for the sake of something else, clearly not all ends are final ends; but the chief good is evidently something final. Therefore, if there is only one final end, this will be what we are seeking, and if there are more than one, the most final of these will be what we are seeking. Now we call that which is in itself worthy of pursuit more final than that which is worthy of pursuit for the sake of something else, and that which is never desirable for the sake of something else more final than the things that are desirable both in themselves and for the sake of that other thing, and therefore we call final without qualification that which is always desirable in itself and never for the sake of something else.

Now such a thing happiness, above all else, is held to be; for this we choose always for self and never for the sake of something else, but honour, pleasure, reason, and every virtue we choose indeed for themselves (for if nothing resulted from them we should still choose each of them), but we choose them also for the sake of happiness, judging that by means of them we shall be happy. Happiness, on the other hand, no one chooses for the sake of these, nor, in general, for anything other than itself.

From the point of view of self-sufficiency, the same result seems to follow; for the final good is thought to be self-sufficient. Now by self-sufficient we do not mean that which is sufficient for a man by himself, for one who lives a solitary life, but also for parents, children, wife, and in general for his friends and fellow citizens, since man is born for citizenship. But some limit must be set to this; for if we extend our requirement to ancestors and descendants and friends' friends we are in for an infinite series. Let us examine this question, however, on another occasion; the self-sufficient we now define as that which when isolated makes life desirable and lacking in nothing; and such we think happiness to be; and further we think it most desirable of all things, without being counted as one good thing among others—if it were so counted it would clearly be made more desirable by the addition of even the least of goods; for that which is added becomes an excess of goods, and of goods the greater is always more desirable. Happiness, then, is something final and self-sufficient, and is the end of action.

Presumably, however, to say that happiness is the chief good seems a platitude, and a clearer account of what it is is still desired. This might perhaps be given, if we could first ascertain the function of man. For just as for a flute-player, a sculptor, or an artist, and, in general, for all things that have a function or activity, the good and the "well" is thought to reside in the function, so would it seem to be for man, if he has a function. Have the carpenter, then, and the tanner certain functions or activities, and has man none? Is he born without a function? Or as eye, hand, foot, and in general each of the parts evidently has a function, may one lay it down that man similarly has a function apart from all these? What then can this be? Life seems to be common even to plants, but we are seeking what is peculiar to man. Let us exclude, therefore, the life of nutrition and growth. Next there would be a life of perception, but it also seems to be common even to the horse, the ox, and every animal. There remains, then, an active life of the element that has a rational principle; of this, one part has such a principle in the sense of being obedient to one, the other in the sense of possessing one and exercising thought. And, as "life of the rational element" also has two meanings, we must state that life in the sense of activity is what we mean; for this seems to be the more proper sense of the term. Now if the function of man is an activity of soul which follows or implies a rational principle, and if we say "so-and-so" and "a good so-and-so" have a function which is the same in kind, e.g. a lyre, and a good lyre-player, and so without qualification in all cases, eminence in respect of goodness being idded to the name of the function (for the function of a lyre-player is to play the lyre, and that of a good lyre-player is to do so well): if this is the case, and we state the function of man to be a certain kind of life, and this to be an activity or actions of the soul implying a rational principle, and the function of a good man to be the good and noble performance of these, and if any action is well performed when it is performed in accordance with the appropriate excellence: if this is the case, human good turns out to be activity of soul in accordance with virtue, and if there are more than one virtue, in accordance with the best and most complete.

But we must add "in a complete life." For one swallow does not make a summer, nor does one day; and so too one day, or a short time, does not make a man blessed and happy.

Let this serve as an outline of the good; for we must presumably first sketch it roughly, and then later fill in the details. But it would seem that any one is capable of carrying on and articulating what has once been well outlined, and that time is a good discoverer or partner in such a work; to which facts the advances of the arts are due; for any one can add what is lacking. And we must also remember what has been said before, and not look for precision in all things alike, but in each class of things such precision as accords with the subject-matter, and so much as is appropriate to the inquiry. For a carpenter and a geometer investigate the right angle in different ways; the former does so in so far as the right angle is useful for his work, while the latter inquires what it is or what sort of thing it is; for he is a spectator of the truth. We must act in the same way, then, in all other matters as well, that our main task may not be subordinated to minor questions. Nor must we demand the cause in all matters alike; it is enough in some cases that the fact be well established, as in the case of the first principles; the fact is the primary thing or first principle. Now of first principles we see some by induction, some by perception, some by a certain habituation, and others too in other ways. But each set of principles we must try to investigate in the natural way, and we must take pains to state them definitely, since they have a great influence on what follows. For the beginning is thought to be more than half of the whole, and many of the questions we ask are cleared up by it.

8   We must consider happiness, however, in the light not only of our conclusion and our premises, but also of what is commonly said about it; for with a true view all the data harmonize, but with a false one the facts soon clash. Now goods have been divided into three classes, and some are described as external, others as relating to soul or to body; we call those that relate to soul most properly and truly goods, and psychical actions and activities we class as relating to soul. Therefore our account must be sound, at least according to this view, which is an old one and agreed on by philosophers. It is correct also in that we identify the end with certain actions and activities; for thus it falls among goods of the soul and not among external goods. Another belief which harmonizes with our account is that the happy man lives well and does well; for we have practically defined happiness as a sort of good life and good action. The characteristics that are looked for in happiness seem also, all of them, to belong to what we have defined happiness as being. For some identify happiness with virtue, some with practical wisdom, others with a kind of philosophic wisdom, others with these, or one of these, accompanied by pleasure or not without pleasure; while others include also external prosperity. Now some of these views have been held by many men and men of old, others by a few eminent persons; and it is not probable that either of these should be entirely mistaken, but rather that they

should be right in at least some one respect or even in most respects.

With those who identify happiness with virtue or someone virtue our account is in harmony; for to virtue belongs virtuous activity. But it makes, perhaps, no small difference whether we place the chief good in possession or in use, in state of mind or in activity. For the state of mind may exist without producing any good result, as in a man who is asleep or in some other way quite inactive, but the activity cannot; for one who has the activity will of necessity be acting, and acting well. And as in the Olympic Games it is not the most beautiful and the strongest that are crowned but those who compete (for it is some of these that are victorious), so those who act win, and rightly win, the noble and good things in life.

Their life is also in itself pleasant. For pleasure is a state of soul, and to each man that which he is said to be a lover of is pleasant; e.g. not only is a horse pleasant to the lover of horses, and a spectacle to the lover of sights, but also in the same way just acts are pleasant to the lover of justice and in general virtuous acts to the lover of virtue. Now for most men their pleasures are in conflict with one another because these are not by nature pleasant, but the lovers of what is noble find pleasant the things that are by nature pleasant; and virtuous actions are such, so that these are pleasant for such men as well as in their own nature. Their life, therefore, has no further need of pleasure as a sort of adventitious charm, but has its pleasure in itself. For, besides what we have said, the man who does not rejoice in noble actions is not even good; since no one would call a man just who did not enjoy acting justly, nor any man liberal who did not enjoy liberal actions; and similarly in all other cases. If this is so, virtuous actions must be in themselves pleasant. But they are also good and noble, and have each of these attributes in the highest degree, since the good man judges well about these attributes; his judgement is such as we have described. Happiness then is the best, noblest, and most pleasant thing in the world, and these attributes are not severed as in the inscription at Delos-

Most noble is that which is justest, and best is health;
But pleasantest is it to win what we love.

For all these properties belong to the best activities; and these, or one- the best- of these, we identify with happiness.

Yet evidently, as we said, it needs the external goods as well; for it is impossible, or not easy, to do noble acts without the proper equipment. In many actions we use friends and riches and political power as instruments; and there are some things the lack of which takes the lustre from happiness, as good birth, goodly children, beauty; for the man who is very ugly in appearance or ill-born or solitary and childless is not very likely to be happy, and perhaps a man would be still less likely if he had thoroughly bad children or friends or had lost good children or friends by death. As we said, then, happiness seems to need this sort of prosperity in addition; for which reason some identify happiness with good fortune, though others identify it with virtue.

9   For this reason also the question is asked, whether happiness is to be acquired by learning or by habituation or some other sort of training, or comes in virtue of some divine providence or again by chance. Now if there is any gift of the gods to men, it is reasonable that happiness should be god-given, and most surely god-given of all human things inasmuch as it is the best. But this question would perhaps be more appropriate to another inquiry; happiness seems, however, even if it is not god-sent but comes as a result of virtue and some process of

learning or training, to be among the most godlike things; for that which is the prize and end of virtue seems to be the best thing in the world, and something godlike and blessed.

It will also on this view be very generally shared; for all who are not maimed as regards their potentiality for virtue may win it by a certain kind of study and care. But if it is better to be happy thus than by chance, it is reasonable that the facts should be so, since everything that depends on the action of nature is by nature as good as it can be, and similarly everything that depends on art or any rational cause, and especially if it depends on the best of all causes. To entrust to chance what is greatest and most noble would be a very defective arrangement.

The answer to the question we are asking is plain also from the definition of happiness; for it has been said to be a virtuous activity of soul, of a certain kind. Of the remaining goods, some must necessarily pre-exist as conditions of happiness, and others are naturally co-operative and useful as instruments. And this will be found to agree with what we said at the outset; for we stated the end of political science to be the best end, and political science spends most of its pains on making the citizens to be of a certain character, viz. good and capable of noble acts.

It is natural, then, that we call neither ox nor horse nor any other of the animals happy; for none of them is capable of sharing in such activity. For this reason also a boy is not happy; for he is not yet capable of such acts, owing to his age; and boys who are called happy are being congratulated by reason of the hopes we have for them. For there is required, as we said, not only complete virtue but also a complete life, since many changes occur in life, and all manner of chances, and the most prosperous may fall into great misfortunes in old age, as is told of Priam in the Trojan Cycle; and one who has experienced such chances and has ended wretchedly no one calls happy.

10   Must no one at all, then, be called happy while he lives; must we, as Solon says, see the end? Even if we are to lay down this doctrine, is it also the case that a man is happy when he is dead? Or is not this quite absurd, especially for us who say that happiness is an activity? But if we do not call the dead man happy, and if Solon does not mean this, but that one can then safely call a man blessed as being at last beyond evils and misfortunes, this also affords matter for discussion; for both evil and good are thought to exist for a dead man, as much as for one who is alive but not aware of them; e.g. honours and dishonours and the good or bad fortunes of children and in general of descendants. And this also presents a problem; for though a man has lived happily up to old age and has had a death worthy of his life, many reverses may befall his descendants--some of them may be good and attain the life they deserve, while with others the opposite may be the case; and clearly too the degrees of relationship between them and their ancestors may vary indefinitely. It would be odd, then, if the dead man were to share in these changes and become at one time happy, at another wretched; while it would also be odd if the fortunes of the descendants did not for some time have some effect on the happiness of their ancestors.

But we must return to our first difficulty; for perhaps by a consideration of it our present problem might be solved. Now if we must see the end and only then call a man happy, not as being happy but as having been so before, surely this is a paradox, that when he is happy the attribute that belongs to him is not to be truly predicated of him because we do not wish to call living men happy, on account of the changes that may befall them, and because we have assumed happiness to be something permanent and by no means easily changed, while a single man may suffer many turns of fortune's wheel. For clearly if we were to keep pace with his fortunes, we should often call the same man happy and again wretched, making the happy man out to be chameleon and insecurely based. Or is this keeping pace with his fortunes quite wrong? Success or failure in life does not depend on these, but human life, as we said, needs these as mere additions, while virtuous activities or their opposites are what constitute happiness or the reverse.

The question we have now discussed confirms our definition. For no function of man has so much permanence as virtuous activities (these are thought to be more durable even than knowledge of the sciences), and of these themselves the most valuable are more durable because those who are happy spend their life most readily and most continuously in these; for this seems to be the reason why we do not forget them. The attribute in question, then, will belong to the happy man, and he will be happy throughout his life; for always, or by preference to everything else, he will be engaged in virtuous action and contemplation, and he will bear the chances of life most nobly and altogether decorously, if he is "truly good" and "foursquare beyond reproach."

Now many events happen by chance, and events differing in importance; small pieces of good fortune or of its opposite clearly do not weigh down the scales of life one way or the other, but a multitude of great events if they turn out well will make life happier (for not only are they themselves such as to add beauty to life, but the way a man deals with them may be noble and good), while if they turn out ill they crush and maim happiness; for they both bring pain with them and hinder many activities. Yet even in these nobility shines through, when a man bears with resignation many great misfortunes, not through insensibility to pain but through nobility and greatness of soul.

If activities are, as we said, what gives life its character, no happy man can become miserable; for he will never do the acts that are hateful and mean. For the man who is truly good and wise, we think, bears all the chances life becomingly and always makes the best of circumstances, as a good general makes the best military use of the army at his command and a good shoemaker makes the best shoes out of the hides that are given him; and so with all other craftsmen. And if this is the case, the happy man can never become miserable; though he will not reach blessedness, if he meet with fortunes like those of Priam.

Nor, again, is he many-coloured and changeable; for neither will he be moved from his happy state easily or by any ordinary misadventures, but only by many great ones, nor, if he has had many great misadventures, will he recover his happiness in a short time, but if at all, only in a long and complete one in which he has attained many splendid successes.

When then should we not say that he is happy who is active in accordance with complete virtue and is sufficiently equipped with external goods, not for some chance period but throughout a complete life? Or must we add "and who is destined to live thus and die as befits his life"? Certainly the future is obscure to us, while happiness, we claim, is an end and something in every way final. If so, we shall call happy those among living men in whom these conditions are, and are to be, fulfilled--but happy men. So much for these questions.

11   That the fortunes of descendants and of all a man's friends should not affect his happiness at all seems a very unfriendly doctrine, and one opposed to the opinions men hold; but since the events that happen are numerous and admit of all sorts of difference, and some come more near to us and others less so, it seems a long--nay, an infinite--task to discuss each in detail; a general outline will perhaps suffice. If, then, as some of a man's own misadventures have a certain weight and influence

on life while others are, as it were, lighter, so too there are differences among the misadventures of our friends taken as a whole, and it makes a difference whether the various suffering befall the living or the dead (much more even than whether lawless and terrible deeds are presupposed in a tragedy or done on the stage), this difference also must be taken into account; or rather, perhaps, the fact that doubt is felt whether the dead share in any good or evil. For it seems, from these considerations, that even if anything whether good or evil penetrates to them, it must be something weak and negligible, either in itself or for them, or if not, at least it must be such in degree and kind as not to make happy those who are not happy nor to take away their blessedness from those who are. The good or bad fortunes of friends, then, seem to have some effects on the dead, but effects of such a kind and degree as neither to make the happy unhappy nor to produce any other change of the kind.

12   These questions having been definitely answered, let us consider whether happiness is among the things that are praised or rather among the things that are prized; for clearly it is not to be placed among potentialities. Everything that is praised seems to be praised because it is of a certain kind and is related somehow to something else; for we praise the just or brave man and in general both the good man and virtue itself because of the actions and functions involved, and we praise the strong man, the good runner, and so on, because he is of a certain kind and is related in a certain way to something good and important. This is clear also from the praises of the gods; for it seems absurd that the gods should be referred to our standard, but this is done because praise involves a reference, to something else. But if praise is for things such as we have described, clearly what applies to the best things is not praise, but something greater and better, as is indeed obvious; for what we do to the gods and

the most godlike of men is to call them blessed and happy. And so too with good things; no one praises happiness as he does justice, but rather calls it blessed, as being something more divine and better.

Eudoxus also seems to have been right in his method of advocating the supremacy of pleasure; he thought that the fact that, though a good, it is not praised indicated it to be better than the things that are praised, and that this is what God and the good are; for by reference to these all other things are judged. Praise is appropriate to virtue, for as a result of virtue men tend to do noble deeds, but encomia are bestowed on acts, whether of the body or of the soul. But perhaps nicety in these matters is more proper to those who have made a study of encomia; to us it is clear from what has been said that happiness is among the things that are prized and perfect. It seems to be so also from the fact that it is a first principle; for it is for the sake of this that we all do all that we do, and the first principle and cause of goods is, we claim, something prized and divine.

13   Since happiness is an activity of soul in accordance with perfect virtue, we must consider the nature of virtue; for perhaps we shall thus see better the nature of happiness. The true student of politics, too, is thought to have studied virtue above all things; for he wishes to make his fellow citizens good and obedient to the laws. As an example of this we have the lawgivers of the Cretans and the Spartans, and any others of the kind that there may have been. And if this inquiry belongs to political science, clearly the pursuit of it will be in accordance with our original plan. But clearly the virtue we must study is human virtue; for the good we were seeking was human good and the happiness human happiness. By human virtue we mean not that of the body but that of the soul; and happiness also we call an activity of soul. But if this is so, clearly the student of

politics must know somehow the facts about soul, as the man who is to heal the eyes or the body as a whole must know about the eyes or the body; and all the more since politics is more prized and better than medicine; but even among doctors the best educated spend much labour on acquiring knowledge of the body. The student of politics, then, must study the soul, and must study it with these objects in view, and do so just to the extent which is sufficient for the questions we are discussing; for further precision is perhaps something more laborious than our purposes require.

Some things are said about it, adequately enough, even in the discussions outside our school, and we must use these; e.g. that one element in the soul is irrational and one has a rational principle. Whether these are separated as the parts of the body or of anything divisible are, or are distinct by definition but by nature inseparable, like convex and concave in the circumference of a circle, does not affect the present question.

Of the irrational element one division seems to be widely distributed, and vegetative in its nature, I mean that which causes nutrition and growth; for it is this kind of power of the soul that one must assign to all nurslings and to embryos, and this same power to fullgrown creatures; this is more reasonable than to assign some different power to them. Now the excellence of this seems to be common to all species and not specifically human; for this part or faculty seems to function most in sleep, while goodness and badness are least manifest in sleep (whence comes the saying that the happy are not better off than the wretched for half their lives; and this happens naturally enough, since sleep is an inactivity of the soul in that respect in which it is called good or bad), unless perhaps to a small extent some of the movements actually penetrate to the soul, and in this respect the dreams of good men are better than those of ordinary people. Enough of this subject, however; let us leave the nutritive faculty alone, since it has by its nature no share in human excellence.

There seems to be also another irrational element in the soul-one which in a sense, however, shares in a rational principle. For we praise the rational principle of the continent man and of the incontinent, and the part of their soul that has such a principle, since it urges them aright and towards the best objects; but there is found in them also another element naturally opposed to the rational principle, which fights against and resists that principle. For exactly as paralysed limbs when we intend to move them to the right turn on the contrary to the left, so is it with the soul; the impulses of incontinent people move in contrary directions. But while in the body we see that which moves astray, in the soul we do not. No doubt, however, we must none the less suppose that in the soul too there is something contrary to the rational principle, resisting and opposing it. In what sense it is distinct from the other elements does not concern us. Now even this seems to have a share in a rational principle, as we said; at any rate in the continent man it obeys the rational principle and presumably in the temperate and brave man it is still more obedient; for in him it speaks, on all matters, with the same voice as the rational principle.

Therefore the irrational element also appears to be twofold. For the vegetative element in no way shares in a rational principle, but the appetitive and in general the desiring element in a sense shares in it, in so far as it listens to and obeys it; this is the sense in which we speak of "taking account" of one's father or one's friends, not that in which we speak of "accounting" for a mathematical property. That the irrational element is in some sense persuaded by a rational principle is indicated also by the giving of advice and by all reproof and exhortation. And if this element also must be said to have a rational principle, that which has a rational principle (as well as that which has not) will be twofold, one subdivision having it in the strict sense and in itself, and the other having a tendency to obey as one does one's father.

Virtue too is distinguished into kinds in accordance with this difference; for we say that some of the virtues are intellectual and others moral, philosophic wisdom and understanding and practical wisdom being intellectual, liberality and temperance moral. For in speaking about a man's character we do not say that he is wise or has understanding but that he is good-tempered or temperate; yet we praise the wise man also with respect to his state of mind; and of states of mind we call those which merit praise virtues.

Book II

1   Virtue, then, being of two kinds, intellectual and moral, intellectual virtue in the main owes both its birth and its growth to teaching (for which reason it requires experience and time), while moral virtue comes about as a result of habit, whence also its name (*ethike*) is one that is formed by a slight variation from the word *ethos* (habit). From this it is also plain that none of the moral virtues arises in us by nature; for nothing that exists by nature can form a habit contrary to its nature. For instance the stone which by nature moves downwards cannot be habituated to move upwards, not even if one tries to train it by throwing it up ten thousand times; nor can fire be habituated to move downwards, nor can anything else that by nature behaves in one way be trained to behave in another. Neither by nature, then, nor contrary to nature do the virtues arise in us; rather we are adapted by nature to receive them, and are made perfect by habit.

Again, of all the things that come to us by nature we first acquire the potentiality and later exhibit the activity (this is plain in the case of the senses; for it was not by often seeing or often hearing that we got these senses, but on the contrary we had them before we used them, and did not come to have them by using them); but the virtues we get by first exercising them, as also happens in the case of the arts as well. For the things we have to learn before we can do them, we learn by doing them, e.g. men become builders by building and lyreplayers by playing the lyre; so too we become just by doing just acts, temperate by doing temperate acts, brave by doing brave acts.

This is confirmed by what happens in states; for legislators make the citizens good by forming habits in them, and this is the wish of every legislator, and those who do not effect it miss their mark, and it is in this that a good constitution differs from a bad one.

Again, it is from the same causes and by the same means that every virtue is both produced and destroyed, and similarly every art; for it is from playing the lyre that both good and bad lyre-players are produced. And the corresponding statement is true of builders and of all the rest; men will be good or bad builders as a result of building well or badly. For if this were not so, there would have been no need of a teacher, but all men would have been born good or bad at their craft. This, then, is the case with the virtues also; by doing the acts that we do in our transactions with other men we become just or unjust, and by doing the acts that we do in the presence of danger, and being habituated to feel fear or confidence, we become brave or cowardly. The same is true of appetites and feelings of anger; some men become temperate and good-tempered, others self-indulgent and irascible, by behaving in one way or the other in the appropriate circumstances. Thus, in one word, states of character arise out of like activities. This is why the activities we exhibit must be of a certain kind; it is because the states of character correspond to the differences between these. It makes no small difference, then, whether we form habits of one kind or of another from our very youth; it makes a very great difference, or rather all the difference.

2   Since, then, the present inquiry does not aim at theoretical knowledge like the others (for we are inquiring not in order to know what virtue is, but in order to become good, since otherwise our inquiry would have been of no use), we must examine the nature of actions, namely how we ought to do them; for these determine also the nature of the states of character that are produced, as we have said. Now, that we must act according to the right rule is a common principle and must be assumed-it will be discussed later, i.e. both what the right rule is, and how it is related to the other virtues. But this must be agreed upon beforehand, that the whole account of matters of conduct must be given in outline and not precisely, as we said at the very beginning that the accounts we demand must be in accordance with the subject-matter; matters concerned with conduct and questions of what is good for us have no fixity, any more than matters of health. The general account being of this nature, the account of particular cases is yet more lacking in exactness; for they do not fall under any art or precept but the agents themselves must in each case consider what is appropriate to the occasion, as happens also in the art of medicine or of navigation.

But though our present account is of this nature we must give what help we can. First, then, let us consider this, that it is the nature of such things to be destroyed by defect and excess, as we see in the case of strength and of health (for to gain light on things imperceptible we must use the evidence of sensible things); both excessive and defective exercise destroys the strength, and similarly drink or food which is above or below a certain amount destroys the health, while that which is proportionate both produces and increases and preserves it. So too is it, then, in the case of temperance and courage and the other virtues. For the man who flies from and fears everything and does not stand his ground against anything becomes a coward, and the man who fears nothing at all but goes to meet every danger becomes rash; and similarly the man who indulges in every pleasure and abstains from none becomes self-indulgent, while the man who shuns every pleasure, as boors do, becomes in a way insensible; temperance and courage, then, are destroyed by excess and defect, and preserved by the mean.

But not only are the sources and causes of their origination and growth the same as those of their destruction, but also the sphere of their actualization will be the same; for this is also true of the things which are more evident to sense, e.g. of strength; it is produced by taking much food and undergoing much exertion, and it is the strong man that will be most able to do these things. So too is it with the virtues; by abstaining from pleasures we become temperate, and it is when we have become so that we are most able to abstain from them; and similarly too in the case of courage; for by being habituated to despise things that are terrible and to stand our ground against them we become brave, and it is when we have become so that we shall be most able to stand our ground against them.

3 We must take as a sign of states of character the pleasure or pain that ensues on acts; for the man who abstains from bodily pleasures and delights in this very fact is temperate, while the man who is annoyed at it is self-indulgent, and he who stands his ground against things that are terrible and delights in this or at least is not pained is brave, while the man who is pained is a coward. For moral excellence is concerned with pleasures and pains; it is on account of the pleasure that we do bad things, and on account of the pain that we abstain from

noble ones. Hence we ought to have been brought up in a particular way from our very youth, as Plato says, so as both to delight in and to be pained by the things that we ought; for this is the right education.

Again, if the virtues are concerned with actions and passions, and every passion and every action is accompanied by pleasure and pain, for this reason also virtue will be concerned with pleasures and pains. This is indicated also by the fact that punishment is inflicted by these means; for it is a kind of cure, and it is the nature of cures to be effected by contraries.

Again, as we said but lately, every state of soul has a nature relative to and concerned with the kind of things by which it tends to be made worse or better; but it is by reason of pleasures and pains that men become bad, by pursuing and avoiding these--either the pleasures and pains they ought not or when they ought not or as they ought not, or by going wrong in one of the other similar ways that may be distinguished. Hence men even define the virtues as certain states of impassivity and rest; not well, however, because they speak absolutely, and do not say "as one ought" and "as one ought not" and "when one ought or ought not," and the other things that may be added. We assume, then, that this kind of excellence tends to do what is best with regard to pleasures and pains, and vice does the contrary.

The following facts also may show us that virtue and vice are concerned with these same things. There being three objects of choice and three of avoidance, the noble, the advantageous, the pleasant, and their contraries, the base, the injurious, the painful, about all of these the good man tends to go right and the bad man to go wrong, and especially about pleasure; for this is common to the animals, and also it accompanies all objects of choice; for even the noble and the advantageous appear pleasant.

Again, it has grown up with us all from our infancy; this is why it is difficult to rub off this passion, engrained as it is in our life. And we measure even our actions, some of us more and others less, by the rule of pleasure and pain. For this reason, then, our whole inquiry must be about these; for to feel delight and pain rightly or wrongly has no small effect on our actions.

Again, it is harder to fight with pleasure than with anger, to use Heraclitus' phrase, but both art and virtue are always concerned with what is harder; for even the good is better when it is harder. Therefore for this reason also the whole concern both of virtue and of political science is with pleasures and pains; for the man who uses these well will be good, he who uses them badly bad.

That virtue, then, is concerned with pleasures and pains, and that by the acts from which it arises it is both increased and, if they are done differently, destroyed, and that the acts from which it arose are those in which it actualizes itself--let this be taken as said.

4   The question might be asked, what we mean by saying that we must become just by doing just acts, and temperate by doing temperate acts; for if men do just and temperate acts, they are already just and temperate, exactly as, if they do what is in accordance with the laws of grammar and of music, they are grammarians and musicians.

Or is this not true even of the arts? It is possible to do something that is in accordance with the laws of grammar, either by chance or at the suggestion of another. A man will be a grammarian, then, only when he has both done something grammatical and done it grammatically; and this means doing it in accordance with the grammatical knowledge in himself.

Again, the case of the arts and that of the virtues are not similar; for the products of the arts have their goodness in themselves, so that it is enough that they should have a certain character, but if the acts that are in accordance with the virtues have themselves a certain character it does not follow that they are done justly or temperately. The agent also must be in a certain condition when he does them; in the first place he must have knowledge, secondly he must choose the acts, and choose them for their own sakes, and thirdly his action must proceed from a firm and unchangeable character. These are not reckoned in as conditions of the possession of the arts, except the bare knowledge; but as a condition of the possession of the virtues knowledge has little or no weight, while the other conditions count not for a little but for everything, i.e. the very conditions which result from often doing just and temperate acts.

Actions, then, are called just and temperate when they are such as the just or the temperate man would do; but it is not the man who does these that is just and temperate, but the man who also does them as just and temperate men do them. It is well said, then, that it is by doing just acts that the just man is produced, and by doing temperate acts the temperate man; without doing these no one would have even a prospect of becoming good.

But most people do not do these, but take refuge in theory and think they are being philosophers and will become good in this way, behaving somewhat like patients who listen attentively to their doctors, but do none of the things they are ordered to do. As the latter will not be made well in body by such a course of treatment, the former will not be made well in soul by such a course of philosophy.

5   Next we must consider what virtue is. Since things that are found in the soul are of three kinds--passions, faculties, states of character, virtue must be one of these. By passions I mean appetite, anger, fear, confidence, envy, joy, friendly

feeling, hatred, longing, emulation, pity, and in general the feelings that are accompanied by pleasure or pain; by faculties the things in virtue of which we are said to be capable of feeling these, e.g. of becoming angry or being pained or feeling pity; by states of character the things in virtue of which we stand well or badly with reference to the passions, e.g. with reference to anger we stand badly if we feel it violently or too weakly, and well if we feel it moderately; and similarly with reference to the other passions.

Now neither the virtues nor the vices are passions, because we are not called good or bad on the ground of our passions, but are so called on the ground of our virtues and our vices, and because we are neither praised nor blamed for our passions (for the man who feels fear or anger is not praised, nor is the man who simply feels anger blamed, but the man who feels it in a certain way), but for our virtues and our vices we are praised or blamed.

Again, we feel anger and fear without choice, but the virtues are modes of choice or involve choice. Further, in respect of the passions we are said to be moved, but in respect of the virtues and the vices we are said not to be moved but to be disposed in a particular way.

For these reasons also they are not *faculties*; for we are neither called good nor bad, nor praised nor blamed, for the simple capacity of feeling the passions; again, we have the faculties by nature, but we are not made good or bad by nature; we have spoken of this before.

If, then, the virtues are neither passions nor faculties, all that remains is that they should be *states of character*.

Thus we have stated what virtue is in respect of its genus.

6 We must, however, not only describe virtue as a state of character, but also say what sort of state it is. We may remark,

then, that every virtue or excellence both brings into good condition the thing of which it is the excellence and makes the work of that thing be done well; e.g. the excellence of the eye makes both the eye and its work good; for it is by the excellence of the eye that we see well. Similarly the excellence of the horse makes a horse both good in itself and good at running and at carrying its rider and at awaiting the attack of the enemy. Therefore, if this is true in every case, the virtue of man also will be the state of character which makes a man good and which makes him do his own work well.

How this is to happen we have stated already, but it will be made plain also by the following consideration of the specific nature of virtue. In everything that is continuous and divisible it is possible to take more, less, or an equal amount, and that either in terms of the thing itself or relatively to us; and the equal is an intermediate between excess and defect. By the intermediate in the object I mean that which is equidistant from each of the extremes, which is one and the same for all men; by the intermediate relatively to us that which is neither too much nor too little- and this is not one, nor the same for all. For instance, if ten is many and two is few, six is the intermediate, taken in terms of the object; for it exceeds and is exceeded by an equal amount; this is intermediate according to arithmetical proportion. But the intermediate relatively to us is not to be taken so; if ten pounds are too much for a particular person to eat and two too little, it does not follow that the trainer will order six pounds; for this also is perhaps too much for the person who is to take it, or too little--too little for Milo, too much for the beginner in athletic exercises. The same is true of running and wrestling. Thus a master of any art avoids excess and defect, but seeks the intermediate and chooses this--the intermediate not in the object but relatively to us.

If it is thus, then, that every art does its work well--by looking to the intermediate and judging its works by this standard (so that we often say of good works of art that it is not possible either to take away or to add anything, implying that excess and defect destroy the goodness of works of art, while the mean preserves it; and good artists, as we say, look to this in their work), and if, further, virtue is more exact and better than any art, as nature also is, then virtue must have the quality of aiming at the intermediate. I mean moral virtue; for it is this that is concerned with passions and actions, and in these there is excess, defect, and the intermediate. For instance, both fear and confidence and appetite and anger and pity and in general pleasure and pain may be felt both too much and too little, and in both cases not well; but to feel them at the right times, with reference to the right objects, towards the right people, with the right motive, and in the right way, is what is both intermediate and best, and this is characteristic of virtue. Similarly with regard to actions also there is excess, defect, and the intermediate. Now virtue is concerned with passions and actions, in which excess is a form of failure, and so is defect, while the intermediate is praised and is a form of success; and being praised and being successful are both characteristics of virtue. Therefore virtue is a kind of mean, since, as we have seen, it aims at what is intermediate.

Again, it is possible to fail in many ways (for evil belongs to the class of the unlimited, as the Pythagoreans conjectured, and good to that of the limited), while to succeed is possible only in one way (for which reason also one is easy and the other difficult- to miss the mark easy, to hit it difficult); for these reasons also, then, excess and defect are characteristic of vice, and the mean of virtue; for men are good in but one way, but bad in many.

Virtue, then, is a state of character concerned with choice, lying in a mean, i.e. the mean relative to us, this being determined by a rational principle, and by that principle by which the man of practical wisdom would determine it. Now it is a mean between two vices, that which depends on excess and that which depends on defect; and again it is a mean because the vices respectively fall short of or exceed what is right in both passions and actions, while virtue both finds and chooses that which is intermediate. Hence in respect of its substance and the definition which states its essence virtue is a mean, with regard to what is best and right an extreme.

But not every action nor every passion admits of a mean; for some have names that already imply badness, e.g. spite, shamelessness, envy, and in the case of actions adultery, theft, murder; for all of these and suchlike things imply by their names that they are themselves bad, and not the excesses or deficiencies of them. It is not possible, then, ever to be right with regard to them; one must always be wrong. Nor does goodness or badness with regard to such things depend on committing adultery with the right woman, at the right time, and in the right way, but simply to do any of them is to go wrong. It would be equally absurd, then, to expect that in unjust, cowardly, and voluptuous action there should be a mean, an excess, and a deficiency; for at that rate there would be a mean of excess and of deficiency, an excess of excess, and a deficiency of deficiency. But as there is no excess and deficiency of temperance and courage because what is intermediate is in a sense an extreme, so too of the actions we have mentioned there is no mean nor any excess and deficiency, but however they are done they are wrong; for in general there is neither a mean of excess and deficiency, nor excess and deficiency of a mean.

7   We must, however, not only make this general statement, but also apply it to the individual facts. For among statements

about conduct those which are general apply more widely, but those which are particular are more genuine, since conduct has to do with individual cases, and our statements must harmonize with the facts in these cases. We may take these cases from our table. With regard to feelings of fear and confidence courage is the mean; of the people who exceed, he who exceeds in fearlessness has no name (many of the states have no name), while the man who exceeds in confidence is rash, and he who exceeds in fear and falls short in confidence is a coward. With regard to pleasures and pains--not all of them, and not so much with regard to the pains--the mean is temperance, the excess self-indulgence. Persons deficient with regard to the pleasures are not often found; hence such persons also have received no name. But let us call them "insensible."

With regard to giving and taking of money the mean is liberality, the excess and the defect prodigality and meanness. In these actions people exceed and fall short in contrary ways; the prodigal exceeds in spending and falls short in taking, while the mean man exceeds in taking and falls short in spending. (At present we are giving a mere outline or summary, and are satisfied with this; later these states will be more exactly determined.) With regard to money there are also other dispositions- a mean, magnificence (for the magnificent man differs from the liberal man; the former deals with large sums, the latter with small ones), an excess, tastelessness and vulgarity, and a deficiency, niggardliness; these differ from the states opposed to liberality, and the mode of their difference will be stated later. With regard to honour and dishonour the mean is proper pride, the excess is known as a sort of "empty vanity," and the deficiency is undue humility; and as we said liberality was related to magnificence, differing from it by dealing with small sums, so there is a state similarly related to proper pride, being concerned with small honours while that is concerned with great. For it is possible to desire honour as one ought, and more than one ought, and less, and the man who exceeds in his desires is called ambitious, the man who falls short unambitious, while the intermediate person has no name. The dispositions also are nameless, except that that of the ambitious man is called ambition. Hence the people who are at the extremes lay claim to the middle place; and we ourselves sometimes call the intermediate person ambitious and sometimes unambitious, and sometimes praise the ambitious man and sometimes the unambitious. The reason of our doing this will be stated in what follows; but now let us speak of the remaining states according to the method which has been indicated.

With regard to anger also there is an excess, a deficiency, and a mean. Although they can scarcely be said to have names, yet since we call the intermediate person good-tempered let us call the mean good temper; of the persons at the extremes let the one who exceeds be called irascible, and his vice irascibility, and the man who falls short an inirascible sort of person, and the deficiency inirascibility.

There are also three other means, which have a certain likeness to one another, but differ from one another: for they are all concerned with intercourse in words and actions, but differ in that one is concerned with truth in this sphere, the other two with pleasantness; and of this one kind is exhibited in giving amusement, the other in all the circumstances of life. We must therefore speak of these too, that we may the better see that in all things the mean is praiseworthy, and the extremes neither praiseworthy nor right, but worthy of blame. Now most of these states also have no names, but we must try, as in the other cases, to invent names ourselves so that we may be clear and easy to follow. With regard to truth, then, the intermediate is a truthful sort of person and the mean may be called truthfulness, while the pretence which exaggerates is boastfulness and the person characterized by it a boaster, and that which understates is mock modesty and the person characterized by it mock-modest. With regard to pleasantness in the giving of amusement the intermediate person is ready-witted and the disposition ready wit, the excess is buffoonery and the person characterized by it a buffoon, while the man who falls short is a sort of boor and his state is boorishness. With regard to the remaining kind of pleasantness, that which is exhibited in life in general, the man who is pleasant in the right way is friendly and the mean is friendliness, while the man who exceeds is an obsequious person if he has no end in view, a flatterer if he is aiming at his own advantage, and the man who falls short and is unpleasant in all circumstances is a quarrelsome and surly sort of person.

There are also means in the passions and concerned with the passions; since shame is not a virtue, and yet praise is extended to the modest man. For even in these matters one man is said to be intermediate, and another to exceed, as for instance the bashful man who is ashamed of everything; while he who falls short or is not ashamed of anything at all is shameless, and the intermediate person is modest. Righteous indignation is a mean between envy and spite, and these states are concerned with the pain and pleasure that are felt at the fortunes of our neighbours; the man who is characterized by righteous indignation is pained at undeserved good fortune, the envious man, going beyond him, is pained at all good fortune, and the spiteful man falls so far short of being pained that he even rejoices. But these states there will be an opportunity of describing elsewhere; with regard to justice, since it has not one simple meaning, we shall, after describing the other states, distinguish its two kinds and say how each of them is a mean; and similarly we shall treat also of the rational virtues.

8   There are three kinds of disposition, then, two of them vices, involving excess and deficiency respectively, and one a virtue, viz. the mean, and all are in a sense opposed to all; for the extreme states are contrary both to the intermediate state and to each other, and the intermediate to the extremes; as the equal is greater relatively to the less, less relatively to the greater, so the middle states are excessive relatively to the deficiencies, deficient relatively to the excesses, both in passions and in actions. For the brave man appears rash relatively to the coward, and cowardly relatively to the rash man; and similarly the temperate man appears self-indulgent relatively to the insensible man, insensible relatively to the self-indulgent, and the liberal man prodigal relatively to the mean man, mean relatively to the prodigal. Hence also the people at the extremes push the intermediate man each over to the other, and the brave man is called rash by the coward, cowardly by the rash man, and correspondingly in the other cases.

These states being thus opposed to one another, the greatest contrariety is that of the extremes to each other, rather than to the intermediate; for these are further from each other than from the intermediate, as the great is further from the small and the small from the great than both are from the equal. Again, to the intermediate some extremes show a certain likeness, as that of rashness to courage and that of prodigality to liberality; but the extremes show the greatest unlikeness to each other; now contraries are defined as the things that are furthest from each other, so that things that are further apart are more contrary.

To the mean in some cases the deficiency, in some the excess is more opposed; e.g. it is not rashness, which is an excess, but cowardice, which is a deficiency, that is more opposed to courage, and not insensibility, which is a deficiency, but self-indulgence, which is an excess, that is more opposed to temperance. This happens from two reasons, one being drawn from the thing itself; for because one extreme is nearer and liker to the intermediate, we oppose not this but rather its contrary to the intermediate. E.g., since rashness is thought liker and nearer to courage, and cowardice more unlike, we oppose rather the latter to courage; for things that are further from the intermediate are thought more contrary to it. This, then, is one cause, drawn from the thing itself; another is drawn from ourselves; for the things to which we ourselves more naturally tend seem more contrary to the intermediate. For instance, we ourselves tend more naturally to pleasures, and hence are more easily carried away towards self-indulgence than towards propriety. We describe as contrary to the mean, then, rather the directions in which we more often go to great lengths; and therefore self-indulgence, which is an excess, is the more contrary to temperance.

9   That moral virtue is a mean, then, and in what sense it is so, and that it is a mean between two vices, the one involving excess, the other deficiency, and that it is such because its character is to aim at what is intermediate in passions and in actions, has been sufficiently stated. Hence also it is no easy task to be good. For in everything it is no easy task to find the middle, e.g. to find the middle of a circle is not for everyone but for him who knows; so, too, anyone can get angry--that is easy--or give or spend money; but to do this to the right person, to the right extent, at the right time, with the right motive, and in the right way, that is not for everyone, nor is it easy; wherefore goodness is both rare and laudable and noble.

Hence he who aims at the intermediate must first depart from what is the more contrary to it, as Calypso advises--

Hold the ship out beyond that surf and spray.

For of the extremes one is more erroneous, one less so; therefore, since to hit the mean is hard in the extreme, we must as a second best, as people say, take the least of the evils; and this will be done best in the way we describe. But we must consider the things towards which we ourselves also are easily carried away; for some of us tend to one thing, some to another; and this will be recognizable from the pleasure and the pain we feel. We must drag ourselves away to the contrary extreme; for we shall get into the intermediate state by drawing well away from error, as people do in straightening sticks that are bent.

Now in everything the pleasant or pleasure is most to be guarded against; for we do not judge it impartially. We ought, then, to feel towards pleasure as the elders of the people felt towards Helen, and in all circumstances repeat their saying; for if we dismiss pleasure thus we are less likely to go astray. It is by doing this, then, (to sum the matter up) that we shall best be able to hit the mean.

But this is no doubt difficult, and especially in individual cases; for it is not easy to determine both how and with whom and on what provocation and how long one should be angry; for we too sometimes praise those who fall short and call them good-tempered, but sometimes we praise those who get angry and call them manly. The man, however, who deviates little from goodness is not blamed, whether he do so in the direction of the more or of the less, but only the man who deviates more widely; for he does not fail to be noticed. But up to what point and to what extent a man must deviate before he becomes blameworthy it is not easy to determine by reasoning, any more than anything else that is perceived by the senses; such things depend on particular facts, and the decision rests with perception. So much, then, is plain, that the intermediate state is in all things to be praised, but that we must incline sometimes towards the excess, sometimes towards the deficiency; for so shall we most easily hit the mean and what is right.

2:12-17 Vanity: Wisdom, Madness, and Folly Under the Sun

[12] And I turned myself to behold wisdom, and madness, and folly: for what can the man do that cometh after the king? even that which hath been already done.

To see wisdom (*chokmah*), madness (*holelah*), folly (*sikluth*). Solomon had previously engaged in a sampling of these, now he turns to a rationally disinterested viewing of the three.

[13] Then I saw that wisdom excelleth folly, as far as light excelleth darkness.

Excels (*yithron*) – same word as in 2:11 (no profit or excelling under the sun), here wisdom excels folly as a polar opposite, yet that excellence notwithstanding, it is still nothing in the under the sun perspective.

[14] The wise man's eyes are in his head; but the fool walketh in darkness: and I myself perceived also that one event happeneth to them all.

The pursuit of understanding is better than not, but the outcome is not altered by the pursuit.

[15] Then said I in my heart, As it happeneth to the fool, so it

happeneth even to me; and why was I then more wise? Then I said in my heart, that this also is vanity.

If the same fate would befall Solomon as the fool, then how can wisdom even be called wisdom? In what way can it be distinguished from foolishness? Any such distinction ultimately is hebel.

[16] For there is no remembrance of the wise more than of the fool for ever; seeing that which now is in the days to come shall all be forgotten. And how dieth the wise man? as the fool.

Could the distinction be that when a wise man is gone he is remembered as being wise? On the contrary, both the wise and the fool are forgotten. So what benefit the pursuit of wisdom?

[17] Therefore I hated life; because the work that is wrought under the sun is grievous unto me: for all is vanity and vexation of spirit.

Hated (*saneti*, Qal perfect, not intensive) not the strongest term he could have used, but still strong. Life was odious to him – grievous (*rah* – lit., evil). Meaninglessness and inner strife.

Philosophical Parallel: Epistemological Grounding

Competing Pre-Socratic Interpretations[37]
The Milesian school was characterized by a persisting monism – that the only conceivable explanation of the nature of things was still one which showed how all things proceed from one and are resolved into the same (Guthrie). They searched for a unity behind the multiplicity of phenomena, seeking a unified worldview.

Thales was at the forefront, posing the question of *arche*, and by his approach has been understood to be the founder of speculative science, as he observed the recycling of water, concluding its priority in all things living is evidence that it is indeed the *arche*, yet mixes this with mythical influences, saying all things are full of gods, that water is the divine, promulgating the cosmological perspective that the earth floated on water, etc. While his represented a departure from the mythological, it was not a complete one, as he first rationalizes myth, a step leading toward his anticipation of modern scientific thought.

Anaximander's alternative to Thales theory of water and the problem it creates (if all is water, why not all wet, and where is room for opposites?): he believed a divine substance he called "*apeiron*" (unbounded or infinite, and perhaps rarer than water yet denser than air) was the *arche*; that it formed a vortex of cold, wet, dry, hot.....spiral like draining water...fits the appearance of cosmology and explains and places boundaries in the earth (cold--earth geosphere, wet--water hydrosphere, dry--air atmosphere, hot--fire pyrosphere, stars, etc...)...this cosmology also resolves the problem of why all is not wet, as Anaximander suggests that opposites separate (by way of conflict) from the *apeiron*. But if Anaximander is correct, then why is the outer atmosphere not all fire? The inner atmosphere hardened except for holes where stars, sun, etc, are visible? Anaximander's cosmogony: separation of a germ (fertile) of hot and cold from the divine substance, became a ring of flame, giving birth to the "heavens," etc. He believed in an unsupported earth.

Anaxemines reckoned the *arche* to be air, and explained change via rarefaction and condensation, in relation to Anaximander's conception of the conflict of opposites, and reduced quality (cold, dense, light, hot, etc.) to quantity – the difference between qualities is quantity. For Anaximander the ultimate constituents of reality are qualitative, for Anaxemines these qualities are a result of different quantities of the one stuff (the constituents). In agreement with Thales and disagreement with Anaximander, Anaxemines believed the earth to require material support.

These three Milesian philosophers, while finding their most substantial disagreement on the nature of *arche* (Thales – water, Anaximander – *apeiron*, Anaxemines – air), were unified in their cosmologies at least to the extent that all three viewed nature as rational, evolutionary, and hylozoist. Additionally, they viewed eternal motion as the cause of life, and that eternal motion as immortal and even divine, being self-caused.

Heraclitus, the self-searching and intensely independent thinking and at times paradoxical Ephesian "Riddler," is noted for his understanding of fire as central and the source of nature, the coincidence of opposites, and his strongly evidenced statement, "You cannot step twice into the same river." The statement epitomizes his doctrine of flux – that everything moves on and nothing is at rest. Aristotle seems to have understood Heraclitus' views to be enjoined to the Milesians' earlier view (an *arche* in eternal motion, yet self-caused), although Heraclitus shows both advancement of and distinction from the Milesian ideas.

Heraclitus appreciated the need for an *arche*, but also recognized the insufficiency of the Milesians' application of it, and thus his innovation was built upon the idea of *arche* but with a transformation of it. The *logos* is the divine (yet material) force which governs nature: fire, as he describes the "whole world order as ever living fire," Not flame, but dry exhalation – this undergirds an ongoing contrast of dry (good) and wet (bad).

Three additional statements of Heraclitus essentially comprise his system of thought: (1) harmony is the product of opposites, thus the basic fact in nature is strife; (2) everything is in continuous motion or change; (3) the world is a living and everlasting fire.

First, "harmony as the product of opposites," is not intended to agree with the Pythagorean idea of harmony (peaceful coexistence), but rather has three aspects: (1) everything is made of opposites and subject to internal tension; (2) the simultaneity of opposites – opposites are not to be viewed as strictly conflicting but rather as complementary [e.g., "in changing it is at rest"]; and (3) as an obvious consequence, strife is the universal creative force. Second, the doctrine of flux stems naturally from the first statement, as even things appearing at rest can be only because of the effort and motion which causes them to appear so (e.g., a strung bow). Third, the world as a living and everlasting fire is the root of Heraclitus' characterization of logos, and betrays a subtle yet important departure from the Milesians' idea of arche: while previously the arche was perceived to be neutral or mediate, Heraclitus' fire is in itself an opposite, which is being equally and necessarily kindled and extinguished in the cosmos. The unity of the logos (the living fire) undergirds nature with a divine ordering assuring the continuation of the cosmos. This ordering resembles that of the Milesians, with fundamental aspects arche and hylozoism observable in Heraclitus.

While there are the aforementioned points of agreement, Heraclitus does not adopt the Milesians' cosmogony. Whereas the Milesian trio reckoned a beginning to the cosmos, Heraclitus denies any beginning, with his logos as an eternal essence of life, in contrast to the Milesian arche which was perceived as the force inaugurating life. But perhaps the most significant distinction between Heraclitus and the Milesians is found in the essential, rather than qualitative or quantitative, change that Heraclitus suggests. He says that a soul dies when it becomes water, water dies when it becomes earth, but from earth water is born, and from water, souls. Recognizing his identification of soul with fire, it is apparent that he is not suggesting simply a balance of opposites, but a more essential and cyclical flux.

Parmenides the Eleatic is committed to the nonexistence of opposites, plurality and change. He thus critiques a number of Heraclitean ideas:

First, he asserts the non-existence of no-thing. If something is, it cannot be said of it that it was or will be.

Second, change is an illusion – the appearance of change is not to be mistaken for change. Heraclitus' idea of change from one to another would have been logically repugnant to Parmenides.

Third, and not unrelated to point two, the senses cannot be trusted. Parmenides was the first to draw the distinction between data from the senses and logos (rational), between sensible and intelligible.

Fourth, and as a logical conclusion of the previous three points, the world had no beginning, as what is must have always been and from what is not nothing could be. Any cosmogony from a single arche is disallowed (if Anaximander's apeiron a unity then no distinctions could have appeared, Anaxemines condensation and rarefaction impossible).

Fifth, reality is bounded and complete (a kind of cue ball universe).

Platonic Dualism[38]

Plato's cosmogony, metaphysics, and epistemology represent a synthesis of two competing pre-Socratic views: Parmenides' monism—the idea that being is unchanged and understood only by reason; and Heraclitus' idea of the hidden reality of constant change ("one cannot step twice into the same river"). Plato seems motivated by a desire to recognize a noumenal and unchanging world and still at the same time explain the appearances of change. Oakeley sees this as central in Plato's metaphysics:

> As a metaphysician Plato felt primarily the need of understanding the world as a unity. In him culminated the search of Greek thought for the One. But this One must be unity of value. (Oakeley, 1926)

Plato's quest for unity is apparent in his divided line theory, which puts forth metaphysical and epistemological foundations: that which changes is in the metaphysical realm of 'becoming', while the unchanging and intelligibly grasped is 'being'. He can thus offer an explanation for the appearances, while at the same time acknowledging unchangeableness in being. He is recognized as "the first to make a sharp distinction between visible, corporeal reality and an intelligible, incorporeal world of Ideas" (Bos, 2002). His system can be charted as follows:

Knowledge	Pure Intelligence	A	**Intelligible world of being**
	Reason	B	
Opinion	Belief	C	**Visible world of becoming**
	Illusion	D	

The D and C levels represent opinion, and find their focus in the visible world of becoming. The B and A levels represent knowledge, and are interactions with the intelligible world of being.

On opinion and the visible world of becoming: the D level represents the lowest level. On the epistemology side, imagination or illusion, and on the metaphysics/ontology side, the interaction is with shadows, images, or reflections. This is where people commonly interact with the visible world of becoming. The C level is the realm of belief or perception where objects or the antecedents of images are perceived.

On knowledge and the intelligible world of being: the B level in epistemology represents deductive reason, while the metaphysics/ontology focuses on the lower forms (mathematics, etc.); the A level represents on the epistemology side, pure thought, and on the metaphysical/ontological side the higher forms – equality, justice, and including goodness – the highest of the forms.

If Plato's metaphysics and epistemology assert a dualistic ontology, his cosmogony accounts for it. Nothing comes into being without sufficient cause, thus the visible, tangible cosmos came into being by divine causation (Tim., 28). God[39] fashioned a single living creature (the universe), as perfect as conceivable (Tim., 29) and containing all life. The universe-god would then function as the creator of mortals (Tim., 69), demonstrating itself to be a visible and supreme god (Tim., 92). Good and evil find their balance likewise in these creative acts: good is ascribed of God in reality (Rep., 379a-c), yet the existence of evil must be explained by some causation other than God, as Plato is direct in his assertion that evil does not originate from God (Rep., 379c). The cosmos is God's only creation (Tim., 30-31), and that divine created being (his children) brought forth the physical realm (Tim., 69) as an expression of perfection. But the physical realm is inadequate for such a task, ultimately veiling (with "evil") the true goodness of God. Arguably the Platonic cosmogony was a significant factor[40] in the later rise of the Gnostic dualism which exalted the (good) spirit over the (evil) flesh, being himself more inclined to an ascetic perspective[41] leaning even to an "other-worldly side" (Stewart, 1915). Vlastos discusses evidence of such a leaning observed in Plato's theory of forms,[42] he says:

> Plato's Form-mysticism is profoundly otherworldly. The ontology of non-sensible, eternal, incorporeal, self existent, contemplable Forms, and of their anthropological correlate, the invisible, immortal, incorporeal transmigrating soul, has far reaching implications for the mind and for the heart...all we can find here are images, copies, shadows of the real world which we shall fully know only when liberated from the "oyster shell."[43]

This otherworldly interpretation perceives death as ally to enlightenment. But what endures, body or soul? Plato is fairly specific in the *Gorgias*:

> Death, it seems to me, is actually nothing but the disconnexion of two things, the soul and the body, from each other. And so when they are disconnected from one another, each of them keeps its own condition very much as it was when the man was alive....(Gor., 524b)

And again in the *Apology*:

> For the state of death is one of two things: either it is virtual nothingness, so that the dead has no consciousness of anything, or it is, as people say, a change and migration of the soul from this to another place. (Apol., 40c)

And finally, in the more mythical presentation of the *Timaeus*:

> Anyone living well during his life would upon death return to his native star, while those failing to live in this regard would return for a second tour of duty, this time as a woman, and if there was further moral failure, the third coming would be as an animal. (Tim., 42; 90-91)

From this personal ontology of the soul and death, built on metaphysical dualism, rises the ethical principle that things done in the body are of significance to the soul, since the soul will subsist beyond the (original) body, while the body is merely an instrument to facilitate (or hinder) the virtue of the soul. Lange argues that Plato's brand of asceticism is not an extreme one (if it can be labeled as asceticism at all):

> Plato, unlike the Neoplatonists and other extremists, does not look upon the body as something utterly despicable and shameful but merely deprecates the limitations it imposes on the spirit. He is not an ascetic who would torture the body and deny the legitimacy of bodily needs (Rep., 571DE). He would merely train the body to be an efficient servant of the mind. (Lange, 1936).

In Lange's reading, it is the physical body that limits the spirit, hence even if Plato is understood as less than ascetic, Vlastos' "otherworldly" appraisal would still be appropriate since the physical body has no eternality or value in itself, but serves as purely instrumental for the ordering of the spirit.

Primary Source Excerpt: Plato: Allegory of the Cave (399-380 BC)[44] (trans. Benjamin Jowett)

[Socrates] And now, I said, let me show in a figure how far our nature is enlightened or unenlightened: --Behold! human beings living in a underground cave, which has a mouth open towards the light and reaching all along the cave; here they have been from their childhood, and have their legs and necks chained so that they cannot move, and can only see before them, being prevented by the chains from turning round their heads. Above and behind them a fire is blazing at a distance, and between the fire and the prisoners there is a raised way; and you will see, if you look, a low wall built along the way, like the screen which marionette players have in front of them, over which they show the puppets.

[Glaucon] I see.

[Socrates] And do you see, I said, men passing along the wall carrying all sorts of vessels, and statues and figures of animals made of wood and stone and various materials, which appear over the wall? Some of them are talking, others silent.

[Glaucon] You have shown me a strange image, and they are strange prisoners.

[Socrates] Like ourselves, I replied; and they see only their own shadows, or the shadows of one another, which the fire throws on the opposite wall of the cave?

[Glaucon] True, he said; how could they see anything but the shadows if they were never allowed to move their heads?

[Socrates] And of the objects which are being carried in like manner they would only see the shadows?

[Glaucon] Yes, he said.

[Socrates] And if they were able to converse with one another, would they not suppose that they were naming what was actually before them?

[Glaucon] Very true.

[Socrates] And suppose further that the prison had an echo which came from the other side, would they not be sure to fancy when one of the passers-by spoke that the voice which they heard came from the passing shadow?

[Glaucon] No question, he replied.

[Socrates] To them, I said, the truth would be literally nothing but the shadows of the images.

[Glaucon] That is certain.

[Socrates] And now look again, and see what will naturally follow if the prisoners are released and disabused of their error. At first, when any of them is liberated and compelled suddenly to stand up and turn his neck round and walk and look towards the light, he will suffer sharp pains; the glare will distress him, and he will be unable to see the realities of which in his former state he had seen the shadows; and then conceive someone saying to him, that what he saw before was an illusion, but that now, when he is approaching nearer to being and his eye is turned towards more real existence, he has a clearer vision,-- what will be his reply? And you may further imagine that his instructor is pointing to the objects as they pass and requiring him to name them, – will he not be perplexed? Will he not fancy that the shadows which he formerly saw are truer than the objects which are now shown to him?

[Glaucon] Far truer.

[Socrates] And if he is compelled to look straight at the light, will he not have a pain in his eyes which will make him turn away to take refuge in the objects of vision which he can see, and which he will conceive to be in reality clearer than the things which are now being shown to him?

[Glaucon] True, he said.

[Socrates] And suppose once more, that he is reluctantly dragged up a steep and rugged ascent, and held fast until he is forced into the presence of the sun himself, is he not likely to be pained and irritated? When he approaches the light his eyes will be dazzled, and he will not be able to see anything at all of what are now called realities.

[Glaucon] Not all in a moment, he said.

[Socrates] He will require to grow accustomed to the sight of the upper world. And first he will see the shadows best, next the reflections of men and other objects in the water, and then the objects themselves; then he will gaze upon the light of the moon and the stars and the spangled heaven; and he will see the sky and the stars by night better than the sun or the light of the sun by day?

[Glaucon] Certainly.

[Socrates] Last of all he will be able to see the sun, and not mere reflections of him in the water, but he will see him in his own proper place, and not in another; and he will contemplate him as he is.

[Glaucon] Certainly.

[Socrates] He will then proceed to argue that this is he who gives the season and the years, and is the guardian of all that is in the visible world, and in a certain way the cause of all things which he and his fellows have been accustomed to behold?

[Glaucon] Clearly, he said, he would first see the sun and then reason about him.

[Socrates] And when he remembered his old habitation, and the wisdom of the cave and his fellow-prisoners, do you not suppose that he would felicitate himself on the change, and pity them?

[Glaucon] Certainly, he would.

[Socrates] And if they were in the habit of conferring honors among themselves on those who were quickest to observe the passing shadows and to remark which of them went before, and which followed after, and which were together; and who were therefore best able to draw conclusions as to the future, do you think that he would care for such honors and glories, or envy the possessors of them? Would he not say with Homer, *Better to be the poor servant of a poor master,* and to endure anything, rather than think as they do and live after their manner?

[Glaucon] Yes, he said, I think that he would rather suffer anything than entertain these false notions and live in this miserable manner.

[Socrates] Imagine once more, I said, such an one coming suddenly out of the sun to be replaced in his old situation; would he not be certain to have his eyes full of darkness?

[Glaucon] To be sure, he said.

[Socrates] And if there were a contest, and he had to compete in measuring the shadows with the prisoners who had never moved out of the cave, while his sight was still weak, and before his eyes had become steady (and the time which would be needed to acquire this new habit of sight might be very considerable) would he not be ridiculous? Men would say of him that up he went and down he came without his eyes; and that it was better not even to think of ascending; and if any one tried to loose another and lead him up to the light, let them only catch the offender, and they would put him to death.

[Glaucon] No question, he said.

[Socrates] This entire allegory, I said, you may now append, dear Glaucon, to the previous argument; the prison-house is the world of sight, the light of the fire is the sun, and you will not misapprehend me if you interpret the journey upwards to be the ascent of the soul into the intellectual world according to my poor belief, which, at your desire, I have expressed whether rightly or wrongly God knows. But, whether true or false, my opinion is that in the world of knowledge the idea of good appears last of all, and is seen only with an effort; and, when seen, is also inferred to be the universal author of all things beautiful and right, parent of light and of the lord of light in this visible world, and the immediate source of reason and truth in the intellectual; and that this is the power upon which he who would act rationally, either in public or private life must have his eye fixed.

[Glaucon] I agree, he said, as far as I am able to understand you.

[Socrates] Moreover, I said, you must not wonder that those who attain to this beatific vision are unwilling to descend to human affairs; for their souls are ever hastening into the upper world where they desire to dwell; which desire of theirs is very natural, if our allegory may be trusted.

[Glaucon] Yes, very natural.

[Socrates] And is there anything surprising in one who passes from divine contemplations to the evil state of man, misbehaving himself in a ridiculous manner; if, while his eyes are blinking and before he has become accustomed to the surrounding darkness, he is compelled to fight in courts of law, or in other places, about the images or the shadows of images of justice, and is endeavoring to meet the conceptions of those who have never yet seen absolute justice?

[Glaucon] Anything but surprising, he replied.

[Socrates] Anyone who has common sense will remember that the bewilderments of the eyes are of two kinds, and arise from two causes, either from coming out of the light or from going into the light, which is true of the mind's eye, quite as much as of the bodily eye; and he who remembers this when he sees any one whose vision is perplexed and weak, will not be too ready to laugh; he will first ask whether that soul of man has come out of the brighter light, and is unable to see because unaccustomed to the dark, or having turned from darkness to the day is dazzled by excess of light. And he will count the one happy in his condition and state of being, and he will pity the other; or, if he have a mind to laugh at the soul which comes from below into the light, there will be more reason in this than in the laugh which greets him who returns from above out of the light into the cave.

[Glaucon] That, he said, is a very just distinction.

[Socrates] But then, if I am right, certain professors of education must be wrong when they say that they can put a knowledge into the soul which was not there before, like sight into blind eyes.

[Glaucon] They undoubtedly say this, he replied.

[Socrates] Whereas, our argument shows that the power and capacity of learning exists in the soul already; and that just as the eye was unable to turn from darkness to light without the whole body, so too the instrument of knowledge can only by the movement of the whole soul be turned from the world of becoming into that of being, and learn by degrees to endure the sight of being, and of the brightest and best of being, or in other words, of the good.

[Glaucon] Very true.

[Socrates] And must there not be some art which will effect conversion in the easiest and quickest manner; not implanting the faculty of sight, for that exists already, but has been turned in the wrong direction, and is looking away from the truth?

[Glaucon] Yes, he said, such an art may be presumed.

[Socrates] And whereas the other so-called virtues of the soul seem to be akin to bodily qualities, for even when they are not originally innate they can be implanted later by habit and exercise, the virtue of wisdom more than anything else contains a divine element which always remains, and by this conversion is rendered useful and profitable; or, on the other hand, hurtful and useless. Did you never observe the narrow intelligence flashing from the keen eye of a clever rogue--how eager he is, how clearly his paltry soul sees the way to his end; he is the reverse of blind, but his keen eyesight is forced into the service of evil, and he is mischievous in proportion to his cleverness.

[Glaucon] Very true, he said.

[Socrates] But what if there had been a circumcision of such natures in the days of their youth; and they had been severed from those sensual pleasures, such as eating and drinking, which, like leaden weights, were attached to them at their birth, and which drag them down and turn the vision of their souls upon the things that are below --if, I say, they had been released from these impediments and turned in the opposite direction, the very same faculty in them would have seen the truth as keenly as they see what their eyes are turned to now.

[Glaucon] Very likely.

[Socrates] Yes, I said; and there is another thing which is likely, or rather a necessary inference from what has preceded, that neither the uneducated and uninformed of the truth, nor yet those who never make an end of their education, will be able ministers of State; not the former, because they have no single aim of duty which is the rule of all their actions, private as well as public; nor the latter, because they will not act at all except upon compulsion, fancying that they are already dwelling apart in the islands of the blest.

[Glaucon] Very true, he replied.

[Socrates] Then, I said, the business of us who are the founders of the State will be to compel the best minds to attain that knowledge which we have already shown to be the greatest of all-they must continue to ascend until they arrive at the good; but when they have ascended and seen enough we must not allow them to do as they do now.

[Glaucon] What do you mean?

[Socrates] I mean that they remain in the upper world: but this must not be allowed; they must be made to descend again among the prisoners in the cave, and partake of their labors and honors, whether they are worth having or not.

[Glaucon] But is not this unjust? he said; ought we to give them a worse life, when they might have a better?

[Socrates] You have again forgotten, my friend, I said, the intention of the legislator, who did not aim at making any one class in the State happy above the rest; the happiness was to be in the whole State, and he held the citizens together by persuasion and necessity, making them benefactors of the State, and therefore benefactors of one another; to this end he created them, not to please themselves, but to be his instruments in binding up the State.

[Glaucon] True, he said, I had forgotten.

[Socrates] Observe, Glaucon, that there will be no injustice in compelling our philosophers to have a care and providence of others; we shall explain to them that in other States, men of their class are not obliged to share in the toils of politics: and this is reasonable, for they grow up at their own sweet will, and the government would rather not have them. Being self-taught, they cannot be expected to show any gratitude for a culture which they have never received. But we have brought you into the world to be rulers of the hive, kings of yourselves and of the other citizens, and have educated you far better and more perfectly than they have been educated, and you are better able to share in the double duty. Wherefore each of you, when his turn comes, must go down to the general underground abode, and get the habit of seeing in the dark. When you have acquired the habit, you will see ten thousand times better than the inhabitants of the cave, and you will know what the several images are, and what they represent, because you have seen the beautiful and just and good in their truth. And thus our State which is also yours will be a reality, and not a dream only, and will be administered in a spirit unlike that of other States, in which men fight with one another about shadows only and are distracted in the struggle for power, which in their eyes is a great good. Whereas the truth is that the State in which the rulers are

most reluctant to govern is always the best and most quietly governed, and the State in which they are most eager, the worst.
[Glaucon] Quite true, he replied.
[Socrates] And will our pupils, when they hear this, refuse to take their turn at the toils of State, when they are allowed to spend the greater part of their time with one another in the heavenly light?
[Glaucon] Impossible, he answered; for they are just men, and the commands which we impose upon them are just; there can be no doubt that every one of them will take office as a stern necessity, and not after the fashion of our present rulers of State.

[Socrates] Yes, my friend, I said; and there lies the point. You must contrive for your future rulers another and a better life than that of a ruler, and then you may have a well-ordered State; for only in the State which offers this, will they rule who are truly rich, not in silver and gold, but in virtue and wisdom, which are the true blessings of life. Whereas if they go to the administration of public affairs, poor and hungering after the' own private advantage, thinking that hence they are to snatch the chief good, order there can never be; for they will be fighting about office, and the civil and domestic broils which thus arise will be the ruin of the rulers themselves and of the whole State.

[Glaucon] Most true, he replied.
[Socrates] And the only life which looks down upon the life of political ambition is that of true philosophy. Do you know of any other?
[Glaucon] Indeed, I do not, he said.
[Socrates] And those who govern ought not to be lovers of the task? For, if they are, there will be rival lovers, and they will fight.
[Glaucon] No question.

[Socrates] Who then are those whom we shall compel to be guardians? Surely they will be the men who are wisest about affairs of State, and by whom the State is best administered, and who at the same time have other honors and another and a better life than that of politics?
[Glaucon] They are the men, and I will choose them, he replied.
[Socrates] And now shall we consider in what way such guardians will be produced, and how they are to be brought from darkness to light, -- as some are said to have ascended from the world below to the gods?
[Glaucon] By all means, he replied.
[Socrates] The process, I said, is not the turning over of an oyster-shell, but the turning round of a soul passing from a day which is little better than night to the true day of being, that is, the ascent from below, which we affirm to be true philosophy?
[Glaucon] Quite so.

Philosophical Parallel: Epistemological Grounding (cont.)

Cartesian Rationalism
Rene Descartes (1596-1650) represented the end of medieval scholasticism (a synthesis of Aristotle's philosophy and romanism). Up to that point religious and scientific focus was geocentric. The Copernican revolution via the heliocentric theory brought a significant shift to scientific thought, and Cartesian epistemology was an important partner in supporting that shift.

Descartes identified two means of determining knowledge: intuition (self-evident principles which cannot be doubted) and deduction (orderly reasoning based upon self-evident principles). Believing in *a priori* innate ideas, he sought a self-evident principle using the method of doubt. Doubting everything he begins to consider what things are certain and how we can know they are certain. He concludes with certainty that he exists because he is thinking (*cogito ergo sum*) and that reason, not experience can provide such certainty. Ultimately, Descartes' reliance on the mechanism of reason undermines the immanency of God and need for and relevance of revelation.

Primary Source Excerpt: Descartes: Meditation II (1641)

Of the Nature of the Human Mind; and that It Is More Easily Known Than the Body
The Meditation of yesterday has filled my mind with so many doubts, that it is no longer in my power to forget them. Nor do I see, meanwhile, any principle on which they can be resolved; and, just as if I had fallen all of a sudden into very deep water, I am so greatly disconcerted as to be unable either to plant my feet firmly on the bottom or sustain myself by swimming on the surface. I will, nevertheless, make an effort, and try anew the same path on which I had entered yesterday, that is, proceed by casting aside all that admits of the slightest doubt, not less than if I had discovered it to be absolutely false; and I will continue always in this track until I shall find something that is certain, or at least, if I can do nothing more, until I shall know with certainty that there is nothing certain. Archimedes, that he might transport the entire globe from the place it occupied to another, demanded only a point that was firm and immovable; so, also, I shall be entitled to entertain the highest expectations, if I am fortunate enough to discover only one thing that is certain and indubitable. I suppose, accordingly, that all the things which I see are false (fictitious); I believe that none of those objects which my fallacious memory represents ever existed; I suppose that I possess no senses; I believe that body, figure, extension, motion, and place are merely fictions of my mind.

What is there, then, that can be esteemed true? Perhaps this only, that there is absolutely nothing certain.

But how do I know that there is not something different altogether from the objects I have now enumerated, of which it is impossible to entertain the slightest doubt? Is there not a God, or some being, by whatever name I may designate him, who causes these thoughts to arise in my mind? But why suppose such a being, for it may be I myself am capable of producing them? Am I, then, at least not something? But I before denied that I possessed senses or a body; I hesitate, however, for what follows from that? Am I so dependent on the body and the senses that without these I cannot exist? But I had the persuasion that there was absolutely nothing in the world, that there was no sky and no earth, neither minds nor bodies; was I not, therefore, at the same time, persuaded that I did not exist? Far from it; I assuredly existed, since I was persuaded. But there is I know not what being, who is possessed at once of the highest power and the deepest cunning, who is constantly employing all his ingenuity in deceiving me. Doubtless, then, I exist, since I am deceived; and, let him deceive me as he may, he can never bring it about that I am nothing, so long as I shall be conscious that I am something. *So that it must, in fine, be maintained, all things being maturely and carefully considered, that this proposition (pronunciatum) I am, I exist, is necessarily true each time it is expressed by me, or conceived in my mind. [emphasis mine]*

But I do not yet know with sufficient clearness what I am, though assured that I am; and hence, in the next place, I must take care, lest perchance I inconsiderately substitute some other object in room of what is properly myself, and thus wander from truth, even in that knowledge (cognition) which I hold to be of all others the most certain and evident. For this reason, I will now consider anew what I formerly believed myself to be, before I entered on the present train of thought; and of my previous opinion I will retrench all that can in the least be invalidated by the grounds of doubt I have adduced, in order that there may at length remain nothing but what is certain and indubitable.

What then did I formerly think I was? Undoubtedly I judged that I was a man. But what is a man? Shall I say a rational animal? Assuredly not; for it would be necessary forthwith to inquire into what is meant by animal, and what by rational, and thus, from a single question, I should insensibly glide into others, and these more difficult than the first; nor do I now possess enough of leisure to warrant me in wasting my time amid subtleties of this sort. I prefer here to attend to the thoughts that sprung up of themselves in my mind, and were inspired by my own nature alone, when I applied myself to the consideration of what I was. In the first place, then, I thought that I possessed a countenance, hands, arms, and all the fabric of members that appears in a corpse, and which I called by the name of body. It further occurred to me that I was nourished, that I walked, perceived, and thought, and all those actions I referred to the soul; but what the soul itself was I either did not stay to consider, or, if I did, I imagined that it was something extremely rare and subtile, like wind, or flame, or ether, spread through my grosser parts. As regarded the body, I did not even doubt of its nature, but thought I distinctly knew it, and if I had wished to describe it according to the notions I then entertained, I should have explained myself in this manner: By body I understand all that can be terminated by a certain figure; that can be comprised in a certain place, and so fill a certain space as therefrom to exclude every other body; that can be perceived either by touch, sight, hearing, taste, or smell; that can be moved in different ways, not indeed of itself, but by something foreign to it by which it is touched [and from which it receives the impression]; for the power of self-motion, as likewise that of perceiving and thinking, I held as by no means pertaining to the nature of body; on the contrary, I was somewhat astonished to find such faculties existing in some bodies.

But [as to myself, what can I now say that I am], since I suppose there exists an extremely powerful, and, if I may so speak, malignant being, whose whole endeavors are directed toward deceiving me? Can I affirm that I possess any one of all those attributes of which I have lately spoken as belonging to the nature of body? After attentively considering them in my own mind, I find none of them that can properly be said to belong to myself. To recount them were idle and tedious. Let us pass, then, to the attributes of the soul. The first mentioned were the powers of nutrition and walking; but, if it be true that I have no body, it is true likewise that I am capable neither of walking nor of being nourished. Perception is another attribute of the soul; but perception too is impossible without the body; besides, I have frequently, during sleep, believed that I perceived objects which I afterward observed I did not in reality perceive. Thinking is another attribute of the soul; and here I discover what properly belongs to myself. This alone is inseparable from me. I am--I exist: this is certain; but how often? As often as I think; for perhaps it would even happen, if I should wholly cease to think, that I should at the same time altogether cease to be. I now admit nothing that is not necessarily true. I am therefore, precisely speaking, only a thinking thing, that is, a mind *(mens sive animus)*, understanding, or reason, terms whose signification was before unknown to me. I am, however, a real thing, and really existent; but what thing? The answer was, a thinking thing.

The question now arises, am I aught besides? I will stimulate my imagination with a view to discover whether I am not still something more than a thinking being. Now it is plain I am not the assemblage of members called the human body; I am not a thin and penetrating air diffused through all these members, or wind, or flame, or vapor, or breath, or any of all the things I can imagine; for I supposed that all these were not, and, without changing the supposition, I find that I still feel assured of my existence. But it is true, perhaps, that those very things which I suppose to be non-existent, because they are unknown to me, are not in truth different from myself whom I know. This is a point I cannot determine, and do not now enter into any dispute regarding it. I can only judge of things that are known to me: I am conscious that I exist, and I who know that I exist inquire into what I am. It is, however, perfectly certain that the knowledge of my existence, thus precisely taken, is not dependent on things, the existence of which is as yet unknown to me: and consequently it is not dependent on any of the things I can feign in imagination. Moreover, the phrase itself, I frame an image, reminds me of my error; for I should in truth frame one if I were to imagine myself to be anything, since to imagine is nothing more than to contemplate the figure or image of a corporeal thing; but I already know that I exist, and that it is possible at the same time that all those images, and in general all that relates to the nature of body, are merely dreams [or chimeras]. From this I discover that it is not more reasonable to say, I will excite my imagination that I may know more distinctly what I am, than to express myself as follows: I am now awake, and perceive something real; but because my perception is not sufficiently clear, I will of express purpose go to sleep that my dreams may represent to me the object of my perception with more truth and clearness. And, therefore, I know that nothing of all that I can embrace in imagination belongs to the knowledge which I have of myself, and that there is need to recall with the utmost care the mind from this mode of thinking, that it may be able to know its own nature with perfect distinctness.

But what, then, am I? A thinking thing, it has been said. But what is a thinking thing? It is a thing that doubts, understands, [conceives], affirms, denies, wills, refuses; that imagines also, and perceives.

Assuredly it is not little, if all these properties belong to my nature. But why should they not belong to it? Am I not that very being who now doubts of almost everything; who, for all that, understands and conceives certain things; who affirms one alone as true, and denies the others; who desires to know more of them, and does not wish to be deceived; who imagines many things, sometimes even despite his will; and is likewise percipient of many, as if through the medium of the senses. Is there nothing of all this as true as that I am, even although I should be always dreaming, and although he who gave me being employed all his ingenuity to deceive me? Is there also any one of these attributes that can be properly distinguished from my thought, or that can be said to be separate from myself? For it is of itself so evident that it is I who doubt, I who understand, and I who desire, that it is here unnecessary to add anything by way of rendering it more clear. And I am as certainly the same being who imagines; for although it may be (as I before supposed) that nothing I imagine is true, still the power of imagination does not cease really to exist in me and to form part of my thought. In fine, I am the same being who perceives, that is, who apprehends certain objects as by the organs of sense, since, in truth, I see light, hear a noise, and feel heat. But it will be said that these presentations are false, and that I am dreaming. Let it be so. At all events it is certain that I seem to see light, hear a noise, and feel heat; this cannot be false, and this is what in me is properly called perceiving *(sentire)*, which is nothing else than thinking.

From this I begin to know what I am with somewhat greater clearness and distinctness than heretofore. But, nevertheless, it still seems to me, and I cannot help believing, that corporeal things, whose images are formed by thought [which fall under the senses], and are examined by the same, are known with much greater distinctness than that I know not what part of myself which is not imaginable; although, in truth, it may seem strange to say that I know and comprehend with greater distinctness things whose existence appears to me doubtful, that are unknown, and do not belong to me, than others of whose reality I am persuaded, that are known to me, and appertain to my proper nature; in a word, than myself. But I see clearly what is the state of the case. My mind is apt to wander, and will not yet submit to be restrained within the limits of truth. Let us therefore leave the mind to itself once more, and, according to it every kind of liberty [permit it to consider the objects that appear to it from without], in order that, having afterward withdrawn it from these gently and opportunely [and fixed it on the consideration of its being and the properties it finds in itself], it may then be the more easily controlled.

Let us now accordingly consider the objects that are commonly thought to be [the most easily, and likewise] the most distinctly known, viz., the bodies we touch and see; not, indeed, bodies in general, for these general notions are usually somewhat more confused, but one body in particular. Take, for example, this piece of wax; it is quite fresh, having been but recently taken from the beehive; it has not yet lost the sweetness of the honey it contained; it still retains somewhat of the odor of the flowers from which it was gathered; its color, figure, size, are apparent (to the sight); it is hard, cold, easily handled; and sounds when struck upon with the finger. In fine, all that contributes to make a body as distinctly known as possible, is found in the one before us. But, while I am speaking, let it be placed near the fire--what remained of the taste exhales, the smell evaporates, the color changes, its figure is destroyed, its size increases, it becomes liquid, it grows hot, it can hardly be handled, and, although struck upon, it emits no sound. Does the same wax still remain after this change? It must be admitted that it does remain; no one doubts it, or judges otherwise. What, then, was it I knew with so much distinctness in the piece of wax? Assuredly, it could be nothing of all that I observed by means of the senses, since all the things that fell under taste, smell, sight, touch, and hearing are changed, and yet the same wax remains.[italics mine]

It was perhaps what I now think, viz., that this wax was neither the sweetness of honey, the pleasant odor of flowers, the whiteness, the figure, nor the sound, but only a body that a little before appeared to me conspicuous under these forms, and which is now perceived under others. But, to speak precisely, what is it that I imagine when I think of it in this way? Let it be attentively considered, and, retrenching all that does not belong to the wax, let us see what remains. There certainly remains nothing, except something extended, flexible, and movable. But what is meant by flexible and movable? Is it not that I imagine that the piece of wax, being round, is capable of becoming square, or of passing from a square into a triangular figure? Assuredly such is not the case, because I conceive that it admits of an infinity of similar changes; and I am, moreover, unable to compass this infinity by imagination, and consequently this conception which I have of the wax is not the product of the faculty of imagination. But what now is this extension? Is it not also unknown? for it becomes greater when the wax is melted, greater when it is boiled, and greater still when the heat increases; and I should not conceive [clearly and] according to truth, the wax as it is, if I did not suppose that the piece we are considering admitted even of a wider variety of extension than I ever imagined, I must, therefore, admit that I cannot even comprehend by imagination what the piece of wax is, and that it is the mind alone (*mens,* Lat., *entendement,* F.) which perceives it. I speak of one piece in particular; for as to wax in general, this is still more evident. But what is the piece of wax that can be perceived only by the [understanding or] mind? It is certainly the same which I see, touch, imagine; and, in fine, it is the same which, from the beginning, I believed it to be. But (and this it is of moment to observe) the perception of it is neither an act of sight, of touch, nor of imagination, and never was either of these, though it might formerly seem so, but is simply an intuition *(inspectio)* of the mind, which may be imperfect and confused, as it formerly was, or very clear and distinct, as it is at present, according as the attention is more or less directed to the elements which it contains, and of which it is composed.

But, meanwhile, I feel greatly astonished when I observe [the weakness of my mind, and] its proneness to error. For although, without at all giving expression to what I think, I consider all this in my own mind, words yet occasionally impede my progress, and I am almost led into error by the terms of ordinary language. We say, for example, that we see the same wax when it is before us, and not that we judge it to be the same from its retaining the same color and figure: whence I should forthwith be disposed to conclude that the wax is known by the act of sight, and not by the intuition of the mind alone, were it not for the analogous instance of human beings passing on in the street below, as observed from a window. In this case I do not fail to say that I see the men themselves, just as I say that I see the wax; and yet what do I see from the window beyond hats and cloaks that might cover artificial machines, whose motions might be determined by springs? But I judge that there are human beings from these appearances, and thus I comprehend, by the faculty of judgment alone which is in the mind, what I believed I saw with my eyes.

The man who makes it his aim to rise to knowledge superior to the common, ought to be ashamed to seek occasions of doubting from the vulgar forms of speech: instead, therefore, of doing this, I shall proceed with the matter in hand, and inquire whether I had a clearer and more perfect perception of the piece of wax when I first saw it, and when I thought I knew it by means of the external sense itself, or, at all events, by the common sense *(sensus communis)*, as it is called, that is, by the imaginative faculty; or whether I rather apprehend it more clearly at present, after having examined with greater care, both what it is, and in what way it can be known. It would certainly be ridiculous to entertain any doubt on this point. For what, in that first perception, was there distinct? What did I perceive which any animal might not have perceived? But when I distinguish the Oval from its exterior forms, and when, as if I had stripped it of its vestments, I consider it quite naked, it is certain, although some error may still be found in my judgment, that I cannot, nevertheless, thus apprehend it without possessing a human mind.

But finally, what shall I say of the mind itself, that is, of myself? for as yet I do not admit that I am anything but mind. What, then! I who seem to possess so distinct an apprehension of the piece of wax, do I not know myself, both with greater truth and certitude, and also much more distinctly and clearly? For if I judge that the wax exists because I see it, it assuredly follows, much more evidently, that I myself am or exist, for the same reason: for it is possible that what I see may not in truth be wax, and that I do not even possess eyes with which to see anything; but it cannot be that when I see, or, which comes to the same thing, when I think I see, I myself who think am nothing. So likewise, if I judge that the wax exists because I touch it, it will still also follow that I am; and if I determine that my imagination, or any other cause, whatever it be, persuades me of the existence of the wax, I will still draw the same conclusion. And what is here remarked of the piece of wax, is applicable to all the other things that are external to me. And further, if the [notion or] perception of wax appeared to me more precise and distinct, after that not only sight and touch, but many other causes besides, rendered it manifest to my apprehension, with how much greater distinctness must I now know myself, since all the reasons that contribute to the knowledge of the nature of wax, or of anybody whatever, manifest still better the nature of my mind? And there are besides so many other things in the mind itself that contribute to the illustration of its nature, that those dependent on the body, to which I have here referred, scarcely merit to be taken into account.

But, in conclusion, I find I have insensibly reverted to the point I desired; for, since it is now manifest to me that bodies themselves are not properly perceived by the senses nor by the faculty of imagination, but by the intellect alone; and since they are not perceived because they are seen and touched, but only because they are understood [or rightly comprehended by thought], I readily discover that there is nothing more easily or clearly apprehended than my own mind. But because it is difficult to rid one's self so promptly of an opinion to which one has been long accustomed, it will be desirable to tarry for some time at this stage, that, by long continued meditation, I may more deeply impress upon my memory this new knowledge.

Excursus: On Descartes' Discourse on the Method

In Discourse I, Descartes discusses his own dissatisfaction with his early education, identifying both the merits and drawbacks of a liberal education, with a view not to the establishment of a superior method which all should follow, but rather to "show in what manner" he has promoted the "good conduct" of his own reason. The merits and drawbacks are points of interest here, as is the standard by which Descartes judges education. I shall return to these issues after laying some pertinent groundwork regarding the broader scope of his project in the Discourse. Of particular importance are Descartes' four rules of scientific method and his proposed practical goal of science.

The four rules are pronounced in *Discourse* II, and can be summarized and explained briefly as follows: (1) accept only that which is certain – be careful to avoid the prejudices of external sources (teachers, writings, etc.); (2) divide the problems into as many parts as possible – this will allow for the detailed problem analysis necessary for resolution; (3) move from simple to complex – this allows for the progression of knowledge; (4) be thorough – be complete in enumerations and general in reviews – omit nothing. These four rules are emblematic of Descartes' full reliance on his own reason as the best instrument for [his own] inquiry. In fact it was the rules' promotion of the ordered use of reason as the apparatus for inquiry that pleased him most about their implementation. By applying these rules he was certain to be "exercising my reason in all things, if not perfectly, at least as well as within my own power and in so doing set a course to eradicate wrong opinions and establish certainty."

Further, of significant introductory importance is Descartes' objective for attaining knowledge, clearly delineated in *Discourse* VI as rooted in practical (rather than speculative) philosophy and precisely as rendering "ourselves as masters and possessors of nature." This intended dominion of nature by man has two identified manifestations: (1) invention for human enjoyment of the fruits of the earth, and (2) the preservation of health as the greatest and most foundational blessing. In light of these central goals Descartes' attitudes toward liberal education may be assessed.

Descartes views his own liberal education as not without its merits, the most notable being its service as a means of determining the limitation of such an education – e.g., learning of the diversity of opinions in the philosophers taught him not to rely on that which he had only learned by example or custom.[45] By his own experience, he was able to discover the lack of certainty in that which is called *learning*. While the judgments wrought by the inquiry are flawed, the content provides a springboard for the realization the judgments are indeed flawed, and that a *method* of learning is necessary.

Such necessity, while unveiled by the merits of this kind of learning, is a result of the flaws in the process and conclusions of a liberal education, several of which Descartes sternly identifies – at least from his own vantage point (he seems not to explicitly impose a blanket condemnation, yet such criticism is implicit). As Descartes recounts his experience, he notes that his was not an unsuccessful one, and that he was not perceived to be lacking in any aspect as a student. The implication here is that while he will only make a judgment on his personal experience, it is likely that his experience is representative rather than exceptional, and that indeed the system is flawed since it is not efficacious to provide "clear and assured knowledge useful for this life."[46] He likens study to travelling, acknowledging that one who travels much is in danger of being ignorant of his own context, and this seems a strong indictment – that the learner who relies on example and custom rather than reason will face such ignorance and lack of certainty. In his assessment of his study of poesy, mathematics, letters, language, literature, theology, philosophy, and even sciences, he sees the result as either irrelevance or uncertainty, suggesting, "one could have built nothing solid on foundations so far from firm." Descartes expounds on this architectural metaphor in *Discourse* II, asserting the advantage of singular over eclectic design in building and city planning as the eclectic does not function as efficiently and has sometimes numerous means to an end – or even uncertain ends. Descartes bemoans the lack of method –the eclecticism of means (and ends) – as producing a less than desirable product.

While Descartes' formal education focused on external elements (perhaps similar to Friere's banking approach of learning, in which information is deposited in the mind of the pupil, without any real critical thought or inquiry taking place), Descartes freed himself to a more internally grounded mode of inquiry – seeking "no other science than that which could be found in myself or at least in the great book of the world." He perceived that the unsystematic or non-methodical approach of education did not lead to certainty and was essentially an admixture of earlier traditions rather than the result of present observations. Descartes' formal education provided the inspiration for his first rule of scientific method: *accept only that which is certain.* The judgments to be learned were often "extravagant and ridiculous" and far from certain, being derived from external sources rather than the use of reason guided by method.

Additionally, the approach resulted in "many errors which might have obscured...natural vision and rendered...less capable of listening to reason." It is here that Descartes' standard for judging education is apparent. He is adamant in his supposition that reason guided by method is the true grounding of knowledge, and he perceives his formal education to be grounded in example and custom apart from reason guided by method. The more he focuses on himself as the object of study, with reason as the instrument, the more "successful" his study is (see the first rule of scientific method). This should replace the less successful focus on speculative philosophy, which is not "very useful in life." This replacement is a more practical philosophy whereby, by way of reason, the learner can be a master and possessor of nature. Thus it could perhaps be said that the quality of an education is determined by (1) how much it "renders one capable to listen to reason," and (2) on how practical it is for purposes of rendering one as master and possessor of nature.

Why a Provisional Moral Code?
Returning to his repeated use of architectural metaphor, Descartes introduces Discourse III by citing the need for a provisional morality that would allow for his continued happiness through resoluteness of action despite a necessary irresoluteness of judgment. He constructs four maxims[47] which are subject to examination and considered for replacement if better maxims are discovered through his advancement in the truth via the method (28). The maxims, even the whole of any moral code, must be submitted to such examination. If not, then the project (the guiding of reason by the method for the more certain knowledge of the truth to the end of mastery and possession of nature) is undermined before it even begins, as that non-provisional morality would provide a guiding method of its own accord which would be in conflict with the principles of the method. Descartes has little respect for certain ancient moral codes (he takes aim particularly at virtue ethics) characterizing them in Discourse I as "built only on sand and mud" (8) and suggesting that the ancient teachers fail to show how virtues can be sufficiently known. He further adds that while he "did nothing but observe the morals of other men" (10) he found them (the morals) to be as diverse and uncertain as the opinions of the philosophers. For Descartes it is not the moral conclusions that are centrally problematic, but rather an insufficiently grounded pre-commitment to any given moral code that causes the difficulty.

As Descartes later implies (Discourse IV), a moral pre-commitment requires a metaphysical grounding which Kennington says is unnecessary and even incompatible with

Descartes' method.[48] Kennington further observes Descartes to be clearly asserting that "we can know the laws of nature without answering the question of the nature of ultimate parts. The metaphysical ultimacy is unnecessary."[49]

Thus Descartes' provisional morality, rather than representing a moral pre-commitment, emerges from his method – not as an end product but as a means to maintaining some appropriate stability while engaging in the process of inquiry. The process of utilizing reason guided by method may or may not end in a reshaping of the axioms – or their abolishment altogether, but in the end it is the method that governs morality, and not the other way around.

On the Publishing of the Discourse

In autobiographical fashion, Descartes gives the reader a front row seat to his decision making process regarding the publication of the Discourse. His arguments for and against publication lend important insight on how he views and values learning, and how it is to be conducted and why.

His arguments are several. First, he is readily aware of contemporary (primarily religious) opposition to Galileo's Dialogue Concerning the Two Chief World Systems. While Descartes had initially decided to publish, the reception Galileo received from the Roman Catholic Church gave him pause. The possibility that he might record some mistaken thoughts made the endeavor that much less appealing.

Next, he believed initially that he had no moral obligation to publish, but as he engages in enquiry he reckons that he cannot keep his findings hidden without "gravely sinning against the law [emphasis mine] that obliges us to procure, so much as we can, the general good of all men." (61) By referencing law it seems he intends a direct reference to the means of facilitating the mastery and possessing of nature – for the maximizing of enjoyment, minimizing of pain, and promotion of health. This law is not a presupposed universal moral principle (his morality is at this point provisional), rather it emerges from the use of reason guided by method as the *telos* or purpose: seeking the general good of man. How then is this law to be kept? It is at this point that Descartes sees significant value in publication: his Discourse provides the answer: reason guided by method.

Additionally, he focuses on development in the field of medicine and observes that there are two impediments to progress: brevity of life and lack of experiments. The remedy for both is that each generation build on the findings of the previous, rather than beginning anew. Such progress requires a constant method. He narrates how his experimental process follows the four rules of the method ((1) accept only that which is certain – be careful to avoid the prejudices of external sources (teachers, writings, etc.); (2) divide the problems into as many parts as possible – this will allow for the detailed problem analysis necessary for resolution; (3) move from simple to complex – this allows for the progression of knowledge; (4) be thorough – be complete in enumerations and general in reviews – omit nothing.) applying them to the context of experimentation and demonstrating that the remedy for brevity of life and lack of experimentation is indeed found (and thus perhaps can only be found) in the appropriation of his method.

Further, he discusses the value of publication as providing an impetus for closer examination of the content due to the additional attention naturally given to a project when one writes for an audience. Such occasion for refinement would improve the overall quality of the project.

At this point a third alternative emerges: perhaps he should have the work published posthumously. Publishing in this manner would be advantageous on two counts: he would not be distracted from progressing in his work by the process of publishing, and he would not be distracted by the controversies that would be certain to appear.

Thus far perhaps his strongest pull toward publication is its utility for the benefit of others. However, he questions its usefulness on grounds that there is much more work to be done in order to derive any real practical value and that work would be most efficiently engaged by him, as the originator of the project. His experience in sharing previous work left him questioning whether future work conducted on the basis of his own would truly be a springboard to greater successes or would instead be received in much the same manner as two common errors in speculative philosophy: either the learner aspires to converse as his mentor without any thought to surpassing him or the learner so reads between the lines that much is attributed to the writer that was not intended and thus the project of the writer is lost.

Descartes is thus left with a dilemma: does he, alone and limited, attempt to further his experiments or does he involve others. It seems that involving others could not bring substantive progress but only financial backing at best. He realizes that he is ultimately compelled to publish by two additional factors: first, if he does not publish his work might be viewed as deficient in some way and Descartes' project would end with him; second, in order to continue progress he needs a great many experiments – too many for him to personally conduct. Thus he must involve others. He must publish. Finally, he fears that if he does not publish, he may give cause for later interlocutors to view him with reproach since he would not have told them what they need to know in order to further the project. Thus Descartes publishes. He introduces what is initially presented as his method under the auspice of an autobiographical account, but it seems apparent that he reckons it to be the method undergirding the proper use of reason for progress to his end, the mastery and possession of nature for the long-lived enjoyment of its fruits.

Philosophical Parallel: Epistemological Grounding (cont.)

Kantian Structuralism
Immanuel Kant (1724-1804) was as influential in epistemology as Copernicus' heliocentric theory was to science. Understanding the noumena as essential reality (things in themselves) and the phenomena as the experiencing of the noumena by mediation of the sense, he synthesized Descartes' rationalism and Hume's empiricism, asserting that knowledge begins with experience but does not arise out of experience. For Kant, the mind was not passive but was active in constructing the external world. Thus reality was not fully external and independent of the self: both reason and experience are necessary. He held that there were essentially three levels or faculties of perceiving:
1. the faculty of sensibility: objects received by the senses; here there are two factors to consider:
    i. space – an outer sense; the mind's form to arrange sensations
    ii. time – an inner sense; objects that appear must do so in time
2. the faculty of understanding: a higher faculty than sensibility; related to objects thought, *a priori* categories of understanding, higher faculty than sensibility (dealt with quantity, quality, relation, modality, etc.)
3. the faculty of reason or pure reason: the highest faculty; reason based on transcendental ideas (self, cosmos, God).

Kant holds substance is an *a priori* category of understanding - without substance experience would be impossible (how would one experience the taste and feel of a tomato if there was no actual tomato?).

Primary Source Excerpt: Kant: Critique of Pure Reason (1781) (trans. J.M.D. Meiklejohn)

I. Of the Difference Between Pure and Empirical Knowledge

That all our knowledge begins with experience there can be no doubt. For how is it possible that the faculty of cognition should be awakened into exercise otherwise than by means of objects which affect our senses, and partly of themselves produce representations, partly rouse our powers of understanding into activity, to compare to connect, or to separate these, and so to convert the raw material of our sensuous impressions into a knowledge of objects, which is called experience? In respect of time, therefore, no knowledge of ours is antecedent to experience, but begins with it.

But, though all our knowledge begins with experience, it by no means follows that all arises out of experience. For, on the contrary, it is quite possible that our empirical knowledge is a compound of that which we receive through impressions, and that which the faculty of cognition supplies from itself (sensuous impressions giving merely the occasion), an addition which we cannot distinguish from the original element given by sense, till long practice has made us attentive to, and skillful in separating it. It is, therefore, a question which requires close investigation, and not to be answered at first sight, whether there exists a knowledge altogether independent of experience, and even of all sensuous impressions? Knowledge of this kind is called a priori, in contradistinction to empirical knowledge, which has its sources a posteriori, that is, in experience

But the expression, "a priori," is not as yet definite enough adequately to indicate the whole meaning of the question above started. For, in speaking of knowledge which has its sources in experience, we are wont to say, that this or that may be known a priori, because we do not derive this knowledge immediately from experience, but from a general rule, which, however, we have itself borrowed from experience. Thus, if a man undermined his house, we say, "he might know a priori that it would have fallen;" that is, he needed not to have waited for the experience that it did actually fall. But still, a priori, he could not know even this much. For, that bodies are heavy, and, consequently, that they fall when their supports are taken away, must have been known to him previously, by means of experience.

By the term "knowledge a priori," therefore, we shall in the sequel understand, not such as is independent of this or that kind of experience, but such as is absolutely so of all experience. Opposed to this is empirical knowledge, or that which is possible only a posteriori, that is, through experience. Knowledge a priori is either pure or impure. Pure knowledge a priori is that with which no empirical element is mixed up. For example, the proposition, "Every change has a cause," is a proposition a priori, but impure, because change is a conception which can only be derived from experience.

IV. Of the Difference Between Analytical and Synthetical Judgements.

In all judgements wherein the relation of a subject to the predicate is cogitated (I mention affirmative judgements only here; the application to negative will be very easy), this relation is possible in two different ways. Either the predicate B belongs to the subject A, as somewhat which is contained (though covertly) in the conception A; or the predicate B lies completely out of the conception A, although it stands in connection with it. In the first instance, I term the judgement analytical, in the second, synthetical. Analytical judgements (affirmative) are therefore those in which the connection of the predicate with the subject is cogitated through identity; those in which this connection is cogitated without identity, are called synthetical judgements. The former may be called explicative, the latter augmentative judgements; because the former add in the predicate nothing to the conception of the subject, but only analyse it into its constituent conceptions, which were thought already in the subject, although in a confused manner; the latter add to our conceptions of the subject a predicate which was not contained in it, and which no analysis could ever have discovered therein. For example, when I say, "All bodies are extended," this is an analytical judgement. For I need not go beyond the conception of body in order to find extension connected with it, but merely analyse the conception, that is, become conscious of the manifold properties which I think in that conception, in order to discover this predicate in it: it is therefore an analytical judgement. On the other hand, when I say, "All bodies are heavy," the predicate is something totally different from that which I think in the mere conception of a body. By the addition of such a predicate, therefore, it becomes a synthetical judgement.

Judgements of experience, as such, are always synthetical. For it would be absurd to think of grounding an analytical judgement on experience, because in forming such a judgement I need not go out of the sphere of my conceptions, and therefore recourse to the testimony of experience is quite unnecessary. That "bodies are extended" is not an empirical judgement, but a proposition which stands firm a priori. For before addressing myself to experience, I already have in my conception all the requisite conditions for the judgement, and I have only to extract the predicate from the conception, according to the principle of contradiction, and thereby at the same time become conscious of the necessity of the judgement, a necessity which I could never learn from experience. On the other hand, though at first I do not at all include the predicate of weight in my conception of body in general, that conception still indicates an object of experience, a part of the totality of experience, to which I can still add other parts; and this I do when I recognize by observation that bodies are heavy. I can cognize beforehand by analysis the conception of body through the characteristics of extension, impenetrability, shape, etc., all which are cogitated in this conception. But now I extend my knowledge, and looking back on experience from which I had derived this conception of body, I find weight at all times connected with the above characteristics, and therefore I synthetically add to my conceptions this as a predicate, and say, "All bodies are heavy." Thus it is experience upon which rests the possibility of the synthesis of the predicate of weight with the conception of body, because both conceptions, although the one is not contained in the other, still belong to one another (only contingently, however), as parts of a whole, namely, of experience, which is itself a synthesis of intuitions.

But to synthetical judgements a priori, such aid is entirely wanting. If I go out of and beyond the conception A, in order to recognize another B as connected with it, what foundation have I to rest on, whereby to render the synthesis possible? I have here no longer the advantage of looking out in the sphere of experience for what I want. Let us take, for example, the proposition, "Everything that happens has a cause." In the conception of "something that happens," I indeed think an existence which a certain time antecedes, and from this I can derive analytical judgements. But the conception of a cause lies quite out of the above conception, and indicates something entirely different from "that which happens," and is consequently not contained in that conception. How then am I able to assert concerning the general conception--"that which happens" -- something entirely different from that conception, and to recognize the conception of cause although not contained in it, yet as belonging to it, and even necessarily? what is here the unknown = X, upon which the understanding rests when it believes it has found, out of the conception A a foreign predicate B, which it nevertheless considers to be connected with it? It cannot be experience, because the principle adduced annexes the two representations, cause and effect, to the representation existence, not only with universality, which experience cannot give, but also with the expression of necessity, therefore completely a priori and from pure conceptions. Upon such synthetical, that is augmentative propositions, depends the whole aim of our speculative knowledge a priori; for although analytical judgements are indeed highly important and necessary, they are so, only to arrive at that clearness of conceptions which is requisite for a sure and extended synthesis, and this alone is a real acquisition.

2:18-23 Vanity:
Labor and Consequence Under the Sun

[18] Yea, I hated all my labour which I had taken under the sun: because I should leave it unto the man that shall be after me.
[19] And who knoweth whether he shall be a wise man or a fool? yet shall he have rule over all my labour wherein I have laboured, and wherein I have shewed myself wise under the sun. This is also vanity.

Solomon, having labored with the skill of wisdom, turned to hatred of his labor (NASB, fruit of labor, implied), as the effect of it was *hebel*. The outcome, that it (the labor and the fruit) be passed to the next generation (worthy or not), destroyed any concept of profit or gain from utility.

[20] Therefore I went about to cause my heart to despair of all the labour which I took under the sun.

I brought my heart to despair of the whole of my labor that I labored under the sun. Both the means and the end was *hebel*. The result was total despair.

[21] For there is a man whose labour is in wisdom, and in knowledge, and in equity; yet to a man that hath not laboured therein shall he leave it for his portion. This also is vanity and a

great evil.

Solomon observed that a man can labor in the highest skill, and yet the labor and the fruit of it goes to one who has not done so. Solomon then reckoned meaninglessness too soft a term and adds that this is a great evil (*rah rabah*). It is worse than meaningless. He will reference evil regularly (more than 20 times) throughout the remainder of the book, but only so emphatically also in 5:13 and 16, which present the opposite scenario as that described here. In this case, the fruit of the labor is given to the next generation who has not earned it. In the latter case one labors, hoards, and loses his riches and the son borne to him has nothing. Despite the altered circumstances, the outcome remains the same: none will take fruit from his labor (5:16).

[22] For what hath man of all his labour, and of the vexation of his heart, wherein he hath laboured under the sun?

If there is no lasting fruit, then what does a man take from his labor?

[23] For all his days are sorrows, and his travail grief; yea, his heart taketh not rest in the night. This is also vanity.

He takes nothing from his labor. He can't even rest well. The means do not matter, nor does the end.

Philosophical Parallel: Utilitarianism

Jeremy Bentham (1748-1832) (along with Hobbes, Locke, and Mill) promotes the principle of utility: that an effect of an action establishes its moral worth. Bentham's consequentialism views

2:18-23 Vanity: Labor and Consequence Under the Sun 163

human nature as subject to two masters: pain and pleasure. The highest end is happiness, which is accomplished by the minimization of pain and the maximization of pleasure.

He recognizes four kinds of sanctions that keep people from being immoral. Each one provides some degree of pain as a consequence to particular kinds of actions; (1) physical sanctions – physical harm, (2) moral sanctions – public opinion, (3) religious – consequences in the afterlife, and (4) political sanctions – by judges and magistrates, e.g., prison, etc. Bentham viewed the latter as most effective. He viewed the principle of utility as most useful not only for guiding the individual but also society, thus the idea of political sanctions grounds the morality of society.

Bentham develops a calculus for measuring the worth of an action based on its accomplishing of pain or pleasure. Bentham's hedonic calculus considers the following factors: intensity – how strong; duration – how long; certainty – how likely to produce pleasure; propinquity – how soon the pleasure how near the consequences; fecundity – how likely to produce more pleasure; purity – whether there is a mixture of pain and pleasure; and extent – a measurement of how many others will be affected.

In short, this "ends justify the means" morality is built not on any absolute standard of good (besides the end of happiness), and is not consistent with Solomon's "good in God's sight" ethic.

Primary Source Excerpt: Bentham: An Introduction to the Principles of Morals and Legislation (1781)

Chapter I: Of The Principle of Utility
I. Nature has placed mankind under the governance of two sovereign masters, *pain* and *pleasure*. It is for them alone to

point out what we ought to do, as well as to determine what we shall do. On the one hand the standard of right and wrong, on the other the chain of causes and effects, are fastened to their throne. They govern us in all we do, in all we say, in all we think: every effort we can make to throw off our subjection, will serve but to demonstrate and confirm it. In words a man may pretend to abjure their empire: but in reality he will remain subject to it all the while. The *principle of utility* recognizes this subjection, and assumes it for the foundation of that system, the object of which is to rear the fabric of felicity by the hands of reason and of law. Systems which attempt to question it, deal in sounds instead of sense, in caprice instead of reason, in darkness instead of light.

But enough of metaphor and declamation: it is not by such means that moral science is to be improved.

II. The principle of utility is the foundation of the present work: it will be proper therefore at the outset to give an explicit and determinate account of what is meant by it. *By the principle of utility is meant that principle which approves or disapproves of every action whatsoever. according to the tendency it appears to have to augment or diminish the happiness of the party whose interest is in question: or, what is the same thing in other words to promote or to oppose that happiness. I say of every action whatsoever, and therefore not only of every action of a private individual, but of every measure of government. [italics mine]*

III. By utility is meant that property in any object, whereby it tends to produce benefit, advantage, pleasure, good, or happiness, (all this in the present case comes to the same thing) or (what comes again to the same thing) to prevent the happening of mischief, pain, evil, or unhappiness to the party whose interest is considered: if that party be the community in general, then the happiness of the community: if a particular individual, then the happiness of that individual.

IV. The interest of the community is one of the most general expressions that can occur in the phraseology of morals: no wonder that the meaning of it is often lost. When it has a meaning, it is this. The community is a fictitious *body,* composed of the individual persons who are considered as constituting as it were its *members.* The interest of the community then is, what?— the sum of the interests of the several members who compose it.

V. It is in vain to talk of the interest of the community, without understanding what is the interest of the individual. A thing is said to promote the interest, or to be *for* the interest, of an individual, when it tends to add to the sum total of his pleasures: or, what comes to the same thing, to diminish the sum total of his pains.

VI. An action then may be said to be conformable to the principle of utility, or, for shortness sake, to utility, (meaning with respect to the community at large) when the tendency it has to augment the happiness of the community is greater than any it has to diminish it.

VII. A measure of government (which is but a particular kind of action, performed by a particular person or persons) may be said to be conformable to or dictated by the principle of utility, when in like manner the tendency which it has to augment the happiness of the community is greater than any which it has to diminish it.

VIII. When an action, or in particular a measure of government, is supposed by a man to be conformable to the principle of utility, it may be convenient, for the purposes of discourse, to imagine a kind of law or dictate, called a law or dictate of utility: and to speak of the action in question, as being conformable to such law or dictate.

IX. A man may be said to be a partizan of the principle of utility, when the approbation or disapprobation he annexes to any action, or to any measure, is determined by and proportioned to the tendency which he conceives it to have to augment or to diminish the happiness of the community: or in other words, to its conformity or unconformity to the laws or dictates of utility.

X. Of an action that is conformable to the principle of utility one may always say either that it is one that ought to be done, or at least that it is not one that ought not to be done. One may say also, that it is right it should be done; at least that it is not wrong it should be done: that it is a right action; at least that it is not a wrong action. When thus interpreted, the words *ought,* and *right* and *wrong* and others of that stamp, have a meaning: when otherwise, they have none.

XI. Has the rectitude of this principle been ever formally contested? It should seem that it had, by those who have not known what they have been meaning. Is it susceptible of any direct proof? it should seem not: for that which is used to prove everything else, cannot itself be proved: a chain of proofs must have their commencement somewhere. To give such proof is as impossible as it is needless.

XII. Not that there is or ever has been that human creature at breathing, however stupid or perverse, who has not on many, perhaps on most occasions of his life, deferred to it. By the natural constitution of the human frame, on most occasions of their lives men in general embrace this principle, without thinking of it: if not for the ordering of their own actions, yet for the trying of their own actions, as well as of those of other men. There have been, at the same time, not many perhaps, even of the most intelligent, who have been disposed to embrace it purely and without reserve. There are even few who have not taken some occasion or other to quarrel with it, either on account of their not understanding always how to apply it, or on account of some prejudice or other which they were afraid to examine into, or could not bear to part with. For such is the stuff that man is made of: in principle and in practice, in a right track and in a wrong one, the rarest of all human qualities is consistency.

XIII. When a man attempts to combat the principle of utility, it is with reasons drawn, without his being aware of it, from that very principle itself. His arguments, if they prove anything, prove not that the principle is *wrong,* but that, according to the applications he supposes to be made of it, it is *misapplied.* Is it possible for a man to move the earth? Yes; but he must first find out another earth to stand upon.

XIV. To disprove the propriety of it by arguments is impossible; but, from the causes that have been mentioned, or from some confused or partial view of it, a man may happen to be disposed not to relish it. Where this is the case, if he thinks the settling of his opinions on such a subject worth the trouble, let him take the following steps, and at length, perhaps, he may come to reconcile himself to it.

1. Let him settle with himself, whether he would wish to discard this principle altogether; if so, let him consider what it is that all his reasonings (in matters of politics especially) can amount to?

2. If he would, let him settle with himself, whether he would judge and act without any principle, or whether there is any other he would judge an act by?

3. If there be, let him examine and satisfy himself whether the principle he thinks he has found is really any separate intelligible principle; or whether it be not a mere principle in words, a kind of phrase, which at bottom expresses neither more nor less than the mere averment of his own unfounded sentiments; that is, what in another person he might be apt to call caprice?

4. If he is inclined to think that his own approbation or disapprobation, annexed to the idea of an act, without any regard to its consequences, is a sufficient foundation for him to judge and act upon, let him ask himself whether his sentiment is to be a standard of right and wrong, with respect to every other man, or whether every man's sentiment has the same privilege of being a standard to itself?

5. In the first case, let him ask himself whether his principle is not despotical, and hostile to all the rest of human race?

6. In the second case, whether it is not anarchial, and whether at this rate there are not as many different standards of right and wrong as there are men? and whether even to the same man, the same thing, which is right today, may not (without the least change in its nature) be wrong tomorrow? and whether the same thing is not right and wrong in the same place at the same time?

and in either case, whether all argument is not at an end? and whether, when two men have said, "I like this," and "I don't like it," they can (upon such a principle) have anything more to say?

7. If he should have said to himself, No: for that the sentiment which he proposes as a standard must be grounded on reflection, let him say on what particulars the reflection is to turn? if on particulars having relation to the utility of the act, then let him say whether this is not deserting his own principle, and borrowing assistance from that very one in opposition to which he sets it up: or if not on those particulars, on what other particulars?

8. If he should be for compounding the matter, and adopting his own principle in part, and the principle of utility in part, let him say how far he will adopt it?

9. When he has settled with himself where he will stop, then let him ask himself how he justifies to himself the adopting it so far? and why he will not adopt it any farther?

10. Admitting any other principle than the principle of utility to be a right principle, a principle that it is right for a man to pursue; admitting (what is not true) that the word *right* can have a meaning without reference to utility, let him say whether there is any such thing as a *motive* that a man can have to pursue the dictates of it: if there is, let him say what that motive is, and how it is to be distinguished from those which enforce the dictates of utility: if not, then lastly let him say what it is this other principle can be good for?

2:24-26 Conclusion: God Is

[24] There is nothing better for a man, than that he should eat and drink, and that he should make his soul enjoy good in his labour. This also I saw, that it was from the hand of God.

Finally, some good news. (But alas, what is good?)
Literally, "nothing good in man" (*ayin tov b'adam*) but for three things (1) that he should eat, (2) that he should drink, and that (3) (lit.) he should see his soul good in his labor. While the third point provides some degree of challenge, the most literal rendering indicates he is not simply to enjoy his labor but to see the good in it for his soul. But Solomon has already decried the meaninglessness of labor, so does this represent a shift? No, rather it represents the idea that the most fundamental elements of life are to be enjoyed with a view to their proper estimation by the soul. How can the soul, with any integrity, assert the goodness of these activities? They are good, but not under the sun. Thus the perspective must expand beyond the sun in order to unveil the value.

[25] For who can eat, or who else can hasten hereunto, more than I?

A textual variant creates some difficulty here, as some Hebrew mss., the Syriac, and LXX read *apart from Him*, while most Hebrew mss. read *apart from I*.

If *I* is correct, the implication is that these aspects of life cannot be enjoyed without Solomon, particularly with a view to the wisdom he is granting the reader in presenting the metaphysical presupposition of God's existence as the underlying meaning for reality.

If *Him* is the correct rendering, then the meaning is even clearer. The basic functions of life cannot be enjoyed apart from Him. Both renderings arrive, by different means, at the same conclusion: God provides meaning and joy in even the simplicities of life.

[26] For God giveth to a man that is good in his sight wisdom, and knowledge, and joy: but to the sinner he giveth travail, to gather and to heap up, that he may give to him that is good before God. This also is vanity and vexation of spirit.

If the variant in the previous verse causes any question it is immediately cleared up in v. 26. God gives to the good (*tov*) man wisdom, knowledge, and joy. None of these things are to be had apart from His giving them. To the sinner, however, he gives (*nathan*) labors to provide for the good (*tov*).

It must be noted that the good is "good before Him" (*tov pani*). Good is a relative term — relative to the Absolute. When discussing the good it can be asked, as it was in the Euthyphro, whether God calls something good because He must or because He wishes. If because He must, then He is subject to some higher absolute standard, and thus He is either not God or He is irrelevant. If because He wishes, then any idea of absolute value of good vanishes. Berkeley had the right idea, reckoning God to be the ultimate perceiver. God determines what is good. He defines what is good. Thus to be good before God is to be good indeed. This reckoning of good is, by the way, the Biblical key to resolving the problem of evil.

So arises the obvious question: how does one become *tov pani*? While Solomon never directly addresses "positional goodness" in Ecclesiastes, he does note that reckoning good is a gift of God (3:13), being good is a reward (5:18), determining with certainty what is ultimately good for a man is not possible from an under the sun perspective (6:12), there is none who does good and never sins (7:20), under the sun the only discernible good is eating, drinking, and being merry, and even that is vanity (8:15), and God will ultimately be the judge of what is good and what is evil (12:14).

Significantly, Solomon leaves this important question completely unanswered. It seems a strange oversight, and indeed it is no oversight. Here is the key: *Solomon's final exhortation is to fear God and keep (shamar, attend to) His commandments (mitzvah) (12:13). It is an exhortation to pursue (1) a right perspective of and (2) right relationship to God. Solomon is not conversing about positional goodness at all, but rather about practical human response to the knowledge of God. One can acknowledge God and still be a sinner. He can walk in disobedience. He can walk in foolishness and meaninglessness, despite the grand blessings provided by God. A New Testament scenario analogous to this would be one who reads Ephesians 1:3 and understands he has every spiritual blessing in the heavenlies in Christ and then disregards the imperative to walk in a manner worthy of the calling (4:1). Position is not the issue. Perspective and practice are. Thus Ecclesiastes also serves as a caution to those who are positionally right with God but whose perspective and practice may not reflect the position.*

Philosophical Parallel: On the Existence of God

Solomon asserts innate ideas originating from God (v. 11). Throughout the book he operates from the first principle that the Sovereign Creator exists. He makes no effort to argue or demonstrate God's existence. It is notable that he uses the term *Elohim* exclusively (all 40 references to God) and does not mention the name Yahweh. While God's name Yahweh is often used as a reminder of His covenant relationship with His people Israel, that relationship is not in view here. Solomon concerns himself instead with the entirety of under the sun existence, thus the broader term would connect with those even who were separate from the commonwealth of Israel. In any case, Solomon works from God rather than working to God. This metaphysical presupposition undergirds his epistemology (Prov. 1:7, 9:10).

While working from this first principle is the Biblical model, the question of God's existence is a significant component of metaphysical inquiry and philosophy of religion.

Anselm's Ontological Argument

Anselm (1033-1109) argued ontologically (from being), to disprove the fool of Psalm 14:1, that the existence of God is self-evident. His argument from *Proslogion* chapter 2 has six basic components:

1. God is that than which no greater can be conceived.
2. God exists in human understanding.
3. It can be conceived that God could exist in reality
4. If an entity exists in reality and in understanding it is greater than if it only existed in understanding.
5. God cannot exist only in human understanding, for it is greater to exist in reality than to not.

6. Thus, God exists in reality.

He adjusts the argument as follows in chapter 3:
1. God is that than which no greater can be conceived.
2. It is greater to be necessary than not.
3. It is necessary that God is necessary.
4. God necessarily exists.

Primary Source Excerpt: Anselm: Proslogion (1077), Chapters 2 and 3 (trans. David Burr)

Chapter 2: That God Really Exists
Therefore, Lord, you who give knowledge of the faith, give me as much knowledge as you know to be fitting for me, because you are as we believe and that which we believe. And indeed we believe you are something greater than which cannot be thought. Or is there no such kind of thing, for "the fool said in his heart, 'there is no God'" (Ps. 14:1, 53:1)? But certainly that same fool, having heard what I just said, "something greater than which cannot be thought," understands what he heard, and what he understands is in his thought, even if he does not think it exists. For it is one thing for something to exist in a person's thought and quite another for the person to think that thing exists. For when a painter thinks ahead to what he will paint, he has that picture in his thought, but he does not yet think it exists, because he has not done it yet. Once he has painted it he has it in his thought and thinks it exists because he has done it. Thus even the fool is compelled to grant that something greater than which cannot be thought exists in thought, because he understands what he hears, and whatever is understood exists in thought. And certainly that greater than which cannot be understood cannot exist only in thought, for if it exists only in thought it could also be thought of as existing in reality as well,

which is greater. If, therefore, that than which greater cannot be thought exists in thought alone, then that than which greater cannot be thought turns out to be that than which something greater actually can be thought, but that is obviously impossible. Therefore something than which greater cannot be thought undoubtedly exists both in thought and in reality.

Chapter 3: That God Cannot be Thought Not to Exist
In fact, it so undoubtedly exists that it cannot be thought of as not existing. For one can think there exists something that cannot be thought of as not existing, and that would be greater than something which can be thought of as not existing. For if that greater than which cannot be thought can be thought of as not existing, then that greater than which cannot be thought is not that greater than which cannot be thought, which does not make sense. Thus that than which nothing can be thought so undoubtedly exists that it cannot even be thought of as not existing.

And you, Lord God, are this being. You exist so undoubtedly, my Lord God, that you cannot even be thought of as not existing. And deservedly, for if some mind could think of something greater than you, that creature would rise above the creator and could pass judgment on the creator, which is absurd. And indeed whatever exists except you alone can be thought of as not existing. You alone of all things most truly exists and thus enjoy existence to the fullest degree of all things, because nothing else exists so undoubtedly, and thus everything else enjoys being in a lesser degree. Why therefore did the fool say in his heart "there is no God," since it is so evident to any rational mind that you above all things exist? Why indeed, except precisely because he is stupid and foolish?

Aquinas' Five Ways

In Thomas Aquinas' (1225-1274) "Five Ways," he disagreed with Anselm's assertion that the existence of God was self-evident, and believing the existence of God must and can be proved, he formulated five major arguments(ways) to that end:

Way 1 – a cosmological, prime mover argument.
Way 2 – a cosmological argument from first cause.
Way 3 – a cosmological argument from necessity: there are two categories of things: possible and contingent, and it is impossible for them to always exist (they must by nature at some point cease to exist) if possible for nothing to exist, then at one time possible nothing existed, yet things must exist, so there must exist one necessary thing which must always have existed and never will cease to exist.
Way 4 – a henological (Greek *heno*, one) argument from perfection and degree: there are differing degrees of goodness, and thus a maximum: God.
Way 5 – a teleological argument (from design): an orderly design needs a designer

Primary Source Excerpt: Thomas Aquinas: The Five Ways (from Summa Theologica, 1170)

The existence of God can be proved in five ways.

The first and more manifest way is the argument from motion. It is certain, and evident to our senses, that in the world some things are in motion. Now whatever is in motion is put in motion by another, for nothing can be in motion except it is in potentiality to that towards which it is in motion; whereas a thing moves inasmuch as it is in act. For motion is nothing else than the reduction of something from potentiality to actuality.

But nothing can be reduced from potentiality to actuality, except by something in a state of actuality. Thus that which is actually hot, as fire, makes wood, which is potentially hot, to be actually hot, and thereby moves and changes it. Now it is not possible that the same thing should be at once in actuality and potentiality in the same respect, but only in different respects. For what is actually hot cannot simultaneously be potentially hot; but it is simultaneously potentially cold. It is therefore impossible that in the same respect and in the same way a thing should be both mover and moved, i.e. that it should move itself. Therefore, whatever is in motion must be put in motion by another. If that by which it is put in motion be itself put in motion, then this also must needs be put in motion by another, and that by another again. But this cannot go on to infinity, because then there would be no first mover, and, consequently, no other mover; seeing that subsequent movers move only inasmuch as they are put in motion by the first mover; as the staff moves only because it is put in motion by the hand. Therefore it is necessary to arrive at a first mover, put in motion by no other; and this everyone understands to be God.

The second way is from the nature of the efficient cause. In the world of sense we find there is an order of efficient causes. There is no case known (neither is it, indeed, possible) in which a thing is found to be the efficient cause of itself; for so it would be prior to itself, which is impossible. Now in efficient causes it is not possible to go on to infinity, because in all efficient causes following in order, the first is the cause of the intermediate cause, and the intermediate is the cause of the ultimate cause, whether the intermediate cause be several, or only one. Now to take away the cause is to take away the effect. Therefore, if there be no first cause among efficient causes, there will be no ultimate, nor any intermediate cause. But if in efficient causes it is possible to go on to infinity, there will be no first efficient cause, neither will there be an ultimate effect, nor any intermediate efficient causes; all of which is plainly false. Therefore it is necessary to admit a first efficient cause, to which everyone gives the name of God.

The third way is taken from possibility and necessity, and runs thus. We find in nature things that are possible to be and not to be, since they are found to be generated, and to corrupt, and consequently, they are possible to be and not to be. But it is impossible for these always to exist, for that which is possible not to be at some time is not. Therefore, if everything is possible not to be, then at one time there could have been nothing in existence. Now if this were true, even now there would be nothing in existence, because that which does not exist only begins to exist by something already existing. Therefore, if at one time nothing was in existence, it would have been impossible for anything to have begun to exist; and thus even now nothing would be in existence--which is absurd. Therefore, not all beings are merely possible, but there must exist something the existence of which is necessary. But every necessary thing either has its necessity caused by another, or not. Now it is impossible to go on to infinity in necessary things which have their necessity caused by another, as has been already proved in regard to efficient causes. Therefore we cannot but postulate the existence of some being having of itself its own necessity, and not receiving it from another, but rather causing in others their necessity. This all men speak of as God.

The fourth way is taken from the gradation to be found in things. Among beings there are some more and some less good, true, noble and the like. But "more" and "less" are predicated of different things, according as they resemble in their different ways something which is the maximum, as a thing is said to be hotter according as it more nearly resembles that which is hottest; so that there is something which is truest, something best, something noblest and, consequently, something which is uttermost being; for those things that are greatest in truth are greatest in being, as it is written in Metaph. ii. Now the maximum in any genus is the cause of all in that genus; as fire, which is the maximum heat, is the cause of all hot things. Therefore there must also be something which is to all beings the cause of their being, goodness, and every other perfection; and this we call God.

The fifth way is taken from the governance of the world. We see that things which lack intelligence, such as natural bodies, act for an end, and this is evident from their acting always, or nearly always, in the same way, so as to obtain the best result. Hence it is plain that not fortuitously, but designedly, do they achieve their end. Now whatever lacks intelligence cannot move towards an end, unless it be directed by some being endowed with knowledge and intelligence; as the arrow is shot to its mark by the archer. Therefore some intelligent being exists by whom all natural things are directed to their end; and this being we call God.

Other Arguments for the Existence of God

Cosmological arguments – from first cause.
Ontological – from being.
Teleological – from design.
Moral argument – primarily Kant, similar to Aquinas' henological argument.
Anthropic – the existence of man is best explained by the existence of God
Pascal's (wager /decision theory –

> "God is, or He is not." But to which side shall we incline? Reason can decide nothing here. There is an infinite

chaos which separated us. A game is being played at the extremity of this infinite distance where heads or tails will turn up.... Which will you choose then? Let us see. Since you must choose, let us see which interests you least. You have two things to lose, the true and the good; and two things to stake, your reason and your will, your knowledge and your happiness; and your nature has two things to shun, error and misery. Your reason is no more shocked in choosing one rather than the other, since you must of necessity choose... But your happiness? Let us weigh the gain and the loss in wagering that God is.... If you gain, you gain all; if you lose, you lose nothing. Wager, then, without hesitation that He is. (*Pensees*, "Thoughts")

Majority argument – the majority of people believe in some deity, thus God exists.

While these arguments to God's existence are convincing to an extent, they generally fall victim to Hume's Stopper: while they may lend credence to the idea of a first cause, they do not sufficiently support their conclusions of the existence of a personal God, let alone the personal God of the Bible.

There is an additional inherent weakness in the arguments, as Aquinas' in particular begins without God and moves to prove Him. But if God must be proven, then He is subject to some greater standard of proof, and that standard itself would be of a higher quality than God (God being subject to it). Such a God would not be a God at all, and certainly not the God of the Bible. Thus to say that God's existence must be proven is to defeat the very possibility of His existence. This is one reason it is so critical to work from the first principle that God exists rather than to seek to establish his existence. It is by no accident that every Biblical writer operates in that manner, and none offers any argument for God's existence.

Presuppositionalism
In epistemology the Biblical perspective is best represented by presuppositionalism and the transcendental argument: reasoning from the fact that we do have experiences or engage in practices of a certain sort to the truth of those conditions without which these experiences or practices would not be possible. Concisely iterated, the transcendental argument says *the existence of God can be proven by the impossibility of the contrary.*

Cornelius Van Til (1895-1987) like Kant, thought rationalism and empiricism were inadequate, though for different reasons than Kant. Van Til thought that the idea of neutrality (that experience and reason can function independently of God) was a poor epistemological base, and one that must arrive at the necessary conclusion of its presuppositions. The necessity of presuppositions and circular reasoning at the outset - the epistemological problem of 'how can we know?' - these issues Kant and others were wrestling with. Van Til believed his permutation of the transcendental argument to be quite effective:

1. all systems must demonstrate circularity in their foundational presuppositions (rationalist must presuppose the reality of reason, empiricists, of experience, etc...in order for the rationalist to defend the authority of reason, he must use reason, etc...)
2. the presuppositional approach (what he refers to as the Biblical worldview), he argues is the only intelligible explanation of the universe: i.e., the laws

of math, logic, etc...meaning, significance, and intelligible discourse...

Example of the two circles...everyone begins with a circle...what then is the right circle? Van Til says, the Biblical one, as it explains reality better than any other. Thus Van Til and other presuppositionalists, like Solomon, work from the premise of God's existence rather than to it.

Arguments Against the Existence of God

Problem of evil – the trilemma: if God is omnipotent, omniscient, and omnibeneficient, then from whence does evil come?
Plurality of revelation – many religious texts, most of them contradicting the other. Which, if any. is correct, and upon what basis?
Argument from poor design – e.g., Voltaire's comment that the nose is perfectly designed to hold glasses. (Hint: if everything is well designed, then why the need for glasses?)
Argument from unbelief – that there is unbelief demonstrates God to be a failure, i.e., nonexistent.
Argument from freewill – argues against an omniscient God
Cosmological argument – self-defeating, argues the necessity of first cause, thus infinite regress.
Transcendental argument against – God would make logic and morality contingent thus invalidating the transcendental argument which suggest they are necessary.

Noted skeptic Bertrand Russell (1872-1970) combines several of these arguments in a challenging, if sometimes illogical and fallacious, critique of Christianity.

Primary Source Excerpt: Bertrand Russell: Why I am Not a Christian (1927)[50]

Introductory note: Russell delivered this lecture on March 6, 1927 to the National Secular Society, South London Branch, at Battersea Town Hall. Published in pamphlet form in that same year, the essay subsequently achieved new fame with Paul Edwards' edition of Russell's book, *Why I Am Not a Christian and Other Essays ....* (1957).

As your Chairman has told you, the subject about which I am going to speak to you tonight is "Why I Am Not a Christian." Perhaps it would be as well, first of all, to try to make out what one means by the word *Christian*. It is used these days in a very loose sense by a great many people. Some people mean no more by it than a person who attempts to live a good life. In that sense I suppose there would be Christians in all sects and creeds; but I do not think that that is the proper sense of the word, if only because it would imply that all the people who are not Christians -- all the Buddhists, Confucians, Mohammedans, and so on -- are not trying to live a good life. I do not mean by a Christian any person who tries to live decently according to his lights. I think that you must have a certain amount of definite belief before you have a right to call yourself a Christian. The word does not have quite such a full-blooded meaning now as it had in the times of St. Augustine and St. Thomas Aquinas. In those days, if a man said that he was a Christian it was known what he meant. You accepted a whole collection of creeds which were set out with great precision, and every single syllable of those creeds you believed with the whole strength of your convictions.

What Is a Christian?

Nowadays it is not quite that. We have to be a little more vague in our meaning of Christianity. I think, however, that there are two different items which are quite essential to anybody calling himself a Christian. The first is one of a dogmatic nature -- namely, that you must believe in God and immortality. If you do not believe in those two things, I do not think that you can properly call yourself a Christian. Then, further than that, as the name implies, you must have some kind of belief about Christ. The Mohammedans, for instance, also believe in God and in immortality, and yet they would not call themselves Christians. I think you must have at the very lowest the belief that Christ was, if not divine, at least the best and wisest of men. If you are not going to believe that much about Christ, I do not think you have any right to call yourself a Christian. Of course, there is another sense, which you find in *Whitaker's Almanack* and in geography books, where the population of the world is said to be divided into Christians, Mohammedans, Buddhists, fetish worshipers, and so on; and in that sense we are all Christians. The geography books count us all in, but that is a purely geographical sense, which I suppose we can ignore. Therefore I take it that when I tell you why I am not a Christian I have to tell you two different things: first, why I do not believe in God and in immortality; and, secondly, why I do not think that Christ was the best and wisest of men, although I grant him a very high degree of moral goodness.

But for the successful efforts of unbelievers in the past, I could not take so elastic a definition of Christianity as that. As I said before, in olden days it had a much more full-blooded sense. For instance, it included he belief in hell. Belief in eternal hell-fire was an essential item of Christian belief until pretty recent times. In this country, as you know, it ceased to be an essential item because of a decision of the Privy Council, and from that decision the Archbishop of Canterbury and the Archbishop of York dissented; but in this country our religion is settled by Act of Parliament, and therefore the Privy Council was able to override their Graces and hell was no longer necessary to a

Christian. Consequently I shall not insist that a Christian must believe in hell.

The Existence of God

To come to this question of the existence of God: it is a large and serious question, and if I were to attempt to deal with it in any adequate manner I should have to keep you here until Kingdom Come, so that you will have to excuse me if I deal with it in a somewhat summary fashion. You know, of course, that the Catholic Church has laid it down as a dogma that the existence of God can be proved by the unaided reason. That is a somewhat curious dogma, but it is one of their dogmas. They had to introduce it because at one time the freethinkers adopted the habit of saying that there were such and such arguments which mere reason might urge against the existence of God, but of course they knew as a matter of faith that God did exist. The arguments and the reasons were set out at great length, and the Catholic Church felt that they must stop it. Therefore they laid it down that the existence of God can be proved by the unaided reason and they had to set up what they considered were arguments to prove it. There are, of course, a number of them, but I shall take only a few.

The First-cause Argument

Perhaps the simplest and easiest to understand is the argument of the First Cause. (It is maintained that everything we see in this world has a cause, and as you go back in the chain of causes further and further you must come to a First Cause, and to that First Cause you give the name of God.) That argument, I suppose, does not carry very much weight nowadays, because, in the first place, cause is not quite what it used to be. The philosophers and the men of science have got going on cause, and it has not anything like the vitality it used to have; but, apart from that, you can see that the argument that there must be a First Cause is one that cannot have any validity. I may say that when I was a young man and was debating these questions very seriously in my mind, I for a long time accepted the argument of the First Cause, until one day, at the age of eighteen, I read John Stuart Mill's Autobiography, and I there found this sentence: "My father taught me that the question 'Who made me?' cannot be answered, since it immediately suggests the further question 'Who made god?'" That very simple sentence showed me, as I still think, the fallacy in the argument of the First Cause. If everything must have a cause, then God must have a cause. If there can be anything without a cause, it may just as well be the world as God, so that there cannot be any validity in that argument. It is exactly of the same nature as the Hindu's view, that the world rested upon an elephant and the elephant rested upon a tortoise; and when they said, "How about the tortoise?" the Indian said, "Suppose we change the subject." The argument is really no better than that. There is no reason why the world could not have come into being without a cause; nor, on the other hand, is there any reason why it should not have always existed. There is no reason to suppose that the world had a beginning at all. The idea that things must have a beginning is really due to the poverty of our imagination. Therefore, perhaps, I need not waste any more time upon the argument about the First Cause.

The Natural-law Argument
Then there is a very common argument from natural law. That was a favorite argument all through the eighteenth century, especially under the influence of Sir Isaac Newton and his cosmogony. People observed the planets going around the sun according to the law of gravitation, and they thought that God had given a behest to these planets to move in that particular fashion, and that was why they did so. That was, of course, a

convenient and simple explanation that saved them the trouble of looking any further for explanations of the law of gravitation. Nowadays we explain the law of gravitation in a somewhat complicated fashion that Einstein has introduced. I do not propose to give you a lecture on the law of gravitation, as interpreted by Einstein, because that again would take some time; at any rate, you no longer have the sort of natural law that you had in the Newtonian system, where, for some reason that nobody could understand, nature behaved in a uniform fashion. We now find that a great many things we thought were natural laws are really human conventions. You know that even in the remotest depths of stellar space there are still three feet to a yard. That is, no doubt, a very remarkable fact, but you would hardly call it a law of nature. And a great many things that have been regarded as laws of nature are of that kind. On the other hand, where you can get down to any knowledge of what atoms actually do, you will find they are much less subject to law than people thought, and that the laws at which you arrive are statistical averages of just the sort that would emerge from chance. There is, as we all know, a law that if you throw dice you will get double sixes only about once in thirty-six times, and we do not regard that as evidence that the fall of the dice is regulated by design; on the contrary, if the double sixes came every time we should think that there was design. The laws of nature are of that sort as regards a great many of them. They are statistical averages such as would emerge from the laws of chance; and that makes this whole business of natural law much less impressive than it formerly was. Quite apart from that, which represents the momentary state of science that may change tomorrow, the whole idea that natural laws imply a lawgiver is due to a confusion between natural and human laws. Human laws are behests commanding you to behave a certain way, in which you may choose to behave, or you may choose not to behave; but natural laws are a description of how things do in fact behave, and being a mere description of what they in fact do, you cannot argue that there must be somebody who told them to do that, because even supposing that there were, you are then faced with the question "Why did God issue just those natural laws and no others?" If you say that he did it simply from his own good pleasure, and without any reason, you then find that there is something which is not subject to law, and so your train of natural law is interrupted. If you say, as more orthodox theologians do, that in all the laws which God issues he had a reason for giving those laws rather than others -- the reason, of course, being to create the best universe, although you would never think it to look at it -- if there were a reason for the laws which God gave, then God himself was subject to law, and therefore you do not get any advantage by introducing God as an intermediary. You really have a law outside and anterior to the divine edicts, and God does not serve your purpose, because he is not the ultimate lawgiver. In short, this whole argument about natural law no longer has anything like the strength that it used to have. I am traveling on in time in my review of the arguments. The arguments that are used for the existence of God change their character as time goes on. They were at first hard intellectual arguments embodying certain quite definite fallacies. As we come to modern times they become less respectable intellectually and more and more affected by a kind of moralizing vagueness.

The Argument from Design
The next step in the process brings us to the argument from design. You all know the argument from design: everything in the world is made just so that we can manage to live in the world, and if the world was ever so little different, we could not manage to live in it. That is the argument from design. It sometimes

takes a rather curious form; for instance, it is argued that rabbits have white tails in order to be easy to shoot. I do not know how rabbits would view that application. It is an easy argument to parody. You all know Voltaire's remark, that obviously the nose was designed to be such as to fit spectacles. That sort of parody has turned out to be not nearly so wide of the mark as it might have seemed in the eighteenth century, because since the time of Darwin we understand much better why living creatures are adapted to their environment. It is not that their environment was made to be suitable to them but that they grew to be suitable to it, and that is the basis of adaptation. There is no evidence of design about it.

When you come to look into this argument from design, it is a most astonishing thing that people can believe that this world, with all the things that are in it, with all its defects, should be the best that omnipotence and omniscience have been able to produce in millions of years. I really cannot believe it. Do you think that, if you were granted omnipotence and omniscience and millions of years in which to perfect your world, you could produce nothing better than the Ku Klux Klan or the Fascists? Moreover, if you accept the ordinary laws of science, you have to suppose that human life and life in general on this planet will die out in due course: it is a stage in the decay of the solar system; at a certain stage of decay you get the sort of conditions of temperature and so forth which are suitable to protoplasm, and there is life for a short time in the life of the whole solar system. You see in the moon the sort of thing to which the earth is tending -- something dead, cold, and lifeless.

I am told that that sort of view is depressing, and people will sometimes tell you that if they believed that, they would not be able to go on living. Do not believe it; it is all nonsense. Nobody really worries about much about what is going to happen millions of years hence. Even if they think they are worrying much about that, they are really deceiving themselves. They are worried about something much more mundane, or it may merely be a bad digestion; but nobody is really seriously rendered unhappy by the thought of something that is going to happen to this world millions and millions of years hence. Therefore, although it is of course a gloomy view to suppose that life will die out -- at least I suppose we may say so, although sometimes when I contemplate the things that people do with their lives I think it is almost a consolation -- it is not such as to render life miserable. It merely makes you turn your attention to other things.

The Moral Arguments for Deity
Now we reach one stage further in what I shall call the intellectual descent that the Theists have made in their argumentations, and we come to what are called the moral arguments for the existence of God. You all know, of course, that there used to be in the old days three intellectual arguments for the existence of God, all of which were disposed of by Immanuel Kant in the *Critique of Pure Reason*; but no sooner had he disposed of those arguments than he invented a new one, a moral argument, and that quite convinced him. He was like many people: in intellectual matters he was skeptical, but in moral matters he believed implicitly in the maxims that he had imbibed at his mother's knee. That illustrates what the psychoanalysts so much emphasize -- the immensely stronger hold upon us that our very early associations have than those of later times.

Kant, as I say, invented a new moral argument for the existence of God, and that in varying forms was extremely popular during the nineteenth century. It has all sorts of forms. One form is to say there would be no right or wrong unless God existed. I am not for the moment concerned with whether there is a difference between right and wrong, or whether there is not: that is another question. The point I am concerned with is that, if you are quite sure there is a difference between right and wrong, then you are in this situation: Is that difference due to God's fiat or is it not? If it is due to God's fiat, then for God himself there is no difference between right and wrong, and it is no longer a significant statement to say that God is good. If you are going to say, as theologians do, that God is good, you must then say that right and wrong have some meaning which is independent of God's fiat, because God's fiats are good and not bad independently of the mere fact that he made them. If you are going to say that, you will then have to say that it is not only through God that right and wrong came into being, but that they are in their essence logically anterior to God. You could, of course, if you liked, say that there was a superior deity who gave orders to the God that made this world, or could take up the line that some of the gnostics took up – a line which I often thought was a very plausible one – that as a matter of fact this world that we know was made by the devil at a moment when God was not looking. There is a good deal to be said for that, and I am not concerned to refute it.

The Argument for the Remedying of Injustice

Then there is another very curious form of moral argument, which is this: they say that the existence of God is required in order to bring justice into the world. In the part of this universe that we know there is great injustice, and often the good suffer, and often the wicked prosper, and one hardly knows which of those is the more annoying; but if you are going to have justice in the universe as a whole you have to suppose a future life to redress the balance of life here on earth. So they say that there must be a God, and there must be Heaven and Hell in order that in the long run there may be justice. That is a very curious argument. If you looked at the matter from a scientific point of view, you would say, "After all, I only know this world. I do not know about the rest of the universe, but so far as one can argue at all on probabilities one would say that probably this world is a fair sample, and if there is injustice here the odds are that there is injustice elsewhere also." Supposing you got a crate of oranges that you opened, and you found all the top layer of oranges bad, you would not argue, "The underneath ones must be good, so as to redress the balance." You would say, "Probably the whole lot is a bad consignment"; and that is really what a scientific person would argue about the universe. He would say, "Here we find in this world a great deal of injustice, and so far as that goes that is a reason for supposing that justice does not rule in the world; and therefore so far as it goes it affords a moral argument against deity and not in favor of one." Of course I know that the sort of intellectual arguments that I have been talking to you about are not what really moves people. What really moves people to believe in God is not any intellectual argument at all. Most people believe in God because they have been taught from early infancy to do it, and that is the main reason.

Then I think that the next most powerful reason is the wish for safety, a sort of feeling that there is a big brother who will look after you. That plays a very profound part in influencing people's desire for a belief in God.

The Character of Christ
I now want to say a few words upon a topic which I often think is not quite sufficiently dealt with by Rationalists, and that is the question whether Christ was the best and the wisest of men. It is generally taken for granted that we should all agree that that was so. I do not myself. I think that there are a good many points upon which I agree with Christ a great deal more than the professing Christians do. I do not know that I could go with

Him all the way, but I could go with Him much further than most professing Christians can. You will remember that He said, "Resist not evil: but whosoever shall smite thee on thy right cheek, turn to him the other also." That is not a new precept or a new principle. It was used by Lao-tse and Buddha some 500 or 600 years before Christ, but it is not a principle which as a matter of fact Christians accept. I have no doubt that the present prime minister [Stanley Baldwin], for instance, is a most sincere Christian, but I should not advise any of you to go and smite him on one cheek. I think you might find that he thought this text was intended in a figurative sense.

Then there is another point which I consider excellent. You will remember that Christ said, "Judge not lest ye be judged." That principle I do not think you would find was popular in the law courts of Christian countries. I have known in my time quite a number of judges who were very earnest Christians, and none of them felt that they were acting contrary to Christian principles in what they did. Then Christ says, "Give to him that asketh of thee, and from him that would borrow of thee turn not thou away." That is a very good principle. Your Chairman has reminded you that we are not here to talk politics, but I cannot help observing that the last general election was fought on the question of how desirable it was to turn away from him that would borrow of thee, so that one must assume that the Liberals and Conservatives of this country are composed of people who do not agree with the teaching of Christ, because they certainly did very emphatically turn away on that occasion.

Then there is one other maxim of Christ which I think has a great deal in it, but I do not find that it is very popular among some of our Christian friends. He says, "If thou wilt be perfect, go and sell that which thou hast, and give to the poor." That is a very excellent maxim, but, as I say, it is not much practiced. All these, I think, are good maxims, although they are a little difficult to live up to. I do not profess to live up to them myself; but then, after all, it is not quite the same thing as for a Christian.

Defects in Christ's Teaching
Having granted the excellence of these maxims, I come to certain points in which I do not believe that one can grant either the superlative wisdom or the superlative goodness of Christ as depicted in the Gospels; and here I may say that one is not concerned with the historical question. Historically it is quite doubtful whether Christ ever existed at all, and if He did we do not know anything about him, so that I am not concerned with the historical question, which is a very difficult one. I am concerned with Christ as He appears in the Gospels, taking the Gospel narrative as it stands, and there one does find some things that do not seem to be very wise. For one thing, he certainly thought that His second coming would occur in clouds of glory before the death of all the people who were living at that time. There are a great many texts that prove that. He says, for instance, "Ye shall not have gone over the cities of Israel till the Son of Man be come." Then he says, "There are some standing here which shall not taste death till the Son of Man comes into His kingdom"; and there are a lot of places where it is quite clear that He believed that His second coming would happen during the lifetime of many then living. That was the belief of His earlier followers, and it was the basis of a good deal of His moral teaching. When He said, "Take no thought for the morrow," and things of that sort, it was very largely because He thought that the second coming was going to be very soon, and that all ordinary mundane affairs did not count. I have, as a matter of fact, known some Christians who did believe that the second coming was imminent. I knew a parson who frightened his congregation terribly by telling them that the second coming was

very imminent indeed, but they were much consoled when they found that he was planting trees in his garden. The early Christians did really believe it, and they did abstain from such things as planting trees in their gardens, because they did accept from Christ the belief that the second coming was imminent. In that respect, clearly He was not so wise as some other people have been, and He was certainly not superlatively wise.

The Moral Problem
Then you come to moral questions. There is one very serious defect to my mind in Christ's moral character, and that is that He believed in hell. I do not myself feel that any person who is really profoundly humane can believe in everlasting punishment. Christ certainly as depicted in the Gospels did believe in everlasting punishment, and one does find repeatedly a vindictive fury against those people who would not listen to His preaching -- an attitude which is not uncommon with preachers, but which does somewhat detract from superlative excellence. You do not, for instance find that attitude in Socrates. You find him quite bland and urbane toward the people who would not listen to him; and it is, to my mind, far more worthy of a sage to take that line than to take the line of indignation. You probably all remember the sorts of things that Socrates was saying when he was dying, and the sort of things that he generally did say to people who did not agree with him.

You will find that in the Gospels Christ said, "Ye serpents, ye generation of vipers, how can ye escape the damnation of Hell." That was said to people who did not like His preaching. It is not really to my mind quite the best tone, and there are a great many of these things about Hell. There is, of course, the familiar text about the sin against the Holy Ghost: "Whosoever speaketh against the Holy Ghost it shall not be forgiven him neither in this World nor in the world to come."

That text has caused an unspeakable amount of misery in the world, for all sorts of people have imagined that they have committed the sin against the Holy Ghost, and thought that it would not be forgiven them either in this world or in the world to come. I really do not think that a person with a proper degree of kindliness in his nature would have put fears and terrors of that sort into the world.

Then Christ says, "The Son of Man shall send forth his His angels, and they shall gather out of His kingdom all things that offend, and them which do iniquity, and shall cast them into a furnace of fire; there shall be wailing and gnashing of teeth"; and He goes on about the wailing and gnashing of teeth. It comes in one verse after another, and it is quite manifest to the reader that there is a certain pleasure in contemplating wailing and gnashing of teeth, or else it would not occur so often. Then you all, of course, remember about the sheep and the goats; how at the second coming He is going to divide the sheep from the goats, and He is going to say to the goats, "Depart from me, ye cursed, into everlasting fire." He continues, "And these shall go away into everlasting fire." Then He says again, "If thy hand offend thee, cut it off; it is better for thee to enter into life maimed, than having two hands to go into Hell, into the fire that never shall be quenched; where the worm dieth not and the fire is not quenched." He repeats that again and again also. I must say that I think all this doctrine, that hell-fire is a punishment for sin, is a doctrine of cruelty. It is a doctrine that put cruelty into the world and gave the world generations of cruel torture; and the Christ of the Gospels, if you could take Him as His chroniclers represent Him, would certainly have to be considered partly responsible for that.

There are other things of less importance. There is the instance of the Gadarene swine, where it certainly was not very kind to the pigs to put the devils into them and make them rush down the hill into the sea. You must remember that He was omnipotent, and He could have made the devils simply go away; but He chose to send them into the pigs. Then there is the curious story of the fig tree, which always rather puzzled me. You remember what happened about the fig tree. "He was hungry; and seeing a fig tree afar off having leaves, He came if haply He might find anything thereon; and when He came to it He found nothing but leaves, for the time of figs was not yet. And Jesus answered and said unto it: 'No man eat fruit of thee hereafter forever' . . . and Peter . . . saith unto Him: 'Master, behold the fig tree which thou cursed is withered away.'" This is a very curious story, because it was not the right time of year for figs, and you really could not blame the tree. I cannot myself feel that either in the matter of wisdom or in the matter of virtue Christ stands quite as high as some other people known to history. I think I should put Buddha and Socrates above Him in those respects.

The Emotional Factor
As I said before, I do not think that the real reason why people accept religion has anything to do with argumentation. They accept religion on emotional grounds. One is often told that it is a very wrong thing to attack religion, because religion makes men virtuous. So I am told; I have not noticed it. You know, of course, the parody of that argument in Samuel Butler's book, *Erewhon Revisited*. You will remember that in *Erewhon* there is a certain Higgs who arrives in a remote country, and after spending some time there he escapes from that country in a balloon. Twenty years later he comes back to that country and finds a new religion in which he is worshiped under the name of the "Sun Child," and it is said that he ascended into heaven. He finds that the Feast of the Ascension is about to be celebrated, and he hears Professors Hanky and Panky say to each other that

they never set eyes on the man Higgs, and they hope they never will; but they are the high priests of the religion of the Sun Child. He is very indignant, and he comes up to them, and he says, "I am going to expose all this humbug and tell the people of Erewhon that it was only I, the man Higgs, and I went up in a balloon." He was told, "You must not do that, because all the morals of this country are bound round this myth, and if they once know that you did not ascend into Heaven they will all become wicked"; and so he is persuaded of that and he goes quietly away.

That is the idea -- that we should all be wicked if we did not hold to the Christian religion. It seems to me that the people who have held to it have been for the most part extremely wicked. You find this curious fact, that the more intense has been the religion of any period and the more profound has been the dogmatic belief, the greater has been the cruelty and the worse has been the state of affairs. In the so-called ages of faith, when men really did believe the Christian religion in all its completeness, there was the Inquisition, with all its tortures; there were millions of unfortunate women burned as witches; and there was every kind of cruelty practiced upon all sorts of people in the name of religion.

You find as you look around the world that every single bit of progress in humane feeling, every improvement in the criminal law, every step toward the diminution of war, every step toward better treatment of the colored races, or every mitigation of slavery, every moral progress that there has been in the world, has been consistently opposed by the organized churches of the world. I say quite deliberately that the Christian religion, as organized in its churches, has been and still is the principal enemy of moral progress in the world.

How the Churches Have Retarded Progress

You may think that I am going too far when I say that that is still so. I do not think that I am. Take one fact. You will bear with me if I mention it. It is not a pleasant fact, but the churches compel one to mention facts that are not pleasant. Supposing that in this world that we live in today an inexperienced girl is married to a syphilitic man; in that case the Catholic Church says, "This is an indissoluble sacrament. You must endure celibacy or stay together. And if you stay together, you must not use birth control to prevent the birth of syphilitic children." Nobody whose natural sympathies have not been warped by dogma, or whose moral nature was not absolutely dead to all sense of suffering, could maintain that it is right and proper that that state of things should continue.

That is only an example. There are a great many ways in which, at the present moment, the church, by its insistence upon what it chooses to call morality, inflicts upon all sorts of people undeserved and unnecessary suffering. And of course, as we know, it is in its major part an opponent still of progress and improvement in all the ways that diminish suffering in the world, because it has chosen to label as morality a certain narrow set of rules of conduct which have nothing to do with human happiness; and when you say that this or that ought to be done because it would make for human happiness, they think that has nothing to do with the matter at all. "What has human happiness to do with morals? The object of morals is not to make people happy."

Fear, the Foundation of Religion

Religion is based, I think, primarily and mainly upon fear. It is partly the terror of the unknown and partly, as I have said, the wish to feel that you have a kind of elder brother who will stand by you in all your troubles and disputes. Fear is the basis of the whole thing -- fear of the mysterious, fear of defeat, fear of death. Fear is the parent of cruelty, and therefore it is no wonder if cruelty and religion have gone hand in hand. It is because fear is at the basis of those two things. In this world we can now begin a little to understand things, and a little to master them by help of science, which has forced its way step by step against the Christian religion, against the churches, and against the opposition of all the old precepts. Science can help us to get over this craven fear in which mankind has lived for so many generations. Science can teach us, and I think our own hearts can teach us, no longer to look around for imaginary supports, no longer to invent allies in the sky, but rather to look to our own efforts here below to make this world a better place to live in, instead of the sort of place that the churches in all these centuries have made it.

What We Must Do
We want to stand upon our own feet and look fair and square at the world -- its good facts, its bad facts, its beauties, and its ugliness; see the world as it is and be not afraid of it. Conquer the world by intelligence and not merely by being slavishly subdued by the terror that comes from it. The whole conception of God is a conception derived from the ancient Oriental despotisms. It is a conception quite unworthy of free men. When you hear people in church debasing themselves and saying that they are miserable sinners, and all the rest of it, it seems contemptible and not worthy of self-respecting human beings. We ought to stand up and look the world frankly in the face. We ought to make the best we can of the world, and if it is not so good as we wish, after all it will still be better than what these others have made of it in all these ages. A good world needs knowledge, kindliness, and courage; it does not need a regretful hankering after the past or a fettering of the free intelligence by

the words uttered long ago by ignorant men. It needs a fearless outlook and a free intelligence. It needs hope for the future, not looking back all the time toward a past that is dead, which we trust will be far surpassed by the future that our intelligence can create.

3:1-10 Conclusion: God Has Ordered the Universe

[1] To everything there is a season, and a time to every purpose under the heaven:

To all a season and a time to every desirable thing under the heaven. There are twenty-eight forthcoming occurrences of a time (*eth*) for opposing activities. There is order. There is design.

[2] A time to be born, and a time to die; a time to plant, and a time to pluck up that which is planted;
[3] A time to kill, and a time to heal; a time to break down, and a time to build up;
[4] A time to weep, and a time to laugh; a time to mourn, and a time to dance;
[5] A time to cast away stones, and a time to gather stones together; a time to embrace, and a time to refrain from embracing;
[6] A time to get, and a time to lose; a time to keep, and a time to cast away;
[7] A time to rend, and a time to sew; a time to keep silence, and a time to speak;
[8] A time to love, and a time to hate; a time of war, and a time of peace.
[9] What profit hath he that worketh in that wherein he laboureth?

The activity of man (labor) is a part of this order and design, and despite the obvious teleological conclusions, there remains no profit (*yithron*) for the worker in his labor. The design in itself does not provide the meaning, but it points directly to it.

[10] I have seen the travail, which God hath given to the sons of men to be exercised in it.

Travail (*inyan*) – better, task (NASB). The task is given (*nathan*) for the purpose of being engaged in. The task is part of the design, yet it has already been described as *hebel* by Solomon. Again, it does not provide meaning but points to it. The arrow points beyond the sun.

Excursus: The Philosophical and Theological Compatibility of Mechanistic Evolution and An Ordered Universe

Introduction
With the early 2008 release of Ben Stein's documentary *Expelled*, discussions of cosmogony and teleological ideas have found themselves once again at the center of public debate. Certainly cosmic origins are not of so little interest that such a commotion should be considered a surprise – of course in recent years there have been heightened efforts both in support of and in opposition to the resumption of some form of creationist curriculum in public schools. Stein's documentary has already proved to be a significant catalyst in the reframing of the national debate, and represents an outcry on the part of many perceiving their belief system to be disenfranchised from the mainstream. How contentious is this issue? One review says the movie

...calls attention to the plight of highly credentialed scholars who have been forced out of prestigious academic positions because the proposed Intelligent Design as a possible alternative to Charles Darwin's 150-year-old theories about the origins of life. Instead of entertaining a debate on the merits of competing theories, the scientific establishment has moved to suppress the ID movement in a "systematic and ruthless" way at odds with America's founding principles, the film asserts.[51]

The high level of controversy surrounding the film is an indicator of the profundity of the issue – both in academia and society at large. At the heart of the issue is the metaphysical question of the teleological – is the universe ordered or is it essentially random. Darwinian theory implies a pervading randomness, yet certain systems such as theistic evolution and intelligent design seek (in some permutations) to redeem evolutionism by granting it a teleological underpinning. But is such redemption possible? Do the philosophical aspects of Darwinism allow for such a move? Heideggerian thinker Hans Jonas conducts an insightful assessment of Darwinism and has much to say about the sought after consistency between Darwinian theory and an ordered universe. Jonas' observations will be considered here as the thesis that, outside of any consideration of special revelation (which will not be addressed here), there is an incompatibility between mechanistic evolutionism and an ordered universe, and that attempts to philosophically justify systems requiring or utilizing both are untenable.

Not all proponents of intelligent design recognize evolution as the agent of origin, but some of the earliest references to ID – in particular those of Helena Blavatsky – demonstrate an acceptance of evolutionism as creative agent.

Additionally a great many theists are willing to accept the evolutionary model as the instrument of creation.

Gap theorist Harry Rimmer acknowledged that the Genesis text did not require anything other than a literal seven-day creation, saying

> ...there is no reason to demand an extensive time period in the days of creation in Genesis, except the desire to be in conformity with the contentions and demands of the evolutionary school of geology. That system of philosophy requires unlimited ages for the unfolding and the gradual development of the creation as it now is and long has been, and calls for multiplied millions of years for each small change in the vast chain of evolving creatures.[52]

At the same time, despite his recognition of a seven day creation week, he makes textual arguments favoring the gap theory – an interpretive license applied in between Genesis 1:1 and 1:2 which would allow for a great amount of time to pass from the original creative act to the beginning of the "revitalizing" creative week. This was a prevalent approach, utilized in accommodation of the development of Darwinian theory. In short, gap theory demonstrates an awareness of obligation on the part of many to justify theology with science and philosophy.

Steven Jay Gould's principle of Non-Overlapping Magesteria (NOMA) suggests a "respectful noninterference"[53] and thus a resolution of the "false conflict between science and religion".[54] Gould rejects the tenets of creationism as "marginal and long-discredited factual claims"[55] and as the passion of "a small group allied to one magesterium [which] tries to impose its irrelevant and illegitimate will upon the other's domain."[56] Not insignificantly, however, he is not opposed to versions of creation which are consistent with NOMA, and specifically

> ...the belief, for example, that God works through laws of evolution over the long time scale determined by geology, and that this style of superintendence may be regarded as a mode of creation.[57]

The key point in relation to the topic at hand is that Gould recommends the co-existence of theism and evolution, suggesting that "[c]reationists do not represent the magisterium of religion,"[58] and that "[t]he enemy is not religion but dogmatism and intolerance."[59] There is an assumed consistency on Gould's part between religion and evolutionism – indeed one that is certainly not present between literal creationism and evolutionary science.

Regarding the mechanizing of the world picture, developing from Copernicus to Newton,[60] Hooykaas suggests

> ...seventeenth century mechanistic philosophy was not a new compromise of Christianity, this time with ancient materialism instead of ancient organicism or idealism, but rather a step towards the Christianization and the emancipation of natural science.[61]

And although this mechanizing represents for Hooykaas a compromise of Christianity, he suggests the mechanistic perspective is superior to the organic one in that it better fits the Biblical model, since it reckons the world to be fabricated rather than generated. Despite the accolades offered for the mechanistic model, Hooykaas reckons that the model possesses significant limitation. He says,

> What nature really is cannot be adequately expressed by the simile of a "machine," and who God really is cannot

be aptly represented by the term "mechanician." It cannot be done even by reducing natural science to mathematics and by calling God...a great mathematician."[62]

Hans Jonas, offering an admittedly "existential interpretation of biological facts,"[63] and seeking to affirm the interdependence between the organic and mind traces the organic interpretation to Plato. He says,

> The God of the Timaeus created the world as the perfect "animal" or visible god, ensouled and intelligent. Looking to the intelligible pattern he formed the changeable in its likeness, and thus as far as possible in his own. For the intelligible and the intelligent are the same. Passive "matter" alone could certainly not be entrusted with preserving throughout change the forms and proportions imprinted on it, nor with providing the force for that motion of change itself by which the fair copy must imitate eternity in time.[64]

While Plato's model was ensouled, the Judeo-Christian model, which Jonas suggests replaced the Platonic one, was a significant contrast. Jonas says,

> The created world of Genesis is not a god and is not to be worshipped instead of God. Nor has it a soul of its own that would account for its activity and its orderliness. It is merely made and is in no sense maker.[65]

While the metaphysic of modern science, Jonas observes, is based on this model, Descartes' momentous modification of the model cannot be underestimated, as it set metaphysics on a new course.

The Teleological Concept Developed and Applied
Rooted in Platonic and Aristotelian philosophy, the teleological concept is epitomized in Socrates' initial inquiries into natural philosophy:

> Do heat and cold, by a sort of fermentation, bring about the organization of animals, as some people say? Is it the blood, or air, or fire by which we think? Or is it none of these...?[66]

Socrates at first drew comfort from Anaxagoras' system of arrangement and causation, with *things* as causation, but then realized certain shortcomings of the method, saying,

> But to say that those things are the cause of my doing what I do, and that I act with intelligence but not from the choice of what is best, would be an extremely careless way of talking. Whoever talks in that way is unable to make a distinction and to see that in reality a cause is one thing, and the thing without which the cause could never be a cause is quite another thing. And so it seems to me that most people, when they give the name of cause to the latter, are groping in the dark, as it were, and are giving it a name that does not belong to it.[67]

Socrates recognizes here that to suggest that things are causes in themselves is to deny the design of function and best utilization of things – such denial being an absurdity to him. Thus a teleological concept is at the heart of Plato's organic concept (and is explained in depth in the creation account of the *Timaeus*).

The teleological inquiry forms a nexus between theology and philosophy by way of Thomas Aquinas' attempts to justify Christian theology as fully competent to hold up under the scrutiny of philosophy. In particular Aquinas argues that God's existence can be proved in five ways, offering philosophical explanation for the certainty of a personal[68] and divine Being. The fifth proof is decidedly teleological, founded on the earlier Platonic conception of obtaining the *best* result:

> The fifth way is taken from the governance of the world. We see that things which lack knowledge, such as natural bodies, act for an end, and this is evident from their acting always, or nearly always, in the same way, so as to obtain the best result. Hence it is plain that they achieve their end, not fortuitously, but designedly. Now whatever lacks knowledge cannot move towards an end, unless it be directed by some being endowed with knowledge and intelligence; as the arrow is directed by the archer. Therefore some intelligent being exists by whom all natural things are directed to their end; and this being we call God.[69]

Aquinas simply complements the Socratic thought of function intended for the best outcome by explaining the origin and definition of the best outcome. Aquinas' proof is a philosophical argument that relies on natural theology for the specifics of its conclusion. In fairness to Aquinas' theological grounding, it should be noted that on several occasions in his discussion of the five ways, Aquinas invites his interlocutors to consider special revelation, but the vast majority of the discussion is centered on argument based on premises that even those unwilling to consider special revelation would be willing to at least entertain.

Perhaps the most notable elucidation of the teleological concept is William Paley's analogical argument based on the existence of a watch. The questions one might ask when discovering a watch are profoundly teleological, and ultimately of great metaphysical import. He says,

> ...the question which irresistibly presses upon our thoughts is, whence this contrivance and design? The thing required is the intending mind, the adapting hand, the intelligence by which that hand was directed...I deny that for the design, the contrivance, the suitableness of means to an end, the adaptation of instruments to a use (all which we discover in a watch,) we have any cause whatever. It is vain therefore, to assign a series of such causes, or to allege that a series may be carried back to infinity; for I do not admit that we have yet any cause at all of the phenomena, still less any series of causes finite or infinite. Here is contrivance, but no contriver; proofs of design but no designer....[70]

For Paley, design requires a designer, the denial of which is atheism. He concludes his work with an admission that among many examples one in particular will stand out - the chief example of the teleological concept in his judgment is human anatomy.[71] Due to this instance alongside a host of others, Paley says,

> I shall not, I believe, be contradicted when I say, that, if one train of thinking be more desirable than another, it is that which regards the phenomena of nature with a constant reference to a supreme intelligent Author.[72]

It is notable that Paley's appeal (and subject matter) is to natural theology, working from Platonic ideas (as did Aquinas) to achieve certain theological suppositions. Both Aquinas and Paley utilized the teleological argument to defend the existence of a divine Architect, but just as the teleological concept that the two used was first utilized outside of a theological context, so it would later be utilized as it had been initially.

In the late nineteenth century, theosophy founder Helena Blavatsky described evolutionary process as a product of intelligent design. Her cosmogony represented a shift from the Aquinas/Paley model which asserted the existence of a personal Designer. She viewed evolution not as the working out of randomness, but rather as guided by "an underlying purposeful intelligence in nature."[73] Blavatsky's teleological concept seems quite compatible with the Platonic model.

Some more recent and increasingly popular permutations of the teleological concept come from such groups as the Intelligent Design Network (IDNet). IDNet defines intelligent design as follows:

> The theory of intelligent design (ID) holds that certain features of the universe and of living things are best explained by an intelligent cause rather than an undirected process such as natural selection. ID is thus a scientific disagreement with the core claim of evolutionary theory that the apparent design of living systems is an illusion.[74]

Within this definition is ample room for a return to the Platonic model, and IDNet recognizes that the controversy may be more philosophical and theological than scientific:

3:1-10 Conclusion: God Has Ordered the Universe

> ID is controversial because of the *implications* of its evidence, rather than the significant *weight* of its evidence. ID proponents believe science should be conducted objectively, without regard to the implications of its findings. This is particularly necessary in origins science because of its historical (and thus very subjective) nature, and because it is a science that unavoidably impacts religion.[75]

While there are obvious theological ramifications, the ID debate is perhaps more philosophical than even scientific – raising the issue of objectivity in science (which ironically is a decidedly philosophical issue).

In summary, I have reviewed some very elementary milestones in the development and application of the teleological concept – not for purposes of argument either in favor or against, but rather simply to provide the contextual setting for the utilization of a particular philosophical construct in attempts to resolve certain theological dilemmas. The teleological concept, as such a philosophical construct, has a very definite metaphysical bearing beyond cosmogony in particular for at least the Platonic, Blavatskyan, and theistic evolutionism models. This influence is evident in at least two important manifestations: (1) being is ordered, and meaningful being is understood by or extracted from that order; and (2) being (in general) is governed by order, and the governing singular being (specific), whether personal or impersonal, is superior to the order. Both would seem necessary in a comprehensive philosophical perspective, and thus arriving at an incompatibility with these manifestations and the instrument of being would indeed be problematic.

The Compatibility Problem

In his essay on the *Philosophical Aspects of Darwinism*,[76] Hans Jonas recognizes a significant flaw in this kind of thinking. He first characterizes the mechanistic model which found prominence in the seventeenth century as a deliberate amelioration of the earlier organic model which tended toward pantheism. The new model assumed design and thus presupposed a designer, but the design was perceived to be so efficient that it was indeed self-functioning – that within its design was the provision of everything necessary for operating to the best end. The epicenter of inquiry was no longer the cosmogony of the ordered system but instead the performance of the structure. Coupled with the shift in focus was a new direction in the defining of origins, which proved influential as later discussions of origin took center stage. Jonas highlights that shift, characterizing prevailing modern physics theory as ultimately concluding that

> ...origin and resulting existence do not differ except in the sense of antecedent and subsequent states of an identical substratum: the producing reality is of the same order as the product, being merely differently located in the infinite time-series of cause and effect.[77]

This represents in Jonas' view a new metaphysical perspective of being – that it is identified with action and process.[78] The metaphysical significance of this shift cannot be underestimated, since in this precedent setting realignment and consequent redefining of being and origins there is a role reversal of the originating principle and its effects. Jonas explains:

> It had mostly been assumed that there must be not only more power but also more perfection in the cause than in the effect. The originating agency must possess more reality that the things originated by it. It must also be superior in formal essence, to account for the degree of form that the derivative things may enjoy...this pattern is completely reversed in the kind of genetic deduction which modern theory inaugurated.[79]

This reversal shows an incompatibility of mechanistic philosophy with (at least previous conceptions of) the teleological – that the designer was initially and remains presently superior to the design. Thus the second manifestation of the (Platonic/Blavatskyan/theistic evolutionary) teleological concept is directly contradicted by the definitions of being and origin which are spawned from that which is designed.

As for the first manifestation – that being is ordered – to this, Jonas responds that existentialism is a more proper understanding than is the teleological concept as a philosophical consequence of mechanistic evolutionism. In demonstrating this Jonas makes two key observations regarding evolution: (1) in contrast to Descartes' conception, the evolutionist model regards structure as "the condition for a specific performance of life, as itself a product of life, the outcome and temporary stopping-place of a continuous dynamism which itself must be termed 'life.'"[80] This is to say that life appears in its means rather than as being endowed with them; and perhaps more significantly (2) that the evolutionary process is devoid of any "teleological directedness."[81] Thus the basic concept of life, for Jonas in this context, is a conjoining of organism and environment – this is a non-teleological system. What then is the outcome? And how is the first previously stated manifestation of the teleological concept (that being is ordered) manipulated?

As the designer no longer holds supremacy over the design, but is now virtually a part of it, the essence of human existence is perceived differently:

> The "image," in the absence of creation, had vanished with the original; and reason had been reduced to a means among means, to be judged by the efficiency of its instrumental role in the survival issue: as a merely formal skill.[82]

Origin and being are redefined but so is knowledge. No longer a tool to investigate the blueprint in order to discover something of the architect, knowledge becomes simply a survival skill. This is, as Jonas suggests, "the nihilistic implication in man's losing a "being" transcending the flux of becoming."[83] The will to power seems then the only remaining appropriate ethical mooring in light of the philosophical consequences of evolution. And while Darwinism may not be the biological father of existentialism, the two are intimately acquainted, as Jonas concludes of Darwinism "...that it conforms and contributes to all the other mental factors out of whose total setting existentialism logically grew."[84] It is at this point that the clearest incompatibility between the teleological concept and mechanistic evolutionism is evident.

Conclusion

Henry Morris describes a not so recent trend in cosmogony: "Creationism is being fitted for new clothes...."[85] Citing E.C. Scott's reference to these new clothes as "neocreationism," Morris explains that neocreationism is not so concerned about adding new clothes but rather removing them. Specifically, neocreationism – including theistic evolutionism, intelligent design, progressive creationism, etc. – is not Biblical creationism in the sense of the ex-nihilo seven-day variety, but rather is fairly unconcerned with the details of the Genesis account or the finer points of evolutionary grounding and process, but instead focuses on the claim that life is an effect of an intelligent architect rather than the fruit of impersonal mechanistic forces. However, as has already been discussed here, a significant contingent of the neocreationist crowd is willing to accept evolution as the engine of creation. Essentially neocreationism is motivated centrally by apologetic sentiments and is powered by teleological arguments that are primarily philosophical rather than theological. (Admittedly, there is difficulty ascertaining in certain contexts where theology ends and philosophy begins [and vice versa], but in this case the appeal to natural theology being profoundly more prominent in neocreationism than any appeal to special revelation, would offer, in this writers' view, evidence that the discussion is primarily philosophical.)

While Henry Morris is an avowed Biblical creationist, Hans Jonas is not. Yet, Jonas' complements Morris' perspective as he voices a philosophical critique that seems fatal to the philosophical viability of such accommodationism.

Can evolutionism be justified with the teleological concept, or is evolutionism better associated with its Lucretian roots and disdain for design? Lucretius' anti-teleological perspective is unmistakable:

> Herein I sorely yearn to have thee shun
> This fault, and as with deep felt dread avoid
> A general error: lest perchance thou deem
> The eye's bright orb hath with design been framed
> That we might look before us...[86]

Lucretius and Darwin, as Jonas indicates, are far more philosophically compatible with existential thought than with any form of teleological conception. Consequently, the (at least) apparent incompatibility between mechanistic evolution and an ordered universe uncovers that such theories as non-theistic intelligent design as well as theistic evolution contain within themselves strange philosophical self-contradictions that might cause one to inquire as to the reason any secularist should need to perceive intelligent design, and that any theist should turn to the evolutionary engine.

3:11-22 Conclusion: God Has a "Beyond the Sun" Program for Man

[11] He hath made everything beautiful in his time: also he hath set the world in their heart, so that no man can find out the work that God maketh from the beginning to the end.

An ordered universe points to a designer. One may argue that there is flawed order or that things break. One may argue about the character of the Designer, but arguing that the order that exists is accidental takes a special kind of faith (and not the kind built on any reasonable grounding). The order doesn't unveil meaning, but points to it.

The whole He has made beautiful (*yapheh*) in His time. What a pregnant statement with several significant implications: (1) He made everything; (2) He made it beautiful, thus beauty has an absolute value as determined by Him (beauty in the eye of *the* Beholder); (3) The beauty of the ordered universe is based on His time. The Designer has a program for His universe.

He has given the always (*ha olam*) in their heart (set eternity in their heart, NASB). God has given a clue to His program for man via an innate awareness of Him within the heart of man. Yet He has hidden the fullness of His program from man. But why?

From the beginning (*merosh*) and unto the end (*suph*) – the Greek of the LXX translates *arche* (beginning, in philosophy - the ultimate principle of reality) and *telous* (goal or purpose, end). Both Greek terms represent monumental pursuits in philosophy. Philosophy seeks to understand both from a naturalistic perspective. Yet Solomon says that man will not, by Divine design, find out either. Quite a contradiction between the two systems.

[12] I know that there is no good in them, but for a man to rejoice, and to do good in his life.

There is nothing good (tov) for them (the sons of men, v.10) but to rejoice and to work (infinitives) good (*tov*) in his life. But how can one rejoice knowing all is vanity? And how can one work good if the end result is the same as working evil? All under the sun is vanity. But not all is under the sun.

[13] And also that every man should eat and drink, and enjoy the good of all his labour, it is the gift of God.

And also every man eats and drinks and sees good in all his labor, a gift of God it is. The most basic of functions (eating, drinking, working) can rightly be perceived as good when received and reckoned to be a gift of God.

[14] I know that, whatsoever God doeth, it shall be forever: nothing can be put to it, nor any thing taken from it: and God doeth it, that men should fear before him.

I know (*yada*) all that God works shall be eternal (*olam*). And here it is: there is eternal significance in all that God does. Eating, drinking, laboring – these things are doings of God. Thus done with God they have meaning, as originally intended. Done apart from God the intrinsic value and meaning of the actions vanish, leaving naught but *hebel*. Why then does God reveal what he has revealed? In order that (LXX has the *hina* purpose clause) man should fear (*yiraw*) Him. The gifts, the design, the order, the labors, all of it – intended to point man to his Creator. Once directed to the Creator, man should respond in fear (much stronger than simply respect, as yiraw is often used of those in terror for their lives [e.g., Gen. 32:11; 46:3, etc.], the LXX translates *phobeo*. Man should respond in fear, knowing that God has a program for him and that he rests in the Sovereign hand of his Creator.

[15] *That which hath been is now; and that which is to be hath already been; and God requireth that which is past.*

God has ordained the cyclical order of the universe.

[16] *And moreover I saw under the sun the place of judgment, that wickedness was there; and the place of righteousness, that iniquity was there.*

The focus shifts from beyond the sun recognition back to the under the sun meaninglessness: the judgment seats of man are corrupt and where righteousness is expected wickedness is found. Solomon here is anticipating the problem of evil: why is there injustice under the sun if there is none beyond the sun?

[17] *I said in mine heart, God shall judge the righteous and the wicked: for there is a time there for every purpose and for every work.*

His abbreviated resolution is stated in several steps: Step 1: God will judge in His time.

[18] I said in mine heart concerning the estate of the sons of men, that God might manifest them, and that they might see that they themselves are beasts.
Step 2: God allows injustice under the sun in order that man may become aware of his fallen estate.

[19] For that which befalleth the sons of men befalleth beasts; even one thing befalleth them: as the one dieth, so dieth the other; yea, they have all one breath; so that a man hath no preeminence above a beast: for all is vanity.
[20] All go unto one place; all are of the dust, and all turn to dust again.

Step 3: From the fall the fate of man and beasts is the same: death from sin. All remain under the curse.

[21] Who knoweth the spirit of man that goeth upward, and the spirit of the beast that goeth downward to the earth?

Step 4: How can a man know of any distinction between him and the beasts? How can he know of eternal significance? The innate awareness of God via (in part) the awareness of justice and injustice.

[22] Wherefore I perceive that there is nothing better, than that a man should rejoice in his own works; for that is his portion: for who shall bring him to see what shall be after him?

Nothing good but takes the reader back to vv.12-14 with all that those verses imply. That is his portion (*cheleq*) – inheritance.

Man cannot observe beyond the sun, as God has limited human perspective. It has been said that the concept of faith is foreign to Solomon in Ecclesiastes, however, it is evident he is exhorting the reader to operate on faith: God's beyond the sun program exists. But God has placed man under the sun. Thus man is prescribed to operate under the sun with a beyond the sun perspective. This sounds remarkably like the definition of faith: "faith is the assurance of things hoped for, the conviction of things not seen" (Heb. 12:1).

Excursus: Environmental Ethics: On the Spirit of Man and Intrinsic Value

Two questions have steered a significant segment of thought, discussion, and consequent development of the identifiable foundations of environmental ethics: *(1) Does man possess any degree of intrinsic value which animals do not share? And (2) Is the human spirit unique in its possession of life after death?* Lynn White's pivotal *On the Historical Roots of our Ecological Crisis*[87] centralizes these questions and draws conclusions contrary in varying degree to a number of religious traditions. Any who would agree with White's conclusions must therefore reevaluate any agreement with these traditions as consistent systems (if they even purport to function as such). While White's critiques, though broad and often not well supported, are certainly pertinent to some traditions, the issues should not be moved from epicenter in the discussion. Throwing the baby out with the bathwater in this case has profound impact.

It is perhaps useful at this point to deal with these two questions in light of White's critiques of religion, and in light of the Biblical record. Comparing and contrasting the two approaches will necessarily present an alternate set of conclusions which not only demand consideration in the ethical debate, but also provide a solid set of moorings for future discussion.

Intrinsic Value: Man or Beast?

White admits limited knowledge of the true cause of or severity of the "ecological crisis," saying "The history of ecological change is still so rudimentary that we know little about what really happened, or what the results were." But despite such uncertainty, there is at first no suggestion for coping with the problem. Asking and answering his own important question, White says, "What shall we do? No one yet knows." White blames "the presuppositions that underlie modern technology and science," and suggests the current crisis is

> The product of an emerging, entirely novel, democratic culture. The issue is whether a democratized world can survive its own implications. Presumably we cannot unless we rethink our axioms.

So what are the presuppositions which White vilifies?

> Since both our technological and our scientific movements got their start, acquired their character, and achieved world dominance in the Middle Ages, it would seem that we cannot understand their nature or their present impact upon ecology without examining medieval assumptions and developments.

White suggests that modern technology is rooted in "ruthlessness toward nature," and traces this ruthlessness to the view that "man and nature are two things, and man is master." But where does he assert this view comes from? In a word – religion: "Human ecology is deeply conditioned by beliefs about our nature and destiny – that is religion." But not just any religion. White points an accusing finger at one tradition directly: "The victory of Christianity over paganism was the greatest psychic revolution in the history of our culture." His indictment continues as he later warns that "We shall continue to have a worsening ecologic crisis until we reject the Christian axiom that nature has no reason for existence save to serve man."

In fairness, White is not condemning Christianity as a whole, but simply the axiom he so readily identifies with the ethical traditions of Christianity and the pedagogy that results from the axiom. (see Appendix I for Specific areas of criticism and disagreement with the Christian text)

Others have labored to redeem the Christian tradition to some degree from White's blanket criticism: Callicott presents J-theism as an alternative interpretation to Lynn White's within the Christian tradition. He identifies

> a countercurrent of thought powerfully and discernibly running in the text of Genesis itself.... Within the general outlines of the traditional scriptural worldview, nonhuman species may have intrinsic value because they are parts of God's creation and God has conferred intrinsic value upon them, either by creating them or by a secondary fiat.[88]

Callicott's defense rests on a non-literal hermeneutic approach to the creation account, seemingly assuming that the literal-grammatical hermeneutic could not possibly offer any solution in such discussions. Hull de-emphasizes hermeneutic significance, saying,

> Regardless of hotly debated interpretations of biblical passages, the monotheism of the Judeo-Christian tradition dramatically changed people's understanding of nature. The landscape existing before the God of Abraham was inspirited, alive with many gods, demons, and ancestors.... Judeo-Christian teachings de-spirited nature by claiming that nature, unlike people, is not caring, feeling, or inspirited. Spirits on Earth exist only in people....[89]

In particular, Hull hones in on the issue of *the spirit* – noting the Biblical distinctions between man and animal. In his defense of the Judeo-Christian tradition he references other hermeneutical traditions (including that of Wendell Berry) which close the value gap between man and beast and redefine the spirit as more universal. It becomes quickly evident that intrinsic value and the nature of the spirit are interrelated issues bearing significant influence on each other.

Upward Mobility of the Spirit
Qoheleth[90] made a significant observation three thousand years ago pertaining to the nature of man and beast. Writing from the purely human perspective[91] he says the following:

> I said to myself concerning the sons of men, "God has surely tested them in order for them to see that they are but beasts." **For the fate of the sons of men and the fate of beasts is the same. As one dies so dies the other; indeed, they all have the same breath and there is no advantage for man over beast, for all is vanity. All go to the same place. All came from the dust and all return to the dust. Who knows that the breath of man ascends upward and the breath of the beast descends downward to the earth?**

> [emphasis mine] I have seen that nothing is better than that man should be happy in his activities, for that is his lot. For who will bring him to see what will occur after him? (Ecclesiastes 3:18-22)

Operating from an empirical perspective, Solomon observes that the senses cannot detect what takes place after the senses cease their functions. His argument then is not a positive assertion of spiritual reality based on sensual empiricism, but rather a critique – based on sensual empiricism – of any other interpretation, asserting that all is vanity, and thus after a number of case studies and arguments, makes the following case:

> The conclusion, when all has been heard, *is:* fear God and keep His commandments, because this *applies to* every person. For God will bring every act to judgment, everything which is hidden, whether it is good or evil. (Ecclesiastes 12:13-14)

It is notable that the Hebrew word translated *person* here is the word *adam*, which references mankind collectively[92] in contradistinction to other living creatures. Solomon's conclusion then, is that while it cannot be observed that there are differing destinations for the spirit of man and the spirit of beast due to the observable reality that both creatures return to the dust, that there is indeed a distinction explainable in this context by transcendental argument – no other proposed explanation of reality offers a consistent and satisfactory explanation for the vanity or emptiness of such human elements as pleasure, wisdom, madness, folly, labor, life, work, aloneness, wealth, honor, and death.[93] The conclusion rests upon the reality of a judgment for humanity after death. But then what happens to the breath of life that God placed within every animal (see Gen. 7:15) upon the death of the animal? Despite the relative silence of the Bible on this matter, this question ultimately has no bearing on the intrinsic value of either man or animal. That there are a number of divergent historical and hermeneutic traditions pertaining to the text is evident at this point. Affect the methodology, and the conclusion will necessarily be impacted. Affect the conclusion, and the praxis will be inevitably changed.

The Solomonic argument provides the basis for an epistemological grounding – a starting point if you will for the consideration of the two key questions identified here. Solomonic wisdom here will ultimately lead to a different assessment of history and hermeneutic than is provided by White or even Callicott and Hull. Thus a new discussion can be embarked upon – one that perhaps should have been engaged long ago. Then again, perhaps the discussion has been ongoing and we have just not been listening.

Like Solomon's wisdom, the book of Job grants us insight into the nature of value and the value of nature. Is White's accusation that "No item in the physical creation had any purpose save to serve man's purposes" hold up theologically? Job 38:25-26 reads,

> Who has cleft a channel for the flood, or a way for the thunderbolt; to bring rain on a land without people, on a desert without a man in it?

It is quite obvious, as this passage, reveals, that God's work does far more than meet the simple needs of man. Solomon and Job present a view of purpose in nature that is hardly utilitarian uniquely for the sake of man. Utilitarian, perhaps, but not for man – rather for God, Who works all things together for His purpose. Ultimately, then, in light of this Biblical perspective, the purpose for nature in some cases have very little to do with man. Therefore, in a discussion of intrinsic value, the idea that man has it while beasts do not cannot be defended Biblically. On the contrary, it becomes evident that neither man nor beast has independent intrinsic value, but both have relative intrinsic value – as being fashioned by the Creator for His own purposes and to His glory. While the Biblical record does indeed demonstrate a difference between man and beast, It never presents man as intrinsically valuable, but rather presents a contrasting view. Note Genesis 6:5 –

> Then the Lord saw that the wickedness of man was great on the earth, and that every intent of the thoughts of his heart was only evil continually.

Man, because of sin, is not the reflection of God as was originally created. Man is therefore incapable of ruling over creation (note the dominion imperative is given before sin[Gen. 1:26] and is not repeated after sin), and is certainly unable to faithfully steward it. The problem, therefore, is not the Biblical tradition, as White implies, rather it is sin. Man has turned his back on creation's Designer. Is it any wonder that creation is then misappropriated?

Conclusion
White's critique of supposedly Christian axioms, along with Callicott's and Hull's hermeneutic alternatives do not adequately address the key issues of intrinsic value and the nature of the spirit. White places too much emphasis on one particular historical interpretation and not enough on the text which moors Christianity (i.e., the Bible, itself). While Callicott and Hull address alternative conclusions by virtue of

hermeneutic methodology, it is fairly odd that neither considered a literal-grammatical hermeneutic approach - which since being the inaugural hermeneutic within both elements of the Judeo-Christian tradition deserves attention. To grasp most accurately the teachings of these traditions this hermeneutic is a necessary consideration.

An accurate assessment of the theology and reasoning of Biblical Christianity (properly contextualizing history and hermeneutic method) results in a much fairer assessment of the ethical conclusions of the religious system. Sadly, when the practice does not match the teaching of a particular system, the worthiness of the system comes under impassible scrutiny. The same is true for both world views – particularly White's and that of the Bible.

Perhaps it would be wise to consider the practical application of the system/worldview taken to its logical end. If done with consideration and objectivity perhaps the Biblical system of stewardship provides an excellent explanation, foundation, and ethic for living with each other.

Assertions by White, and Biblical Responses
Assertion by White: "implicit faith in perpetual progress – "rooted in and indefensible apart from Judeo-Christian teleology."

Biblical Approach: Perpetual progress is a Darwinian idea not a Biblical one:

Genesis 6:5 – Then the Lord saw that the wickedness of man was great on the earth, and that every intent of the thoughts of his heart was only evil continually.

Psalm 9:15 – The nations have sunk down in the pit which they have made; In the net which they hid, their own foot has been caught.

White: "God created Eve as an afterthought to keep man from being lonely."

Biblical: Genesis 1:27 – God created man in His own image, in the image of God He created him; male and female He created them.

Matthew 19:4 – And He answered and said, "Have you not read that He who created them from the beginning made them male and female.

Matthew 19:5 – ...and said, 'for this reason a man shall leave his father and mother and be joined to his wife, and the two shall become one flesh."

Matthew 19:6 – "So they are no longer two, but one flesh. What therefore God has joined together, let no man separate."

White: "God planned all of this explicitly for man's benefit and rule."

Biblical: No, He planned all of this for His benefit and rule:

Psalm 24:1 – The earth is the Lord's, and all it contains, The world, and those who dwell in it.

Colossians 1:16 – For by Him all things were created, *both* in the heavens and on earth, visible and invisible... all things have been created through Him and for Him.

Romans 1:20 – For since the creation of the world His invisible attributes, His eternal power and divine nature, have been clearly seen, being understood through what has been made, so that they are without excuse.

Revelation 4:11 – "Worthy are You, our Lord and our God, to receive glory and honor and power; for You created all things, and because of Your will they existed, and were created."

White: "No item in the physical creation had any purpose save to serve man's purposes."

Biblical: Colossians 1:16 – For by Him all things were created, *both* in the heavens and on earth, visible and invisible... all things have been created through Him and for Him.

Nothing was made to serve man's purposes alone.

White: "Christianity is the most anthropocentric religion the world has seen."

Biblical: Biblical Christianity is the *only* ethic that is decidedly not anthropocentric and egocentric; rather it is theocentric.

Isaiah 2:22 – Stop regarding man, whose breath of life is in his nostrils; For why should he be esteemed?

Isaiah 40:15 – Behold, the nations are like a drop from a bucket, And are regarded as a speck of dust on the scales...

Isaiah 40:17 – All the nations are as nothing before Him, They are regarded by Him as less than nothing and meaningless....

Isaiah 40:26 – Lift up your eyes on high And see who has created these *stars,* The One who leads forth their host by number, He calls them all by name; Because of the greatness of His might and the strength of *His* power, Not one *of them* is missing.

John 3:30 – "He must increase, but I must decrease.

White: "Man shares, in great measure, God's transcendence of nature."

Biblical: Genesis 2:7 – Then the LORD God formed man of dust from the ground, and breathed into his nostrils the breath of life; and man became a living being.

Genesis 3:19 – By the sweat of your face You will eat bread, 'til you return to the ground, because from it you were taken; For you are dust, And to dust you shall return."

Isaiah 55:8-9 – "For My thoughts are not your thoughts, Nor are your ways My ways," declares the Lord. "For *as* the heavens are higher than the earth, So are My ways higher than your ways And My thoughts than your thoughts.

White: "It is God's will that man exploit nature for his proper ends... Christianity made it possible to exploit nature in a mood of indifference to the feelings of natural objects."

Biblical: Proverbs 12:10 – A righteous man has regard for the life of his animal, But *even* the compassion of the wicked is cruel.

Deuteronomy 25:4 – "You shall not muzzle the ox while he is threshing.

White: "Man's effective monopoly on spirit in this world was confirmed, and the old inhibitions to the exploitation of nature crumbled. Christian dogma of man's transcendence of and rightful mastery over nature..."

Biblical: Genesis 7:15 – So they went into the ark to Noah, by twos of all flesh in which was the breath of life.

Genesis 1:28-30 – God blessed them; and God said to them, "Be fruitful and multiply, and fill the earth, and subdue it; and rule over the fish of the sea and over the birds of the sky and over every living thing that moves on the earth." Then God said, "Behold, I have given you every plant yielding seed that is on the surface of all the earth, and every tree which has fruit yielding seed; it shall be food for you; and to every beast of the earth and to every bird of the sky and to everything that moves on the earth which has life, I have given every green plant for food"; and it was so.

After sin the mandate changed:

Genesis 9:1 – And God blessed Noah and his sons and said to them, "Be fruitful and multiply, and fill the earth."

No longer was there the dominance because of sin: sin made man incapable of properly managing creation:

Genesis 9:9-10 – "Now behold, I Myself do establish My covenant with you, and with your descendants after you; and with every living creature that is with you, the birds, the cattle, and every beast of the earth with you; of all that comes out of the ark, even every beast of the earth."

3:11-22 Conclusion: God Has a "BTS" Program for Man

White: "The Christian axiom which must be rejected in order to avoid a worsening of the current ecological crisis..." What is that axiom? *"**Nature has no reason for existence save to serve man.**"*

Biblical: Psalm 19:1 – The heavens are telling of the glory of God; And their expanse is declaring the work of His hands.

Romans 1:20 – For since the creation of the world His invisible attributes, His eternal power and divine nature, have been clearly seen, being understood through what has been made, so that they are without excuse.

White: "Orthodox Christian arrogance toward nature..."

Biblical: Genesis 8:1 – But God remembered Noah and all the beasts and all the cattle that were with him in the ark;

Genesis 8:17 – "Bring out with you every living thing of all flesh that is with you, birds and animals and every creeping thing that creeps on the earth, that they may breed abundantly on the earth, and be fruitful and multiply on the earth."

Job 12:7-10 – "But now ask the beasts, and let them teach you; And the birds of the heavens, and let them tell you. "Or speak to the earth, and let it teach you; And let the fish of the sea declare to you. "Who among all these does not know That the hand of the Lord has done this, In whose hand is the life of every living thing, And the breath of all mankind?

Biblical Christianity never made the assertions White suggests. From where, then, did such ideas arise?

White: The roots of our trouble are largely religious, the remedy must also be essentially religious.

Biblical: White is correct here. The problem, according to the Bible is sin. Sin corrupts. There is a coming redemption, but in the meantime, we are to be faithful stewards with all that is entrusted to us.

Romans 8:20-21 – For the creation was subjected to futility, not willingly, but because of Him who subjected it, in hope that the creation itself also will be set free from its slavery to corruption into the freedom of the glory of the children of God.

4:1-3 Vanity: Life and Oppression Under the Sun

[1] So I returned, and considered all the oppressions that are done under the sun: and behold the tears of such as were oppressed, and they had no comforter; and on the side of their oppressors there was power; but they had no comforter.

Turning again to his empirical investigation, he focused on a comprehensive observation of tyranny and oppression (*ashuq*). Behold (*lo* – emphatic) the tears of the oppressed, as they stood with no comforter (*nacham*) (*parakalon* in the LXX). The oppressors had power (*koach* – force) but the oppressed had no help or comfort. This grievous injustice went continually without remedy.

[2] Wherefore I praised the dead which are already dead more than the living which are yet alive.

This was so egregious to Solomon that he concluded this injustice by itself was enough to make life unworthy of sustaining.

[3] Yea, better is he than both they, which hath not yet been, who hath not seen the evil work that is done under the sun.

Better never to exist than to either participate in or observe the injustice of oppression. These three verses contain some of the harshest language in Ecclesiastes, and certainly one of the strongest conclusions: if for no other reason than oppression, life is not worth living. This conclusion is more hopeless than even suicidal nihilism.

Philosophical Parallel: Marxism

In *Das Kapital*, Karl Marx (1818 – 1883) sought to "lay bare the economic law of modern society." Marx felt philosophy was useful for interpreting but not changing history. Theology he viewed as no better for the righting of injustices he observed. Economics, on the other hand provided a much more efficacious instrument to facilitate change. Marx focused his attention on historical change as a result of class conflict. He and Friedrich Engels (1820-1895) traced five epochs of human history based on economic principles and class conflict: (1) primitive and communal, (2) slave, (3) feudal, (4) capitalist – they viewed capitalism as a refined form of the slave and feudal epochs, and characterized the epoch as comprised of class conflict between the bourgeois (exploitive owners) and the proletariat (degraded, exploited, and alienated workers), particularly grieving the commoditization of labor and perceived consequent dehumanization of the workers; and in nearly prophetic fashion (5) socialist and communist, characterized by the ideal that "each should give according to his ability and receive only according to his needs."

Marx' and Engels' communist model sought to mandate and enforce the reversal of human depravity (e.g., greed, oppression, etc.) by three primary means: (1) the abolition of private property, (2) the abolition of classes (including any and all family relations), and (3) the abolition of religion.

By the abolition of private property, communism undermines the right that Locke viewed as necessary to self-preservation and as foundational in his iteration of democracy (one cannot preserve themselves for long without food, shelter, clothing, etc.). Marx would have the individual fully dependent on the state in order to eliminate the practical effects of human depravity. Locke recognized that man had certain natural rights granted by God, and esteemed property rights as necessarily one of them.

Marx observes the same injustices Solomon decries, but while Solomon recognizes there is no under the sun solution, Marx seeks to eliminate all distinctions, thereby creating a functional egalitarian society. But such an oppression-free society can only be created if governed with vigorous enforcement by the most empowered and oppressive man-made state ever proposed. Sinners beware...

Primary Source Excerpt: Marx and Engels, A Communist Manifesto (1848)

A spectre is haunting Europe — the spectre of communism. All the powers of old Europe have entered into a holy alliance to exorcise this spectre: Pope and Tsar, Metternich and Guizot, French Radicals and German police-spies.

Where is the party in opposition that has not been decried as communistic by its opponents in power? Where is the opposition that has not hurled back the branding reproach of communism, against the more advanced opposition parties, as well as against its reactionary adversaries?

Two things result from this fact:

I. Communism is already acknowledged by all European powers to be itself a power.

II. It is high time that Communists should openly, in the face of the whole world, publish their views, their aims, their tendencies, and meet this nursery tale of the Spectre of Communism with a manifesto of the party itself.

To this end, Communists of various nationalities have assembled in London and sketched the following manifesto, to be published in the English, French, German, Italian, Flemish and Danish languages.

Bourgeois and Proletarians

The history of all hitherto existing society is the history of class struggles.

Freeman and slave, patrician and plebeian, lord and serf, guild-master and journeyman, in a word, oppressor and oppressed, stood in constant opposition to one another, carried on an uninterrupted, now hidden, now open fight, a fight that each time ended, either in a revolutionary reconstitution of society at large, or in the common ruin of the contending classes.

In the earlier epochs of history, we find almost everywhere a complicated arrangement of society into various orders, a manifold gradation of social rank. In ancient Rome we have patricians, knights, plebeians, slaves; in the Middle Ages, feudal lords, vassals, guild-masters, journeymen, apprentices, serfs; in almost all of these classes, again, subordinate gradations.

The modern bourgeois society that has sprouted from the ruins of feudal society has not done away with class antagonisms. It has but established new classes, new conditions of oppression, new forms of struggle in place of the old ones.

Our epoch, the epoch of the bourgeoisie, possesses, however, this distinct feature: it has simplified class antagonisms. Society as a whole is more and more splitting up into two great hostile camps, into two great classes directly facing each other — Bourgeoisie and Proletariat.

From the serfs of the Middle Ages sprang the chartered burghers of the earliest towns. From these burgesses the first elements of the bourgeoisie were developed.

The discovery of America, the rounding of the Cape, opened up fresh ground for the rising bourgeoisie. The East-Indian and Chinese markets, the colonisation of America, trade with the colonies, the increase in the means of exchange and in commodities generally, gave to commerce, to navigation, to industry, an impulse never before known, and thereby, to the revolutionary element in the tottering feudal society, a rapid development.

The feudal system of industry, in which industrial production was monopolised by closed guilds, now no longer sufficed for the growing wants of the new markets. The manufacturing system took its place. The guild-masters were pushed on one side by the manufacturing middle class; division of labour between the different corporate guilds vanished in the face of division of labour in each single workshop.

Meantime the markets kept ever growing, the demand ever rising. Even manufacture no longer sufficed. Thereupon, steam and machinery revolutionized industrial production. The place of manufacture was taken by the giant, Modern Industry; the place of the industrial middle class by industrial millionaires, the leaders of the whole industrial armies, the modern bourgeois.

Modern industry has established the world market, for which the discovery of America paved the way. This market has given an immense development to commerce, to navigation, to communication by land. This development has, in its turn, reacted on the extension of industry; and in proportion as industry, commerce, navigation, railways extended, in the same proportion the bourgeoisie developed, increased its capital, and pushed into the background every class handed down from the Middle Ages.

We see, therefore, how the modern bourgeoisie is itself the product of a long course of development, of a series of revolutions in the modes of production and of exchange.

Each step in the development of the bourgeoisie was accompanied by a corresponding political advance of that class. An oppressed class under the sway of the feudal nobility, an armed and self-governing association in the medieval commune: here independent urban republic (as in Italy and Germany); there taxable "third estate" of the monarchy (as in France); afterwards, in the period of manufacturing proper, serving either the semi-feudal or the absolute monarchy as a counterpoise against the nobility, and, in fact, cornerstone of the great monarchies in general, the bourgeoisie has at last, since the establishment of Modern Industry and of the world market, conquered for itself, in the modern representative State, exclusive political sway. The executive of the modern state is but a committee for managing the common affairs of the whole bourgeoisie.

The bourgeoisie, historically, has played a most revolutionary part.

(section omitted...)

All previous historical movements were movements of minorities, or in the interest of minorities. The proletarian movement is the self-conscious, independent movement of the immense majority, in the interest of the immense majority. The proletariat, the lowest stratum of our present society, cannot stir, cannot raise itself up, without the whole superincumbent strata of official society being sprung into the air.

Though not in substance, yet in form, the struggle of the proletariat with the bourgeoisie is at first a national struggle. The proletariat of each country must, of course, first of all settle matters with its own bourgeoisie.

In depicting the most general phases of the development of the proletariat, we traced the more or less veiled civil war raging within existing society, up to the point where that war breaks out into open revolution, and where the forcible overthrow of the bourgeoisie lays the foundation for the sway of the proletariat.

Hitherto, every form of society has been based, as we have already seen, on the antagonism of oppressing and oppressed classes. But in order to oppress a class, certain conditions must be assured to it under which it can, at least, continue its slavish existence. The serf, in the period of serfdom, raised himself to membership in the commune, just as the petty bourgeois, under the yoke of the feudal absolutism, managed to develop into a bourgeois. The modern labourer, on the contrary, instead of rising with the process of industry, sinks deeper and deeper below the conditions of existence of his own class. He becomes a pauper, and pauperism develops more rapidly than population and wealth. And here it becomes evident, that the bourgeoisie is unfit any longer to be the ruling class in society, and to impose its conditions of existence upon society as an over-riding law. It is unfit to rule because it is incompetent to assure an existence to its slave within his slavery, because it cannot help letting him sink into such a state, that it has to feed him, instead of being fed by him. Society can no longer live under this bourgeoisie, in other words, its existence is no longer compatible with society.

The essential conditions for the existence and for the sway of the bourgeois class is the formation and augmentation of capital; the condition for capital is wage-labour. Wage-labour rests exclusively on competition between the labourers. The advance of industry, whose involuntary promoter is the bourgeoisie, replaces the isolation of the labourers, due to competition, by the revolutionary combination, due to association. The development of Modern Industry, therefore, cuts from under its feet the very foundation on which the bourgeoisie produces and appropriates products. What the bourgeoisie therefore produces, above all, are its own grave-diggers. Its fall and the victory of the proletariat are equally inevitable.

Proletarians and Communists
In what relation do the Communists stand to the proletarians as a whole? The Communists do not form a separate party opposed to the other working-class parties.

They have no interests separate and apart from those of the proletariat as a whole. They do not set up any sectarian principles of their own, by which to shape and mould the proletarian movement.

The Communists are distinguished from the other working-class parties by this only: (1) In the national struggles of the proletarians of the different countries, they point out and bring to the front the common interests of the entire proletariat, independently of all nationality. (2) In the various stages of development which the struggle of the working class against the bourgeoisie has to pass through, they always and everywhere represent the interests of the movement as a whole.

The Communists, therefore, are on the one hand, practically, the most advanced and resolute section of the working-class parties of every country, that section which pushes forward all others; on the other hand, theoretically, they have over the great mass of the proletariat the advantage of clearly understanding the lines of march, the conditions, and the ultimate general results of the proletarian movement.

The immediate aim of the Communists is the same as that of all other proletarian parties: formation of the proletariat into a class, overthrow of the bourgeois supremacy, conquest of political power by the proletariat.

The theoretical conclusions of the Communists are in no way based on ideas or principles that have been invented, or discovered, by this or that would-be universal reformer. They merely express, in general terms, actual relations springing from an existing class struggle, from a historical movement going on under our very eyes. The abolition of existing property relations is not at all a distinctive feature of communism.

All property relations in the past have continually been subject to historical change consequent upon the change in historical conditions. The French Revolution, for example, abolished feudal property in favour of bourgeois property.

The distinguishing feature of Communism is not the abolition of property generally, but the abolition of bourgeois property. But modern bourgeois private property is the final and most complete expression of the system of producing and appropriating products, that is based on class antagonisms, on the exploitation of the many by the few.

In this sense, the theory of the Communists may be summed up in the single sentence: Abolition of private property. [emphasis mine]

We Communists have been reproached with the desire of abolishing the right of personally acquiring property as the fruit of a man's own labour, which property is alleged to be the groundwork of all personal freedom, activity and independence.

Hard-won, self-acquired, self-earned property! Do you mean the property of petty artisan and of the small peasant, a form of property that preceded the bourgeois form? There is no need to abolish that; the development of industry has to a great extent already destroyed it, and is still destroying it daily. Or do you mean the modern bourgeois private property?

But does wage-labour create any property for the labourer? Not a bit. It creates capital, i.e., that kind of property which exploits wage-labour, and which cannot increase except upon condition of begetting a new supply of wage-labour for fresh exploitation. Property, in its present form, is based on the antagonism of capital and wage labour. Let us examine both sides of this antagonism. To be a capitalist, is to have not only a purely personal, but a social status in production. Capital is a collective product, and only by the united action of many members, nay, in the last resort, only by the united action of all members of society, can it be set in motion. Capital is therefore not only personal; it is a social power.

When, therefore, capital is converted into common property, into the property of all members of society, personal property is not thereby transformed into social property. It is only the social character of the property that is changed. It loses its class character. Let us now take wage-labour.

The average price of wage-labour is the minimum wage, i.e., that quantum of the means of subsistence which is absolutely requisite to keep the labourer in bare existence as a labourer. What, therefore, the wage-labourer appropriates by means of his labour, merely suffices to prolong and reproduce a bare existence. We by no means intend to abolish this personal appropriation of the products of labour, an appropriation that is made for the maintenance and reproduction of human life, and that leaves no surplus wherewith to command the labour of others. All that we want to do away with is the miserable character of this appropriation, under which the labourer lives merely to increase capital, and is allowed to live only in so far as the interest of the ruling class requires it.

In bourgeois society, living labour is but a means to increase accumulated labour. In Communist society, accumulated labour is but a means to widen, to enrich, to promote the existence of the labourer. In bourgeois society, therefore, the past dominates the present; in Communist society, the present dominates the past. In bourgeois society capital is independent and has individuality, while the living person is dependent and has no individuality.

And the abolition of this state of things is called by the bourgeois, abolition of individuality and freedom! And rightly so. The abolition of bourgeois individuality, bourgeois independence, and bourgeois freedom is undoubtedly aimed at. By freedom is meant, under the present bourgeois conditions of production, free trade, free selling and buying. But if selling and buying disappears, free selling and buying disappears also. This talk about free selling and buying, and all the other "brave words" of our bourgeois about freedom in general, have a meaning, if any, only in contrast with restricted selling and buying, with the fettered traders of the Middle Ages, but have no meaning when opposed to the Communistic abolition of buying and selling, of the bourgeois conditions of production, and of the bourgeoisie itself.

You are horrified at our intending to do away with private property. But in your existing society, private property is already done away with for nine-tenths of the population; its existence for the few is solely due to its non-existence in the hands of those nine-tenths. You reproach us, therefore, with intending to do away with a form of property, the necessary condition for whose existence is the non-existence of any property for the immense majority of society. In one word, you reproach us with intending to do away with your property. Precisely so; that is just what we intend.

From the moment when labour can no longer be converted into capital, money, or rent, into a social power capable of being monopolized, i.e., from the moment when individual property can no longer be transformed into bourgeois property, into capital, from that moment, you say, individuality vanishes. You must, therefore, confess that by "individual" you mean no other person than the bourgeois, than the middle-class owner of property. This person must, indeed, be swept out of the way, and made impossible.

Communism deprives no man of the power to appropriate the products of society; all that it does is to deprive him of the power to subjugate the labour of others by means of such appropriations. It has been objected that upon the abolition of private property, all work will cease, and universal laziness will overtake us. According to this, bourgeois society ought long ago to have gone to the dogs through sheer idleness; for those of its members who work, acquire nothing, and those who acquire anything do not work. The whole of this objection is but another expression of the tautology that there can no longer be any wage-labour when there is no longer any capital.

All objections urged against the Communistic mode of producing and appropriating material products, have, in the same way, been urged against the Communistic mode of producing and appropriating intellectual products. Just as, to the bourgeois, the disappearance of class property is the disappearance of production itself, so the disappearance of class culture is to him identical with the disappearance of all culture. That culture, the loss of which he laments, is, for the enormous majority, a mere training to act as a machine.

But don't wrangle with us so long as you apply to our intended abolition of bourgeois property the standard of your bourgeois notions of freedom, culture, law, etc. Your very ideas are but the outgrowth of the conditions of your bourgeois

4:1-3 Vanity: Life and Oppression Under the Sun 249

production and bourgeois property, just as your jurisprudence is but the will of your class made into a law for all, a will whose essential character and direction are determined by the economical conditions of existence of your class.

The selfish misconception that induces you to transform into eternal laws of nature and of reason, the social forms springing from your present mode of production and form of property – historical relations that rise and disappear in the progress of production – this misconception you share with every ruling class that has preceded you. What you see clearly in the case of ancient property, what you admit in the case of feudal property, you are of course forbidden to admit in the case of your own bourgeois form of property.

Abolition [Aufhebung] of the family! Even the most radical flare up at this infamous proposal of the Communists. On what foundation is the present family, the bourgeois family, based? On capital, on private gain.[emphasis mine] In its completely developed form, this family exists only among the bourgeoisie. But this state of things finds its complement in the practical absence of the family among the proletarians, and in public prostitution. The bourgeois family will vanish as a matter of course when its complement vanishes, and both will vanish with the vanishing of capital. Do you charge us with wanting to stop the exploitation of children by their parents? To this crime we plead guilty.

But, you say, we destroy the most hallowed of relations, when we replace home education by social. [emphasis mine] And your education! Is not that also social, and determined by the social conditions under which you educate, by the intervention direct or indirect, of society, by means of schools, andc.? The Communists have not invented the intervention of society in education; they do but seek to alter the character of that intervention, and to rescue education from the influence of the ruling class.

The bourgeois clap-trap about the family and education, about the hallowed co-relation of parents and child, becomes all the more disgusting, the more, by the action of Modern Industry, all the family ties among the proletarians are torn asunder, and their children transformed into simple articles of commerce and instruments of labour.

But you Communists would introduce community of women, screams the bourgeoisie in chorus. The bourgeois sees his wife a mere instrument of production. He hears that the instruments of production are to be exploited in common, and, naturally, can come to no other conclusion that the lot of being common to all will likewise fall to the women. He has not even a suspicion that the real point aimed at is to do away with the status of women as mere instruments of production. For the rest, nothing is more ridiculous than the virtuous indignation of our bourgeois at the community of women which, they pretend, is to be openly and officially established by the Communists. The Communists have no need to introduce community of women; it has existed almost from time immemorial. Our bourgeois, not content with having wives and daughters of their proletarians at their disposal, not to speak of common prostitutes, take the greatest pleasure in seducing each other's wives.

Bourgeois marriage is, in reality, a system of wives in common and thus, at the most, what the Communists might possibly be reproached with is that they desire to introduce, in substitution for a hypocritically concealed, an openly legalised community of women. For the rest, it is self-evident that the abolition of the present system of production must bring with it the abolition of the community of women springing from that system, i.e., of prostitution both public and private.

The Communists are further reproached with desiring to abolish countries and nationality. The working men have no country. We cannot take from them what they have not got. Since the proletariat must first of all acquire political supremacy, must rise to be the leading class of the nation, must constitute itself the nation, it is so far, itself national, though not in the bourgeois sense of the word.

National differences and antagonism between peoples are daily more and more vanishing, owing to the development of the bourgeoisie, to freedom of commerce, to the world market, to uniformity in the mode of production and in the conditions of life corresponding thereto. The supremacy of the proletariat will cause them to vanish still faster. United action, of the leading civilised countries at least, is one of the first conditions for the emancipation of the proletariat. In proportion as the exploitation of one individual by another will also be put an end to, the exploitation of one nation by another will also be put an end to. In proportion as the antagonism between classes within the nation vanishes, the hostility of one nation to another will come to an end.

The charges against Communism made from a religious, a philosophical and, generally, from an ideological standpoint, are not deserving of serious examination. Does it require deep intuition to comprehend that man's ideas, views, and conception, in one word, man's consciousness, changes with every change in the conditions of his material existence, in his social relations and in his social life? What else does the history of ideas prove, than that intellectual production changes its character in proportion as material production is changed? The ruling ideas of each age have ever been the ideas of its ruling class. When people speak of the ideas that revolutionise society, they do but express that fact that within the old society the elements of a new one have been created, and that the dissolution of the old ideas keeps even pace with the dissolution of the old conditions of existence.

When the ancient world was in its last throes, the ancient religions were overcome by Christianity. When Christian ideas succumbed in the 18th century to rationalist ideas, feudal society fought its death battle with the then revolutionary bourgeoisie. The ideas of religious liberty and freedom of conscience merely gave expression to the sway of free competition within the domain of knowledge. "Undoubtedly," it will be said, "religious, moral, philosophical, and juridical ideas have been modified in the course of historical development. But religion, morality, philosophy, political science, and law, constantly survived this change." "There are, besides, eternal truths, such as Freedom, Justice, etc., that are common to all states of society. But Communism abolishes eternal truths, it abolishes all religion, and all morality, instead of constituting them on a new basis; it therefore acts in contradiction to all past historical experience." What does this accusation reduce itself to? *The history of all past society has consisted in the development of class antagonisms, antagonisms that assumed different forms at different epochs. [emphasis mine]* But whatever form they may have taken, one fact is common to all past ages, viz., the exploitation of one part of society by the other. No wonder, then, that the social consciousness of past ages, despite all the multiplicity and variety it displays, moves within certain common forms, or general ideas, which cannot completely vanish except with the total disappearance of class antagonisms.

The Communist revolution is the most radical rupture with traditional relations; no wonder that its development involved the most radical rupture with traditional ideas. But let us have done with the bourgeois objections to Communism.

We have seen above, that the first step in the revolution by the working class is to raise the proletariat to the position of ruling class to win the battle of democracy. The proletariat will use its political supremacy to wrest, by degree, all capital from the bourgeoisie, to centralize all instruments of production in the hands of the State, i.e., of the proletariat organized as the ruling class; and to increase the total productive forces as rapidly as possible.

Of course, in the beginning, this cannot be effected except by means of despotic inroads on the rights of property, and on the conditions of bourgeois production; by means of measures, therefore, which appear economically insufficient and untenable, but which, in the course of the movement, outstrip themselves, necessitate further inroads upon the old social order, and are unavoidable as a means of entirely revolutionising the mode of production.

These measures will, of course, be different in different countries. Nevertheless, in most advanced countries, the following will be pretty generally applicable:

1. Abolition of property in land and application of all rents of land to public purposes.

2. A heavy progressive or graduated income tax.

3. Abolition of all rights of inheritance.

4. Confiscation of the property of all emigrants and rebels.

5. Centralisation of credit in the banks of the state, by means of a national bank with State capital and an exclusive monopoly.

6. Centralisation of the means of communication and transport in the hands of the State.

7. Extension of factories and instruments of production owned by the State; the bringing into cultivation of waste-lands, and the improvement of the soil generally in accordance with a common plan.

8. *Equal liability of all to work. Establishment of industrial armies, especially for agriculture.*

9. *Combination of agriculture with manufacturing industries; gradual abolition of all the distinction between town and country by a more equable distribution of the populace over the country.*

10. *Free education for all children in public schools. Abolition of children's factory labour in its present form. Combination of education with industrial production, etc. [italics mine]*

When, in the course of development, class distinctions have disappeared, and all production has been concentrated in the hands of a vast association of the whole nation, the public power will lose its political character. Political power, properly so called, is merely the organised power of one class for oppressing another. If the proletariat during its contest with the bourgeoisie is compelled, by the force of circumstances, to organise itself as a class, if, by means of a revolution, it makes itself the ruling class, and, as such, sweeps away by force the old conditions of production, then it will, along with these conditions, have swept away the conditions for the existence of class antagonisms and of classes generally, and will thereby have abolished its own supremacy as a class.

In place of the old bourgeois society, with its classes and class antagonisms, we shall have an association, in which the free development of each is the condition for the free development of all.

Socialist and Communist Literature (section omitted)

Position of the Communists in Relation to the Various Existing Opposition Parties
In short, the Communists everywhere support every revolutionary movement against the existing social and political order of things. In all these movements, they bring to the front,

as the leading question in each, the property question, no matter what its degree of development at the time. Finally, they labour everywhere for the union and agreement of the democratic parties of all countries.

The Communists disdain to conceal their views and aims. They openly declare that their ends can be attained only by the forcible overthrow of all existing social conditions. Let the ruling classes tremble at a Communistic revolution. The proletarians have nothing to lose but their chains. They have a world to win. WORKING MEN OF ALL COUNTRIES, UNITE!

Excursus: An Introductory Survey of the Problem of Evil

The seemingly unavoidable contradiction between the existence of a personal God and the reality of evil provides a crucial point of entry not only for discussion both of (1) argument for and against the existence of God and (2) the nature and character of such a God, but also, as Neiman suggests, the problem of evil is itself an organizing principle for history of philosophy.[94] Thus the theologian will not be the only interlocutor on the subject, but rather in fact the philosopher must also dedicate significant energies to understanding and ultimately dealing with the problem. Perhaps if Neiman is correct, the problem has even less to do with philosophy of religion than with philosophy itself, or then again, as I would suggest the problem of evil affords *an example of the unbreakable bond between religion and philosophy and the resultant necessity of interdisciplinarity between the two.*

Noting the significance, then, of the issue, this present discussion will (1) identify major theorists and their statements of the problem within context, and (2) will give attention to various attempts at resolution also within a chronological context. I will neither offer critiques of these various attempts nor propose a theodicy, nor will I attempt to offer a comprehensive discussion of pertinent thinkers and their views. The focus here will be an introductory survey intended to provide a working and historically informed definition of the problem of evil from theological and philosophical vantage points.

Just as philosophical inquiry has a grand tradition of attempting paradox resolution, it is often these very same postulated resolutions that create further paradoxes. In pre-Socratic natural philosophy, for example, Parmenides, seeking to ground monism more appropriately proposed a theory of reality which suggested that reality was both motionless and limited, thus requiring his 'cue-ball' kind of world – spherical and homogeneous.[95] His cosmology begs questions though - questions such as how motion can be accounted for in a motionless reality and how pluralities which can be observed in appearance can be accounted for in a singular reality. While Parmenides certainly attempts to resolve these issues, the questions give rise to further evolution in thought – note the shift from monism to pluralism. Empedocles proposes an entire cosmology which would justify Parmenides' approach but which would also deal with the paradox of appearances more effectively. To accomplish this feat, Empedocles develops a position that includes four elements (air, water, earth, and fire) and two significant forces (love and strife). With each advance and development, the cosmologies grow more and more complex and the questions grow more difficult.

This kind of dilemma is not unique to pre-Socratic natural philosophy, but also finds its way into later metaphysics. The problem of evil (both moral and natural) is one such issue which, when historically examined, exemplifies the predicament of creating more questions than answers. Can it be said that the problem of evil is a mere creation of philosophical inquiry, or is it a case study for paradox resolution within philosophical inquiry? How is Neiman (for example) justified in identifying evil (and its related problems) as the underlying issue in history of philosophy? An examination of the problem as defined and dealt with in historical context can go a long way in helping us to come to grips with the significance and structure of the problem itself, and can perhaps provide an impetus for resolution.

The Problem of Evil in Ancient Philosophy

Preliminary Religious Characterizations
Most conservative biblical scholars acknowledge the book of Job as one of the earliest biblical books, dating its content around 2000 BC, and contemporary to patriarchal times (i.e., Abraham, etc.). As such, Job provides a very early inquiry into the purpose of evil. Job 10:7 offers Job's essential statement of the problem: "According to Thy knowledge I am indeed not guilty; yet there is no deliverance from Thy hand." Job here questions God's allowance of evil in his life despite his perceived innocence. Eliphaz, Bildad, and Zophar all rebuke Job, presenting as a theodicy the idea that God possesses a kind of justice which would only allow evil for punishment of sin, and concludes that Job must have been stained by sin. Yet another perspective arises, that of Elihu, who argues that "Surely, God will not act wickedly, and the Almighty will not pervert justice.... If He should determine to do so, if He should gather to Himself His spirit and His breath, all flesh would perish together, and man would return to dust." (34:12,14-15) Elihu's argument revolves around the character of God being unimpeachable and unquestionable. The problem of evil in the book of Job is not that evil exists, but rather that the presence of evil at times does not seem justified by circumstances. This perspective on the

problem is represented regularly in later biblical texts such as Habakkuk[96] (7th century BC), and Romans[97] (1st century AD). Throughout the biblical record there is arguable univocality in favor of a theodicy.

Zoroastrianism is decidedly dualistic and monotheistic. In one particular strain Ahura Mazda (Ormuzd) is the benevolent deity in opposition to the evil Ahriman who possessed nearly equal power. Ormuzd, lacking the ability at present to fully eradicate evil, cannot be described as fully omnipotent, but will one day possess such capability, at which point evil will be eliminated. Thus history is outlined by the struggle against evil – a struggle which will at some point have a resolution which will in itself eliminate not only evil, but consequently any paradoxes associated with the existence of evil.

The Qur'an presents Allah as responsible for both good and evil, doing what he wishes (Qur'an 3:40) even to the point of testing by instrument of both good and evil (Qur'an 21:35), and thus the Qur'an does not concern itself with resolution. In fact, there has been little systematic emphasis on theodicy within Islam. Later traditions do point to the need for evil as a kind of resistive complement to the moral.[98]

While the Judeo-Christian, Zoroastrian, and Islamic bases are more univocal in their responses – owing to a primarily monotheistic starting point - polytheistic, pantheistic, and non-theistic traditions place lesser emphasis on the need for resolution to the problem of evil, as they essentially do not hold to the existence of the kind of deity whose existence alongside that of evil that would create a significant paradox. Yet they all must deal with the existence and origin of suffering and evil in at least some regard, and most of them do in various degree.

Hindu tradition provides diversity in addressing the issue. At least three particular varieties of description can be identified: (1) that of the Vedas, which present an ongoing dualistic (good vs. evil) conflagration, (2) that of the pantheistic literature (Upanishads, etc.), which relates evil to the cosmic cycle in relation to karma, and (3) that of the Epics and Puranas, which describe a kind of anthropomorphic theism in which the gods are responsible for both good and evil. Rem Edwards suggests that Eastern religions (including both Hinduism and Buddhism)

> fully develop the idea that evil originates in sheer finitude and fragmentariness of perspective and in the desire for fragmentary goals and objects...and see evil as originating to some extent in immorality, for the sufferings of this world are partly if not entirely the working out of one's Karma.[99]

While not tendering a systematic theodicy – particularly in the matter of the origin of evil - Hinduism does offer a means of dealing with the existence of evil and (at least) minimizing its effect: namely, the eternality of the soul provides a setting (through a sequence of births and temporal existence) whereby one can learn to avoid ignorance and associated actions which afford negative karmic results - including suffering and evil.

Not unlike Hindu explanations, the Buddhist approach to evil and suffering is largely characterized by the relationship of evil to karma. Buddhism posits the *Four Noble Truths,*[100] in which suffering can be limited and even eliminated by the right kinds of thought and action. However, a key distinguishing characteristic of Buddhism is its rejection of the existence of an omnibenevolent (or any other) deity, with partial justification in the asserted paradox of evil, as presented in the following verses from the 13th century *Bhuridatta Jataka:*[101]

If the creator of the world entire
They call God, of every being be
the Lord
Why does he order such
misfortune
And not create concord?

If the creator of the world entire
They call God, of every being be
the Lord
Why prevail deceit, lies and
ignorance
And he such inequity and injustice
create?

If the creator of the world entire
They call God, of every being be
the Lord
Then an evil master is he, (O
Aritta)
Knowing what's right did let
wrong prevail!

Bearing marked resemblance to Epicurus' riddle, these verses illustrate an aspect of the grounding for Buddhist rejection of theism. There is, within Buddhist tradition, no need for a theologically driven theodicy, yet the paradox of suffering still exists without explanation.

Within the various religious traditions there is broad agreement that evil exists and that it is a central theme in the comparative doctrines, yet justification for the existence of evil and magnitude of the paradox differs significantly from belief system to belief system. While each system gives at least some attention to the problem, it seems readily apparent that within the Christian tradition one will find the greatest consideration of and more numerous propositions for resolution of the problem. Perhaps the problem of evil is a central issue for the biblical system, since it is more *precisely* definitive of the character of God than it is in any other system.

Plato (428-348 B.C.)
In Plato's dialogue between Socrates and Euthyphro, Socrates asks "Is the pious loved by the gods because it is pious, or is it pious because it is loved by the gods?" The question reflects a dilemma related to the problem of evil. If the former is affirmed then the gods are governed by an absolute standard which would necessarily be superior to them by virtue of its governance. If the latter is affirmed then any absolute standard of piety (or goodness) must be dismissed. If the latter is affirmed then the gods (or God) could not accurately be described as absolutely good since there would be no absolute standard of good, but again if the former is affirmed then the gods (or God) could not be described as all powerful, since they (or He) would be governed by piety (or goodness).

While Plato provides an epistemological basis for further discussion of the problem of evil, he would not have recognized the existence of evil as presenting any difficulty to explain. Evil offers a counterbalance to good and "evils can never pass away, for there must always remain something which is antagonistic to good" (*Theaetetus* 176). Regarding moral evil (absence of good, virtue, etc., related to ignorance), it is to the soul as physical evil (disease) is to the body – each type of evil brings about the destruction of its host (*Republic*, Book X, 608). In life and death comes a kind of divine justice, as Plato's *Apology* recounts Socrates statement that "no evil can happen to a good man either in life or after death" (41d). But the very existence of evil is attributed in the *Timaeus* to the demiurge's creation not as *ex nihilo*, but rather from preexisting and imperfect materials. Here Plato identifies a dichotomy in causation between the necessary and the divine, the latter of which is recognizable as nature permits happiness, and the former being prerequisite to the divine (*Timaeus*, 36:69). While Plato did believe in the benevolence of the deity, he would not accept the premise of the creative deity possessing omnipotence, thus in Platonic thinking there is no paradox regarding the existence of evil, for it is necessary.

Epicurus (341-270 B.C.)

Although there is no extant form of Epicurus' characterization of the problem, he is generally credited as the first to state it, and he does so in the form of a trilemma, which as understood by Hume could be structured as follows: if God is omnipotent, omniscient, and omnibenevolent, then how can evil exist in a world made by God? First-century (BC) atomist Lucretius represents significant Epicurean influence, and his poem *De Rerum Natura* provides an important source for Epicurean doctrine, as Lucretius argues against the teleological on grounds (among others) that there is frailty and evil present for which cannot be accounted in a teleological system. Third-century theologian Lanctantius provides perhaps the strongest early evidence of Epicurus' statement of the trilemma, as he propounds an apologetic responding directly to Epicurus:

> What happiness, then, can there be in God, if He is always inactive, being at rest and un-moveable? if He is deaf to those who pray to Him, and blind to His worshippers? [lacking omniscience] What is so worthy of God, and so befitting to Him, as providence? [lacking omnipotence]

> But if He cares for nothing [lacking omnibenevolence], and foresees nothing, He has lost all His divinity [note: Epicurus' necessary conclusion]. What else does he say, who takes from God all power and all substance, except that there is no God at all? [notes mine][102]

And again, regarding two particular horns of the problem:

> God, says Epicurus, regards nothing [premise 1: lacking omnibenevolence]; therefore He has no power [conclusion: lacking omnipotence]. For he who has power must of necessity regard affairs [premise 2: inferential relationship between omnibenevolence and omnipotence]. For if He has power, and does not use it, what so great cause is there that, I will not say our race, but even the universe itself, should be contemptible in His sight?[103]

While Epicurus' goal was not to assert atheism (he didn't, but rather posited that if gods existed they were of no concern, being themselves either unconcerned or impotent regarding human affairs), his elucidation of the problem of evil in particular and resultant complexities in the teleological idea provides momentum for the atheistic worldview, and thus with Epicurus (as characterized by Lucretius, Lanctantius, and later Hume) the problem of evil becomes a pivot point of discussion not only in regard to theism but cosmogony and cosmology in general. The teleological nature of the issue causes the problem of evil to be of significance to a number of fields within philosophical inquiry.

Plotinus (205-270 A.D.)

Relating evil to matter itself, Plotinus sees matter as having potential for good but being in itself (and unaided) a primary evil. While this in itself seems a significant contradiction in Plotinus' approach, his characterization of evil not as an objective state of being but rather as the absence (although not completely so) of good, importantly provides the Neoplatonic context for iteration and solution of the problem. Evil is in the realm of non-being. Plotinus explains:

> If such be the Nature of Beings and of That which transcends all the realm of Being, Evil
> cannot have place among Beings or in the Beyond-Being; these are good. *There remains, only, if Evil exist at all, that it be situate in the realm of Non-Being,* [emphasis mine] that it be some mode, as it were, of the Non-Being, that it have its seat in something in touch with Non-Being or to a certain degree communicate in Non-Being. By this Non-Being, of course, we are not to understand something that simply does not exist, but only something of an utterly different order from Authentic-Being: there is no question here of movement or position with regard to Being; the Non-Being we are thinking of is, rather, an image of Being or perhaps something still further removed than even an image. Now this (the required faint image of Being) might be the sensible universe with all the impressions it engenders, or it might be something of even later derivation, accidental to the realm of sense, or again, it might be the source of the sense-world or something of the same order entering into it to complete it. Some conception of it would be reached by thinking of measurelessness as opposed to measure, of the unbounded against bound, the unshaped against a

principle of shape, the ever-needy against the self-sufficing: think of the ever-undefined, the never at rest, the all-accepting but never sated, utter dearth; and make all this character not mere accident in it but its equivalent for essential-being, so that, whatsoever fragment of it be taken, that part is all lawless void, while whatever participates in it and resembles it becomes evil, though not of course to the point of being, as itself is, Evil-Absolute.[104]

Plotinus' dichotomy is evident: being and beyond-being is good, and while non-being does indeed exist, it is essentially distinct from authentic being. Thus evil does not exist as an objective hypostasis, and certainly not as a co-equal and opposing force to deity.

The impact that the Neoplatonic definition of evil would have on future discussion is truly immeasurable, and Plotinus' characterization is an instinctive entry point for the medieval philosophers.

The Problem of Evil in Medieval Philosophy

It is early in this era that we see a turn toward more theological interpretations of the problem, and perhaps for two reasons: (1) As the rise in philosophy observed in the presocratics can be attributed to directed effort toward naturalistic explanations, there was a reluctance on the part of more than a few to adopt the materialist framework. While natural philosophy was constructing the problem and attempting materialist solutions, moral philosophy was not immune to the pursuit and found itself in need of similarly contrived resolutions on the topic. Also of significance, (2) natural philosophy declined (at least) with Socrates' shift toward moral philosophy and perhaps can be credited to lack of development in contemporary scientific methods. The naturalists could only extend tested theories so far, thus microcosm presented greater need and opportunity for advancement than did macrocosm.

But how to explain the human experience relating to interaction with evil in metaphysical terms? This question would find primacy in the philosophy of the medievals.

Gnosticism

As a developed synthesis of Platonic cosmogony (as presented in *Timaeus*) and epistemological premises gnosticism found itself impacting the problem. Evil's existence, in gnostic tradition, was attributed to the failure of the demiurge's potency – an absolute denial of omnipotence, and thus as in Plato, the problem of evil was a non-issue. Such justifications on grounds of rejecting omnipotence were untenable to the groundings of the Western theological minds that would soon rise as the Biblical text became a focal point for the bonding of theological presupposition with philosophical justification.

In practice, the foundations of gnosticism were characteristically dualistic, viewing the material as corrupt and that relating to gnosis as more pure. As a result, two particular strains of orthodoxy become evident: (1) that which would de-emphasize the significance of the material/corrupt and thus promote licentiousness, and (2) that which would highlight the significance of the material/corrupt and in accordance promote asceticism. Later thinkers would respond (generally) critically toward both.

Irenaeus (c115-c200 A.D.)

Working from a theistic standpoint and a Biblical context, Irenaeus opposed Gnostic premises, responding directly to them (perhaps most notably in *Against Heresies*). He affirmed omnipotence and offered an alternative solution in two forms.

First, Irenaeus redefined the epistemological grounding on the issue, appealing to the Biblical text as the source of objective truth, consequently dismissing Platonic cosmogony as untenable.

Second, he redefined anthropological cosmogony, operating from the basic premise that human free will is prerequisite to human good or perfection. This presupposes that God did not create perfection (in mankind at least). Rather perfection comes through the proper appropriation of autonomy. While natural evil provides opportunity and occasion for the person's growth, moral evil is then an outcome of free will appropriated to disobedience, and is not due directly or necessarily to the corporeal nature of humanity (as in gnosticism). He is specific on this point, saying,

> Those persons, then, who possess the earnest of the Spirit, and who are not enslaved by the lusts of the flesh, but are subject to the Spirit, and who in all things walk according to the light of reason, does the apostle properly term "spiritual," because the Spirit of God dwells in them. *Now, spiritual men shall not be incorporeal spirits; but our substance, that is, the union of flesh and spirit, receiving the Spirit of God, makes up the spiritual man.* [emphasis mine][105]

Thus the spiritual man is one who has received the Spirit of God in union with the flesh (and spirit). In gnostic tradition such redemption of the flesh would have been impossible, yet for Irenaeus, in accordance with his epistemological foundationalism (holding revelation as foundational) is able to argue for a theodicy that neither denies the omnipotence of God nor the existence of evil. While he would certainly face significant hermeneutic challenges in defending his conception of man and his place in the cosmos, he nevertheless succeeds in providing an alternative in both areas of knowledge and cosmogony of evil, and as a result is influential in restructuring the debate. Also notable here is the role given to free will, which further colors future discussion and again illustrates the centrality of the problem of evil in connecting philosophy and theology.

Augustine (354-430 A.D.)
From his foundational assertion that God is "supremely and equally and unchangeably good"[106] Augustine argues admittedly[107] from the Neoplatonic standpoint that evil is the privation of good. He distinguishes between natural evil as penal consequence and moral evil as the fruit of free will appropriated in disobedience. Augustine attributes significance to the existence of evil, but not at the expense of God's omnipotence or omnibenevolence. Thus evil must serve those two qualities in a utilitarian sense. He says,

> And in the universe, even that which is called evil, when it is regulated and put in its own place, only enhances our admiration of the good; for we enjoy and value the good more when we compare it with the evil. For the almighty God, who, as even the heathen acknowledge, has supreme power over all things, being Himself supremely good, would never permit the existence of anything evil among His works, if He were not so omnipotent and good that He can bring good even out of evil. For what is that which we call evil but the absence of good?[108]

Evil is only allowed inasmuch as God is powerful enough to bring from it greater good. And Augustine is careful to characterize evil not as an independent substance of equal quality to that of the good, but rather simply as the absence of good. In illustration of this he discusses a wound as a defect in the flesh which when health is restored ceases to exist. The wound does not continue existence elsewhere, and thus should not be seen as an entity in itself but rather as the privation of function or health. Evil functions in the same manner.

It should also be noted that Augustine believed good to be extracted from evil even to the point of *supreme* good. Evil contributes in an important way to cosmic order: privation of good is a necessary and divine implement serving an almost aesthetic overview of existence. The principle of plenitude begins to emerge here.

Finally, for Augustine, evil finds its origin and impetus as being intimately connected to human free will. God in His goodness allows free will, the utilization of which must possibly result in a turning from God. Augustine notes that the turning itself is the central issue, not the alternative chosen. He says,

> For when the will relinquishes that which is superior to itself, and turns to that which is inferior, it becomes evil not because that toward which it turns is evil, but because the turning is evil.[109]

Thus the turning itself results in the privation of the ideal and offers contingencies not readily identifiable with any overall good, yet when viewed in perspective of the whole, there is an aesthetic sense in which the whole is (and must be) deemed good. This creates another separate yet related problem with which Augustine must deal – and one beyond the scope of this present discussion: the compatibility of human free will with the divine perfections of omniscience, omnipotence, and omnibenevolence. The manner in which he deals with these issues necessarily impacts his conception of theodicy.

Anselm of Canterbury (1033-1109 A.D.)

Anselm, like Augustine, preferred to see creature-volition as the means whereby the responsibility for the existence of evil is placed elsewhere other than at the feet of God, and in so doing protected the attribute of omnibenevolence, a necessary consequence to his ontological defense of the existence of God. Anselm's argument is as follows:

> something greater than which cannot be thought exists in thought.... And certainly that greater than which cannot be understood cannot exist only in thought, for if it exists only in thought it could also be thought of as existing in reality as well, which is greater. If, therefore, that than which greater cannot be thought exists in thought alone, then that than which greater cannot be thought turns out to be that than which something greater actually can be thought, but that is obviously impossible. Therefore something than which greater cannot be thought undoubtedly exists both in thought and in reality.[110]

The argument requires "that than which greater cannot be thought" to possess the highest degree of perfection, and thus Anselm narrows the debate to exclude the possibility of diminishing the perfections of God in order to resolve the problem of evil. For Anselm, as was also the case with Augustine, creature-volition seemed the best option. In discussing freedom of the will, Anselm emphasizes not freedom *from* but rather freedom *to*. This active element of freedom does not, for Anselm, in its protection especially of omnibenevolence, violate omnipotence or omniscience, despite its potential to create scenarios which could be described as evil, as that freedom finds its very origin and enablement in divine mandate. The significant contribution here is the centrality of omnibenevolence in the trilemma.

Aquinas (1225-1274 A.D.)
Isaiah 45:7 reads in the KJV as follows: "I form the light, and create darkness: I make peace, and create evil: I the Lord do all these things."
Aquinas counters a syllogistic argument based on this passage: (P1) God created everything, (P2) Evil is something, (C) Therefore, God created evil. The second premise causes difficulty for Aquinas as he, consistent with Neoplatonic thinking, argues against evil as a *substance*. He says,

> ... As the term good signifies "perfect being," so the term evil signifies nothing else than "privation of perfect being." In its proper acceptance, privation is predicated of that which is fitted by its nature to be possessed, and to be possessed at a certain time and in a certain manner. Evidently, therefore, a thing is called evil if it lacks a perfection it ought to have. Thus if a man lacks the sense of sight, this is an evil for him. But the same lack is not an evil for a stone, for the stone is not equipped by nature to have the faculty of sight.[111]

Aquinas solidifies for medieval philosophy the definition of evil as privation rather than essence. Like those before him he recognizes that this definition requires human volition in order to account for privation, and that evil as a penalty is introduced by God in order to supply justice. This accommodation is a significant one, as it additionally introduces an intersection between theological philosophy and naturalistic philosophy by way of a world ordered by justice. The teleological emphasis here ties the problem of evil and theodicies of this order to the concepts of necessity, justice, and plenitude – factors not exclusive to the religious or the secular, but rather shared by both. Thus while Aquinas remains perhaps the medieval era's most provocative advocate of theological philosophy, he also plays an important role in uniting the interests of the religious and the secular as he frames the problem of evil in terms which can be engaged from either grounding.

William of Ockham (1288-1347 A.D.)

Whereas previous thinkers regarded omnibenevolence as the attribute least predisposed to redefinition, Ockham shared no such regard. He suggested that there existed in the volition of God distinction between *potentia absoluta* (absolute power) and *potentia ordinata* (ordained power). Feinberg explains the division:

> The distinction between the two powers doesn't mean that God acts sometimes with order and other times without it. It means that God can, and has, in fact, decided to do certain things according to the laws which He *freely* establishes, i.e., de potentia ordinata. On the other hand, God has absolute power (potentia absoluta) to do anything that doesn't imply a contradiction....[112]

The result for Ockham is a non-absolute standard of good: God is not obligated to act in a certain manner because that action is good, rather it is good because He declares it to be so. Thus in Ockham's estimation the standard of good is God Himself. Some, like Barnhart, believe that such a move robs the term *goodness* of any real meaning and results in a cruel and tyrannical deity. Barnhart indicts such a deity as

> ...not only [knowing] who would go to hell, he actually created them to go there...[this] is not unfair because God is not subject to the principle of fairness. He is above it.[113]

For Ockham, this redefinition represented an ironclad theodicy, but it invited criticism as the very nature of good and God was in need of reassessment. Such analysis would be furthered with the dawn of the Reformation and the rise of the Modern Era of philosophy.

The Problem of Evil in Modern Philosophy

Calvin (1509-1564 A.D.)

Calvin resolutely disregards human volition as a means of absolving God for evil's existence, and thus rejects earlier mainstream theodicies. In Ockham, however, Calvin finds an agreeable response to the problem, and builds upon Ockham's foundation – his conception of good. Calvin minces no words when describing the root of good:

> The will of God is the supreme rule of righteousness, so that everything which he wills must be held to be righteous by the mere fact of his willing it. Therefore, when it is asked why the Lord did so, we must answer, Because he pleased. But if you proceed farther to ask why he pleased, you ask for something greater and more sublime than the will of God, and nothing such can be found.[114]

Calvin's lofty view of God excels his concept of good as a standard. God is Himself the standard, and as in Ockham, the problem of evil, at least as formally conceived disintegrates. A new problem, however, rises in its place – the nature of divine justice. Calvin anticipates this, offering,

> First, they ask why God is offended with his creatures who have not provoked him by any previous offense; for to devote to destruction whomsoever he pleases, more resembles the caprice of a tyrant than the legal sentence of a judge; and, therefore, there is reason to expostulate with God, if at his mere pleasure men are, without any desert of their own, predestinated to eternal death. If at any time thoughts of this kind come into the minds of the pious, they will be sufficiently armed to repress them, by considering how sinful it is to insist on knowing the causes of the divine will, since it is itself, and justly ought to be, the cause of all that exists. For if his will has any cause, there must be something antecedent to it, and to which it is annexed; this it were impious to imagine.[115]

For Calvin, not only is God the standard of good, but also that of order. He supplies a teleological grounding based in His volition and acting as causative of all things. All things, then, work in accordance with His justice, and that justice imbues the cosmos with order much like paint encompasses the canvas and provides the implement for intelligibility of meaning and design in the resulting artwork.

Descartes (1596-1560 A.D.)

Descartes follows Augustinian theory in two particular areas: (1) assertion of human volition, and (2) evil as a non-essence. But Descartes adds an important component to the discussion. To this point omnipotence was the attribute most commonly limited in efforts to construct a theodicy. Descartes focuses on this feature as well, but rather than limiting it he expands it to the degree that God can even perform contradictions if He so desires. This is related to the idea of contingency that Descartes supports, as Nussbaum explains,

> For him, not only is it the case that causal laws could have been different, had God willed it so; more radically, the laws of mathematics and of logic themselves could have been different as well.[116]

Thus God could have chosen other permutations of organizing laws, but in accord with Anselm's view of the perfection of God, Descartes recognizes that this world is the best possible, and that as God determines what laws will be, they then become necessary. Contingency, then, exists but with limits at the point where the contingent becomes the real. At this point the real becomes necessary. So while Descartes does utilize the free-will explanation in his theodicy, two additional ingredients are observable: (1) the possibility of contradiction due to superomnipotence, or the divine possession of power which can contradict without self-defeat, generates a course in which the problem of evil becomes a non sequitur, and (2) his concept of contingency which offers a teleological explanation for the presence of evil. It should be noted in this context that in addition to these specific theodical elements, Descartes also provides an intersection of philosophy and theology, as his theodicy is distinctly philosophical. Janowski observes that

> *Descartes' prime concern is Certitude or Truth* [emphasis mine], while the classical theodicies deal with the existence of moral evil.... Although Descartes tried not to

meddle with theological and moral issues, it is clear from his treatment of the good and the true – both of which, according to him, were established by God – that they are two aspects of the same problem.[117]

For Descartes epistemological consistency, grounded in reason, was central in his theodicy, thus expanding discussions of theodicy into the realm of epistemology.

Spinoza (1632-1677 A.D.)

Spinoza adopts, as Nussbaum categorizes him, a primarily modal approach to theodicy, espousing causal determinism and advocating necessity rather than contingency. Whereas Spinoza acknowledges contingency in an epistemological sense, he categorically denies it in the natural sense.[118] Spinoza's affinity for necessity corresponds with his emphasis on plenitude (Lovejoy's term) – the idea that all that can be must be. With a view toward a 'greater good' theodicy, Spinoza held that all that exists must do so of necessity. Evil exists in similar fashion to the Neoplatonic conception as privation rather than essence – on this point Spinoza agrees with Augustine. The point of departure for Spinoza is causation, whereas Augustine viewed evil as caused by wrongheaded choices, Spinoza perceives evil as that which is suffered due to external forces acting on the individual. Yet good and evil are not absolute, as he describes in *The Ethics*, they both emerge equally from the perfect nature of a (panentheistic) deity:

> If all things follow from a necessity of the absolutely perfect nature of God, why are there so many imperfections in nature? Such, for instance, as things corrupt to the point of putridity, loathsome deformity, confusion, evil, sin, etc....the perfection of things is to be

reckoned only from their own nature and power; things are not more or less perfect, according as they delight or offend the human senses, or according as they are serviceable or repugnant to mankind.[119]

The elements of necessity and perfection are in view for Spinoza, and flowing from his panentheistic perspective of God — He does not make creative determinations but rather supports and sustains by way of omnipotence - Spinoza creates for himself tremendous latitude in defining of good. The principle of perfection when conjoined with necessity yields varying degrees of perfection including evil as privation of higher degrees of the same. He says in this regard,

To those who ask why God did not so create all men, that they should be governed only by reason, I give no answer but this: because matter was not lacking to him for the creation of every degree of perfection from highest to lowest; or more strictly, because the laws of his nature are so vast, as to suffice for the production of everything conceivable by an infinite intelligence....[120]

Here is a form of greater-good theodicy which must of necessity include each degree of perfection, even to the negative extreme. Spinoza's theodicy, due to its emphasis on plenitude, invites aesthetic critique rather than purely rational assessment, thus affording a point of intersection between philosophical critique and theological dogma.

Leibniz (1646-1716 A.D.)
For Leibniz, the problem of evil is a supreme inquiry. He seems particularly motivated to address the issue that a world containing evil seems a malfunction on the part of its creator if

indeed that creator possesses perfection. Like Spinoza, Leibniz recognizes the principle of perfection as a reality, yet whereas for Spinoza the best possible world is a product of divine power, for Leibniz, it is a product of divine choice actuated in necessity. For both thinkers the actual world is the best possible one, thus while the path differs substantially the destination in this regard is the same. God as perfect is obligated to create the best possible world, He will to do so, and He in fact does so.

Leibniz' theodicy also relies on plenitude, as demonstrated in part by his deployment of aesthetic illustration of the nature of evil as both necessary and as privation. He says,

> . . . to say that the painter is the author of all that is real in the two paintings, without however being the author of what is lacking or the disproportion between the larger and the smaller painting. . . . In effect, what is lacking is nothing more than a simple result of an infallible consequence of that which is positive, without any need for a distinct author [of that which is lacking].[121]

In this case divine authorship is defended against the malfunction claim. Evil has a necessary role in what appears to be a less than ideal world, a role which Leibniz identifies as emerging in three manifestations: (1) metaphysical evil – the degeneration inherent in the limits of the substance(s) of which the world is made, (2) natural evil – the pain and suffering experienced in the world, and (3) moral evil – that which inevitably results in natural evil.[122] Evil, then, completes the picture and is the result of no malfunction at all.

Hume (1711-1776 A.D.)
Leading up to Hume, theodicy grew to be an increasingly central issue not only in theological discussion but also in philosophical

inquiry – for some (such as Leibniz) it was a primary stimulus. Hume's empiricism brought no less emphasis on the topic but did, however, generate dramatically disparate conclusions. Countering in particular the teleological concept, Hume attacks theism mercilessly. While epistemology may be his primary battleground, the problem of evil attracts much of his attention. It is notable that for Hume arriving at a theodicy was not his ambition, rather he sought to obliterate traditional notions of God. Having already countered to his own satisfaction *a priori* arguments for God's existence, Hume attacks what he believes to be the last bastion of grounding for belief in God – the teleological idea.

If able to demonstrate that God is indifferent to good and evil, He can be made irrelevant and even nonsensical. As a result any theistically based teleological idea would be moot. To accomplish this Hume relies on an ancient iteration of the problem – that of Epicurus. He reminds theists that

> Epicurus's old questions are yet unanswered. Is he willing to prevent evil, but not able? then he is impotent. Is he able, but not willing? then he is malevolent. Is he both able and willing? whence then is evil?[123]

In Hume's analysis of Epicurus, a more formalized argument begins to take shape. Unless terminology is redefined (as it is in previous theodicies), there are only three possibilities: (1) God is not omnipotent, (2) God is not omnibenevolent, (3) evil does not exist.

Hume will not allow any redefinition of evil, as in his *Dialogues Concerning Natural Religion*[124] he lists a number of moral and natural evils which are painfully evident to all. In so doing he concludes against a cosmos initiated by either concern for its creatures or by divine volition, saying:

> Were all living creatures incapable of pain, or were the world administered by particular volitions, evil never could have found access into the universe: and were animals endowed with a large stock of powers and faculties, beyond what strict necessity requires; or were the several springs and principles of the universe so accurately framed as to preserve always the just temperament and medium; there must have been very little ill in comparison of what we feel at present. What then shall we pronounce on this occasion?[125]

Once *a priori* ideas of inherent goodness are vanquished (theistic or otherwise), such goodness can only be derived from experience, and Hume has an easy time of dismissing that possibility:

> But let us still assert, that as this goodness is not antecedently established, but must be inferred from the phenomena, there can be no grounds for such an inference, while there are so many ills in the universe, and while these ills might so easily have been remedied, as far as human understanding can be allowed to judge on such a subject.[126]

Having established the groundlessness of the idea of teleological goodness, Hume closes the issue with a resounding indictment derived from simple observation:

> But inspect a little more narrowly these living existences, the only beings worth regarding. How hostile and destructive to each other! How insufficient all of them for their own happiness! How contemptible or odious to the

spectator! The whole presents nothing but the idea of a blind Nature, impregnated by a great vivifying principle, and pouring forth from her lap, without discernment or parental care, her maimed and abortive children![127]

As representative of Hume, these statements fasten theological conceptions of evil and notions of the character of God to theories of knowledge, and they additionally raise questions of the nature of good which leads further into ethical discussions. For Hume, theology and philosophy are too connected, and he wishes to extricate philosophical inquiry from the grips of unverifiable religious notions. Insofar as this is his objective, Hume becomes perhaps the lead protagonist for theodicy. Any attempt at theodicy which does not at least consider the colossal issues he raises will be found deficient or partial at best.

Kant (1724-1804 A.D.)
In contrast to Hume, Kant sought to extrapolate systematic order in the cosmos. Like Hume, his epistemological grounding necessitated certain conclusions – while Hume's empiricism supplied an *a priori* opposition to the metaphysical, Kant's structuralism furnished a means for explaining the existence of evil in a manner not fully incompatible with a theistic outlook. For Kant *radical evil* is self-inflicted on those who *will* corruptly. Kant's metaphysical conception of radical evil relates directly to his deontological ethics. Connection can likewise be drawn from the basic issues of theodicy to moral duty in Kant, thus generating a point of intersection between metaphysics and ethics. If evil for Kant is such a pivotal issue, then how does he account for its presence?

> We shall say, therefore, of the character (good or evil) distinguishing man from other possible rational beings,

that it is innate in him. Yet in doing so we shall ever take the position that nature is not to bear the blame (if it is evil) or take the credit (if it is good), but that man himself is its author.[128]

Evil is not divinely inspired but rather is intrinsic within the person and inextricably connected to the utilization of free choice. Kant continues:

> To have a good or an evil disposition as an inborn natural constitution does not here mean that it has not been acquired by the man who harbors it, that he is not author of it, but rather, that it has not been acquired in time (that he has always been good, or evil, from his youth up). The disposition, i.e., the ultimate subjective ground of the adoption of maxims, can be one only and applies universally to the whole use of freedom. Yet this disposition itself must have been adopted by free choice, for otherwise it could not be imputed.[129]

Whereas Kant attributes the existence of evil within human character to the (corrupt) deployment of free choice, he acknowledges three distinct degrees of evil: (1) frailty of human nature, (2) impurity of the human heart, and (3) wickedness of the human heart – the propensity toward evil. Evil is found to differing degree universally within human nature – so much so, in fact, that Kant says it is "woven into human nature."[130] As such, to become free from evil is the "greatest prize,"[131] and to fail to be such is man's own fault. In deriving such conclusions Kant relies on two theodical components: (1) free will as source of origin and causation of evil, and (2) the principle of plenitude. In his representation of the latter, Kant reckons the end game as the establishment of an ethical commonwealth – the founding of a kingdom of God on earth. As free choice plays an important role in this, evil is a necessity in this drama.

Conclusion

From a synthesis of historical views on the problem of evil from the pre-Socratic through the modern era, two primary definitions emerge: one, elucidated primarily in medieval theology from a monotheistic vantage point, revolves around harmonizing the concurrent existences of God and evil; and the second, from pre-Socratic and modern naturalistic grounding, centers on the question of whether the cosmos is teleological. Whether from aesthetic motivation or otherwise – the question of teleology persists.

The problem, from a monotheistic perspective, is dependent upon three perfections attributed to God: omniscience, omnipotence, and omnibenevolence. If any one of the three fail, then God (as defined) cannot exist. The existence of evil seems to threaten at any time at least one of these perfections. The problem, then, as gleaned from historical thinkers could be formally structured as follows:[132]

Premise 1: If G is X then G is A (If God is existent then God is omniscient)
Premise 2: If G is X then G is B (If God is existent then God is omnipotent)
Premise 3: If G is X then G is C (If God is existent then God is omnibenevolent)
Premise 4: If D is X then G is not A (If evil is existent then God is not omniscient)
Premise 5: If D is X then G is not B (If evil is existent then God is not omnipotent)

Premise 6: If D is X then G is not C (If evil is existent then God is not omnibenevolent)
Premise 7: D is X (evil is existent)
Conclusion: G is not X (God is not existent)

Given the positive truth value of the premises, the conclusion necessarily follows. This obviously creates a very significant theological conundrum which can only be resolved if it can be shown that any one of the premises is false.

If Premise 1 is false, then omniscience is *not* prerequisite to the existence of God. God theoretically could possess omnipotence and omnibenevolence and yet lack omniscience, the lacking of which allows for the existence of evil without logically nullifying His existence. In this case, God is powerful enough to eliminate evil, and he is morally perfect enough to want it eliminated, but He does not have the knowledge either that it exists, or of how it should be eliminated. If Premise 2 is false, then God has the necessary knowledge and the desire to eliminate evil but lacks the power to do so. If Premise 3 is false, then God has both the knowledge and the power to eliminate evil but does not desire to do so. If Premises 4, 5, or 6 is false, then the existence of evil does not constitute a contradiction to one or more of the perfections asserted of God. If Premise 7 is false, then there is no problem at all, since evil is non-existent.

From a naturalistic perspective, and independent of theological considerations, the second permutation of the problem discusses the plausibility of good, order, and ultimately purpose within the cosmos despite apparent contradictions brought by suffering within nature, for example, and relies on the same basic logical structure. Such a problem could be formalized in the following manner:

Premise 1: If N is P then N is G (If nature is purposed then nature is good)
Premise 2: If N is P then N is O (If nature is purposed then nature is orderly)
Premise 3: If S is R then N is not G (If suffering is a reality then nature is not good)
Premise 4: If S is R then N is not O (If suffering is a reality then nature is not orderly)
Premise 5: S is R (suffering is a reality)
Conclusion: N is not P (nature is not purposed)

As evidenced from a historical overview and resultant definitions, the problem of the existence of evil has confounded theologian and philosopher alike and is not isolated exclusively within either category of thought. Insomuch as it is true that both disciplines must confront the issue, it seems that at least two considerations should be made.

First, a working definition of the problem from each standpoint (such as those here provided) should be perceived. Any problem to be resolved requires at least general agreement on the part of the participants regarding core definitions. And while I am not suggesting that the definitions offered here necessarily provide finality in this regard, I do suggest that these particular formulations, derived from the problem as historically iterated, provide a reduction of terms apt to facilitate comparative analysis of proposed solutions, rendering more readily visible presuppositions and other such factors which would significantly impact conclusions. In short, a definition extracted from a plurality of theorists addressing the problem over time will allow for broader and even interdisciplinary critique, thus deepening the analysis.

Second, as this kind of analysis takes place a reduced-term definition provides greater opportunity for a broader interdisciplinary testing of ideas. Philosophical attempts at resolving the issue – or reframing the issue so as not to require resolution – when held to the light (or darkness) of theology must meet challenges it might not otherwise wish to consider. The core premises of naturalistic philosophy may be examined in this context, and in light of such testing will either be shown to want further refinement or will be strengthened even further in its convictions. Likewise, theological efforts, when informed by naturalistic argument, must question its very basis of authority. Is it grounded properly? Is it hermeneutically sound? The testing which philosophical inquiry brings provides opportunity for heightened precision which might not be otherwise motivated. The informing of one discipline by the other, then, gives occasion for strengthening or dismissal of views as the case may demand.

With these two considerations in view, and in light of the historical inquiry and the problem's ramifications for epistemology, metaphysics, ethics, and aesthetics, there may be perhaps no more fertile ground for interdisciplinary inquiry between philosophy and theology than the problem of evil.

4:4-6 Vanity: Survival and Rivalry Under the Sun

[4] Again, I considered all travail, and every right work, that for this a man is envied of his neighbour. This is also vanity and vexation of spirit.

Having considered the wearying effort (both the labor and the skill to engage in it) required to subsist, Solomon sees a pervasive strife, a rivalry or envy (*qinah*) (*zelos* in the LXX) between a man and his neighbor (*rea*) – a term implying a very close associate. Even close relationships do not supersede the rivalry inherent in the pursuit of survival. The rivalry is meaningless and results in inner strife.

[5] The fool foldeth his hands together, and eateth his own flesh.

The one who does not strive to subsist consumes himself. To some degree, the "rat race" is unavoidable. Seeking to remove oneself fully from meaningless labors of subsistence is foolishness and self-destructive. What a grievous choice to be had here.
    There are three approaches highlighted in vv. 5-6. The first is found in v. 5: two empty hands.

[6] Better is an handful with quietness, than both the hands full with travail and vexation of spirit.

The second option is one handful of labor (and thus vexation of spirit) and one handful of restfulness or quietness (*nachath*). The third option is inferior to the second, and represents two fistfuls of labor (and thus vexation of spirit). Note the term translated by the KJV as handful is *kaph* (open palm) while the second reference is *chophen* (closed fist). The one who grasps labor in this way – double fisted, in earnest – is especially vexed. There is common grace to be seen here, in the appropriation of balance between labor and rest.

Philosophical Parallel: Social Contract

Thomas Hobbes (1588-1679 A.D.) observed the rivalry involved in subsistence and sought to remedy it by means of social agreement. He held that God created man, but yet man's existence, he says, is "solitary, poor, nasty, brutish, and short." While this seems a striking contradiction (why would a good God create such a miserable existence?), the solution is found in man operating in the image of God by creating an artificial man, just as God had created natural man. He describes people as like wolves who struggle after the same things – with the ultimate goal of each person as self-preservation. Each person has the right to self-preservation and the right to punish any would violate that natural right. This creates the rivalry and the chaos. Conditions can be bettered, however, when two parties give up their right to execute judgment on the other. They pass that right on to a third party called the Leviathan (from Job's monster), otherwise defined as the commonwealth or state. Thus there is a social contract, enforceable by the third party.

In Hobbes' construct, the solution to the misery of life is an under the sun solution – yes, there is acknowledgment of God as Creator, but Hobbes did not look to God for solutions to common problems instead believing that the responsibility rests on man's shoulders to improve his fate.

While the social contract has proven particularly useful as a social political system (democracy is perhaps the most shining example), it is also applied as an ethical system. This use is far more tenuous, as morality is determined by agreement of society. When the sentiment of society changes, so do definitions of good and evil. For example, oppressive and degrading slavery was prevalent in the United States in the early nineteenth century. In the twenty-first century it is almost universally viewed to be a grave evil. What changed?

The social contract was not inaugurated by Hobbes, but he certainly added a good deal of refinement to it. Previous thinkers such as Plato are highly critical of social contract - particularly in the form of democracy. Plato, for example, believed society should be governed by philosopher kings in an aristocracy (rule by the best), and that the democratic social contract represented rule by the mob, the many, the ignorant, the weak, etc. Hobbes' version of social contract reckoned that all men were created equal and entitled to pursue survival, but that various advantages and disadvantages had to be offset. Plato held that advantages and disadvantages should be maintained according to nature.

Primary Source Excerpt: Hobbes: The Leviathan (1651 A.D.)

INTRODUCTION

NATURE (the art whereby God hath made and governs the world) is by the art of man, as in many other things, so in this also imitated, that it can make an artificial animal. For seeing life is but a motion of limbs, the beginning whereof is in some principal part within, why may we not say that all automata (engines that move themselves by springs and wheels as doth a watch) have an artificial life? For what is the heart, but a spring; and the nerves, but so many strings; and the joints, but so many wheels, giving motion to the whole body, such as was intended by the Artificer? Art goes yet further, imitating that rational and most excellent work of Nature, man. For by art is created that great LEVIATHAN called a COMMONWEALTH, or STATE (in Latin, CIVITAS), which is but an artificial man, though of greater stature and strength than the natural, for whose protection and defence it was intended; and in which the sovereignty is an artificial soul, as giving life and motion to the whole body; the magistrates and other officers of judicature and execution, artificial joints; reward and punishment (by which fastened to the seat of the sovereignty, every joint and member is moved to perform his duty) are the nerves, that do the same in the body natural; the wealth and riches of all the particular members are the strength; salus populi (the people's safety) its business; counsellors, by whom all things needful for it to know are suggested unto it, are the memory; equity and laws, an artificial reason and will; concord, health; sedition, sickness; and civil war, death. Lastly, the pacts and covenants, by which the parts of this body politic were at first made, set together, and united, resemble that fiat, or the Let us make man, pronounced by God in the Creation.

To describe the nature of this artificial man, I will consider First, the matter thereof, and the artificer; both which is man. Secondly, how, and by what covenants it is made; what are the rights and just power or authority of a sovereign; and what it is that preserveth and dissolveth it. Thirdly, what is a Christian Commonwealth. Lastly, what is the Kingdom of Darkness.

Concerning the first, there is a saying much usurped of late, that wisdom is acquired, not by reading of books, but of men. Consequently whereunto, those persons, that for the most part can give no other proof of being wise, take great delight to show what they think they have read in men, by uncharitable censures of one another behind their backs. But there is another saying not of late understood, by which they might learn truly to read one another, if they would take the pains; and that is, Nosce teipsum, Read thyself: which was not meant, as it is now used, to countenance either the barbarous state of men in power towards their inferiors, or to encourage men of low degree to a saucy behaviour towards their betters; but to teach us that for the similitude of the thoughts and passions of one man, to the thoughts and passions of another, whosoever looketh into himself and considereth what he doth when he does think, opine, reason, hope, fear, etc., and upon what grounds; he shall thereby read and know what are the thoughts and passions of all other men upon the like occasions. I say the similitude of passions, which are the same in all men,- desire, fear, hope, etc.; not the similitude of the objects of the passions, which are the things desired, feared, hoped, etc.: for these the constitution individual, and particular education, do so vary, and they are so easy to be kept from our knowledge, that the characters of man's heart, blotted and confounded as they are with dissembling, lying, counterfeiting, and erroneous doctrines, are legible only to him that searcheth hearts. And though by men's actions we do discover their design sometimes; yet to do it without comparing them with our own, and distinguishing all circumstances by which the case may come to be altered, is to decipher without a key, and be for the most part deceived, by too much trust or by too much diffidence, as he that reads is himself a good or evil man.

But let one man read another by his actions never so perfectly, it serves him only with his acquaintance, which are but few. He that is to govern a whole nation must read in himself, not this, or that particular man; but mankind: which though it be hard to do, harder than to learn any language or science; yet, when I shall have set down my own reading orderly and perspicuously, the pains left another will be only to consider if he also find not the same in himself. For this kind of doctrine admitteth no other demonstration.

CHAPTER XIII OF THE NATURAL CONDITION OF MANKIND AS CONCERNING THEIR FELICITY AND MISERY

NATURE hath made men so equal in the faculties of body and mind as that, though there be found one man sometimes manifestly stronger in body or of quicker mind than another, yet when all is reckoned together the difference between man and man is not so considerable as that one man can thereupon claim to himself any benefit to which another may not pretend as well as he. For as to the strength of body, the weakest has strength enough to kill the strongest, either by secret machination or by confederacy with others that are in the same danger with himself.

And as to the faculties of the mind, setting aside the arts grounded upon words, and especially that skill of proceeding upon general and infallible rules, called science, which very few have and but in few things, as being not a native faculty born with us, nor attained, as prudence, while we look after somewhat else, I find yet a greater equality amongst men than that of strength. For prudence is but experience, which equal time equally bestows on all men in those things they equally apply themselves unto. That which may perhaps make such equality incredible is but a vain conceit of one's own wisdom, which almost all men think they have in a greater degree than the vulgar; that is, than all men but themselves, and a few others, whom by fame, or for concurring with themselves, they approve. For such is the nature of men that howsoever they may acknowledge many others to be more witty, or more eloquent or more learned, yet they will hardly believe there be many so wise as themselves; for they see their own wit at hand, and other men's at a distance. But this proveth rather that men are in that point equal, than unequal. For there is not ordinarily a greater sign of the equal distribution of anything than that every man is contented with his share.

From this equality of ability ariseth equality of hope in the attaining of our ends. And therefore if any two men desire the same thing, which nevertheless they cannot both enjoy, they become enemies; and in the way to their end (which is principally their own conservation, and sometimes their delectation only) endeavour to destroy or subdue one another. And from hence it comes to pass that where an invader hath no more to fear than another man's single power, if one plant, sow, build, or possess a convenient seat, others may probably be expected to come prepared with forces united to dispossess and deprive him, not only of the fruit of his labour, but also of his life or liberty. And the invader again is in the like danger of another. And from this diffidence of one another, there is no way for any man to secure himself so reasonable as anticipation; that is, by force, or wiles, to master the persons of all men he can so long till he see no other power great enough to endanger him: and this is no more than his own conservation requireth, and is generally allowed. Also, because there be some that, taking pleasure in contemplating their own power in the acts of conquest, which they pursue farther than their security requires, if others, that otherwise would be glad to be at ease within modest bounds, should not by invasion increase their power, they would not be able, long time, by standing only on their defence, to subsist. And by consequence, such augmentation of dominion over men being necessary to a man's conservation, it ought to be allowed him.

Again, men have no pleasure (but on the contrary a great deal of grief) in keeping company where there is no power able to overawe them all. For every man looketh that his companion should value him at the same rate he sets upon himself, and upon all signs of contempt or undervaluing naturally endeavours, as far as he dares (which amongst them that have no common power to keep them in quiet is far enough to make them destroy each other), to extort a greater value from his contemners, by damage; and from others, by the example.

So that in the nature of man, we find three principal causes of quarrel. First, competition; secondly, diffidence; thirdly, glory.

The first maketh men invade for gain; the second, for safety; and the third, for reputation. The first use violence, to make themselves masters of other men's persons, wives, children, and cattle; the second, to defend them; the third, for trifles, as a word, a smile, a different opinion, and any other sign of undervalue, either direct in their persons or by reflection in their kindred, their friends, their nation, their profession, or their name.

Hereby it is manifest that during the time men live without a common power to keep them all in awe, they are in that condition which is called war; and such a war as is of every man against every man. For war consisteth not in battle only, or the act of fighting, but in a tract of time, wherein the will to contend by battle is sufficiently known: and therefore the notion of time is to be considered in the nature of war, as it is in the nature of weather. For as the nature of foul weather lieth not in a shower or two of rain, but in an inclination thereto of many days together: so the nature of war consisteth not in actual fighting, but in the known disposition thereto during all the time there is no assurance to the contrary. All other time is peace.

Whatsoever therefore is consequent to a time of war, where every man is enemy to every man, the same consequent to the time wherein men live without other security than what their own strength and their own invention shall furnish them withal. In such condition there is no place for industry, because the fruit thereof is uncertain: and consequently no culture of the earth; no navigation, nor use of the commodities that may be imported by sea; no commodious building; no instruments of moving and removing such things as require much force; no knowledge of the face of the earth; no account of time; no arts; no letters; no society; and which is worst of all, continual fear, and danger of violent death; and the life of man, solitary, poor, nasty, brutish, and short.

It may seem strange to some man that has not well weighed these things that Nature should thus dissociate and render men apt to invade and destroy one another: and he may therefore, not trusting to this inference, made from the passions, desire perhaps to have the same confirmed by experience. Let him therefore consider with himself: when taking a journey, he arms himself and seeks to go well accompanied; when going to sleep, he locks his doors; when even in his house he locks his chests; and this when he knows there be laws and public officers, armed, to revenge all injuries shall be done him; what opinion he has of his fellow subjects, when he rides armed; of his fellow citizens, when he locks his doors; and of his children, and servants, when he locks his chests. Does he not there as much accuse mankind by his actions as I do by my words? But neither of us accuse man's nature in it. The desires, and other passions of man, are in themselves no sin. No more are the actions that proceed from those passions till they know a law that forbids them; which till laws be made they cannot know, nor can any law be made till they have agreed upon the person that shall make it.

It may peradventure be thought there was never such a time nor condition of war as this; and I believe it was never generally so, over all the world: but there are many places where they live so now. For the savage people in many places of America, except the government of small families, the concord whereof dependeth on natural lust, have no government at all, and live at this day in that brutish manner, as I said before. Howsoever, it may be perceived what manner of life there would be, where there were no common power to fear, by the manner of life which men that have formerly lived under a peaceful government use to degenerate into a civil war.

But though there had never been any time wherein particular men were in a condition of war one against another, yet in all times kings and persons of sovereign authority, because of their independency, are in continual jealousies, and in the state and posture of gladiators, having their weapons pointing, and their eyes fixed on one another; that is, their forts, garrisons, and guns upon the frontiers of their kingdoms, and continual spies upon their neighbours, which is a posture of war. But because they uphold thereby the industry of their subjects, there does not follow from it that misery which accompanies the liberty of particular men.

To this war of every man against every man, this also is consequent; that nothing can be unjust. The notions of right and wrong, justice and injustice, have there no place. Where there is no common power, there is no law; where no law, no injustice. Force and fraud are in war the two cardinal virtues. Justice and injustice are none of the faculties neither of the body nor mind. If they were, they might be in a man that were alone in the world, as well as his senses and passions. They are qualities that relate to men in society, not in solitude. It is consequent also to the same condition that there be no propriety, no dominion, no mine and thine distinct; but only that to be every man's that he can get, and for so long as he can keep it. And thus much for the ill condition which man by mere nature is actually placed in; though with a possibility to come out of it, consisting partly in the passions, partly in his reason.

The passions that incline men to peace are: fear of death; desire of such things as are necessary to commodious living; and a hope by their industry to obtain them. And reason suggesteth convenient articles of peace upon which men may be drawn to agreement. These articles are they which otherwise are called the laws of nature, whereof I shall speak more particularly in the two following chapters.

4:7-12 Vanity: Egocentrism and Aloneness Under the Sun

[7] Then I returned, and I saw vanity under the sun.

And I turned and observed vanity under the sun. The activity observed is different. The result is the same.

[8] There is one alone, and there is not a second; yea, he hath neither child nor brother: yet is there no end of all his labour; neither is his eye satisfied with riches; neither saith he, For whom do I labour, and bereave my soul of good? This is also vanity, yea, it is a sore travail.

There was one and not a second. All he has is the pursuit of self-interest. There is no end (*qetz*, purpose, direction; *perasmos* in the LXX – trial or outcome) to all his labor. Self-interest is also devoid of meaning.

[9] Two are better than one; because they have a good reward for their labour.
[10] For if they fall, the one will lift up his fellow: but woe to him that is alone when he falleth; for he hath not another to help him up.
[11] Again, if two lie together, then they have heat: but how can one be warm alone?
[12] And if one prevail against him, two shall withstand him;

and a threefold cord is not quickly broken.

Solitude might be sought in order for one to be more effective in the pursuit of self-interest. But self-interest is fruitless, thus solitude has no advantage. Companionship, on the other hand, at least has practical value, if not lasting meaning.

Philosophical Parallel: Ethical Egoism

Ayn Rand (1905-1982 A.D.) wrote *The Virtue of Selfishness* (among other works), in which she promotes ethical egoism or rational selfishness — the idea that one should pursue self-interest exclusively. Rand views altruistic ethics (morality based on the other as beneficiary) as foolish — even dangerous. She rejects (1) mysticism [her term] — which asserts morality as originating from God, (2) neomysticism — which replaces God with society and grounds ethics in social good, (3) emotionalism, and (4) personal whim as grounds for moral value. She believes she has resolved the is / ought problem with the basic premise that one exists (descriptive) therefore one should (prescriptive) pursue the interests of that existence. She defines value and virtue not in traditional terms: value is what one acts to gain or keep, while virtue is the means by which one gains or keeps it.

Rand's brand of egoism is rational, thus it does not infringe on others, but rather interacts through trade. She sees this as beneficial since those who trade in this context do so as equals. Thus her social political views, consistent with her ethics, are strongly capitalist.

Solomon underscores the vanity of pursuing one's own self-interests: it is empty and lonely. If one cooperates with others, there shall be perhaps more under the sun profit, but the emptiness remains.

4:13-16 Vanity: Foolishness Under the Sun

[13] Better is a poor and a wise child than an old and foolish king, who will no more be admonished.

Teachability and wisdom is better (*tov*) than power with foolishness (*k'sil*, or *aphrona* in the LXX).

[14] For out of prison he cometh to reign; whereas also he that is born in his kingdom becometh poor.

The wise man can navigate from prison to rulership. Thus wisdom has practical value.

[15] I considered all the living which walk under the sun, with the second child that shall stand up in his stead.

Despite the practical value of wisdom utilized to ascend to the throne, people will gravitate to the next leader.

[16] There is no end of all the people, even of all that have been before them: they also that come after shall not rejoice in him. Surely this also is vanity and vexation of spirit.

The people who came before were unsatisfied with the present leader just as the people to come will be. Thus the practical value of wisdom for attaining rulership is meaninglessness and strife.

Philosophical Parallel: Nietzsche's Will to Power

Nietzsche wrote in The Gay Science that God is dead, meaning that notions of God are irrelevant. The discovery of which is worthy of celebration, as mankind is now free from superstition and moral restraint. What then becomes the basis of ethics? For Nietzsche, it is the will to power – self-overcoming, self-mastery, self-realization.

Will to power has two ethical orientations:
1. master morality – strong will, nobility, equate self-fulfillment with "the good," psychologically honest ...morality=self-glorification
2. slave morality – condemn the master morality (sour grapes – traits beyond their reach), reaction, negation, resentment

Nietzsche believed Jews and Christians to hold the slave morality, describing Christianity as a fatal and seductive lie, thinking that unbelief was actually a precondition of greatness.

While Christianity was his primary example, he believed there was another inferior type: traditional, customary: herd morality. Herd moralists seek simply the life of the herd, whereas slave moralists seek to change their situation. For Nietzsche, all ethical framework was humanistic, weighted toward master morality and toward autonomy and self-expression. The ideal of this is manifest in the application of will to power resulting in the *ubermensch* (overman or superman). The *ubermensch* possesses spiritual superiority, well-being, and an excess of strength...Caesar with the soul of Jesus Christ. Nietzsche's ultimate meaning and value in life is essentially: become who you are.

Excursus: On the Will to Power: Nietzsche's Pedigree

The flow of Nietzsche's thought is notably distinct from more systematic philosophers (e.g., Kant) in that his perspective on moral value does not advance from previously defined epistemological and metaphysical conceptions. In fact, a reverse progression is evident as he begins his inquiry with a question of value (GM:3) while epistemological and metaphysical outlooks emerge only later from his skepticism on the original subject. In observing this priority of the ethical/moral issue, this writer believes Nietzsche's thought can be appropriately traced in pedigree to demonstrate the ethical/moral presuppositions which chart the course for his broader worldview, as well as some perhaps significant inconsistencies which may undermine the practical value[133] of his project.

Operating from the framework of Geuss' five characteristics of pedigree[134] ((1) seeks a positive valorization of some item, (2) starting from singular origin, (3) an actual source of value, (4) tracing an unbroken line of succession from origin to item of value, and (5) steps preserve value) this discussion will trace a pedigree of Nietzschean thought to achieve the aforementioned ends.

Philippa Foot in her discussion of *Nietzsche's Revaluation of Value* appropriately observes that "a confrontation with Nietzsche is a difficult thing to arrange," and further describes his valuation project as "intrinsically puzzling" (how *can* one value values?).[135] Geuss attempts just such an arrangement in his assessment of Nietzsche's genealogy of morals.[136] Geuss defines genealogy for his particular usage in contrast[137] to a pedigree composed of five elements: (1) seeks a positive valorization of some item, (2) starting from singular origin, (3) an actual source of value, (4) tracing an unbroken line of succession from origin to item of value, and (5) steps preserve value. While Geuss' concern is genealogy, pedigree[138] nonetheless could play a valuable role in a discussion of the development of Nietzschean valuation, particularly as a device to trace his ethical presuppositions and resultant epistemological and metaphysical conclusions to their culmination in Nietzsche's crowning achievement – a prescriptive moral doctrine, the import of which is not lost on his interlocutors, as Salter says, "...he does propose *a constructive moral principle* [emphasis mine], and it is likely that this will be counted his chief significance in the future." (Salter, NMA, 1915).

(1) Seeks a Positive Valorization of Some Item
Arguably, Nietzsche's journey begins at the age of thirteen with a valorization of an "immoral or at least immoralistic *a priori.*" (GM:3) "Brought up on strict religious principles, he had learned to set up a particular value on veracity, regarding it oddly as a strictly Christian virtue...." (Benn, 1908). His skepticism of absolute moral value is perhaps the central presupposition grounding his project. His three stage view (premoral, moral, ultramoral)[139] of history shows the primacy of his moral skepticism. As in Marx's five stage[140] economic view of history which culminated in Marx's ideal, so Nietzsche's historical panorama likewise culminates in his own ideal of beyond good and evil:

> Is it not possible, however, that the necessity may now have arisen of again making up our minds with regard to the reversing and fundamental shifting of values, owing to a new self-consciousness and acuteness in man-is it not possible that we may be standing on the threshold of a period which to begin with, would be distinguished negatively as ultra-moral .... ?[141]

Nietzsche's view pursues justification for his moral skepticism with, as Bakewell suggests, religious fervor:

> Nietzsche is not primarily a philosopher, not a scientist, but, rather, a poet, a poet with the mission to preach a new philosophy which shall be, as no other philosophy is, or ever has been, in accordance with science and reality. But this new philosophy is also a religion, and Nietzsche is its prophet. (Bakewell, 1899)

Arguably, Nietzsche shows a prior commitment to this skepticism, and he maintains it consistently throughout his canon. In particular, he shows opposition to morality in the pejorative sense (MPS[142]) on the following grounds. First, MPS views happiness as good and suffering as bad. But happiness, or well-being is not an appropriate end in itself, as Nietzsche would strongly disagree with Aristotle's virtue ethics which concludes in favor of happiness as final end. Happiness eliminates life's rough edges, reducing man, in Nietzsche's fitting analogy, to sand. Well-being quickly makes man ridiculous and contemptible. On the contrary, Nietzsche views suffering as necessary and prerequisite for human excellence. Nietzsche credits dealing with suffering as creating all enhancements of man thus far. Clearly, happiness provides quite an antithesis to Nietzsche's formula for success in life, and MPS is a fundamental contributor to this flawed system of valuation. Additionally, MPS favors altruism and un-egoism – a tendency which furthers pity and other herd tendencies. Finally, MPS favors egalitarianism which is roadblock for the higher man.

Notably, he is not merely attempting to cast down MPS, but is seeking to replace it as the central interpretation of the human condition, offering an alternate explanation of human experience, and one which he certainly considers superior – on the basis of its avoidance of moral absolutism and the accompanying conceptions of noumenal reality[143] apart from phenomena. While one could conduct a biographical inquiry into Nietzsche's background and circumstances in order to discover some motivation for such an a priori commitment, no such account of his motivation is needed. It is enough to assert that the agreement between his initial skepticism and resulting doctrines shows an (at least) a posteriori valorization of the value of immoralism or skepticism of moral absolutes.

(2) Starting From Singular Origin

Robinson describes Nietzsche as "a classic example of a philosopher motivated from the beginning and throughout his career by an ineradicable and insane prejudice against all forms of religion, and especially of the Christian religion."[144] While Salter believes Robinson to have far overstated this prejudice, it is a noteworthy theme in Nietzsche and seems to represent a unifying premise for his overall project. Foot characterizes this special objection as to Christian morality rather than simply Christianity per se;[145] noting that it is the one professing Christian virtue (not Christianity itself) who is "a sick individual, deeply malicious to himself and others."[146] And as Leiter observes, "Nietzsche's concern is with MPS as an ideology – not the prevalence of actions in accord with MPS." (Leiter, 2002, 86) In support of Leiter's reading is Nietzsche's discussion of the priestly-aristocratic method of valuation (GM:7-9) in which Christianity is simply emblematic of a greater and overarching problem. Regardless of the specific object of disdain, MPS is assuredly in view, thus Nietzsche's "immoralist *a priori*" offers the grounding for his entire project.

Foot describes aptly N's purpose in assaulting Christianity on account of the perception that it favored the weak at the expense of the strong and was thus the most vital of instruments in the degradation of humanity. Foot identifies two prongs of attack: (1) what appears praiseworthy as Christian virtue is a farce, and is instead motivated by malice, and (2) even as judged by its own aims it is a "bad" morality – as it is driven by pity, by pity a great deal of harm is done. The system is thus the epitome of MPS and is highly destructive.[147]

(3) Actual Source of Value
For Nietzsche there is a standard for measuring truth and goodness (Salter, 1915): valuable in serving life but not governing it – "truths" not affirming life have no binding authority:

> If the highest reach of life is the measure of things, then good comes to be what tends that way, and bad what tends in an opposite direction. There are lines of procedure now, possible actions, feelings, thoughts, institutions, laws that harmonize with movement toward the desired goal – they are then to be furthered; other courses are to be opposed. (Salter, NMA, 1915)

If Nietzsche's standard is binding, alternate (traditional) morality is problematic, and has a less than objective base and questionable authority: "morality is nothing more (therefore no more) than obedience to customs, of whatever kind they may be; customs, however, are the traditional way of behaving and evaluating." (D:1:9)

The correspondence theory of truth identifies as truth that which corresponds to fact, being objective and absolute. Clearly, Nietzsche is opposed to the absolute value of truth. The coherence theory of truth posits that the more consistent the system, the more truthful. Nietzsche seems to take no interest in consistency or coherence, leaving the pragmatic theory of truth – that which works is that which is true – as the remaining option. But Geuss rightly observes that Nietzsche views things both true and untrue as useful at times, thus the pragmatic theory seems not to fit Nietzsche's perspective of truth either. Geuss suggests that Nietzsche is uninterested in theories of truth, but is instead occupied with the question: "How and why does the will-to-truth come about."

The question seems to fit Nietzsche's project, but to disregard the question of the nature of truth as having no relevance seems to gloss over crucial steps that might have otherwise either strengthened or destroyed his argument.
Leiter here recognizes a potential conflict in Nietzsche's critique of truth and his clear prescription of his moral theory as truth, but he solves the problem through a charitable reading, reminding the interlocutor that Nietzsche's critique of will to truth is on grounds that the truth uncovered is harmful to life, while his moral theory represents (a) truth which is life affirming and noble. (Leiter, 2002, 280)

(4) Tracing an Unbroken Line of Succession from Origin to Item of Value
How can Nietzsche's thought be traced from origin (anti MPS sentiment) to item of value (immoralist a priori)? While these two conceptions are closely related, they remain distinct as the immoralist a priori is the valorized presupposition, emerging at the first in anti-MPS sentiment. It is at this point that Nietzsche's epistemological and metaphysical grounding facilitates the promulgation of the presupposition through anti MPS sentiment: in short, agreeable cognitive theory and metaphysical considerations are needed to justify the validity of the end result as emerging from the beginning point.

Leiter observes that Nietzsche has little concern for theories of knowledge and has in fact no fully developed theory of mind. (Leiter, 2002, 87). Any binding theory of knowledge would require an acknowledgement of relevant noumenal reality

– an admission Nietzsche seems profoundly unwilling to make - perhaps because the greater consequence of such an admission would be the authoritative nature of truth not necessarily affirming to life – the very basis of MPS. Additionally, Nietzsche perceives will to truth as seductive and worthy of suspicion (BGE 1:1-2) and seems convinced that "the way does not exist" (Z:III:SoG:2). Thus his epistemology, though not easily quantifiable, is not inconsistent with his ethical presupposition.

Neitzsche's perspectivism serves him well on this point as a metaphysical grounding: his denial of relevant noumenal reality (the world is not real – Salter, NPR, 1915) with his affirmation of phenomena (reality interpreted is relevant reality – we make the world real – Salter, NPR, 1915) is again consistent with his opposition to MPS. He is decidedly naturalistic, rejecting in no uncertain terms any degree of otherworldliness and condemning those who would offer an opposing interpretation:

> I entreat you, my brothers, remain true to the earth, and do not believe those who speak to you of superterrestrial hopes! They are poisoners, whether they know it or not. They are despisers of life, atrophying and self-poisoned men, of whom the earth is weary: so let them be gone! (Z:ZP:3)

His commitment to naturalism is profound, leaving some to interpret that loyalty as akin to religious fervor:

> The instinct for something perfect, or as perfect as the conditions of existence will allow, is, I take it, the ruling impulse in Nietzsche. Essentially he was a religious man...As I read him, deep instincts of reverence preponderate in him, instincts that have their ordinary food and sustenance in the thought of God. But as his

> scientific conscience forbade him that belief, the instincts were driven to seek other satisfaction and found it measurably in the thought of the possibilities of mankind. (Salter, NMA, 1915)

Leiter observes another potential riddle here: despite numerous statements favoring some form of naturalism, Nietzsche seems to distance from naturalism, citing it as a form of asceticism (GM:III:25). Again, Leiter resolves the inconsistency through a charitable reading, asserting that while Nietzsche does shun a type of naturalism which would relate to asceticism, he holds to a naturalism which is "fundamentally non-ascetic," since it frees the higher man from the false conceptions of MPS. (Leiter, 2002, 283)

As in Salter's observation, Nietzsche's metaphysics is driven by a prior commitment to naturalism, and is necessary - along with his (non) epistemology - for the cogency of his presupposition and conclusion.

(5) Steps Preserve Value
Bakewell describes Nietzsche's teachings at first glance to be "so bizarre, so absurd, so blasphemous, that one is tempted to set them aside as simply unworthy of consideration" (Bakewell, 1899), but through deeper inquiry, and despite numerous prima facie inconsistencies, it seems evident that Nietzsche indeed succeeds at putting forth a unified doctrine of moral skepticism. His goal? Affirmation of life. MPS is unacceptable - despite its success at averting suicidal nihilism – since it degrades and subjugates life. His critique of MPS is

> ...no more than a strong way of saying that much of what passes for absolutely right and good is only true within certain very narrow limitations, and that there are

impulses, supposed to be very virtuous, which tend on the whole to do mankind more harm than good. (Benn, 1908)

Nietzsche's project achieves the same end – dismissing suicidal nihilism, but does it with a powerful side effect: explaining human experience, and in particular giving suffering a meaning, in a hopeful way. While his model is highly prescriptive, Nietzsche seems insistent that his conception is not in itself MPS with a different face, but is merely "a truth," he says: "This is my good and evil; he has silenced thereby the mole and the dwarf who says: 'Good for all, evil for all'" (Z:III:SoG:2), and again: "Unchanging good and evil does not exist...And he who has to be a creator in good and evil, truly, has first to be a destroyer and break values." (Z:II:OSO)

This creation of good and evil is a crucial point for Nietzsche, and requires a better explanation than that of the traditional four-step process in the development of good and evil: (1) usefulness – unegoistic acts were called good by those to whom they were useful, (2) forgetting – due to the routine praising of said acts, the reason for the praise (usefulness) was forgotten, and (3) the routine praise, as it continued, gave way to (4) the error of viewing the unegoistic act to be good in itself. Nietzsche seems to take issue with this four-step diagnosis at one crucial point: the determination of the goodness of the unegoistic act is not made by those to whom it useful, but rather it is made by the one committing the act – specifically the noble, mighty, etc. This attribution of goodness gives rise to a promulgated superiority on the part of the unegoistic actor – the conditions for which find themselves most satisfactory in a decline of the aristocracy. Nietzsche's primary (or at least initial) disagreement here is a matter of perspective.

With certainty, Nietzsche dismisses ontological good and evil, yet still reckons good and bad to be important factors in the human condition. Particularly, good is that which affirms life — even life itself:

> And now what is the final aim which Nietzsche proposes? It is no other than life, and particularly the highest ranges of life. Man is higher than the animal, and there may be something higher than man, i.e., than man as we ordinarily know him. (Salter, NMA, 1915)

What then is reality? Nietzsche translates it with the hermeneutic key that is will to power as the highest expression of affirmation of life:

> That is your entire will, you wisest men; it is a will to power; and that is so even when you talk of good and evil and of the assessment of values.... Where I found a living creature, there I found will to power; and even in the will of the servant I found the will to be master. (Z:II:OSO)

This will, while expressed in all life, is epitomized in the higher man: "The Overman is the meaning of the earth. Let your will say: The Overman shall be the meaning of the earth!" (Z:ZP:3)

This Overman possesses five requisite characteristics: (1) he is motivated by intense commitment to responsibility and work, the higher man is distinctively individualistic and approaches others as instruments - making something out of them which would contribute to his greater project; (2) the higher man possesses an instinctive drivenness and commitment governed by the organizing idea (Leiter speaks of the goal of completing the unifying project); (3) the higher man is healthy and resilient: he is a non-pessimist, focused on self-restoration; (4) the higher man is unafraid of eternal recurrence — this represents an unconditional welcoming of events including suffering; and (5) the higher man is self-reverent —

noble, rather than submitting to the rules and values of the ages, he determines them by way of a self-reverence that both keeps him from the mediocrity of submission to MPS, and frees him as a determinate force of values. (Leiter, 2002, 115-122)

Such a man seems, in Nietzsche's estimation worthy of the original presupposed moral skepticism. The Overman is the culmination of Nietzsche's project, justifying the (at times questionable) steps taken to arrive at this ideal affirmation of life. The Overman, by way of will to power, provides a more plausible alternate narrative to the prevailing MPS and ascetic ideal. But does Nietzsche work from his presupposed a priori skepticism to the Overman, or does he justify the Overman by method of moral skepticism? He adds to the intrigue of this question when he says, "Our whole procedure is only morality turning against its previous form."[148] The pedigree of Nietzschean thought offers, in this writer's opinion, a plausible narrative of explanation for Nietzsche's impetus and priority, however, it determines neither with certainty. The value, then, of such an inquiry lies not in any definitive conclusions, but rather as a hermeneutic device for interpreting key elements of Nietzschean thought.

5:1-20 Conclusion: Fear God and Enjoy His Gifts

Solomon here moves from the recounting of his findings to the imperative mood, challenging his readers to take action based on the vanities demonstrated thus far.

(4:17, Heb.[149]) [1] Keep thy foot when thou goest to the house of God, and be more ready to hear, than to give the sacrifice of fools: for they consider not that they do evil.

Guard (*sh'mor*, imptv.) your foot...watch your step. Beware the sacrifice of fools (*k'sil*, same as in 4:13). A readiness to hear (*shama*) is the means to avoid such a sacrifice – en evil (*rah*) sacrifice.

While the under the sun thinking man listens only to that which is under the sun, Solomon commands an eagerness to hear. Hear what? The teachings and commandments of God (special revelation). In these previous Old Testament instances *shama* was used as a universal imperative for the people of Israel: for example,

"Hear, O Israel, the statutes and judgments which I speak in your ears this day, that ye may learn them and keep, and do them." (Deut. 5:1)

"Hear therefore, O Israel, and observe to do it; that it may be well with thee, and that ye may increase mightily, as the LORD God of thy fathers hath promised thee...." (Deut. 6:3)

"Hear, O Israel: The Lord our God is one LORD." (Deut. 6:4)

Importantly these commands relate to the hearing of the word of God, and the expected results of fearing God and acting in obedience.

[2] Be not rash with thy mouth, and let not thine heart be hasty to utter anything before God: for God is in heaven, and thou upon earth: therefore let thy words be few.

Be not rash (*bahal, speude* in the LXX) – hasty (NASB).

Let not the heart be rapid (*tachunato* in the LXX) to bring forth anything before God.

God is in heaven (no def. art. here), you are on the land (*ha arutz*, includes the def. art.) – contrast similar in concept to Isaiah 55:8-11. God not only has ordered under the sun, and thus He is intimately acquainted with all in that realm, but He far excels that as well. Man, on the other hand, is limited to a very incomplete under the sun perspective.

[3] For a dream cometh through the multitude of business; and a fool's voice is known by multitude of words.

Dreams have many causes and foolishness is associated with many words. Speak carefully.

[4] When thou vowest a vow unto God, defer not to pay it; for he hath no pleasure in fools: pay that which thou hast vowed.

5:1-20: Conclusion: Fear God and Enjoy His Gifts

[5] Better is it that thou shouldest not vow, than that thou shouldest vow and not pay.

As the Sovereign Creator, God has no need to receive the vows (*neder*, promises) of men, yet He takes them seriously, and Solomon here gives an insight to unveil the mystery of what is the advantage under the sun for the wise and the disadvantage for fools: God does not delight in fools (*k'sil*). As the Sovereign, and the One bearing the greater and proper perspective of the true nature of things, mankind must concern himself with how God valuates things. Foolishness is no delight to Him, and thus should be of no delight to us. This represents more than a divine command mode of valuation; better stated it represents a divine character mode of valuation: the value of an action can be determined by the level of delight (or lack thereof) God takes in it.

[6] Suffer not thy mouth to cause thy flesh to sin; neither say thou before the angel, that it was an error: wherefore should God be angry at thy voice, and destroy the work of thine hands?

Solomon uses the unpaid vow as an example of this ethic. Such foolish behavior angers (*qatsaph*) (*orge* in the LXX – wrath) God. God metes out consequences to such foolishness: He may (in His time and at His discretion) destroy the work (*ma'asah*) of the fool's hands. By avoiding such foolishness, one keeps his work or activity from risk (not of being destroyed simply, but rather of being destroyed as a consequence for foolishness – there is a significant beyond the sun distinction between these two.)

[7] For in the multitude of dreams and many words there are also divers vanities: but fear thou God.

Dreams and words are subject to *hebel*, but the fear of God is not. Thus the imperative is the grounding of wisdom: fear God.

[8] If thou seest the oppression of the poor, and violent perverting of judgment and justice in a province, marvel not at the matter: for he that is higher than the highest regardeth; and there be higher than they.

The reader is not to be surprised by oppression (*osheq* - injury) or violence (denial, NASB) of justice and righteousness, for the Highest One is higher than those who guard (*shamar*) or preside over judgment. God sees, God allows, God recompenses. Thus He is to be feared.

[9] Moreover the profit of the earth is for all: the king himself is served by the field.

And a good land is for all, a king to a field or land is serving himself (niphal participle, *ne'evad* - reflexive). An example of the injustice observed in the previous verse: the land is for all, yet the king makes it serve him. Only divine oversight can fully remedy such injustices, and human efforts guided by the fear of God can minimize them for a time.

Philosophical Parallel: Consensual Democracy

John Locke (1632-1704), in addition to his import in the field of epistemology, is one of the most significant contributors to the present day ideas of consensual democracy. The Declaration of Independence and Constitution borrow heavily from his ideas.

Similar to Hobbes' social contract and self-preservation, Locke's ideas are distinct in his understanding of state of nature:

nature is the workmanship of God, who grants beings natural rights, including self-preservation, property rights (this is a critical point for Locke, that property rights are a fundamental part of the right to self-preservation – without property rights there can be no self-preservation. Note the contrast with Marxism on this point), personal liberty, and the right to punish violators of the law of nature.

Since natural law has no intrinsic civil law, there is need of a political society of indifferent judges (akin to Hobbes' Leviathan). By consenting to join society individuals give up (only) the right of punishment to the executive branch of society. The rule of law is the basis of society, thus government stewards law (by consent of the people). Locke discusses as well the importance of representative government, with checks and balances (he sees three branches: executive [having judiciary power] legislative, and federative [to make war and peace alliances].

Locke's system does not seek (in contrast to Marxism) to resolve the depravity of human nature, but only to guarantee that basic natural rights are protected. Locke recognizes these natural rights as originating from God, and as a result his governmental system, insofar as it acknowledges God as first principle and operates accordingly, is not in conflict with Solomonic principles.

Primary Source Excerpt: Locke: The Second Treatise of Civil Government (1690)

From Chapter VIII: Of the Beginning of Political Societies.
Sec. 95. MEN being, as has been said, by nature, all free, equal, and independent, no one can be put out of this estate, and subjected to the political power of another, without his own consent. The only way whereby any one divests himself of his

natural liberty, and puts on the bonds of civil society, is by agreeing with other men to join and unite into a community for their comfortable, safe, and peaceable living one amongst another, in a secure enjoyment of their properties, and a greater security against any, that are not of it. This any number of men may do, because it injures not the freedom of the rest; they are left as they were in the liberty of the state of nature. When any number of men have so consented to make one community or government, they are thereby presently incorporated, and make one body politic, wherein the majority have a right to act and conclude the rest.

Sec. 96. For when any number of men have, by the consent of every individual, made a community, they have thereby made that community one body, with a power to act as one body, which is only by the will and determination of the majority: for that which acts any community, being only the consent of the individuals of it, and it being necessary to that which is one body to move one way; it is necessary the body should move that way whither the greater force carries it, which is the consent of the majority: or else it is impossible it should act or continue one body, one community, which the consent of every individual that united into it, agreed that it should; and so everyone is bound by that consent to be concluded by the majority. And therefore we see, that in assemblies, impowered to act by positive laws, where no number is set by that positive law which impowers them, the act of the majority passes for the act of the whole, and of course determines, as having, by the law of nature and reason, the power of the whole.

Sec. 97. And thus every man, by consenting with others to make one body politic under one government, puts himself under an obligation, to every one of that society, to submit to the determination of the majority, and to be concluded by it; or else this original compact, whereby he with others incorporates into one society, would signify nothing, and be no compact, if he be left free, and under no other ties than he was in before in the state of nature. For what appearance would there be of any compact? what new engagement if he were no farther tied by any decrees of the society, than he himself thought fit, and did actually consent to? This would be still as great a liberty, as he himself had before his compact, or anyone else in the state of nature hath, who may submit himself, and consent to any acts of it if he thinks fit.

Sec. 98. For if the consent of the majority shall not, in reason, be received as the act of the whole, and conclude every individual; nothing but the consent of every individual can make anything to be the act of the whole: but such a consent is next to impossible ever to be had, if we consider the infirmities of health, and avocations of business, which in a number, though much less than that of a common-wealth, will necessarily keep many away from the public assembly. To which if we add the variety of opinions, and contrariety of interests, which unavoidably happen in all collections of men, the coming into society upon such terms would be only like Cato's coming into the theatre, only to go out again. Such a constitution as this would make the mighty Leviathan of a shorter duration, than the feeblest creatures, and not let it outlast the day it was born in: which cannot be supposed, till we can think, that rational creatures should desire and constitute societies only to be dissolved: for where the majority cannot conclude the rest, there they cannot act as one body, and consequently will be immediately dissolved again.

Sec. 99. Whosoever therefore out of a state of nature unite into a community, must be understood to give up all the power, necessary to the ends for which they unite into society, to the majority of the community, unless they expresly agreed in any number greater than the majority. And this is done by barely agreeing to unite into one political society, which is all the compact that is, or needs be, between the individuals, that enter into, or make up a commonwealth. And thus that, which begins and actually constitutes any political society, is nothing but the consent of any number of freemen capable of a majority to unite and incorporate into such a society. And this is that, and that only, which did, or could give beginning to any lawful government in the world...

Sec. 100-118 omitted.

Sec. 119. Every man being, as has been shewed, naturally free, and nothing being able to put him into subjection to any earthly power, but only his own consent; it is to be considered, what shall be understood to be a sufficient declaration of a man's consent, to make him subject to the laws of any government. There is a common distinction of an express and a tacit consent, which will concern our present case. Nobody doubts but an express consent, of any man entering into any society, makes him a perfect member of that society, a subject of that government. The difficulty is, what ought to be looked upon as a tacit consent, and how far it binds, i.e. how far any one shall be looked on to have consented, and thereby submitted to any government, where he has made no expressions of it at all. And to this I say, that every man, that hath any possessions, or enjoyment, of any part of the dominions of any government, doth thereby give his tacit consent, and is as far forth obliged to obedience to the laws of that government, during such enjoyment, as anyone under it;

whether this his possession be of land, to him and his heirs forever, or a lodging only for a week; or whether it be barely travelling freely on the highway; and in effect, it reaches as far as the very being of any one within the territories of that government.

Sec. 120. To understand this the better, it is fit to consider, that every man, when he at first incorporates himself into any common-wealth, he, by his uniting himself thereunto, annexed also, and submits to the community, those possessions, which he has, or shall acquire, that do not already belong to any other government: for it would be a direct contradiction, for anyone to enter into society with others for the securing and regulating of property; and yet to suppose his land, whose property is to be regulated by the laws of the society, should be exempt from the jurisdiction of that government, to which he himself, the proprietor of the land, is a subject. By the same act therefore, whereby any one unites his person, which was before free, to any common-wealth, by the same he unites his possessions, which were before free, to it also; and they become, both of them, person and possession, subject to the government and dominion of that common-wealth, as long as it hath a being. Whoever therefore, from thenceforth, by inheritance, purchase, permission, or otherways, enjoys any part of the land, so annexed to, and under the government of that common-wealth, must take it with the condition it is under; that is, of submitting to the government of the common-wealth, under whose jurisdiction it is, as far forth as any subject of it.

Sec. 121. But since the government has a direct jurisdiction only over the land, and reaches the possessor of it, (before he has actually incorporated himself in the society) only as he dwells upon, and enjoys that; the obligation any one is under, by virtue of such enjoyment, to submit to the government, begins and ends with the enjoyment; so that whenever the owner, who has given nothing but such a tacit consent to the government, will, by donation, sale, or otherwise, quit the said possession, he is at liberty to go and incorporate himself into any other commonwealth; or to agree with others to begin a new one, *in vacuis locis*, in any part of the world, they can find free and unpossessed: whereas he, that has once, by actual agreement, and any express declaration, given his consent to be of any commonwealth, is perpetually and indispensably obliged to be, and remain unalterably a subject to it, and can never be again in the liberty of the state of nature; unless, by any calamity, the government he was under comes to be dissolved; or else by some public act cuts him off from being any longer a member of it.

Sec. 122. But submitting to the laws of any country, living quietly, and enjoying privileges and protection under them, makes not a man a member of that society: this is only a local protection and homage due to and from all those, who, not being in a state of war, come within the territories belonging to any government, to all parts whereof the force of its laws extends. But this no more makes a man a member of that society, a perpetual subject of that common-wealth, than it would make a man a subject to another, in whose family he found it convenient to abide for some time; though, whilst he continued in it, he were obliged to comply with the laws, and submit to the government he found there. And thus we see, that foreigners, by living all their lives under another government, and enjoying the privileges and protection of it, though they are bound, even in conscience, to submit to its administration, as far forth as any denison; yet do not thereby come to be *subjects or members of that common-wealth*. Nothing can make any man so, but his actually entering into it by positive engagement, and express promise and compact. This is that, which I think, concerning the beginning of political societies, and that consent which makes any one a member of any common-wealth.

5:1-20: Conclusion: Fear God and Enjoy His Gifts (cont.)

[10] He that loveth silver shall not be satisfied with silver; nor he that loveth abundance with increase: this is also vanity.

The principle is that human greed (e.g., the king's in v. 9) is never satiated. Thus cultivating and acquiring is meaningless.

[11] When goods increase, they are increased that eat them: and what good is there to the owners thereof, saving the beholding of them with their eyes?

With primarily non-mechanized production of goods in Solomon's day, in order for there to be great increase of goods, there must be increase in labor, and thus a net percentage decrease in net profit. The more one produces the higher the cost. Thus what is the value of producing more?

[12] The sleep of a labouring man is sweet, whether he eat little or much: but the abundance of the rich will not suffer him to sleep.

Sweet is the sleep of the worker (*abad*) or slave (*doulou*, in the LXX) whether little or much he eats. Note the principle of opposition at work in these examples: where there is advantage there is also disadvantage (the increase of production vs. increase in cost and sweet sleep vs. relative poverty). Thus any advantage under the sun is not really advantage.

[13] There is a sore evil which I have seen under the sun, namely, riches kept for the owners thereof to their hurt.
[14] But those riches perish by evil travail: and he begetteth a son, and there is nothing in his hand.
[15] As he came forth of his mother's womb, naked shall he return to go as he came, and shall take nothing of his labour, which he may carry away in his hand.
[16] And this also is a sore evil, that in all points as he came, so shall he go: and what profit hath he that hath laboured for the wind?

A sore evil or evil disease (*ra'ah cholah*), Solomon will reference this example twice as such (the second occurrence in v. 16): the one who hoards his wealth, which then perishes in an evil affair (*b'inyan ra*) (a bad investment, NASB), he begets a son who enters the world with nothing, nor shall he take anything out of the world. Twice called an evil disease, this illustrates the total emptiness of any pursuit, as - in an under the sun perspective - there is no lasting product.

[17] All his days also he eateth in darkness, and he hath much sorrow and wrath with his sickness.

The previous examples also represent best case scenarios: the worker who sleeps sweetly, the increase in production, etc., for not all workers sleep sweetly, as there are many things that can disturb sleep; likewise, increase in cost does not guarantee increase in production. Even in the best case scenario there is no lasting advantage.

Hobbes' dreary description of life (solitary, poor, nasty, brutish and short) is not unlike Solomon's conclusion here: Just as in all his days in darkness (*b'choshek*) he eats and has sorrow great (*ka'as rabah*) and sickness (*qatzeph*) and indignation (*chaliu*, or evil, or disease). This *is* the human condition under the sun. What then *ought* man to do?

[18] Behold that which I have seen: it is good and comely for one to eat and to drink, and to enjoy the good of all his labour that he taketh under the sun all the days of his life, which God giveth him: for it is his portion.

It is good (*tov*) and beautiful (*yapheh*, fitting, NASB) to eat and to drink and to see goods (*tova*) in all his labor or activity which he works under the sun all the days of his life which God has given to him for it is his portion. God has granted to man a portion – an allotment – to function and to see the goods in that functioning. With an under the sun perspective one cannot see the goods in the activity, for there seems no lasting product. Yet, with a beyond the sun perspective, the goods are evident.

[19] Every man also to whom God hath given riches and wealth, and hath given him power to eat thereof, and to take his portion, and to rejoice in his labour; this is the gift of God.

To rejoice (*samach*, be glad) in his effort (*ba'amalu*) this is a gift (*mattath*, or *doma* in the LXX) of God. (To each man that He gives it.)

[20] For he shall not much remember the days of his life; because God answereth him in the joy of his heart.

How is this to be perceived as a gift? Man does not (or shall not) often recount or consider (*y'zakar*, Qal imperfect) days (*yomi*) of his life, for God answers (*ma'anah*) him in gladness of his heart.

The daily grind and the cycles of life are not the primary instrument God uses to answer mankind's questions regarding ultimate meaning. He gives gladness of heart, that man might see the beauty of life with Him and might by experiencing the lack thereof recognize that life under the sun without a beyond the sun perspective is not what man was designed to do.

6:1-12 Vanity: Riches, Wealth, and Honor Under the Sun

Solomon turns once again from his message of hope to the recounting of the futility he has observed:

[1] There is an evil which I have seen under the sun, and it is common among men:
[2] A man to whom God hath given riches, wealth, and honour, so that he wanteth nothing for his soul of all that he desireth, yet God giveth him not power to eat thereof, but a stranger eateth it: this is vanity, and it is an evil disease.

It is common (*rab*) or abundant.

Yet God giveth him not power (*shalat*) – as in 5:19, but a strange man (*ish nakri*) he eats it.

Meaninglessness and an evil disease – to the man of 5:19 God gives the power to enjoy eating, drinking and seeing goods in labor. To this man, He does not. Common grace can be seen in that God does give (*nathan*) the many provisions, yet God has not empowered (should not be read as not given, as in the KJV) this man to eat, but instead gives to another. Under the sun this is futility and an evil malady. One might question the goodness of God at this point; nonetheless, Solomon marches forward on the premise that God gives and holds back as He chooses, and

He as Sovereign Creator has the right and the perspective to do so. Nonetheless, such acts of God must be viewed under the sun as quite awful. This presents a marked contrast between a naturalistic worldview and a Biblical one: what God views as appropriate man questions and even despises.

[3] If a man beget an hundred children, and live many years, so that the days of his years be many, and his soul be not filled with good, and also that he have no burial; I say, that an untimely birth is better than he.

[4] For he cometh in with vanity, and departeth in darkness, and his name shall be covered with darkness.

One whose life is long and productive but not filled with joy and honor, better the miscarriage or abortion (ha nephel) than he. What a harsh statement: better to have never escaped the womb alive than to live under the sun in such a manner.

[5] Moreover he hath not seen the sun, nor known any thing: this hath more rest than the other.

The miscarriage or abortion has neither seen or known, and thus, taking a shortcut to the grave skips the futility that comes with "seeing the sun."

[6] Yea, though he live a thousand years twice told, yet hath he seen no good: do not all go to one place?

If the end result is the same – a home in *sheol*, the grave, what profit is there in seeing the under the sun existence?

[7] All the labour of man is for his mouth, and yet the appetite is not filled.

The basic needs of life are never fully satiated, and man pursues survival so that he can delay the inevitable day of his death. To what end?

[8] For what hath the wise more than the fool? what hath the poor, that knoweth to walk before the living?

If the final destination be the same for all, then what is the significance in avoiding foolishness and poverty?

[9] Better is the sight of the eyes than the wandering of the desire: this is also vanity and vexation of spirit.

Better the view (*mareh*) of the eyes than the wandering (*mehalak*, or walking) spirit (*nephesh*). The wandering spirit (the one with no direction or purpose) is meaningless and inner strife. Why is the view of the eyes better? Solomon has extolled the goodness of seeing (or observing) the goods in all the activities of life (3:13; 5:18).

[10] That which hath been is named already, and it is known that it is man: neither may he contend with him that is mightier than he.

Despite the ignorance of each new generation, man is well defined, and he cannot rule as an equal with (*diyn im*) the mightier (*shehatqeyf*) than him. This is a strong contrast between impotent man and omnipotent God.

[11] Seeing there be many things that increase vanity, what is man the better?

Many things can increase the already pervasive

meaninglessness. What better (*ma yother*) to (or for) man (*l'adam*)? Or, if the pursuit of many things only make the situation worse, then what is a better path for man to take?

[12] *For who knoweth what is good for man in this life, all the days of his vain life which he spendeth as a shadow? for who can tell a man what shall be after him under the sun?*

For who can answer '*what is good?*' with certainty? Who knows (*yada*) what is good (*tov*) for a man during his fleeting life? This is the quintessential philosophical question. Solomon will answer it, and already has: only God knows, and only God can prescribe for man with absolute certainty. Who can tell the future under the sun?

Philosophy with pride takes up the task of seeking to find the ought for man, but surely even philosophy would cower at the prospect that discovering *the ought* is not possible without first having a certainty of *the what will be.*

Thus there is no under the sun advantage of riches, wealth, honor – or even wisdom, without the absolute certainty that only God can provide. Even the secularist is beginning to understand the impossibility of certainty under the sun.

Excursus: Postmodernism and Globalism: Concentric Forces Impacting Theology

Characterizations

Postmodernism

The premodern world was one of traditional authorities – feudal lords and ecclesiastical hierarchies – which shaped society in every respect. From economics to education (in most cases, lack thereof), the individual was not a unit of impact, but rather a means to an end. The problem then, was not one of authority,

6:1-12 Vanity: Riches, Wealth, and Honor Under the Sun 333

but rather one of terribly abused and falsely assumed authorities.

But by the fifteenth and sixteenth centuries, the power base of these authorities began to buckle, in no small part due to the Reformation, begun in 1517, and of course pre-Reformation developments, including Gutenburg's printing press (1445) and William Tyndale's (illegal) use of it, as he translated the New Testament into the common vernacular in 1526. English citizens were able for the first time to read the Bible in their own tongue, and what resulted was a sweeping recognition that the religious system which dominated their society bore no resemblance to what was described on the actual pages of the Holy Book. Also of immeasurable import was Columbus' 1492 voyage, which, even as it shrunk the world, made the horizon that much broader. The previously unthinkable became plausible. The world was indeed much bigger than it had earlier seemed.

By the late eighteenth century, and inspired in no small part by the Reformation and the scientific progress of Galileo (1564-1642 A.D.) and Newton (1643-1727 A.D.), the era of Enlightenment brought with it a new momentum leading to, "a distinct epoch of historical development marking the inauguration of the economic and socio-cultural disruptions which founded industrial capitalism and the nation-state."[150] The modern world was born, with a view toward the progress of man in understanding, and to at least some degree, conquering the world around him. The collective trust had shifted from the traditional authorities of premodernity to the power of individual reason in the modern age. Descartes' *cogito ergo sum* created an inviting epistemology wherein reason bridged cultural and religious gaps. The great hope was now fixed upon the idea of collective progress and agreement – primarily through the vehicle of reason. But even as technological progress increased by virtue of reason and the scientific method, world war, holocaust, and numerous other sociopolitical, socioeconomic and religious failures proved the two ideas of progress and agreement to be unachievable by the modern mindset.

Fueled by Kierkegard's subjectivity and Nietzche's rejection of absolutes, post-World War II into the 1960's brought a rapid development of postmodernist ideas and methodology, acknowledging the failures of the modern era. Derrida (deconstruction), Foucault (society and power), Lyotard (literary theory and critique of the metanarrative), and Baudrillard (social theory) are just a few key developers of postmodernism, and these gave rise to a new postmodern era.

Postmodernism is a way of doing science – of interpreting the world in an age of postmodernity. It is decidedly not modern and seeks to correct errors of modernity. As Vanhoozer puts it

> Postmodern[ism] is largely a reaction to the subject-object distinction and to its concomitant assumption that truth can be discovered by induction and deduction.[151]

Rozzi, et al, provide a secular scientific perspective on the delineations between the three eras, particularly in the context of scientific observation:

> Pre-Modern represents the emphasis on observation of the natural world started by scholars toward the end of the Middle-Ages. Modern, includes the scientist, who no longer perceives natural beings of processes in themselves but rather as phenomena represented in his/her mind, that may or may not correspond with the "external" material world. Post-Modern, emphasizes the influences of the social and cultural context upon

scientific observations and explanations. (Rozzi, et al, 1998)

Due to its consideration of previously de-emphasized factors (namely social and cultural context), postmodernism is perceived by its adherents as a much better way – willing, of course, to utilize implements of modernity, but unwilling to submit to the modern ideas of inevitable progress through rationality and science,[152] and certainly refusing to submit to any singularity of truth beside the relative realities of cultural impact.

It is at this point that postmodernity and post-modernism are most easily distinguishable, with postmodernity referencing a specific era and postmodernism encompassing *a broad and somewhat unsystematic mode of interpretation.*

Globalization
Thomas Friedman describes globalization as developing in three major stages. Globalization 1.0 begins in 1492 with Columbus' voyage to the New World and concludes around 1800. This was an era fueled by nationalism. The focus here is particularly on the country as a unit. Globalization 2.0 spanned roughly 1800-2000, and was energized by multinational commerce. The basic unit here is the corporation. Globalization 3.0, Friedman asserts, began with the dawning of the twenty-first century, and finds it distinctiveness in its empowering of individuals to act globally.[153] Of course here, the basic unit is the individual. Note the progression from larger units of impact (country) to smaller (individual). And while Friedman draws the chronological boundaries, Bauman draws the significance, iterating globalization as

> The intractable fate of the world, an irreversible process; it is also a process which affects us all in the same measure and in the same way. We are all being "globalized...."[154]

Clearly, (and by very definition) this process has broad impact. The process defined, for some, focuses on the integration of world markets, whereas on a broader scale it must also include the integration of diverse cultural elements. Appadurai characterizes the world of today as "an interactive system in a sense that is strikingly new,"[155] emphasizing that previous sustained cultural interaction came through the catalysts of warfare and religion (e.g., conversion efforts of missionaries). But in recent times, the agora has become the arena of commonality enabling sustained cultural interaction. Consequently, as global marketplace interaction increases, so does non-trade (the arts, philosophies, worldviews, traditions, etc. – the marketplace of ideas) cultural interaction. To this point, cultural globalization has been largely dependent on marketplace globalization (a relationship mourned by many).

Connections

In postmodernity, borders of all types are becoming increasingly obsolete. Previously national borders are now becoming transnational. Transnational trade agreements and proposals such as NAFTA[156], FTAA[157] and CAFTA[158] all find their genesis in recognition of the inefficiencies of physical borders, and seek to create a new and broad borderlessness for efficient trade.

Paralleling this transnational movement is the decline of the nation-state. Appadurai observes that an examination of the present status of worldwide nation-states will reveal that

...border wars, culture wars, runaway inflation, massive immigrant populations, or serious flights of capital threaten sovereignty in many of them. Even where state sovereignty is apparently intact, state legitimacy is frequently insecure. Even in nation-states as apparently secure as the United States, Japan, and Germany, debates about race rights, membership and loyalty, citizenship and authority are no longer culturally peripheral.[159]

Impacted by the growing fluidity of corporate entities and the rise of supranational agencies, the nation state, with its hard and fast physical borders, is moving toward extinction. The face of national sovereignties has seemingly changed forever, leaving whom in control? Bauman's answer:

...no one now seems to be in control. Worse still – it is not clear what "being in control" could, under the circumstances, be like.[160]

So, it is at this point that Bauman has unpacked the real heart of globalization:

The deepest meaning conveyed by the idea of globalization is that of the indeterminate, unruly, and self propelled character of world affairs; the absence of a centre, of a controlling desk, of a board of directors, of a managerial office. Globalization is Jowitt's "new world disorder" under another name.[161]

This power vacuum of sorts seems a recent reality. Previously, global politics represented a struggle for each state to maintain its sovereignty. More recently, the global scene has produced efforts to enable groups of states to work congruously. These latest efforts necessarily reduce the individual state's sovereignty and give birth to a new set of masters who govern very indirectly through pressure upon national governments.[162] The focus of the state then becomes local control as defined by the new global authorities – thus the state maintains its identity and a degree of its power while divesting itself of its own sovereignty, a condition which greatly inhibits the ability of those at the local level to impact change:

> One of the most seminal consequences of the new global freedom of movement is that it becomes increasingly difficult, perhaps altogether impossible, to re-forge social issues into effective collective action.[163]

It seems however that while willing to tolerate a global power vacuum, the collective states are not at all eager for this organized power vacuum to be filled by a single entity. To assuage Orwellian fears the process of globalization is made palatable by a philosophical accomplice – the postmodernism-driven idea that new world disorder is tenable and can be maintained indefinitely. The globalizing quest is for uniformity, leading to conformity, the dark side of which is intolerance.[164] Postmodernism hopes to provide an antidote to this dark side, providing the methodological framework for an egalitarian society with no one at the top who can administer such undesirable intolerance. As long as the postmodernist mindset is maintained, the globalization process can continue with minimal alarm for those most impacted by the process.

Globalization and postmodernism share a notable interdependence: postmodernism *needs* globalization in order to heighten the awareness and advancement of plurality of voice

6:1-12 Vanity: Riches, Wealth, and Honor Under the Sun

and diversity; globalization *needs* postmodernism in order to make palatable newly developing global power structures.

Consequences

The Decline of Absolute Truth

From the postmodernist perspective, with the passing of the (supposedly) premodern idea that truth can be achieved through revelation and the modern idea that truth is derived from reason, all that remains is the conclusion that truth can only be obtained within a cultural framework, and even this allowance there is purported to be a multiplicity of truth due to differences in hermeneutic methodology, and thus, there is no basis for absolute truth. In fact, the only absolute matter of reality here is that there can be no absolute truth independent of its cultural context and impact. Revelation and reason both become by-products of culture, and nothing more. Biblical claims of authority and super-relevance (2 Tim. 3:16-17; 2 Pet. 1:20-21) become simple literary devices and offer no confidence of legitimacy. Culturally the result is reminiscent of theocratic Israel during the twelfth-tenth centuries BC, when every man did what was right in his own eyes (Judg. 17:6).

The Hermeneutic Problem

A focus on broader cultural/theological referents has contributed to the neglect of detailed analysis of what the Bible actually teaches. The postmodernist emphasis on cultural relevance produces a theology developing from the outside in – from cultural response as a hermeneutic key to understanding the textual base.

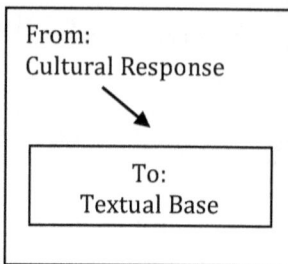 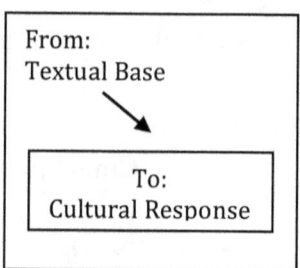

Lynn White, in his groundbreaking 1967 article demonstrates this *response* hermeneutic, when he makes such statements as:

> God planned all of this [creation] explicitly for man's benefit and rule; no item in the physical creation had any purpose save to serve man's purposes.... Christianity is the most anthropocentric religion the world has ever seen...[and] Christianity made it possible to exploit nature in a mood of indifference to the feelings of natural objects.... (White, 1967)

These conclusions can be drawn from a near-historical cultural response hermeneutic, but stand in contradistinction to necessary conclusions of the literal grammatical-historical hermeneutic (applied to such passages as Ps. 24:1; Is. 2:22; 40:15-17, 26; Jn. 3:30; Rom. 1:20; Col. 1:16, etc.).

White's claims are significant to his major argument that the (failed) modern idea of progress is "rooted in and indefensible apart from a Judeo-Christian teleology" and it serves as a justification for his thesis:

> We shall continue to have a worsening ecologic crisis until we reject the Christian axiom that nature has no reason for existence save to serve man. (White, 1967)

Inarguably this is a hermeneutic issue the impact of which is truly monolithic.

The Pluralizing of Voice and the Rise of Fundamentalism

The postmodernist perspective is characterized by an impassioned rejection of certain foundations of the modern era. The problems (real and perceived) of the present world are placed at the footstep of the modern era. White describes his solution to ecological crisis, saying

> As a beginning we should try to clarify our thinking by looking, in some historical depth, at the presuppositions that underlie modern technology and science. Science was traditionally aristocratic, speculative, intellectual in intent; technology was lower-class, empirical, action oriented. The quite sudden fusion of these two towards the middle of the 19th century, is surely related to the slightly prior and contemporary democratic revolutions which, by reducing social barriers, tended to assert a functional unity of brain and hand. Our ecological crisis is the product of an emerging, entirely novel, democratic culture. The issue is whether a democratized world can survive its own implications. Presumably we cannot unless we rethink our axioms. (White, 1967)

Presuppositions and foundational axioms are to blame, and of course White ties these to the Judeo-Christian foundation, which therefore must be dismissed and replaced with something more effective at dealing with such problems as the ecological one.

Additionally, globalization has brought a heightened awareness of diverse belief systems, as interaction with dissimilar religious systems becomes more feasible due to technological advance and ease of travel (and more necessary for the maintenance of the manufactured jungle[165]). The dialogue is not complete without a plurality of voices. As Ott argues in his discussion on the importance of peer review in theological consensus building,

> Not only will the results of a theology forged in global dialogue be potentially richer, but the community of believers is likely to be better served by such a theology.[166]

Presumably, in the ever globalizing marketplace of ideas theology should serve its constituency. It should solve problems – at the very least it should not contribute to them. (But in a *revelation* centered theology, the theology must simply follow that which is revealed. Such things as constituency and problem solving are not in view – once again, the nature of revelation is a pivotal issue.)

From this pluralizing of authoritative voices in theological matters has arisen an important byproduct: the identification and characterization of fundamentalism. Those voices which seem to reject the shift to postmodernity (and consequently globalization) are categorized as fundamentalist (due to their desire to resist change and hold fast basic tenets of their particular belief systems), and are summarily dismissed as valued voices in the marketplace of ideas. Karen Armstrong illustrates the negative connotation of fundamentalism (in America) when she says,

> Fundamentalists have no time for democracy, pluralism, religious tolerance, peacekeeping, free speech and separation of church and state. Christian fundamentalists reject the discoveries of biology and physics about the origins of life and insist that the Book of Genesis is scientifically sound in every detail.[167]

Evidently it is not simply plurality of voice that is desired, but rather plurality of voice sharing a particular degree of diversity and nonresistant to the particular changes that come with a postmodernist/globalization program. Certain voices are unwelcome in the public square – misrepresented or not.

Authority and Pedagogy
In Friere's critique of the banking concept[168] of education he offers a definition which gives impetus for a new pedagogy:

> Implicit in the banking concept is the assumption of a dichotomy between human beings and the world: a person is merely *in* the world, not *with* the world of with others; the individual is spectator, not re-creator. In this view, the person is not a conscious being (*corpo consciente*); he or she is rather the possessor of *a* consciousness: an empty "mind" passively open to the reception of deposits of reality from the world outside.[169]

Friere decries the narrative approach, instead preferring a problem-posing[170] approach, which, he claims, serves as a liberating praxis, overcoming such undesirables as authoritarianism, elite intellectualism, and false perceptions of reality. Friere's emancipatory pedagogy serves as a launching pad of sorts for postmodernist pedagogical methodologies. The answers lie in the process of continually asking questions.[171] Dialogue within a cultural context is paramount, and narration is de-emphasized.

With growing epistemological and pedagogical emphasis on *culture,* the question of authoritative basis must be addressed – particularly the relationship between revelation and culture. Ott identifies three differing approaches to this question: (1) revelation and culture are in opposition, (2) revelation and culture are equals, (3) revelation is determinative and culture is reflective.[172] Ott prefers the third, saying

> In this process, ideally, all will reflect together the glory of God and realize the mission of God in ways, greater, clearer, and brighter than possible from merely a single cultural reference point. Globalizing theology in this sense is not a homogenizing but a harmonizing of local expressions and an amplification of the overarching concern.[173]

In postmodernist thought, cultural elements of context carry the greatest weight and such revelation is dismissed as premodern superstition. Globalization reveals many worldwide traditions that would seem to justify such a dismissal. Pedagogical methodologies and foundations increasingly reflect this perspective on authority. Theology as a result moves away from dealing in matters of authority and becomes a vehicle for quasi cultural enrichment and pedagogical application.

Conclusion
How deeply does postmodernism and the process of globalization affect theology? There is much work to do in answering this question, and only a very little of it has been done here.

But one thing becomes clear at this point, in the mind of this writer: these two concentric forces, along with their various spokespersons and permutations of theoretical foundations, operate together in a curious way, presenting (1) a new humanist methodology, rejecting the failed methodologies of previous generations, and seeking a new anthropocentric means; and (2) a type of secular apocalyptic – realizing (in many cases correctly) the dismal failures of human aspirations, honing in on some of the impending and devastating consequences, and desperately trying to formulate solutions. Great pains are taken by these searchers to avoid Orwell's *1984* kind of world, but in fact these very forces seem to be bringing that world upon us. Can the new world disorder really hold up? Is it tenable to expect that a power vacuum can indeed be maintained indefinitely? What if not?

This writer can't help but wonder what impact a literal grammatical-historical hermeneutic applied to the Biblical prophetic writers would have on these in their search for solutions. Perhaps an understanding of the nature of truth and revelation unclouded by cultural response hermeneutics and epistemologies based in relativity could even offer much more than just solutions, but additionally could explain where this mess came from in the first place.

7:1-8:17 Conclusion: Well-Being Comes Through "Beyond the Sun" Perspective

Solomon answers the question of 6:11: What is the better (*yithron*) for man? His answer is contained in the first 14 verses, and is focused on goods (*tov*). From 7:15-8:17 he recounts what he has seen and what he has tested and draws the conclusion that gladness of heart trumps them all (refer back to 5:20 – God answers man with gladness of heart).

[1] A good name is better than precious ointment; and the day of death than the day of one's birth.

A good (*tov*) name is desirable (*tov*).
The day of death better than birth, for the travails shall be past.

[2] It is better to go to the house of mourning, than to go to the house of feasting: for that is the end of all men; and the living will lay it to his heart.

Better to attend a funeral than a party (e.g., wedding), as it turns the focus beyond the sun (to questions of eternal significance).

[3] Sorrow is better than laughter: for by the sadness of the countenance the heart is made better.

A sad face makes the heart better, considering the ailment (silliness, foolishness, meaninglessness) since it is brought by consideration of eternity (from the previous verses).

[4] The heart of the wise is in the house of mourning; but the heart of fools is in the house of mirth.

Again, better the funeral than the party, the focus of the heart reflects this comparison.

[5] It is better to hear the rebuke of the wise, than for a man to hear the song of fools.

The rebuke of the wise grants insight into a beyond the sun perspective. The song of fools distracts from true reality.

[6] For as the crackling of thorns under a pot, so is the laughter of the fool: this also is vanity.

The laughter of a fool prima facie appears productive and pleasant, but is ultimately meaningless.

[7] Surely oppression maketh a wise man mad; and a gift destroyeth the heart.

Certain kinds of behavior can curtail wisdom: the opposition of pleasure (accepting a bribe) and pain (encountering oppression). Neither are particularly helpful.

[8] Better is the end of a thing than the beginning thereof: and the patient in spirit is better than the proud in spirit.

A restatement of v.1; the end is better because there is final resolution.

Longsuffering (*arek*) is better than loftiness or pride (*gabah*). The patient spirit seeks out the end of a matter. The proud one rejoices at a hopeful beginning.

[9] Be not hasty in thy spirit to be angry: for anger resteth in the bosom of fools.

Quickness to anger is a characteristic of foolishness.

[10] Say not thou, What is the cause that the former days were better than these? for thou dost not inquire wisely concerning this.

Such a question is foolish, since it does not recognize the cyclical order of things, looking for an alternate explanation.

[11] Wisdom is good with an inheritance: and by it there is profit to them that see the sun.

Widsom is good alongside or with inheritance: lit., wisdom is good like an inheritance is good. There is profit from both for those under the sun.

[12] For wisdom is a defence, and money is a defence: but the excellency of knowledge is, that wisdom giveth life to them that have it.

Wisdom is a defense (*tsel*) as is money, but wisdom excels money in that wisdom makes alive or preserves life.

[13] Consider the work of God: for who can make that straight, which he hath made crooked?

Refer to 1:15 – the crooked cannot be straightened; it is God who makes crooked (*avath*, upside down). Man cannot right what is upside down under the sun. For if it is upside down, God has made it upside down for His purposes.

[14] In the day of prosperity be joyful, but in the day of adversity consider: God also hath set the one over against the other, to the end that man should find nothing after him.

Refer to 3:4; there is a time for joy and a time for consideration. He designed both in order that man cannot know (by reason or experience) what shall come after him.

[15] All things have I seen in the days of my vanity: there is a just man that perisheth in his righteousness, and there is a wicked man that prolongeth his life in his wickedness.

Returning to the results of his investigation, Solomon notes the upside down nature of things: the pious dies while he is doing right, while the wicked, while doing evil, prolongs his life.

[16] Be not righteous over much; neither make thyself over wise: why shouldest thou destroy thyself?

Do not increase righteousness (better, piety) and wisdom...it is not that extended life is necessarily desired (he has already stated the end is better than the beginning), but rather that excessive piety and wisdom (akin to what Paul refers to as "to exceed what is written...." (1 Cor. 4:6) results in ruination.

[17] Be not over much wicked, neither be thou foolish: why shouldest thou die before thy time?

Excess in wickedness and foolishness is also ruination. This is not permission for wickedness in moderation, for as Solomon reckons all men to be wicked (cf. 7:20, 8:11 and 9:3), he encourages that it go no further, for it is ruination.

Thus, piety and wickedness bring the same result. Human constructs of morality are inherently problematic as they derive from an evil heart. Trying to resolve the evils of the heart by way of inventions of the evil heart result in the same ruination as comes from excessive wickedness.

Philosophical Parallel: Piety and Moral Theory Of Obligation

Kant's ethical framework is known as deontological ethics (from the Greek, *deon*, meaning duty) or the moral theory of obligation.

Kant recognized that reason does not result in happiness, thus it must serve some other purpose: namely to produce a will that is good in itself. The will is the determinate factor in morality. As one can act in conformity with duty and not be acting morally (but rather amorally), he must act from duty in order for his actions to be considered moral. The distinction between the two approaches is found in the goodness of the will (a prerequisite to happiness), or the motivation for the action. Kant prescribes an inner piety based not on the action itself or the effect intended from the action, but on acting for the right reasons. Kant is decidedly anti-consequentialist.

Although Kant acknowledges God as a transcendental principle, he does not view morality as divine mandate. Reason determines that which is moral and the will either executes it or does not.

Kant identifies two kinds of imperatives: (1) hypothetical – an if-then command applicable only to those who are seeking the resulting condition of the if; (2) categorical – this is applicable to everyone (he says: I ought never to act except in such a way that I could also will that my maxim should become a universal law.[174])

The Kantian ethic is individualistic and poses challenges in building consensus. Each person becomes his own legislator. This kind of piety, is not consistent with Solomon's exhortation to obey divine commands, and finds its critique in Ecclesiastes 7:15-17.

Primary Source Excerpt: Kant: Fundamental Principles of the Metaphysics of Morals (1785 A.D.)

Section II: Transition from Popular Moral Philosophy to the Metaphysic of Morals

If we have hitherto drawn our notion of duty from the common use of our practical reason, it is by no means to be inferred that we have treated it as an empirical notion. On the contrary, if we attend to the experience of men's conduct, we meet frequent and, as we ourselves allow, just complaints that one cannot find a single certain example of the disposition to act from pure duty. Although many things are done in conformity with what duty prescribes, it is nevertheless always doubtful whether they are done strictly from duty, so as to have a moral worth. Hence there have at all times been philosophers who have altogether denied that this disposition actually exists at all in human actions, and have ascribed everything to a more or less refined self-love. Not that they have on that account questioned the soundness of the conception of morality; on the contrary, they spoke with sincere regret of the frailty and corruption of human nature, which, though noble enough to take its rule an idea so worthy of respect, is yet weak to follow it and employs reason which ought to give it the law only for the purpose of providing for the interest of the inclinations, whether singly or at the best in the greatest possible harmony with one another.

In fact, it is absolutely impossible to make out by experience with complete certainty a single case in which the maxim of an action, however right in itself, rested simply on moral grounds and on the conception of duty. Sometimes it happens that with the sharpest self-examination we can find nothing beside the moral principle of duty which could have been powerful enough to move us to this or that action and to so great a sacrifice; yet we cannot from this infer with certainty that it was not really some secret impulse of self-love, under the false appearance of duty, that was the actual determining cause of the will. We like them to flatter ourselves by falsely taking credit for a more noble motive; whereas in fact we can never, even by the strictest examination, get completely behind the secret springs of action; since, when the question is of moral worth, it is not with the actions which we see that we are concerned, but with those inward principles of them which we do not see.

Moreover, we cannot better serve the wishes of those who ridicule all morality as a mere chimera of human imagination over stepping itself from vanity, than by conceding to them that notions of duty must be drawn only from experience (as from indolence, people are ready to think is also the case with all other notions); for or is to prepare for them a certain triumph. I am willing to admit out of love of humanity that even most of our actions are correct, but if we look closer at them we everywhere come upon the dear self which is always prominent, and it is this they have in view and not the strict command of duty which would often require self-denial. Without being an enemy of virtue, a cool observer, one that does not mistake the wish for good, however lively, for its reality, may sometimes doubt whether true virtue is actually found anywhere in the world, and this especially as years increase and the judgement is partly made wiser by experience and partly, also, more acute in observation. This being so, nothing can secure us from falling away altogether from our ideas of duty, or maintain in the soul a well-grounded respect for its law, but the clear conviction that although there should never have been actions which really sprang from such pure sources, yet whether this or that takes place is not at all the question; but that reason of itself, independent on all experience, ordains what ought to take place, that accordingly actions of which perhaps the world has hitherto never given an example, the feasibility even of which might be very much doubted by one who founds everything on experience, are nevertheless inflexibly commanded by reason; that, e.g., even though there might never yet have been a sincere friend, yet not a whit the less is pure sincerity in friendship required of every man, because, prior to all experience, this duty is involved as duty in the idea of a reason determining the will by a priori principles.

When we add further that, unless we deny that the notion of morality has any truth or reference to any possible object, we must admit that its law must be valid, not merely for men but for *all rational creatures generally*, not merely under certain contingent conditions or with exceptions but *with absolute necessity*, then it is clear that no experience could enable us to infer even the possibility of such apodictic laws. For with what right could we bring into unbounded respect as a universal precept for every rational nature that which perhaps holds only under the contingent conditions of humanity? Or how could laws of the determination of our will be regarded as laws of the determination of the will of rational beings generally, and for us only as such, if they were merely empirical and did not take their origin wholly a priori from pure but practical reason?

Nor could anything be more fatal to morality than that we should wish to derive it from examples. For every example of it that is set before me must be first itself tested by principles of morality, whether it is worthy to serve as an original example, i.e., as a pattern; but by no means can it authoritatively furnish the conception of morality. Even the Holy One of the Gospels must first be compared with our ideal of moral perfection before we can recognise Him as such; and so He says of Himself, "Why call ye Me (whom you see) good; none is good (the model of good) but God only (whom ye do not see)?" But whence have we the conception of God as the supreme good? Simply from the *idea* of moral perfection, which reason frames *a priori* and connects inseparably with the notion of a free will. Imitation finds no place at all in morality, and examples serve only for encouragement, i.e., they put beyond doubt the feasibility of what the law commands, they make visible that which the practical rule expresses more generally, but they can never authorize us to set aside the true original which lies in reason and to guide ourselves by examples.

If then there is no genuine supreme principle of morality but what must rest simply on pure reason, independent of all experience, I think it is not necessary even to put the question whether it is good to exhibit these concepts in their generality (*in abstracto*) as they are established *a priori* along with the principles belonging to them, if our knowledge is to be distinguished from the *vulgar* and to be called philosophical. In our times indeed this might perhaps be necessary; for if we collected votes whether pure rational knowledge separated from everything empirical, that is to say, metaphysic of morals, or whether popular practical philosophy is to be preferred, it is easy to guess which side would preponderate.

This descending to popular notions is certainly very commendable, if the ascent to the principles of pure reason has first taken place and been satisfactorily accomplished. This implies that we first found ethics on metaphysics, and then, when it is firmly established, procure a hearing for it by giving it a popular character. But it is quite absurd to try to be popular in the first inquiry, on which the soundness of the principles depends. It is not only that this proceeding can never lay claim to the very rare merit of a true *philosophical popularity*, since there is no art in being intelligible if one renounces all thoroughness of insight; but also it produces a disgusting medley of compiled observations and half-reasoned principles. Shallow pates enjoy this because it can be used for every-day chat, but the sagacious find in it only confusion, and being unsatisfied and unable to help themselves, they turn away their eyes, while philosophers, who see quite well through this delusion, are little listened to when they call men off for a time from this pretended popularity, in order that they might be rightfully popular after they have attained a definite insight.

We need only look at the attempts of moralists in that favourite fashion, and we shall find at one time the special constitution of human nature (including, however, the idea of a rational nature generally), at one time perfection, at another happiness, here moral sense, there fear of God. a little of this, and a little of that, in marvelous mixture, without its occurring to them to ask whether the principles of morality are to be sought in the knowledge of human nature at all (which we can have only from experience); or, if this is not so, if these principles are to be found altogether *a priori*, free from everything empirical, in pure rational concepts only and nowhere else, not even in the smallest degree; then rather to adopt the method of making this a separate inquiry, as pure practical philosophy, or (if one may use a name so decried) as metaphysic of morals, to bring it by itself to completeness, and to require the public, which wishes for popular treatment, to await the issue of this undertaking.

Just as pure mathematics are distinguished from applied, pure logic from applied, so if we choose we may also distinguish pure philosophy of morals (metaphysic) from applied (viz., applied to human nature). By this designation we are also at once reminded that moral principles are not based on properties of human nature, but must subsist a priori of themselves, while from such principles practical rules must be capable of being deduced for every rational nature, and accordingly for that of man.

Such a metaphysic of morals, completely isolated, not mixed with any anthropology, theology, physics, or hyperphysics, and still less with occult qualities (which we might call hypophysical), is not only an indispensable substratum of all sound theoretical knowledge of duties, but is at the same time a desideratum of the highest importance to the actual fulfillment of their precepts. For the pure conception of duty, unmixed with any foreign addition of empirical attractions, and, in a word, the conception of the moral law, exercises on the human heart, by way of reason alone (which first becomes aware with this that it can of itself be practical), an influence so much more powerful than all other springs which may be derived from the field of experience, that, in the consciousness of its worth, it despises the latter, and can by degrees become their master; whereas a mixed ethics, compounded partly of motives drawn from feelings and inclinations, and partly also of conceptions of reason, must make the mind waver between motives which cannot be brought under any principle, which lead to good only by mere accident and very often also to evil.

[Footnote to the word "springs" in the above paragraph.] I have a letter from the late excellent Sulzer, in which he asks me what can be the reason that moral instruction, although containing much that is convincing for the reason, yet accomplishes so little? My answer was postponed in order that I might make it complete. But it is simply this: that the teachers themselves have not got their own notions clear, and when they endeavour to make up for this by raking up motives of moral goodness from every quarter, trying to make their physic right strong, they spoil it. For the commonest understanding shows that if we imagine, on the one hand, an act of honesty done with steadfast mind, apart from every view to advantage of any kind in this world or another, and even under the greatest temptations of necessity or allurement, and, on the other hand, a similar act which was affected, in however low a degree, by a foreign motive, the former leaves far behind and eclipses the second; it elevates the soul and inspires the wish to be able to act in like manner oneself. Even moderately young children feel this impression, ana one should never represent duties to them in any other light. [End of footnote.]

From what has been said, it is clear that all moral conceptions have their seat and origin completely *a priori* in the reason, and that, moreover, in the commonest reason just as truly as in that which is in the highest degree speculative; that they cannot be obtained by abstraction from any empirical, and therefore merely contingent, knowledge; that it is just this purity of their origin that makes them worthy to serve as our supreme practical principle, and that just in proportion as we add anything empirical, we detract from their genuine influence and from the absolute value of actions; that it is not only of the greatest necessity, in a purely speculative point of view, but is also of the greatest practical importance, to derive these notions and laws from pure reason, to present them pure and unmixed, and even to determine the compass of this practical or pure rational knowledge, i.e., to determine the whole faculty of pure practical reason; and, in doing so, we must not make its principles dependent on the particular nature of human reason, though in speculative philosophy this may be permitted, or may even at times be necessary; but since moral laws ought to hold good for every rational creature, we must derive them from the general concept of a rational being. In this way, although for its *application* to man morality has need of anthropology, yet, in the first instance, we must treat it independently as pure philosophy, i.e., as metaphysic, complete in itself (a thing which in such distinct branches of science is easily done); knowing well that unless we are in possession of this, it would not only be vain to determine the moral element of duty in right actions for purposes of speculative criticism, but it would be impossible to base morals on their genuine principles, even for common practical purposes, especially of moral instruction, so as to produce pure moral dispositions, and to engraft them on men's minds to the promotion of the greatest possible good in the world.

But in order that in this study we may not merely advance by the natural steps from the common moral judgment (in this case very worthy of respect) to the philosophical, as has been already done, but also from a popular philosophy, which goes no further than it can reach by groping with the help of examples, to metaphysic (which does allow itself to be checked by anything empirical and, as it must measure the whole extent of this kind of rational knowledge, goes as far as ideal conceptions, where even examples fail us), we must follow and clearly describe the practical faculty of reason, from the general rules of its determination to the point where the notion of duty springs from it.

Everything in nature works according to laws. Rational beings alone have the faculty of acting according *to the conception of laws*, that is according to principles, i.e., have a will. Since the deduction of actions from principles requires *reason*, the will is nothing but practical reason. If reason infallibly determines the will, then the actions of such a being which are recognized as objectively necessary are subjectively necessary also, i.e., the will is a faculty to choose *that only* which reason independent of inclination recognizes as practically necessary, i.e., as good. But if reason of itself does not sufficiently determine the will, if the latter is subject also to subjective conditions (particular impulses) which do not always coincide with the objective conditions; in a word, if the will does not *in itself* completely accord with reason (which is actually the case with men), then the actions which objectively are recognized as necessary are subjectively contingent, and the determination of such a will according to objective laws is *obligation*, that is to say, the relation of the objective laws to a will that is not thoroughly good is conceived as the determination of the will of a rational being by principles of reason, but which the will from its nature does not of necessity follow.

The conception of an objective principle, in so far as it is obligatory for a will, is called a command (of reason), and the formula of the command is called an imperative.

All imperatives are expressed by the word ought [or shall], and thereby indicate the relation of an objective law of reason to a will, which from its subjective constitution is not necessarily determined by it (an obligation). They say that something would be good to do or to forbear, but they say it to a will which does not always do a thing because it is conceived to be good to do it. That is practically *good*, however, which determines the will by means of the conceptions of reason, and consequently not from subjective causes, but objectively, that is on principles which are valid for every rational being as such. It is distinguished from the pleasant, as that which influences the will only by means of sensation from merely subjective causes, valid only for the sense of this or that one, and not as a principle of reason, which holds for everyone.

[Footnote to the previous paragraph in Kant.] The dependence of the desires on sensations is called inclination, and this accordingly always indicates a *want*. The dependence of a contingently determinable will on principles of reason is called an *interest*. This therefore, is found only in the case of a dependent will which does not always of itself conform to reason; in the Divine will we cannot conceive any interest. But the human will can also *take an interest* in a thing without therefore acting *from interest*. The former signifies the *practical* interest in the action, the latter the *pathological* in the object of the action. The former indicates only dependence of the will on principles of reason in themselves; the second, dependence on principles of reason for the sake of inclination, reason supplying only the practical rules how the requirement of the inclination may be satisfied. In the first case the action interests me; in the second the object of the action (because it is pleasant to me). We have seen in the first section that in an action done from duty we must look not to the interest in the object, but only to that in the action itself, and in its rational principle (viz., the law). [End of footnote.]

A perfectly good will would therefore be equally subject to objective laws (viz., laws of good), but could not be conceived as *obliged* thereby to act lawfully, because of itself from its subjective constitution it can only be determined by the conception of good. Therefore no imperatives hold for the Divine will, or in general for a *holy* will; *ought* is here out of place, because the volition is already of itself necessarily in unison with the law. Therefore imperatives are only formulae to express the relation of objective laws of all volition to the subjective imperfection of the will of this or that rational being, e.g., the human will.

Now all *imperatives* command either *hypothetically* or *categorically*. The former represent the practical necessity of a possible action as means to something else that is willed (or at least which one might possibly will). The categorical imperative would be that which represented an action as necessary of itself without reference to another end, i.e., as objectively necessary.

Since every practical law represents a possible action as good and, on this account, for a subject who is practically determinable by reason, necessary, all imperatives are formulae determining an action which is necessary according to the principle of a will good in some respects. If now the action is good only as a means *to something else*, then the imperative is *hypothetical*; if it is conceived as good *in itself* and consequently as being necessarily the principle of a will which of itself conforms to reason, then it is *categorical*.

Thus the imperative declares what action possible by me would be good and presents the practical rule in relation to a will which does not forthwith perform an action simply because it is good, whether because the subject does not always know that it is good, or because, even if it know this, yet its maxims might be opposed to the objective principles of practical reason.

Accordingly the hypothetical imperative only says that the action is good for some purpose, *possible* or *actual*. In the first case it is a problematical, in the second an assertorial practical principle. The categorical imperative which declares an action to be objectively necessary in itself without reference to any purpose, i.e., without any other end, is valid as an apodictic (practical) principle.

Whatever is possible only by the power of some rational being may also be conceived as a possible purpose of some will; and therefore the principles of action as regards the means necessary to attain some possible purpose are in fact infinitely numerous. All sciences have a practical part, consisting of problems expressing that some end is possible for us and of imperatives directing how it may be attained. These may, therefore, be called in general imperatives of skill. Here there is no question whether the end is rational and good, but only what one must do in order to attain it. The precepts for the physician to make his patient thoroughly healthy, and for a poisoner to ensure certain death, are of equal value in this respect, that each serves to effect its purpose perfectly. Since in early youth it cannot be known what ends are likely to occur to us in the course of life, parents seek to have their children taught *a great many things*, and provide for their *skill* in the use of means for all sorts of arbitrary ends, of none of which can they determine whether it may not perhaps hereafter be an object to their pupil, but which it is at all events *possible* that he might aim at; and this anxiety is so great that they commonly neglect to form and correct their judgment on the value of the things which may be chosen as ends.

There is *one* end, however, which may be assumed to be actually such to all rational beings (so far as imperatives apply to them, viz., as dependent beings), and, therefore, one purpose which they not merely *may* have, but which we may with certainty assume that they all actually *have* by a natural necessity, and this is *happiness*. The hypothetical imperative which expresses the practical necessity of an action as means to the advancement of happiness is assertorial. We are not to present it as necessary for an uncertain and merely possible purpose, but for a purpose which we may presuppose with certainty and *a priori* in every man, because it belongs to his being. Now skill in the choice of means to his own greatest well-being may be called *prudence*, in the narrowest sense. And thus the imperative which refers to the choice of means to one's own happiness, i.e., the precept of prudence, is still always *hypothetical;* the action is not commanded absolutely, but only as means to another purpose.

[Footnote to the word "prudence' in the above paragraph.] The word prudence is taken in two senses: in the one it may bear the name of knowledge of the world, in the other that of private prudence. The former is a man's ability to influence others so as to use them for his own purposes. The latter is the sagacity to combine all these purposes for his own lasting benefit. This latter is properly that to which the value even of the former is reduced, and when a man is prudent in the former sense, but not in the latter, we might better say of him that he is clever and cunning, but, on the whole, imprudent.

Finally, there is an imperative which commands a certain conduct immediately, without having as its condition any other purpose to be attained by it. This imperative is categorical. It concerns not the matter of the action, or its intended result, but its form and the principle of which it is itself a result; and what is essentially good in it consists in the mental disposition, let the consequence be what it may. This imperative may be called that of morality.

There is a marked distinction also between the volitions on these three sorts of principles in the *dissimilarity* of the obligation of the will. In order to mark this difference more clearly, I think they would be most suitably named in their order if we said they are either *rules* of skill, or *counsels* of prudence, or *commands* (*laws*) of morality. For it is *law* only that involves the conception of an *unconditional* and objective necessity, which is consequently universally valid; and commands are laws which must be obeyed, that is, must be followed, even in opposition to inclination. *Counsels*, indeed, involve necessity, but one which can only hold under a contingent subjective condition, viz., they depend on whether this or that man reckons this or that as part of his happiness; the categorical imperative, on the contrary, is not limited by any condition, and as being absolutely, although practically, necessary, may be quite properly called a command. We might also call the first kind of imperatives *technical* (belonging to art), the second *pragmatic* (to welfare), the third *moral* (belonging to free conduct generally, that is, to morals).

[Footnote to the word "pragmatic' in the above paragraph.] It seems to me that the proper signification of the word *pragmatic* may be most accurately defined in this way. For *sanctions* are called pragmatic which flow properly not from the law of the states as necessary enactments, but from *precaution* for the general welfare. A history is composed pragmatically when it teaches *prudence*, i.e., instructs the world how it can provide for its interests better, or at least as well as, the men of former time. [End of footnote.]

Now arises the question, how are all these imperatives possible? This question does not seek to know how we can conceive the accomplishment of the action which the imperative ordains, but merely how we can conceive the obligation of the will which the imperative expresses. No special explanation is needed to show how an imperative of skill is possible. Whoever wills the end, wills also (so far as reason decides his conduct) the means in his power which are indispensably necessary thereto. This proposition is, as regards the volition, analytical; for, in willing an object as my effect, there is already thought the causality of myself as an acting cause, that is to say, the use of the means; and the imperative educes from the conception of volition of an end the conception of actions necessary to this end. Synthetical propositions must no doubt be employed in defining the means to a proposed end; but they do not concern the principle, the act of the will, but the object and its realization. E.g., that in order to bisect a line on an unerring principle I must draw from its extremities two intersecting arcs; this no doubt is taught by mathematics only in synthetical propositions; but if I know that it is only by this process that the intended operation can be performed, then to say that, if I fully will the operation, I also will the action required for it, is an analytical proposition; for it is one and the same thing to conceive something as an effect which I can produce in a certain way, and to conceive myself as acting in this way.

If it were only equally easy to give a definite conception of happiness, the imperatives of prudence would correspond exactly with those of skill, and would likewise be analytical. For in this case as in that, it could be said: "Whoever wills the end, wills also (according to the dictate of reason necessarily) the indispensable means thereto which are in his power." But, unfortunately, the notion of happiness is so indefinite that although every man wishes to at. it, yet he never can say definitely and consistently what it is that he really wishes and wills. The reason of this is that all the elements which belong to the notion of happiness are altogether empirical, i.e., they must be borrowed from experience, and nevertheless the idea of happiness requires an absolute whole, a maximum of welfare in my present and all future circumstances. Now it is impossible that the most clear-sighted and at the same time most powerful being (supposed finite) should frame to himself a definite conception of what he really wills in this. Does he will riches, how much anxiety, envy, and snares might he not thereby draw upon his shoulders? Does he will knowledge and discernment, perhaps it might prove to be only an eye so much the sharper to show him so much the more fearfully the evils that are now concealed from him, and that cannot be avoided, or to impose more wants on his desires, which already give him concern enough. Would he have long life? Who guarantees to him that it would not be a long misery? Would he at least have health? how often has uneasiness of the body restrained from excesses into which perfect health would have allowed one to fall? and so on. In short, he is unable, on any principle, to determine with certainty what would make him truly happy; because to do so he would need to be omniscient. We cannot therefore act on any definite principles to secure happiness, but only on empirical counsels, e.g. of regimen, frugality, courtesy, reserve, etc., which experience teaches do, on the average, most promote well-being. Hence it follows that the imperatives of prudence do not, strictly speaking, command at all, that is, they cannot present actions objectively as practically *necessary*; that they are rather to be regarded as counsels (*consilia*) than precepts *praecepta* of reason, that the problem to determine certainly and universally what action would promote the happiness of a rational being is completely insoluble, and consequently no imperative respecting it is possible which should, in the strict sense, command to do what makes happy; because happiness is not an ideal of reason but of imagination, resting solely on empirical grounds, and it is vain to expect that these should define an action by which one could attain the totality of a series of consequences which is really endless. This imperative of prudence would however be an analytical proposition if we assume that the means to happiness could be certainly assigned; for it is distinguished from the imperative of skill only by this, that in the latter the end is merely possible, in the former it is given; as however both only ordain the means to that which we suppose to be willed as an end, it follows that the imperative which ordains the willing of the means to him who wills the end is in both cases analytical. Thus there is no difficulty in regard to the possibility of an imperative of this kind either.

On the other hand, the question how the imperative of *morality* is possible, is undoubtedly one, the only one, demanding a solution, as this is not at all hypothetical, and the objective necessity which it presents cannot rest on any hypothesis, as is the case with the hypothetical imperatives. Only here we must never leave out of consideration that we *cannot* make out by *any example*, in other words empirically, whether there is such an imperative at all, but it is rather to be feared that all those which seem to be categorical may yet be at bottom hypothetical. For instance, when the precept is: Thou shalt not promise deceitfully; and it is assumed that the necessity of this is not a mere counsel to avoid some other evil, so that it should mean: Thou shalt not make a lying promise, lest if it become known thou shouldst destroy thy credit, but that an action of this kind must be regarded as evil in itself, so that the imperative of the prohibition is categorical; then we cannot show with certainty in any example that the will was determined merely by the law, without any other spring of action, although it may appear to be so. For it is always possible that fear of disgrace, perhaps also obscure dread of other dangers, may have a secret influence on the will. Who can prove by experience the non-existence of a cause when all that experience tells us is that we do not perceive it? But in such a case the so-called moral imperative, which as such appears to be categorical and unconditional, would in reality be only a pragmatic precept, drawing our attention to our own interests and merely teaching us to take these into consideration.

We shall therefore have to investigate *a priori* the possibility of a categorical imperative, as we have not in this case the advantage of its reality being given in experience, so that [the elucidation of] its possibility should be requisite only for its explanation, not for its establishment. In the meantime it may be discerned beforehand that the categorical imperative alone has the purport of a practical law; all the rest may indeed be called principles of the will but not laws, since whatever is only necessary for the attainment of some arbitrary purpose may be considered as in itself contingent, and we can at any time be free from the precept if we give up the purpose; on the contrary, the unconditional command leaves the will no liberty to choose the opposite; consequently it alone carries with it that necessity which we require in a law.

Secondly, in the case of this categorical imperative or law of morality, the difficulty (of discerning its possibility) is a very profound one. It is an a priori synthetical practical proposition; and as there is so much difficulty in discerning the possibility of speculative propositions of this kind, it may readily be supposed that the difficulty will be no less with the practical.

[Footnote to the words "practical proposition in the above paragraph.] I connect the act with the will without presupposing any condition resulting from any inclination, but *a priori*, and therefore necessarily (though only objectively, i.e., assuming the idea of a reason possessing full power over all subjective motives). This is accordingly a practical proposition which does not deduce the willing of an action by mere analysis from another already presupposed (for we have not such a perfect will), but connects it immediately with the conception of the will of a rational being, as something not contained in it.

In this problem we will first inquire whether the mere conception of a categorical imperative may not perhaps supply us also with the formula of it, containing the proposition which alone can be a categorical imperative; for even if we know the tenor of such an absolute command, yet how it is possible will require further special and laborious study, which we postpone to the last section.

When I conceive a hypothetical imperative, in general I do not know beforehand what it will contain until I am given the condition. But when I conceive a categorical imperative, I know at once what it contains. For as the imperative contains besides the law only the necessity that the maxims shall conform to this law, while the law contains no conditions restricting it, there remains nothing but the general statement that the maxim of the action should conform to a universal law, and it is this conformity alone that the imperative properly represents as necessary.

[Footnote to the phrase "necessity that the maxims" in the above paragraph.] A maxim is a subjective principle of action, and must be distinguished from the *objective principle*, namely, practical law. The former contains the practical rule set by reason according to the conditions of the subject (often its ignorance or its inclinations), so that it is the principle on which the subject *acts*; but the law is the objective principle valid for every rational being, and is the principle on which it *ought to act* that is an imperative.

There is therefore but one categorical imperative, namely, this: Act only on that maxim whereby thou canst at the same time will that it should become a universal law. *[italics mine]*

Now if all imperatives of duty can be deduced from this one imperative as from their principle, then, although it should remain undecided what is called duty is not merely a vain notion, yet at least we shall be able to show what we understand by it and what this notion means.

Since the universality of the law according to which effects are produced constitutes what is properly called nature in the most general sense (as to form), that is the existence of things so far as it is determined by general laws, the imperative of duty may be expressed thus: *Act as if the maxim of thy action were to become by thy will a universal law of nature.*

7:1-8:17 Conclusion: Well-Being Comes Through "Beyond the Sun" Perspective" (cont.)

Qoheleth VII (cont.)

[18] *It is good that thou shouldest take hold of this; yea, also from this withdraw not thine hand: for he that feareth God shall come forth of them all.*

Pay heed to the avoidance of both extremes in accordance with the fear of God, for extreme piety (being wise in one's own eyes, as in Proverbs 3:7) and further wickedness are not good. He that fears God shall come forth from them all (with both, as in NASB, not the best here…note the LXX rendering – *ta panta*, the all). The fear of God delivers from the unacceptable extremes.

[19] *Wisdom strengtheneth the wise more than ten mighty men which are in the city.*
Wisdom of more benefit than mighty men.

[20] *For there is not a just man upon earth, that doeth good, and sinneth not.*

An inarguable statement of the universal depravity of man. Built on the previous statement of the value of wisdom.

Just – (*tsadiq*, just or righteous).

[21] *Also take no heed unto all words that are spoken; lest thou hear thy servant curse thee:*

Beware of the multiplying of words, as in 5:2, 7. Recognize their vanity and do not take them too personally.

[22] For oftentimes also thine own heart knoweth that thou thyself likewise hast cursed others.

For proof of the foolishness and certainty of a multiplicity of words, he exhorts the reader to examine his own heart.

[23] All this have I proved by wisdom: I said, I will be wise; but it was far from me.

In his investigation, he demonstrates all these things to be true, but as far as extracting a character of wisdom form all the wise statements, he found that far more difficult.

[24] That which is far off, and exceeding deep, who can find it out?

The what is (*shehayah*) is remote and deep deep (*amoq amoq*, emphasis by repetition). Now Solomon is digressing into the is / ought problem: the ought cannot be determined until the what will be is known, and the is cannot be discerned either, due to its remoteness and exceeding depth. Here is another nail in the coffin of under the sun morality.

[25] I applied mine heart to know, and to search, and to seek out wisdom, and the reason of things, and to know the wickedness of folly, even of foolishness and madness:

Appealing yet again to the thoroughness of his investigation and the certainty of his findings...

[26] And I find more bitter than death the woman, whose heart is snares and nets, and her hands as bands: whoso pleaseth God

shall escape from her; but the sinner shall be taken by her.

Worse or more bitter (*marah*) than death is being ensnared by a terrible woman: the one following after God will not be caught in her snare.

[27] Behold, this have I found, saith the preacher, counting one by one, to find out the account:

See, I have found this...one to one (*echad l'echad*) to find a reason (*cheshbon*) or explanation (NASB). He compares women to find why the heart is so.

[28] Which yet my soul seeketh, but I find not: one man among a thousand have I found; but a woman among all those have I not found.

What yet sought (*biq'shah*, my soul, Piel 3fs of *baqash* – note the feminine personification of the soul, along with the Piel intensive: the soul, she has earnestly sought)...I have not found: among a thousand Solomon can find one good man, among a thousand women (quite literally, in his case) he has found none.

This underscores his (I believe King Lemuel to be a name or surname of Solomon) earlier observations of the true value of an excellent wife (Prov. 31).

[29] Lo, this only have I found, that God hath made man upright; but they have sought out many inventions.

This is not a condemnation of technology proper, but rather of man's particular inventions to lower himself to the point that a good man and a good woman should be so hard to discover.

Qoheleth VIII

[1] Who is as the wise man? and who knoweth the interpretation of a thing? a man's wisdom maketh his face to shine, and the boldness of his face shall be changed.

A direct challenge to the reader: who would be like the wise man? Who would know the interpretation of a matter? Who would have his countenance (*panyim*, face) reflect wisdom? Those who would obey his forthcoming imperatives:

[2] I counsel thee to keep the king's commandment, and that in regard of the oath of God.

First, be obedient to the king, based on the oath of God, i.e., the Davidic Covenant reiterated (cf. Ps. 89:28).

[3] Be not hasty to go out of his sight: stand not in an evil thing; for he doeth whatsoever pleaseth him.

Second, loyalty to the king

[4] Where the word of a king is, there is power: and who may say unto him, What doest thou?

Since he has authority (divinely mandated, in the case of the Israelite monarchy).

[5] Whoso keepeth the commandment shall feel no evil thing: and a wise man's heart discerneth both time and judgment.

The loyal and submissive subject will not meet evil consequences, and the wise man knows time and judgment: the appropriate response to the royal command.

[6] Because to every purpose there is time and judgment, therefore the misery of man is great upon him.

Because (*kiy*, because or for - same as in the first clause) the evil of man is great upon him: a broad statement of the cyclical meaninglessness from the fall. The oppressiveness of the cycles under the sun is associated with the evil of man here.
[7] For he knoweth not that which shall be: for who can tell him when it shall be?

Again, the finitude of man's perspective: if he cannot tell what will be, he cannot tell the is or the ought.

[8] There is no man that hath power over the spirit to retain the spirit; neither hath he power in the day of death: and there is no discharge in that war; neither shall wickedness deliver those that are given to it.
No man has authority to retain the spirit (*ruach*) in the day of his death, just as the soldier has no authority to discharge in war, neither does wickedness have any efficacy to deliver (*yimalet*, piel intensive, deliver with certainty).

[9] All this have I seen, and applied my heart unto every work that is done under the sun: there is a time wherein one man ruleth over another to his own hurt.

The recurrent appeal to the thoroughness of the investigation and the certainty of the findings...specifically on this occasion in regard to oppression by the wicked, and how they are not served by their wickedness.

[10] And so I saw the wicked buried, who had come and gone from the place of the holy, and they were forgotten in the city where they had so done: this is also vanity.

The wicked (oppressor) who had come and gone from the holy place (thus possibly including high priests), upon burial is forgotten. This is meaningless.

[11] Because sentence against an evil work is not executed speedily, therefore the heart of the sons of men is fully set in them to do evil.

Delay of consequence is a perversion of justice and reinforces evil. Thus the scenario of v. 10 is meaningless, because the wicked oppressor did not receive the consequences for his actions.

[12] Though a sinner do evil an hundred times, and his days be prolonged, yet surely I know that it shall be well with them that fear God, which fear before him:
[13] But it shall not be well with the wicked, neither shall he prolong his days, which are as a shadow; because he feareth not before God.

Despite the sometimes prolonged days of the wicked, it is and shall be good (*tov*, in the imperfect) for those who fear God. Furthermore, the wicked shall not cause his days to be prolonged.

[14] There is a vanity which is done upon the earth; that there be just men, unto whom it happeneth according to the work of the wicked; again, there be wicked men, to whom it happeneth according to the work of the righteous: I said that this also is

vanity.

When the righteous reaps what should seemingly be the inheritance of the wicked, and vice versa, this is meaningless: it is not reflective of universal justice.

[15] Then I commended mirth, because a man hath no better thing under the sun, than to eat, and to drink, and to be merry: for that shall abide with him of his labour the days of his life, which God giveth him under the sun.

I commended rejoicing (*simchah*)...no good (*tov*) under the sun than to eat drink and to rejoice (infinitive of *samach*). He has previously qualified rejoicing as seeing the goods in labor (2:24-25) and as a means whereby God answers man (5:20).

[16] When I applied mine heart to know wisdom, and to see the business that is done upon the earth: (for also there is that neither day nor night seeth sleep with his eyes)

I gave (*nathan*) my heart to know wisdom and to observe the task (*ha inyan*) even to the extent of sleeplessness...

[17] Then I beheld all the work of God, that a man cannot find out the work that is done under the sun: because though a man labour to seek it out, yet he shall not find it; yea further; though a wise man think to know it, yet shall he not be able to find it.

I observed all the business (*mahaseh*) of God: that not able is man to discover the business that has been done under the sun....

Despite the most earnest of pursuits, man cannot discover it.

Even a wise man, thinking he has discovered it, cannot.

Thus, since God has made the is, the ought, and the what will be unattainable to man through either the use of reason or experience, all that man can know of them is through that which God reveals. True understanding and resultant well-being, then, comes only from the beyond the sun perspective that God provides.

9:1-10 Conclusion: The Urgency of Life Under the Sun

[1] For all this I considered in my heart even to declare all this, that the righteous, and the wise, and their works, are in the hand of God: no man knoweth either love or hatred by all that is before them.

The righteous, the wise and their works are in the hand of God...whether love or whether hate, not knows the man what is before him (before his face). Man sees with such a limited perspective. He must recognize God's involvement.

[2] All things come alike to all: there is one event to the righteous, and to the wicked; to the good and to the clean, and to the unclean; to him that sacrificeth, and to him that sacrificeth not: as is the good, so is the sinner; and he that sweareth, as he that feareth an oath.

One event (*miqreh*) for all: death; this remains the natural order (Heb. 9:27, although not without exceptions: rapture, etc.), irrespective of the manner of life.

[3] This is an evil among all things that are done under the sun, that there is one event unto all: yea, also the heart of the sons of men is full of evil, and madness is in their heart while they live, and after that they go to the dead.

The evil (*ra'ah*) of life: death, and the life (particularly the heart of men) that precedes it is full of evil and madness.

[4] For to him that is joined to all the living there is hope: for a living dog is better than a dead lion.

There is hope...of death (v.5), yet here Solomon extols life (better to be an ignoble living creature than a noble dead creature), where he had previously decried it under the sun (6:3). As the beyond the sun perspective begins to fully emerge, life is shown to have value and meaning.

[5] For the living know that they shall die: but the dead know not anything, neither have they any more a reward; for the memory of them is forgotten.

The hope or confidence of the living is death, thus perhaps the living can still take matters to heart (7:2). But the dead (1) know nothing, (2) have no present under the sun reward (as in 5:18) since he has no present under the sun occupation, and (3) are forgotten by those under the sun.

[6] Also their love, and their hatred, and their envy, is now perished; neither have they any more a portion forever in anything that is done under the sun.

Confirmation of v. 5: the dead are blotted out from under the sun. That is the what is. Establishing that, Solomon moves to the ought:

[7] Go thy way, eat thy bread with joy, and drink thy wine with a merry heart; for God now accepteth thy works.

Walk, eat with rejoicing (*simchah*) your bread, and drink in a good (*tov*) heart your wine. The reader is to walk in the functions of life with a particular kind of perspective – the kind that brings rejoicing and goodness of heart. Only the beyond the sun perspective, beginning with the fear of God, can have such an outcome (3:12-14). Of this one it is certain that "already approved (*ratsah*) God has your works (*ma'asyka*)."

[8] Let thy garments be always white; and let thy head lack no ointment.

Therefore, take pleasure in the simple things of life: care for and cover well your body (investment in the body would without the fear of God be meaningless)

[9] Live joyfully with the wife whom thou lovest all the days of the life of thy vanity, which he hath given thee under the sun, all the days of thy vanity: for that is thy portion in this life, and in thy labour which thou takest under the sun.

Observe life with a woman (no definite article) whom (singular, thus the definite article of the previous is implied) you have loved (*ahav'ta*, Qal imperfect) all the days (pertaining to the imperative observe) of your fleeting (NASB, as he has established that there is meaning, perhaps the intention here is transitory or fleeting rather than meaningless, however, all previous uses of *hebel* seem directly to imply the latter) or meaningless life (if meaningless is the better rendering, then it references the under the sun life as meaningless, but can be enjoyed in a meaningful beyond the sun way).

[10] Whatsoever thy hand findeth to do, do it with thy might; for

there is no work, nor device, nor knowledge, nor wisdom, in the grave, whither thou goest.

Here is the principle of urgency stated: work now, for your work has eternal value and you cannot do it once you complete the days of your under the sun life.

9:11-10:19 Conclusion: The Apparatus for Life Under the Sun: Wisdom > Strength

Returning from the *ought* to the *is*, Solomon confirms the superiority of wisdom:

[11] I returned, and saw under the sun, that the race is not to the swift, nor the battle to the strong, neither yet bread to the wise, nor yet riches to men of understanding, nor yet favour to men of skill; but time and chance happeneth to them all.

Men possessing swiftness, strength, wisdom, and learning: time (*eth*) and happening (*pega*, chance) light upon (*qarah*, Qal imperfect, overtake, NASB) them all. Is there any advantage in these four?

[12] For man also knoweth not his time: as the fishes that are taken in an evil net, and as the birds that are caught in the snare; so are the sons of men snared in an evil time, when it falleth suddenly upon them.

Analogy of fishes and birds meeting their demise...so man does not know his time (*eth*) –that which overtakes him.

[13] This wisdom have I seen also under the sun, and it seemed great unto me:

He considers a great (*gadol*) wisdom...a particular observation:

[14] There was a little city, and few men within it; and there came a great king against it, and besieged it, and built great bulwarks against it:

[15] Now there was found in it a poor wise man, and he by his wisdom delivered the city; yet no man remembered that same poor man.

The wisdom was not efficacious to cause the man to be remembered, but it was enough to save the city.

[16] Then said I, Wisdom is better than strength: nevertheless the poor man's wisdom is despised, and his words are not heard.

Thus wisdom excelled strength, although it is not esteemed or heeded.

[17] The words of wise men are heard in quiet more than the cry of him that ruleth among fools.

Wise words in quiet are heard more than the cry of the ruler in fools (*k'sil*). Contrasting result to v. 17: the words of the wise are not heeded by the masses, but are reckoned in the quiet as wise words indeed. Wisdom in its simplicity excels strength.

[18] Wisdom is better than weapons of war: but one sinner destroyeth much good.

Wisdom excels the weapons (*k'liy*) of war – vv.14-15: the wise man delivered the city; but one who leads astray (*chote*) destroys much good (*tov*). Wisdom is good, but one who walks not in accordance with wisdom destroys good.

Thus wisdom, in the diagnosis of what is, excels strength as the best instrument for conducting the under the sun life.

Philosophical Parallel: Platonic Aristocracy

Solomon is impressed by the wisdom of the poor wise man that helped rescue a city. The victory was not accomplished by a great king or a complex system of governance, but rather by simple wisdom.

Plato envisioned a very different means whereby city states could remain secure. In his *Republic* (specifically Book V regarding the context discussed here) he presents his utopian ideal of society as an aristocracy: a rule by the best. He believed society to be simply a larger representation of the individual psyche, thus the class system he promotes reflects his tripartite view of the soul (appetite, spirit, reason). His division of labor represents a harmonious order and priority of purposes among the citizenry. Positions are distributed (by the experts) based on skill, training, and aptitude. The three classes of society are: (1) the artisans – this is the business (lower) class governed by the appropriation of appetite; (2) the auxiliaries (the lower group within the guardian class) – this is the soldier class, motivated by spirit and demonstrating courage, the lived communally and were allowed no property and could not even handle gold or silver to ensure they remained free from corruption; (3) the philosopher kings (the upper guardian class) – these were the best, the wise, who always considered the interests of the state above their own – these were the experts who determined the suitability of the rest of society for their given roles based on merit and eugenics. Plato promoted systematized breeding within the guardian class to maintain the quality of the overall class (sexual relationships were held in common, but breeding was controlled, and children did not belong to parents but were trained by the city state), however, within the artisan class breeding was not regulated and familial relationships were more acceptable.

Notably Solomon sees wisdom as foundational to social political success (vanity though it may be), yet not exclusively in any class of people. Plato, on the other hand, views wisdom as more exclusive and not readily achievable by the common man. Solomon's epistemology disputes Plato's perspective here, and thus Plato's Aristocracy as well.

9:11-10:19 Conclusion: The Apparatus for Life Under the Sun: Wisdom > Strength (cont.)

Qoheleth X

[1] Dead flies cause the ointment of the apothecary to send forth a stinking savour: so doth a little folly him that is in reputation for wisdom and honour.

Dead flies stink up the ointment, so is a little foolishness (*sikluth*) compared to wisdom and honor (see 9:18).

[2] A wise man's heart is at his right hand; but a fool's heart at his left.

A wise heart to his right and a fool's heart to his left...while I chuckle at the potential for political humor here, the passage is simply elucidating the dramatic contrast between the wise man and the fool.

[3] Yea also, when he that is a fool walketh by the way, his wisdom faileth him, and he saith to everyone that he is a fool.

The fool in his ordinary conduct demonstrates himself a fool, that is the nature of foolishness.

[4] If the spirit of the ruler rise up against thee, leave not thy place; for yielding pacifieth great offences.

Solomon returns to a brief foray in the ought: Leave (*nuach*) not thy standing (*maqom*) for yielding (*marpe*) leaves (*nuach*) great crimes. Persevere in the face of a ruler's unjust wrath, as yielding (not fighting back) leaves or alleviates the great crimes.

[5] There is an evil which I have seen under the sun, as an error which proceedeth from the ruler:

Back to the is...further folly from a ruler behaving badly:

[6] Folly is set in great dignity, and the rich sit in low place.

This is the general observation with specific examples and other truisms and ironies to follow: folly is exalted while (true) richness is not esteemed. There is a strange irony to life.

[7] I have seen servants upon horses, and princes walking as servants upon the earth.

Servants (those deserving to be) upon horses, princes (those deserving to be) walking as servants. An ironic example of v. 6.

[8] He that diggeth a pit shall fall into it; and whoso breaketh an hedge, a serpent shall bite him.

More irony: the one who digs a pit falls prey to it, and the one who breaks a hedge (*gader*, a wall) is bitten by a snake.

[9] Whoso removeth stones shall be hurt therewith; and he that cleaveth wood shall be endangered thereby.

The one who quarries (NASB) stones may be hurt by them, likewise the one who cuts (*baqa*, splits, NASB) wood.

[10] If the iron be blunt, and he do not whet the edge, then must he put to more strength: but wisdom is profitable to direct.

Wisdom excels strength: the simple sharpening of an axe makes the task require less strength – this likewise is ironic.

[11] Surely the serpent will bite without enchantment; and a babbler is no better.

On to a simile: the serpent bites without invitation and no better to a babbler the tongue.

[12] The words of a wise man's mouth are gracious; but the lips of a fool will swallow up himself.
[13] The beginning of the words of his mouth is foolishness: and the end of his talk is mischievous madness.

Wise vs. foolish speech is contrasted.

[14] A fool also is full of words: a man cannot tell what shall be; and what shall be after him, who can tell him?

Despite the foolishness of the fool's words, he still multiplies them. Yet man cannot know what will be, thus the ought: do not multiply foolish words (5:2-7).

[15] The labour of the foolish wearieth every one of them, because he knoweth not how to go to the city.

The fool is so opposed to laboring that he is ignorant of the most basic tasks.

[16] Woe to thee, O land, when thy king is a child, and thy princes eat in the morning!

Immaturity and pursuit of self-interests among leadership is devastating....

Woe (*iy*) to you land: addressed in the vocative sense, land is personified....

[17] Blessed art thou, O land, when thy king is the son of nobles, and thy princes eat in due season, for strength, and not for drunkenness!

The contrast to v. 16: Blessed (*esher*, happy; *makaria* in the LXX) is the land (using the same literary device as in v. 16) when leadership functions according to design: for the benefit of the land and people.

[18] By much slothfulness the building decayeth; and through idleness of the hands the house droppeth through.

Laziness effectively tears down.

[19] A feast is made for laughter, and wine maketh merry: but money answereth all things.

Two examples to demonstrate the contrasting nature of a third: a feast for laughter, wine for making to rejoice (*samach*), and money for answering (*anah*) all (*kol*). Feasts and wine serve one primary purpose; money is broadly useful.

Throughout this section Solomon has focused on the "is": that wisdom applied to the most basic functions of life is superior to strength and also foolishness. Solomon, in accurately assessing the *is* can then move to the more prescriptive elements of discussing the *ought*.

10:20-11:8 Conclusion: Apply Wisdom Under the Sun

While the chapter division waits until after verse 20, the final verse of chapter 10 begins a prescriptive discussion – a series of imperatives; thus I include it here with chapter 11. He centers the exhortations on practical sundry applications of wisdom.

[20] Curse not the king, no not in thy thought; and curse not the rich in thy bedchamber: for a bird of the air shall carry the voice, and that which hath wings shall tell the matter.

Note the parallelism: two prohibitions, two consequences…

Not in your thought (*madda'ka*, knowledge) or your inner chamber…that "a little birdie" should carry that whispered curse from the inner chamber is imaginable. But from the thoughts? Solomon warns to apply wisdom not just in speech but also to govern the thoughts, as they have a tendency to make themselves known.

Qoheleth XI

[1] Cast thy bread upon the waters: for thou shalt find it after many days.

Jewish tradition (Talmud, Midrash, Targum) interprets this is an imperative to charity which will not go unrewarded. This, or perhaps a general principle of investment might be intended. It seems the generosity imperative is the best interpretation.

[2] Give a portion to seven, and also to eight; for thou knowest not what evil shall be upon the earth.
Don't put your eggs in one basket. Diversify. You do not know the what will be. Hence, the wisdom in protecting against the evil that may suddenly appear on the earth (*ha arutz*).

[3] If the clouds be full of rain, they empty themselves upon the earth: and if the tree fall toward the south, or toward the north, in the place where the tree falleth, there it shall be.

Where a tree falls, there it is. Brilliant, Solomon! Sounds so obvious, yet he is speaking of the certainty of events: i.e., the evil of v. 2. Adversity will come as surely as a raincloud must empty itself and as surely as the location of a fallen tree.

[4] He that observeth the wind shall not sow; and he that regardeth the clouds shall not reap.

Observation (*shamar*, heeding) and seeing (*ra'ah*) are not the means to sowing and reaping. Action is. Wisdom recognizes the need for action in its appropriate time.

[5] As thou knowest not what is the way of the spirit, nor how the bones do grow in the womb of her that is with child: even so thou knowest not the works of God who maketh all.

Building on v. 4, as man does not know from whence comes the spirit (*ruach*, or wind) or the impetus for the formation of bones in the womb, man does not know the activity (*ma'asah*) of God who has made the whole, or all. Observation and seeing are warranted, but not to the exclusion of tasks necessary for survival, since they are limited and cannot bring the answers to the most important questions of life (useful nonetheless, but typically doesn't put food on the table).

[6] In the morning sow thy seed, and in the evening withhold not thine hand: for thou knowest not whether shall prosper, either this or that, or whether they both shall be alike good.

Work diligently constantly for you do not know which efforts will bear fruit.

[7] Truly the light is sweet, and a pleasant thing it is for the eyes to behold the sun:

It is good (*tov*) to see (*ra'ah*) the sun (*shemesh*). To see the sun is previously established metaphor for life under the sun (7:11). Thus to live is good.

[8] But if a man live many years, and rejoice in them all; yet let him remember the days of darkness; for they shall be many. All that cometh is vanity.

Rejoice (*yis'mach*) – he shall rejoice, or let him rejoice (NASB). He can rejoice by the previously identified means (cf. 3:12-14) of seeing good in his labor.

And remember (*yiz'kor*, imperative) – he should mark his days of darkness (*choshek*, cf. 5:17) for they will increase (*rabah*).

All that will come is vanity (*hebel*). Because of this, he should take joy and remembrance in all of it, so that he does not view it as vanity (with an under the sun perspective) but by rejoicing in and marking his days, he will be able to maintain the proper evolution of them and see the eternal significance that they possess.

11:9-10 Conclusion: Enjoy Life with a "Beyond the Sun" Perspective

As Solomon nears the apex of his thesis, the imperatives grow stronger and more direct:

[9] Rejoice, O young man, in thy youth; and let thy heart cheer thee in the days of thy youth, and walk in the ways of thine heart, and in the sight of thine eyes: but know thou, that for all these things God will bring thee into judgment.

Rejoice (*semach*), O young man (his initial intended readership was one) in thy youth – notably, Solomon is passing on this profound wisdom to his young son. These matters are not beyond the comprehension of the young, and should not be avoided during ones youth. He demands his young son to heed his words and act upon them.

And you shall cheer your heart (notice the heart is governed by volition here, contrary to Hume) all the days of your youth and walk in the ways of your heart and in the seeings of your eyes.

The heart (the inner man, perhaps even reason) and the eyes (the seat of the empirical) are the instruments God has given whereby man can discern. Yet at the core, and due to the fall and the consequent increasing of the chasm between under the sun and beyond the sun, man is as if blind (Is. 59:10) and his heart is desperately sick (Jer. 17:9). Nonetheless, if he uses these

instruments, guided by proper perspective of God (in this case, knowing that God will judge all actions, thus all actions have eternal significance), they are functional. If not, he is being guided into futility by these very same instruments.
[10] Therefore remove sorrow from thy heart, and put away evil from thy flesh: for childhood and youth are vanity.

Again, volition trumps the passions....

Remove sorrow (*ka'as*, vexation) and evil (*ra*) from your body (*basar*, flesh). The vexation and the calamity that so torments the under the sun perceiver has no place in the beyond the sun vantage point. It is fitting that these things should be removed.

Childhood and youth are vanity (*hebel*) perhaps fleeting is a better rendering here: You get one opportunity to enjoy your youth properly, and you can only make the most of the opportunity with a view to the right perspective of and relation to God. Any alternate approach to life (especially during youth) robs the young one of the only means of grasping meaning and value in the days of life.

Philosophical Parallel: Lucretian Atomism

Lucretius, an early evolutionistic thinker (99-55 BC), wrote an epic poem, *On the Nature of Things*, espousing the doctrine of atomism. His primary purpose was to support an anti-metaphysical animus. He seeks to explain the phenomena in materialistic terms. There is no need for the "gods," and since the gods are not in this world or outside it (having no real substantial existence at all), as a result humanity should have no fear of post-mortem divine judgment. Taking this stance – controversial even at the time of its original proposal – Lucretius must elucidate an alternative explanation for the appearances of things, and even their inner nature and inner workings. Specifically, he argues that substance is eternal – that there exists first things, and that nothing is derived from nothing. Among these "first things" are two things in particular which exist of themselves (and hence are not from nothing, but are everlasting): body and void. That substance which cannot be further reduced (body, comprised of atoms), and the vacuity that allows for movement, etc (void).

Perhaps the central tenet of his initial argument is the presupposition associated with his concept that nothing can come from nothing. The premise that nothing can come from nothing would seemingly eliminate the possibility of any kind of fiat *ex nihilo* creation (as a pre-existent deity or deities engaging in a first creative act would have ultimately had to begin with nothing). But this assertion would also seem to logically dismiss the possibility that any "first things" could exist, lest they not be eternal. And if it is presupposed that they do exist uncreated and thus are eternal, then the need to explain their origin evaporates, but yet upon what basis can Lucretius justify his presupposition? It seems as though this point becomes both his strongest argument and his weakest concurrently. The point is the strongest (if the presupposition is granted) because it makes logically impossible the first creative works of metaphysical beings, and thus directs the mind to look for a reasonable alternative – which Lucretius offers as body and void. Yet the point is also weakest because in order for it to possess a certain efficacy it is first required that the presupposition be granted: namely, that there are first things which are substantial and are yet eternal. His argument here bears strong resemblance to the introduction of Carl Sagan's *The Cosmos*, which states with its inaugural words, "the cosmos is all that is, was, and ever will be." Upon what basis of authority can such a statement be made?

Only upon a materialist presupposition, which if accepted, is self-authenticating and draws the necessary authority to invite consideration of the system as a whole. But if the materialist presupposition is challenged, then indeed Sagan's perspective, and Lucretius' alike, may be challenged as well.

Lucretius, beginning with the materialist assumption, defends the assumption by the assumption itself, yet he cannot be accused of circular reasoning, as any approach seemingly requires a self-authenticating starting point.

12:1-7 Conclusion: Remember Your Creator

Having completed the recounting of his investigation and its results and having given a number of imperatives that naturally flow from them, Solomon, before concluding his exhortation, will fashion one final illustration of the truth he seeks to instill in his son:

[1] Remember now thy Creator in the days of thy youth, while the evil days come not, nor the years draw nigh, when thou shalt say, I have no pleasure in them;

Remember (*yi'zkor*, imperative) your Creator (*bara*) in days in your youth. Be mindful of your Creator. Do not walk through your youth with a naturalistic or materialistic perspective. Be mindful during the good years, for the dark days are coming...

[2] While the sun, or the light, or the moon, or the stars, be not darkened, nor the clouds return after the rain:

While (*ad*), better, before...the dark and gloomy days....

[3] In the day when the keepers of the house shall tremble,

So begins a metaphorical look at the dark days. The aging of the body is portrayed as the decay of a house:

The guarders (*shamar*) – the arms...

and the strong men shall bow themselves,

The legs...

and the grinders cease because they are few,

The teeth...

and those that look out of the windows be darkened,

The eyes...

[4] And the doors shall be shut in the streets, when the sound of the grinding is low,

The lips shall close as speaking declines (also possibly loss of hearing)...

The metaphor shifts now from a singular metaphor (house) to a mixed metaphor portraying the various aspects of aging and decay:

and he shall rise up at the voice of the bird,

Difficulty in sleep...

and all the daughters of music shall be brought low;

The increasing faintness of hearing (and possibly decline of voice)...

[5] Also when they shall be afraid of that which is high, and fears shall be in the way,

With decreasing strength comes increasing helplessness – which is accompanied by fear...

and the almond tree shall flourish,

The hair grows white, and as the almond tree casts off its blossoms, so the old man his hair...

and the grasshopper shall be a burden,

Properly, the locust (*chagab*) – the implication seems the loss of motion and flexibility...

and desire shall fail:

Caperberry (*abiyonah*) symbolic of the desire of taste...

because man goeth to his long home, and the mourners go about the streets:

Because (*ki*) – better, for man goes to the grave and the mourners go about in the street...

[6] Or ever the silver cord be loosed,

As in the cord holding a lamp, if it be removed (*rachaq*) or broken the lamp crashes to the ground: death...

or the golden bowl be broken,

As in the bowl which holds the oil for the lamp. If the bowl be broken, the oil leaks out, thus extinguishing the lamp: death...

or the pitcher be broken at the fountain,

The broken pitcher holds no water: the inability of the container (the body) to hold life, perhaps a reference to the heart as being unable to pump blood, in either case: death...

or the wheel broken at the cistern.

The broken wheel can pump no water...also perhaps a reference to the heart, in either case: death...

[7] Then shall the dust return to the earth as it was:

The fulfillment of the Adamic curse (Gen. 3:19)

and the spirit shall return unto God who gave it.

This is a very striking phrase: earlier, Solomon acknowledged that in an under the sun perspective, no one can be certain of the destination of the spirit and whether such is different for man and beasts (3:20-21). Here, speaking with the enlightenment of the beyond the sun perspective, he speaks with certainty. The spirit (*ruach*, same as in 3:20) returns to God who gave it.

This speaks of the continuance of existence for the spirit, despite the failing of the flesh. The awareness of this reality speaks to the importance of recognizing the eternal significance of all activity through the proper perspective of and relation to God. Such awareness is innate (3:11) if we will but listen, and represents a marvelous contrast to the naturalistic under the sun viewpoint that can boast no certainty about anything.

Excursus: Contrasting Hume's Naturalistic Viewpoint with Calvin's Innate Awareness of Deity

John Calvin (1509-1564) and David Hume (1711-1776), though separated in time by two centuries, both play key roles in the development of Western ethical theory. Calvin, with his spiritual approach, provided perhaps the most comprehensive theological and ethical framework since Augustine. Hume, decidedly secular in his premises, contributed much to Western philosophy during the Scottish Enlightenment, not the least of which is his sentiment based theory of ethics. Calvin and Hume begin with somewhat contradictory premises, and their conclusions are equally as diverse. I provide an introduction to their premises and conclusions – in particular, highlighting some of the key distinctions setting the two approaches apart from each other.

Calvin's Rationality vs. Hume's Sentiment
Calvin begins his *Institutes of the Christian Religion* by emphasizing that there is interlocking need for knowledge of God and knowledge of self, and that one cannot be had without the other.[175] In his discussion Calvin is observed to be doggedly persistent in his implied assertion of the necessity for evaluating reality through the lens of human reason.[176] Despite Calvin's reliance upon reason, he presents it not as serving its own ends, but rather reason serves as an instrument providing awareness of and knowledge of God. Calvin suggests an awareness of divinity in the human mind which renders all men cognizant of the divine majesty.[177] Calvin argues that all humanity possesses this awareness, although some repress it in rebellion.

Hume was convinced that the human world could be explained not in terms of the working of reason but in terms of the working of feeling.[178] For Hume, reason is not the final authority. He says,

> The whole is a riddle, an enigma, an inexplicable mystery. Doubt, uncertainty, suspense of judgment, appear the only result of our most accurate scrutiny concerning this subject. But such is the frailty of human reason, and such the irresistible contagion of opinion, that even this deliberate doubt could scarcely be upheld, did we not enlarge our view, and, opposing one species of superstition to another, set them a quarrelling; while we ourselves, during their fury and contention, happily make our escape into the calm, though obscure, regions of philosophy.[179] [How does this quote relate to the reason/feeling distinction?]

Hume's statement here typifies his view of the limitedness of human reason. Here he identifies the frailty of human reason, a characteristic of reason which gives cause for de-emphasis without negating its significance altogether. Hume understands reason to play a key role, but emphasizes to a greater degree the importance of sentiment. In fact, he values sentiment even over virtue itself – suggesting that sentiment provides the impetus for achieving virtue. Hume's sentiment is the centerpiece of his ethical theory. He vividly describes the relationship between sentiment and ethics:

> Extinguish all the warm feelings and prepossessions in favour of virtue, and all disgust or aversion to vice; render men totally indifferent towards these distinctions; and morality is no longer a practical study, nor has any tendency to regulate our lives and actions.[180]

His conclusion ultimately, though, sees both as important elements, as he suggests that both reason and sentiment work together, saying that they concur in almost all moral determinations and conclusions.[181] In Hume's view, the two complement one another and provide a springboard to an effectual ethical base.

Calvin's Inner and Outer Man vs. Hume's Moral Synthesis
Calvin's ethic is dependent entirely upon the immortality of the soul. He argues vigorously against Aristotle's assertion that the soul is inseparable from the body. Calvin's conclusion is that to deny the immortality of the soul is to deprive God of His right[182] - here Calvin is appealing to the rights of God as Creator – to deny the eternal nature of the soul is to deny the image of God in man and to steal from God the apex of His creation. This is a vital point of call for Calvin's theology, as he highlights in this regard the grave mistake of confusing the creature with the Creator. His line of reasoning gives admission that without the existence of God and consequent immortality of the soul, his system is ineffectual, yet at the same time he even derides any suggestion that such non-existence and lack of immortality could be possible.

Hume, on the other hand, is convinced that the emphasis on the two natures of man is incoherent, that while Calvin would conclude that the inner life is thus the domain of religion, not of morality[183], Hume must insist that the inner and the outer aspects of human life are unified in morality.[184] The crux of ethical foundation then is religion for Calvin, and morality for Hume. Calvin, basing his ethical argument upon the authority of God can see no usefulness for law outside of the reality of such spiritual things, while Hume seeks to justify a system of value and morals entirely separate from religious considerations.[185]

Calvin's Futurity vs. Hume's Temporality

As necessary to Calvin as the immortality of the soul is the idea of future life. He says,

> Knowledge of this sort [of God], then, ought not only to arouse us to the worship of God but also to awaken and encourage us to the hope of future life.[186]

Hume, on the other hand, viewed the present as of the highest value. Schneewind characterizes Hume's argument as being comprehensively temporal, saying,

> We seek a calm and enjoyable life here, it is after all quite attainable, we need and ask for nothing better. Once we understand our own nature and the world we live in, we will not be troubled by the threats and exhortations of Calvin and his ilk. We will go on our way making our own lives and those of others happy, no longer frightened by ghosts or misled by fanatics.[187]

Of particular note in Schneewind's comment is the obvious disdain for Calvin's ethical theory based [primarily here] on this temporality – classifying "Calvin and his ilk" as "fanatics." Futurity must be, in this light, simply considered as one of Hume's *inexplicable mysteries*, and would thus have no merit as a foundation for ethical considerations. It could certainly be argued that Calvin's ethic relies on futurity. Hume ridicules Calvin's idea as simply being the product of wishful thinking:

> The comfortable views exhibited by the belief of futurity are ravishing and delightful. But how quickly they vanish

on the appearance of its terrors, which keep a more firm and durable possession of the human mind!188

The contrast between Calvin and Hume is indeed striking.

Calvin's Chief End vs. Hume's Secular Morality (Benevolence, Happiness)
Calvin's chief end is enumerated in the forthcoming *Westminster Confession* which elucidates that the chief end of man is to glorify God and enjoy him forever. Calvin's epistemological foundation then find as its elementary precepts several basic ideas: (1) God is sovereign; (2) Man is flawed and fallen; (3) Man is created for God's own purposes; and (4) ultimately that purpose is to glorify God.

As a result of Calvin's epistemological keys, his ethical argument is found in his deduced function of morality – not as utilitarian for producing any particular product in man, but instrumental in bringing glory to God – morality is a means to the chief end that is Calvin's doxological purpose.189

Hume also seems to reckon ethical moorings as means to a particular end. Hume indicates that morals serve as means whereby habits are aligned to bring about the greater happiness. Hume says,

> The end of all moral speculations is to teach us our duty; and, by proper representations of the deformity of vice and beauty of virtue, beget correspondent habits, and engage us to avoid the one, and embrace the other.190

Why, though, should one avoid one and embrace the other? The ultimate motivation is defined with precision:

> Upon the whole, then, it seems undeniable, *that* nothing can bestow more merit on any human creature than the sentiment of benevolence in an eminent degree; and *that* a *part*, at least, of its merit arises from its tendency to promote the interests of our species, and bestow happiness on human society.[191]

Hume's secular morality focuses its attention in the provision of happiness for each other – benevolence which provides happiness for the other while at the same time providing happiness for the one. Calvin's ethic then focuses on the pleasure of God, while Hume's serves the pleasure of man.

Calvin's Theology Stated as an Ethical Foundation

While Calvin's theology includes the basic elements discussed here, including rationality, dual nature, belief in an afterlife, and doxological purpose, the nuances of his theology were later elucidated by his followers. Calvin's theology came to be identified by the acronym *tulip:*

Total Depravity – man is condemned in Adam, and steeped in sin, having no ability to achieve such ends as virtue or goodness. Man must therefore rely on the redeeming power of God in order to hold any worthiness whatsoever.

Unconditional Election – God elects those whom He will redeem, and due to the depravity of man, there is no intrinsic value in man whereby he should be redeemed. The sovereignty of God is emphasized here.

Limited Atonement – the death of Christ paid only for the sins of those who are unconditionally elected.

Irresistible Grace – due to man's inability to either warrant or accomplish his own redemption, God must call the elect to Himself, and as a result, this calling is effectual.

Perseverance of Saints – since man has nothing to do with his own redemption, he can't lose it; the elect will abide in faith, ultimately resulting in salvation.

These five points emerge from core elements of Calvin's ethical theory: total depravity keeps man from enjoying the possibility of a sentiment based ethic, as he has no ability to have proper sentiments; unconditional election correlates to the chief end – highlighting the sovereignty of God, therefore providing the impetus for doxological purpose; limited atonement, and irresistible grace parallel the dual nature, as each deals with the new life element; and perseverance of saints provides a corollary to futurity.

Calvin's ethic, despite its several insufficiencies, is commendably built upon the sovereignty of God, the reality of the spiritual world, and the incapacity of man.

Hume's Secular Moral Sentiment Stated as an Ethical Foundation
Calvin and Hume disagreed strongly on the origin of religion, as Calvin held the awareness of it was as intrinsic to human nature as that human nature itself, while Hume had other ideas entirely, as Schneewind emphasizes,

> Hume proposes a variety of causes [for religious beliefs]: mainly, ignorance of real natural causes, and the fear and hope that result from this ignorance; then confusion and uncontrolled imagination; finally the use of fear and confusion by various groups to maintain power.[192]

This seems perhaps a direct response on Hume's part to Calvin's arguments to the contrary, as Calvin insists the following:

> ...it is utterly vain for some men to say that religion was invented by the sublety and craft of a few to hold the simple folk in thrall by this device and that those very persons who originated the worship of God for others did not in the least believe that any God existed.[193]

Despite Calvin's assertions, Hume stands firm against intrinsic awareness of the divine:

> It would appear, therefore, that this preconception springs not from an original instinct or primary impression of nature, such as gives rise to self-love, affection between the sexes, love of progeny, gratitude, resentment; since every instinct of this kind has been found absolutely universal in all nations and ages, and has always a precise determinate object, which it inflexibly pursues.[194]

Hume concludes that religious belief is not universal (and thus – Calvin's brand in particular – is not perhaps an authentic ethical base) as other sentiments surely must be, but rather is invented for more utilitarian purposes, if not altogether stemming from ignorance and superstition. Hume thus finds it quite natural to detach morality from religion, and thus has no fear that with a desirable decrease in religious beliefs there would be a resultant decline in moral sensitivities. Hume strives to present an epistemological base founded on a purely secular system of moral sentiment. His contrasts with Hobbes' framework, although similarly secular, as Hobbes presents a bleak view of human nature bent on self-love and self-interest redeemed only by the qualities of the social contract. Hume, on the contrary, appeals to moral sentiment – and the idea that man can take joy in the successes of others, building his case that humanity is not entirely self-serving. Thus Hume's world is potentially a feel-good Utopia wherein the golden rule is applied without the follower being bound to its Proclaimer.[195]

> ...Hume thought he was able to show that morality is always, in the long run, concerned with making human life enjoyable. Life is not a matter of frightened and painful preparation for another world, as the Calvinists held.[196]

Hume may have acknowledged the possibility of a deity existing (albeit with consistent skepticism regarding any revelation of such),[197] and he seems to have some affection for deism,[198] although Warburton's accusations that Hume promoted atheism[199] seems at least partially accurate, as certainly Hume is, at the very least, a practical atheist. Hume's ultimate goal seems to be, simply stated, to present "a universe where there is no God who rewards and punishes,"[200] yet one in which people are sufficiently motivated to conduct themselves in a moral way. In short, the theological underpinnings of morality are removed,[201] yet Hume proposes that morality still stands nonetheless – and even flourishes. In fact, Hume views religion as even being harmful to the notion of morality, saying,

> ...the greatest crimes have been found, in many instances, compatible with a superstitious piety and devotion. Hence it is justly regarded as unsafe to draw any certain inference in favor of a man's morals from the fervor or strictness of his religious exercises, even though he himself believe them sincere. Nay, it has been observed that enormities of the blackest dye have been rather apt

to produce superstitious terrors, and increase the religious passion.[202]

(While Hume's accusations here seem particular relevant today, one would have to question whether he is entirely fair in his considerations...rather than generalize about "religious fervor" [as does Lynn White later regarding the influence of so-called "Christian" teachings on western environmental ethics], perhaps he should make a calculated examination of a number of specific religious systems...Hume paints with [I think] too broad a brush.)

Thus in freeing humanity from the moors of religion, Hume frees us *from* the terrors resulting from superstitions and religious devotions and passions, and frees us *to* a morality of philanthropic sentiment. Indeed, Hume says, morality is determined by sentiment.[203]

Conclusion

While Hume appeals to religion sometimes as superstition, Calvin argues that the existence of superstition is a reality, but that "true religion" can be easily distinguished from such superstition, and that superstitions are not a part of a well-informed faith.[204] These contrasting premises provide an example of Hume's seeming lack of consideration for the possibility a legitimate faith or of the veracity of the Bible. Hume views religion as wholly artificial and certainly not the product of propositional revelation. Calvin is at odds with this epistemological foundation. Through Calvin's eyes we can observe a transcendental foundation for ethics, based on the necessary existence of God and specificity of revealed Scripture. The results are two dramatically opposed ethical foundations. Hume appeals to the authority of man – ultimately the collective happiness of man – for his ethical moorings. Calvin appeals to the authority of God as revealed on the pages of Scripture. These two views could not be more diametrically opposed, and if there is any reality in the law of non-contradiction, then the two cannot both be correct. Even postmodernist efforts to couch the two arguments within a context compatible for varying purposes fall far short of presenting a cohesive synthesis.

As certainly as the two do not coincide, it seems also as certain that one or the other would be legitimate, as the two views present such stark contrasts in their premises – if Hume's premises are faulty, his system falls flat, as would Calvin's if his premises are flawed. Each appeals to a final authority which legitimizes the system. For Hume, it is happiness. For Calvin, it is submission to a sovereign God. For Hume, the scope is limited to the here and now. For Calvin, the scope broadens into eternity. Calvin would accuse Hume of confusing the creature with the Creator, while Hume would probably disagree only in denying the pertinence of such a Creator.

Ethical systems are not founded without much systematic consideration. Both Calvin and Hume essentially present fairly comprehensive worldviews. How does one choose one over the other? Upon what basis? Upon what authority? Calvin's divine revelation? Hume' sentiment and understanding of human nature?

Regarding this question, Pascal formulated his wager - dealing here with the consequence of belief vs. the consequence of unbelief, and thus determining that since the consequence of unbelief was far greater than that of belief, belief was the logical and appropriate conclusion. Ironically, while Pascal concludes in favor of religion, his wager is actually contradicted by the words of the Apostle Paul who said that "If we have hoped in Christ in this life only, we are of all men most to be pitied." (1 Corinthians 15:19)

While Pascal's wager certainly is no sound basis for religious belief, certainly in respect to the issue of ethical foundation – in a discussion in which *utility* is not foreign - particularly in a comparison of Calvin's and Hume's approach – Pascal's query comes readily to mind.

12:8-14 Conclusion: Life with God Is Not Vanity

Here Solomon sums up his exhortation, first with a confirmation of his qualification to make the exhortation, and finally with the conclusion itself:

[8] Vanity of vanities, saith the preacher; all is vanity.

A reiteration of the opening assertion.

[9] And moreover, because the preacher was wise, he still taught the people knowledge; yea, he gave good heed, and sought out, and set in order many proverbs.

He was wise, he taught (*lamad*, as with a goad or with skill and directness) knowledge, listened, examined, and he arranged many proverbs (*m'shalim*, I believe, a confirmation of his authorship of the Book with the same name). If this constitutes a confirmation of his authoring of Proverbs, it would also speak to his authority as a writer of God-inspired writings.

[10] The preacher sought to find out acceptable words: and that which was written was upright, even words of truth.

Acceptable (*chephets*, desirable or pleasurable) words and trustworthy words rightly...

To *Qoheleth*, words mattered. He sought precision in the choosing of his words.

[11] The words of the wise are as goads, and as nails fastened by the masters of assemblies, which are given from one shepherd.

Goads (*dorbon*) spur to action, thus the words of the wise are not merely speculative (knowledge for the sake of knowledge).

Like nails well struck nails are masters of these collections (*asuppah*, collections better than assemblies here). The masters (*ba'aly*) are given (*nathan*) by one Shepherd (*mera'ah echad*). There is ultimately only one source of *true* knowledge.

[12] And further, by these, my son, be admonished: of making many books there is no end; and much study is a weariness of the flesh.

By these...i.e., the gift of the one Shepherd (the word of God) be enlightened (*hizaher*, Niphal imperative, 2ms) – a passive: you are to allow them to enlighten you. They will do the enlightening, you just heed them.

Since there is but one source of truth, beware (imperative implied) extensive dedication to writing and study (it can be unending and wearying).

[13] Let us hear the conclusion of the whole matter: Fear God, and keep his commandments: for this is the whole duty of man.

The conclusion then, from the singular source of truth is:

(1) Fear God and (2) keep His commandments. This is for all men (This applies to every person, NASB).

[14] For God shall bring every work into judgment, with every secret thing, whether it be good, or whether it be evil.

A reason is given for the imperatives: For God shall bring every work (*ma'aseh*, activity) to a verdict (*mishphat*). He shall determine what is good (*tov*) and what is evil (*ra'ah*).

If every action is so examined by God, then the ought is clear: fear God (we must reckon Him to have sovereign rights as Creator in order to reckon Him as the rightful Judge, thus we must perceive Him rightly) and keep his commandments (do those things in which He delights, do not do those in which He doesn't). How can we know His commandments? Only by listening to His word.

Thus Solomon has resolved not just the is / ought problem, but he has resolved the is/ought/ what will be problem:

The is: God is, and He has placed man under the sun.
The ought: fear God and keep His commandments.
The what will be: God will judge every action under the sun.

A beyond the sun perspective of life really makes things quite simple.

Excursus: The Commandments of Jesus: The Ethics of the Gospels

The teachings of Jesus, as recorded in the four New Testament Gospels, provide a system of ethics precisely based yet not comprehensively enunciated. The breadth of subject matter and the systematic continuity of Jesus' teachings have led even secularists such as Bertrand Russell to declare that Jesus possessed "a very high degree of moral goodness."[205]

The goal here is to examine in brief introduction this moral goodness in its various categories, in order to (1) isolate a systematic ethical system (with appropriate divisions) easily comparable with other contrasting or complementary systems with similar divisions, and (2) provide a point of entry to an examination of the New Testament ethic in its broader context with a view to the overall continuity which the plurality of New Testament writers maintain.

Outside of the four Gospels and the immediate context of Jesus' earthly ministry an overarching Biblical framework for ethics is present. First heard as an utterance by God (Lev. 11:44) and later offered by Peter as a reminder (1 Pet. 1:16) are the words, "be holy for I am holy." Based on the relation of mankind to the Creator (made in His image), the created is to reflect the holiness of the Creator. This is perhaps the simplest form of the Biblical basis for ethics and morality. Being fashioned in the likeness of the Divine obligates the created by relation and by imperative as duty bound to reflect the Creator properly.

Since the holiness imperative holds the ethical key it is notable that Jesus does not mention it in any of the four Gospels. Rather He relates to Israel in the context of a second level ethic[206] or an application of the holiness imperative: the Mosaic Law. At this point it must be understood that while the holiness imperative finds its first elucidation in the context of the Mosaic Law, the imperative by logic and by nature precedes the giving of the Law. Man is created in the image of a holy God (Gen. 1:26; Ex. 3:4-6), and even before the giving of the Law recognizes his obligation to holiness (Gen. 3:7; 4:1-8; 6:9; 12:1-3; 15; 22; etc.). The Mosaic Law provided an application of the holiness imperative in bilateral contract form specifically to the nation of

Israel (and no other). It is into this context (one with which the Jewish mind was very familiar) that Jesus injects another application of the holiness imperative. Since the bilateral Mosaic covenant had been previously broken by Israel (Jer. 31:32), it could not serve as (among other things) an ethical base for future generations. Jesus brings the message of a coming prophesied kingdom based upon unilateral covenants and which could not be cancelled out by any moral failure by Israel.[207] In fact, Jesus offers that very kingdom at the outset of His earthly ministry. For those with whom the unilateral covenants would be fulfilled (Israel), this was good news indeed – the *euangellion*.

Ethical Foundations

The *euangellion* constitutes the basic content of Jesus' message, and as such gives some insight into Jesus' particular application of the holiness imperative and the resulting ethical foundations. *Euangellion* is mentioned some 110 times in the New Testament, and a cursory examination of the usage will reveal two primary contexts.

The Gospel of the Kingdom – The National Element

In such passages as Mt. 4:23, 9:35; Mk. 1:14; Lk. 16:16, etc., the *euangellion* is used in a genitive sense in relation to the kingdom. This is certainly the most common usage, and fits well with the emphasis on a prophesied kingdom (2 Sam. 7, etc.) legitimately offered to the nation of Israel. Notably, Matthew is the only one of the four Gospel writers who refers to the kingdom of heaven, and he does so over 30 times. This is significant, as Matthew's purpose is to demonstrate Christ as the King who possesses the authority to rule over the prophesied kingdom which the nation of Israel would enjoy. Matthew thus presents God's eternal and heavenly kingdom as coming to earth in its consummation under the rulership of Jesus. Kingdom of heaven emphasizes, then, the heavenly rule come to earth.

The other writers use the term kingdom of God exclusively. In keeping with their various emphases (Mark – Jesus as Servant of God; Luke – Jesus as Son of Man; John – Jesus as Son of God, and God incarnate) their references to the kingdom highlight its relation in a genitive sense to God. Jesus' involvement in and rulership over this kingdom is a testimony to His unique relation to God.

Regardless of the very important facets of the titling of the kingdom, the kingdom is itself a major emphasis of Jesus' teaching, and pertaining to Israel constitutes a key national element providing another second level ethical base.

The Gospel of Salvation – The Personal Element
While the *euangellion* of the kingdom provided a national hope for Israel accompanied by an aspect of individual responsibility, a second element of the *euangellion* emerges in the writings of Paul, Peter, and John. The two tiered nature of the gospel is seen in Acts 8:12, as Luke recounts the preaching of Philip as the gospel (1) of the kingdom and (2) of the name of Jesus Christ. Paul and Peter in particular both emphasize the second element.

Paul references the *euangellion* some 58 times, and defines the *euangellion* in 1 Cor. 15:1-8 and Rom. 1:16-17 as that which provides personal salvation. This *euangellion* is related in the genitive sense to Christ – it is the gospel of and about Him. It was to be universally proclaimed as the ability[208] of God for salvation to the Jew first and also to the Greek. Paul does not emphasize Matthew's kingdom of heaven, but rather in Rom. 9-11 explains that the national restoration is being delayed by an intercalation generally characterized as the church age. Paul unveils (Eph. 2-3) the mystery that Jew and Gentile participate together in this age as the church body. As Paul seems the primary theologian of the early church and since the kingdom fulfillment would come only after the completion of the intercalation that is the church, the kingdom element of the *euangellion* is deemphasized to some degree in favor of the personal element of salvation.

Peter cites the *euangellion* three times in his first letter, emphasizing a tie to salvation and the sufferings of Christ (1 Pet. 1:10-12) and offering a reminder that the *euangellion*, in addition to requiring belief (Mk. 1:15; Acts 15:7) should be obeyed (1 Pet. 4:17). While Peter's *euangellion* is forward looking in an eschatological sense, it seems most related to individual salvation, as was Paul's, rather than to the national restoration element.

Interestingly, John does not reference the *euangellion* proper even once in his Gospel account, yet his emphasis on the identity of Jesus ties his message contextually and directly (Jn. 20:30-31) to the element of individual salvation. John later recounts witnessing an angel having an eternal gospel to be proclaimed universally, a message centrally of the fear of God and coming judgment (Rev. 14:6-7). That this *euangellion* was both universally proclaimed and contained an imperative (fear God and give Him glory) which was not ethno-specific ties it also to the second element. It is significant that John presents new birth as prerequisite to entry into the kingdom of God (Jn. 3:3).

Each of the early church age writers then places strong emphasis on the element of personal salvation, while recognizing the kingdom element as an eschatological one. But is this *euangellion* of personal salvation foreign to the gospel which Christ proclaimed? And if not, then why does Jesus seem to emphasize the kingdom element, while his disciples focus on the personal salvation element? These issues form an important context for the framework of Biblical ethics.

Jesus' National Emphasis

The *euangellion* that Christ proclaimed was that of the kingdom. His earliest public proclamations recorded by Matthew (Mt. 4:17) and Mark (Mk. 1:15) included the assertion that the kingdom was at hand and the repentance imperative. Notably, the audience of both the imperative and the proclamation of imminence was Jewish, and as is evidenced from Matthew's Gospel, this kingdom was offered as the legitimate fulfillment of such early covenants as the Abrahamic and Davidic. In this light, then, Jesus made an offer to that present generation which could have been accepted by the fulfillment of the imperative (i.e., repent and believe, from Mk. 1:15). The emphasized element of the *euangellion* was that which immediately and most urgently pertained to the audience. The King was here, and His kingdom was being offered. Once the kingdom was not accepted (Mt. 12-13) Jesus began to speak in parables, veiling the truth from those who had rejected, while at the same time asserting that the kingdom would still be actualized in the future. From that point of rejection Jesus' message shifts from the national emphasis to focus on the individual.

By the time the disciples began their proclamations and writing, this national emphasis had already been prophesied by Jesus as purely eschatological, and notably each of the three writers previously mentioned – Paul, Peter, and John all dealt extensively with eschatological material focusing to varying degrees on both the individual and the national.

Jesus' Individual Focus

Jesus spoke of spiritual rebirth as a preliminary for entrance into the kingdom of God (Jn. 3:3) and explained its taking place as through belief in Him (Jn. 3:16). In so doing, Jesus Himself introduced the two elements of the *euangellion*. In this presentation a spiritual position is required in order to participate in the physical blessings that would accompany the kingdom of heaven. In like fashion Jesus described the richness of being a disciple of the kingdom of heaven (Mt. 13:52). Importantly this description emphasizes, after the national rejection of the offered kingdom, a *now* element of the kingdom. In other words, it was in the present possible to pursue the kingdom – to live with a kingdom ethic – despite an absence, in actualization, of the kingdom. In short, those present in the kingdom would exhibit a certain kind of ethic (Mt. 5-7), and if by virtue of the new birth access to the kingdom of God was granted, [209] then it would seem quite appropriate that the kingdom ethic would be applicable to all who participate in spiritual rebirth.

Jesus also introduced a new corporate entity, the church, to be built upon Himself and by Himself. [210] Paul later expands on this entity, asserting direct revelation from Jesus. Both Jesus and Paul emphasize individual responsibility in the context of the church, just as was also emphasized in the context of the kingdom, and both connect the individual in some fashion to the kingdom. In short, the kingdom ethic would be pertinent not only to those who would physically inherit the kingdom of heaven – namely those of Israel preceding and succeeding the church age (as literal fulfillment of Abrahamic and Davidic promises) but also to the participants of the church age as members of the body of Christ – Jew and Gentile. The kingdom ethic as presented by Jesus can be seen as a critical element of Biblical ethical framework, and is at times very impactful toward the specific outworking of ethics in the Gospels.

Ethical Outworking: The Value of Life

The Dignity of Life and the Valuation of the Other
Mt. 18:12-13; Lk. 15:4-6; Mt. 7:12; Lk. 6:31
Characters from Dostoevsky's *The Brothers Karamazov* illustrate well the connectedness of the ethical base to valuation of the other. Dmitry asks how one can be virtuous without God.[211] Ivan previously deals with the same question, attempting a resolution, saying,

> Destroy a man's belief in immortality and not only will his ability to love wither away within him, but, along with it, the force that impels him to continue his existence on earth. Moreover, nothing would be immoral then, everything would be permitted....[212]

At stake in Dostoevsky's polyphony is the origin of ethics, the resolution of which issue is assumed by this writer.[213] The concern dealt with here is not the origin but rather how valuation of the other is defined by the ethical base and is a primary outworking of it. Ivan Karamazov's assumption is that without a base there can be no valuation of the other. Barnhart, while asserting a naturalistic origin of ethics, suggests that cooperation is morality in action,[214] and ultimately cooperation requires a means of valuation of the other. Even when working from an opposing set of presuppositions than those assumed here[215] the primacy of valuation is emphasized. Assuming here the ethical base as a form of divine-command, what then is Jesus' framework for the dignity of life and how is valuation of the other connected to it?

Jesus assumes much and reveals little new information regarding the ontological value of human life, standing on the valuation base of the creation account. Jesus references God as

Father even of those described as evil (Mt. 7:11), a fatherhood relationship presumably tied to the act (Mt. 19:4) and ongoing maintenance (Mt. 6:26) of creation. Jesus is not recorded as having repeated the *made in His image* descriptive, yet it permeates His teaching. In short, human value is presupposed in Jesus' ministry. Without it, even the kingdom message makes little sense. Jefferson, et al, later illustrate this presumption of value, asserting that men are created equal and endowed with certain inalienable rights by virtue of the creation act is a "self-evident truth." Already the established base of the ethical system, it needs not be defended or expounded. Much like the prophets of Israel never offered an apologetic for the existence of Yahweh – His existence was presupposed.

The presupposition of ontological human value is justified by a number of specific actions on God's part as communicated early in Jesus' earthly ministry. God provides, among other things: (1) a means whereby persons can be fed and live (Mt. 4:4), (2) opportunity for entrance into His kingdom (4:17), (3) means for blessing and happiness (Mt. 5:1-12), (4) basic cosmic structure enabling the coexistence of both righteous and unrighteous (Mt. 5:45), and ultimately a means of spiritual rebirth and fellowship with God based on Jesus' sacrifice (Jn. 3:1-21).

Economic value is assessed in terms of individual worth, as the example of the lost sheep illustrates. The shepherd's value of the one sheep finds several justifications: (1) the sheep has intrinsic value as a sheep, (2) the sheep has community value as a part of a flock, (3) the sheep has genitive value as the shepherd's charge, and (4) in light of ontological value, the shepherd is willing to expend great energy and find occasion for great rejoicing over its rescue.

If then there is an intrinsic value of human life which God acts initially to inject and continuously to maintain, then there is to be a pertinent application of the holiness imperative on the part of humanity. The Golden Rule (Mt. 7:12), is a next-step premise in valuation of life. One must value others as God values the one. This is more than simply an ethic of reciprocity as it is extended beyond the limits of reciprocity – namely it is an expression of *agapé* love extending even to those who hate the individual and will provide no reward (Lk. 6:35). Reward is in view not from the person (or enemy) being loved but from God, again stemming from ontological value.

The Human Priority
Mt. 6:25-34; 12:11-12

Lynn White, in his historical critique of the Judeo-Christian ethic makes several pertinent assertions: that God planned all this explicitly for man's benefit and rule, that no item in the physical creation had any purpose save to serve man's purposes, and that Christianity is the most anthropocentric religion the world has ever seen. White argues that the Biblical record thus provides impetus for exploitation of nature, is ultimately the root of the ecological crisis, and must therefore be rejected (White, 1967).

Hull frames the argument perhaps more efficiently, highlighting the central issue of intrinsic value as relating to the idea of spirit:

> Regardless of hotly debated interpretations of biblical passages, the monotheism of the Judeo-Christian tradition dramatically changed people's understanding of nature. The landscape existing before the God of Abraham was inspirited, alive with many gods, demons, and ancestors.... Judeo-Christian teachings de-spirited nature by claiming that nature, unlike people, is not

caring, feeling, or inspirited. Spirits on Earth exist only in people....[216]

While White badly misrepresents purpose in creation[217] and anthropocentrism,[218] Hull, although not entirely accurate in his assessment, seems to uncover the real issue: an intrinsic distinction between humanity and the rest of creation and the seeming priority of humanity afforded by the distinction.

Jesus' teaching is clear on the matter. He presupposes the individual's value as greater than that of the birds of the air and the fields of grass, and yet God expends effort to feed these birds and clothe these fields. Here is implied intrinsic value even of birds and grassy fields as being the products of God's creative act and attentive maintenance. Also, in Jesus' argument that it is indeed lawful to pull a man from a pit on the Sabbath (and thus do labor, thus seemingly disobeying the imperative), He provides the premise that any man would without hesitation remove a sheep from the same predicament. By using this analogy, He demonstrates that in the economy of his listeners, at least, the sheep is assumed to possess intrinsic value.

The question here is not really of intrinsic value, as the person, the sheep and the grassy field possess that. Rather the question is of priority and the logical application of priority in an ethical sense.

Jesus in each instance makes human priority clear: man is worth more than birds, than sheep, than a field. Yet, built into the economy of previous revelation was the awareness of intrinsic value of both beast (Gen. 1:19-22) and field (Lev. 25:3-7) and the imperative to respect and protect both (Deut. 25:4; Prov. 12:10-11; Ecc. 5:9). The ethical framework upon which Jesus built left no room for abuse or misuse of beast or field.

Ethical Outworking: Social Political

Race, Gender and Class Interaction
Lk. 10:30-37; Jn. 4:7-9; Mt. 20:1-16

Jesus' reference to the Samaritan in the Luke 10 parable is significant as it underscores a key racial issue of the day and thereby provides opportunity for Jesus to present an ethic of race.

In 721BC, the northern ten tribes of Israel — often referenced by the Hebrew prophets as Samaria (after the north-central city and region) were taken into captivity by Assyria. Oddly though, the Assyrian captors did not remove the inhabitants to the degree that the Babylonian captors would do to the southern tribes. Rather the Assyrians brought in their own people into the fertile land, bringing about over time occasion and opportunity for intermarriage between Assyrian and Jew in the Samarian region. Later the progeny of such unions came to be known as Samaritans and would be frowned upon and even hated in Israel as they did not possess pure Jewish blood. The distinctions and segregation were so great that the Samaritans even established their own location and system of worship, being unwelcome to participate in the traditions at Jerusalem.

As Jesus reinforces to the lawyer the imperative to love God and one's neighbor, He provides an example in which the Samaritan demonstrates heroically this kind of love for (probably) a Jewish man. In doing so Jesus illustrates that this kind of love is transcendent, even overruling the most severe of racial distinctions.

Jesus does demonstrate, like Paul later, a focus on the Jew first, even to the initial exclusion of the Gentile and Samaritan (Mt. 10:5-7) this emphasis develops from a prophetic base. Later, the message would be proclaimed also to the other (Mt. 10:18; 12:21; Acts. 1:8).

John likewise presents an encounter that Jesus has with a Samaritan woman. Leaving Judea, Jesus travels north to Galilee. The common route would have led him close to the Jordan, yet the text explains that He had to travel through Samaria. Once arriving in Samaria, Jesus has social interaction with a person who has three strikes against her: (1) she is a Samaritan – Jews avoided interaction with Samaritans, (2) she is a woman – Jewish men generally avoided interaction with women, (3) she appears to have been an outcast of some sort, perhaps even a woman of ill repute, judging by the time of day during which she comes to draw water and that she is unaccompanied in doing so. The woman is quite surprised that Jesus addresses her, and as the account progresses, Jesus offers her salvation, even remaining in the city making proclamation on a larger scale.

Jesus' recognition and inclusion of women here and elsewhere in the context of ministry (Mk. 15:41; Lk. 8:1-3) is significant, as Jesus acknowledges distinctions, and ultimately does not fully eliminate them,[219] but the message proclaimed – of love and salvation – provides a means and even imperative for harmonious living with a base of equality and value.

In the same way, Jesus recognizes class distinctions (e.g., tax gatherers as lowly, Mt. 21:32), but is emphatic that those most esteemed now would not necessarily find themselves esteemed so highly in the kingdom – the first shall be last and the last, first. There are two elements which drive this conclusion (1) the kingdom and afterlife concept of rewards, and (2) a focus on the internal attitudes and motivation rather than on the external activity. Things are not always as they seem, and only God who judges the heart can see things as they really are.

Class distinctions in the present context are therefore temporal and not of any lasting significance.

Relation to Governmental Authority
Mt. 22:17-21; Mk. 12:14-17; Lk. 20:22-25; Mt. 20:25-28; 28:18; Jn. 18:36; 19:10-11

Jesus' stance on the proper response to governmental authority is exemplified in the simple statement, "render to Caesar the things that are Caesar's and to God the things that are God's." This statement presupposes even some degree of division between sacred and political. Jesus does not here imply that the things of Caesar are somehow outside of God's jurisdiction, but rather that there is a hierarchy of sorts in the political realm. Specifically applied in this case, paying a poll tax to Caesar violates no law of God, and Caesar is in fact given his authority by God (Jn. 19:11), therefore that which Caesar commands which is not in conflict with that which God has commanded is to be obeyed. Yet, conflicts do arise. One such later conflict involves Peter and the apostles, commissioned by Jesus to proclaim the *euangellion*, yet prohibited by government to do so (Acts. 5:28-29). In such a case, the apostles recognize their duty to obey God rather than men. Such conflicts should be minimal, as Paul later explains that the qualities which are borne of the Spirit are violations of no law (Gal. 5:22-23).

Also notable in this context is the kingdom idea. The scope of the kingdom initially offered (in fulfillment of the Davidic promise) was to be an earthly kingdom, yet as it was at the present rejected, it remained a heavenly kingdom - thus Jesus' statement to Pilate that His kingdom was not of this world. This is important, as it illustrates along with the wheat and the tares (Mt. 13:29-30), a necessary passivity on the part of the people of God in executing judgment for spiritual wrongdoing. Neither the Jews of that age nor the church of the

12:8-14 Conclusion: Life with God Is Not Vanity   431

next age were to be agents of God's judgment as Israel had been early in her history (Deut. 7:2-10). Jesus often spoke of a day of judgment to be initiated at His second coming (Mt. 24:30) under the authority of the Father and given to Jesus (Jn. 5:22). While Jesus could not necessarily be called a pacifist (e.g., surely saving a life, Mk. 3:4, or defending a little one was a worthy cause of violence, Mt. 18:6), He clearly was not interested in the inauguration of His kingdom by use of force on the part of His followers (Jn. 18:10-11). Thus any violence intended for the advance the kingdom of God could not be justified by appealing to the teaching of Jesus, but would constitute man's usurping of Jesus' own authority – the authority of judgment which the Father gave the Son, and the Son gave to no one.

Ethical Outworking: Sex, Gender and Family

The Sanctity of Marriage and Gender Equality
Mt. 19:1-12; 22:23-33 / Mk. 10:1-12; 12:18-27
The school of Shammai interpreted Moses' allowance of divorce (Deut. 24:1) in a very strict manner, concluding that a woman could only be divorced for occasion of adultery, while the Hillel school took a broadly liberal stance, allowing for divorce for virtually any triviality. Hillel's interpretation was the popular contemporary view, and contributed to an attitude that women were no more than to be the property of men.[220]

When confronted with the two views in a Pharisaical attempt to ensnare Jesus, He responded by appealing to neither of the contemporary traditions but rather to the original declaration of marital purpose (Gen. 1:27; 2:24). In doing so, Jesus works constructively from this original paradigm rather than reductively from Moses' divorce permissive. This illustrates several keys in Jesus' determinative approach to ethical resolution: (1) an acknowledgment of progressive revelation — later statements will find their conceptual framework in earlier statements; (2) the Scriptures rather than tradition as the base of authority; and (3) the awareness of an ethical construct handed down by God rather than developed as convention.

In the case of marriage the ethical construct is as follows: (1) the participants are created by God in equality, (2) the participants are designed as opposite and complementary, (3) the participants are to find relational priority in each other, thus decreasing the relational priority of other relationships, and (4) the participants are to enjoy a union that is accomplished both by the participants themselves through a physical act, and by God, apparently at the metaphysical level yet also through the physical act. The key conclusion is that *marriage is a divinely approved and facilitated unity between two created equals*, and thus at least the Hillel interpretation was built on a flawed premise. As Pentecost eloquently phrases it, the Pharisees viewed marriage as a social institution governed by laws of men, while Christ viewed marriage as a divine institution governed by the laws of God.[221]

Later, Jesus is tested by the Sadducees who, not holding to resurrection, present the problem of a woman having seven husbands in sequence asking whose she would be in the resurrection. Again, Jesus rebukes the hermeneutics of His testers, appealing to the authority of Scriptures and the power of God. It is notable here that *in the resurrection* has a distinctly futuristic sense, and this identification of what will be *in the resurrection* cannot be applied to previous circumstances.[222] In particular there would be no marriage among the resurrected analogous to the angels in heaven.[223] While dealing with some of these details, Jesus highlights the real issue — that there is a resurrection. He appeals to Ex. 3:6, an emphatic record that God is the God of the living, and thus His character necessitates resurrection.

It is at this point that the eschatological kingdom element is in view. The relationship of man and woman in marriage is both ontological and economic in the present world, yet in the resurrection, this relationship will change in an economic sense, although the underlying ontological premises of equality as divinely created beings will not. In the most straightforward teachings of Jesus on marriage and its sanctity there is no room to conclude as the Hillel school had previously done, that women were simply property and resources to be managed. Even if one were to argue in favor of an existing inequality from certain elements of the Mosaic value system of sons and daughters (e.g., Ex. 21:7), it is notable that Jesus' appeal to the creation account provides an ontological premise of value for man and woman that is never altered nor rescinded.

Internal vs. External Purity
Mt. 5:17-48; 15:17-20; Mk. 7:15-23
The Mosaic Law at this point stood in its legal authority as a contract broken (Jer. 31:32). In its ethical authority, as a means of demonstrating rather than achieving righteousness, it remained a focus of centrality in Jewish life. Jesus indicates that its value extended beyond its legal authority (a concept upon which Paul later elaborates in Gal. 3:24), and provides specific example in the Sermon on the Mount. His approach is exemplified in the Mt. 5:27-28 intensification of the adultery prohibition.

In its legal contract sense the Mosaic Law was a means whereby Israel would on their part demonstrate a unique ethical system pointing to the character of Yahweh as holy and God would on His part allow Israel to remain peacefully in the land and reap its benefits (Ex. 19). But as the Hebrew prophets repeatedly attested, this contract was not upheld by the nation, and thereby became legally invalid in the sense that God would not be obligated to honor the conditions of the covenant. In Jeremiah's prophesy of a new covenant the old one is acknowledged to have been broken. However, upon Israel's return from the exile which served as a consequence for breaking this covenant, the Mosaic Law was not abandoned. It had served additionally as Israel's ethical framework. Just as the character of God remained unchanged, the means of (dimly) reflecting it did as well. Yet, Jesus presents the essence of the law as being more than outward obedience to it.

Jesus reveals the means of violating the seventh commandment. The physical act constituted a violation of the letter of the law, but it was the internal response of the heart that violated the essence of the law. Looking upon a woman in lust constituted adultery. Whereas many could claim innocence according to the letter, perhaps none could claim innocence according to Jesus' definition. The holiness imperative is restated as the perfection imperative (Mt. 5:48) – a standard which of course none could achieve. Jesus is here emphasizing that holiness and perfection are really reflective of the same standard and one that his listeners could not attain.

While Jesus had unveiled an internal intensification, oddly enough, the rabbinic traditions had offered their own enhancements (including such things as cleansing of hands before eating) that could only focus on the external. Jesus dismisses these enhancements not as useless for hygienic purposes but certainly as useless for any element of holiness, emphasizing that the internal uncleanness is the true defilement.

In discussion of ethics this internal focus emphasizes being a certain kind of character by managing the internal rather than simply doing ethical things in management of the external. For the Jewish mind under influence of the rabbinic traditions this would have been very difficult to handle, but of course this is Jesus' purpose – to demonstrate both on a national and individual scale the need for a redeeming Messiah who could provide the means to relation with a perfect and holy God.

Ethical Outworking: Ideal Ethics vs. Situation Ethics

Inevitably, it seems, conflicts arise between apparent ethical goods. Kant's categorical imperative emphasizes universalizeability and also appeals to higher order principles in ethical decision making, in recognition of the possible situational conflicts between ethical goods. Fletcher offers only three possible means of ethical decision making: (1) legalistic, (2) antinomian, and (3) situational.[224] Fletcher criticizes the legalistic, citing Miller's characterization of legalism as the immorality of morality.[225]

To illustrate the problem, one could ask specifically what would be Jesus' response to Dietrich Bonhoeffer's 1944 plot to kill Hitler. A more general query would consider how Jesus would resolve apparent ethical conflicts of this sort. One of the difficulties in answering this question lies in the fact that Jesus often presents an ideal and does not elucidate contingency. For example He presents the necessity of forgiveness but does not deal with issues such as enabling one to continue in wrongdoing; He emphasizes the undesirability of divorce but does not address the role of the parents in raising the children who are products of the failed marriage. Likewise, He commands love for one's enemies but never addresses what action should be taken if one's enemy stands as an immediate threat to his life (i.e., the issue of self-defense). This lack of specificity indicates that Jesus was more concerned with broad ethical elements related to the holiness imperative and the kingdom economy – namely personal holiness in an internal sense, rather than the very specific machinations of external expression in the rabbinic traditions. But how then to resolve ethical conflicts when they arise? It appears that the answer could have two components: (1) a reframing of the conflict, and (2) a hierarchy of valuation.

Reframing
Mt. 22:17-22, 25-32; Mk. 12:14-17, 18-27
In the pharisaical concoction that was the poll tax question Jesus reframes the conflict by dealing with specifics. Namely that the coin bore the likeness and inscription of Caesar, and thus the coin was Caesar's. In being the originator of the coin Caesar in a sense had sovereign rights as creator and therefore the rightful authority to demand it as payment in the poll tax. Adding a broader perspective to the issue caused the conflict to evaporate and left Jesus' interrogators in amazement.

In Jesus' wilderness temptation at the hands of Satan, three conflicts are presented. In the first two temptations Satan provides an unsolicited is/ought resolution. Jesus' identity should warrant a certain kind of behavior. Was Jesus certain of His identity? He could prove it by demonstrating His power in a certain manner. In third temptation, Satan offers Him a glorious alternative to the fate which awaited Jesus. In each of these three instances, Jesus does not engage Satan nor defend His identity, rather He appeals to that which is written, thus reframing the conflict in light of previous Scripture. There was no is/ought problem, and Jesus had no need for Satan's alternative. Scripture offered the more accurate perspective than the one Satan had initially framed.

In a further test, the Sadducees present a conflict regarding the permanence of marriage, asking to which of seven sequential husbands a woman would belong in the resurrection.

Jesus reframed the question, addressing their true concern – the issue of afterlife, the reality of which the Sadducees denied.

Reframing is not necessarily the resolution of a conflict, rather it redefines the conflict as a non-conflict, and in so doing dismisses a great many perceived conflicts. Those conflicts which remain conflicts even after reframing are seen with new and brighter perspectives enabling at least perhaps a simpler resolution than previously anticipated. But how are these conflicts resolved?

Hierarchy of Divine Valuation
Mt. 5:29-30; 12:1-8, 10-12; Jn. 9:1-3

God, after he created man in His image declared this new creation to be good. God created man possessing among other things, eyes. If God had wished for man not to possess eyes He would not have given them to him, but He did indeed give man eyes. In two instances we see at work the principle of hierarchy of valuation applied in regard to man's eyes.

In Jesus first major oratory, it is pronounced that man should pluck out his right eye if it would cause him to stumble (Mt. 5:29). On the surface, this would seem a ridiculous proposition, but if compared to a modern medical situation in which a cancerous limb is to be removed in order that the patient may escape with his life (a reframing of sorts), the situation is granted a somber realism. In both examples – the one given by Jesus and the medical one – there is a calculus at work. The conclusion is that the whole of the human life is worth more than any of its parts. The parts have significant intrinsic value, but the whole possesses more. The principle of the lesser of two evils is at work. Regardless of the degree of literalness Jesus intended here, man is in this example encouraged to forego the greater of two evils by means of embracing the lesser.

In another instance Jesus passes a man born blind. When the disciples query the reason for the blindness, Jesus identifies the purpose as somewhat utilitarian: that the works of God might be displayed in him. Here the ideal is foregone not on man's part, but on God's. In this case the lesser good (the eyesight of the man) is discarded in favor of the greater (God's works displayed). This second illustration provides the economic premise vitally necessary for ethical conflict resolution. In order to decide based on any hierarchy of valuation, value must be assessed. But who determines value? In Jesus' ethical calculus, God does. Thus hierarchy of valuation becomes hierarchy of Divine valuation.

Conclusion

While Jesus' teaching provides a definitive ethical base, it may not provide the systematic details one might look for in an ethical system. If Jesus was primarily focused on providing an ethical system, as His motivation is often characterized to have been, then perhaps one would expect a more comprehensive presentation. But His teaching provided a hierarchy of its own – priorities of content which impacted the levels of content. He first presented the kingdom and the ethical characteristics of those representing the kingdom, then spiritual rebirth by virtue of belief in Him, and then an ongoing exposition played out in His own actions regarding the content of belief – namely the outworking of His identity, i.e., His sacrificial and substitutionary work. In short, He had bigger fish to fry than simply to provide a comprehensive ethical framework.

This is not to say that His focus on the eternal precluded any interest in the temporal; as a matter of fact it is in His connection of the two realms that the magnificence of His ethical base really comes into view. What is more important, man's relationship with God or his relationship to his fellow man? Matthew 5:23-24 gives Jesus' perspective:

> Therefore if you are presenting your offering at the altar, and there remember that your brother has something against you, leave your offering there before the altar and go; first be reconciled to your brother, and then come and present your offering.

Jesus ties the worship of God to one's right relation with his brother. In the overarching scheme, God has primacy, as indicated by the imperative to love God first and then one's neighbor. Yet the interconnectedness of treating fellow humanity ethically with maintaining fellowship with God is undeniable. John would later characterize the one proclaiming his love for God yet maintaining a hatred of his brother as a liar. Thus despite the nonsystematic nature of Jesus' ethic, His reaffirmation of the love mandate with its inherent valuation calculus provides a broad and comprehensive base thoughtfully applicable to any ethical conflict or circumstance.

Postscript

When Nation X mandates within its constitution the elimination of Nation Y, is there any possibility that both of two conditions can exist: (1) Nation X is successful in its core goals and (2) Nation X and Nation Y coexist peacefully? Of course not. And as we see the impossibility of this situation played out in the Middle East every day, we see the same type of contradiction between naturalistic philosophy, which insists at its very core on an atheistic premise, and Biblical wisdom, which opposes the former aggressively.

It is critical then that the believer recognizes two fundamental principles:

First, God is, and He is a rewarder of those who seek Him (Heb. 11:6). Naturalistic philosophy begins with the premise that God is not. There is no common ground here. While philosophy in its purest form should be a love of true wisdom, grounded in the fear of God, naturalistic philosophy allows for no such undergirding. Thus to answer the questions of life we cannot turn to both philosophy and God's word, since the two provide discordant answers to important questions. Occasionally the two will agree, but only in cases in which philosophy borrows from God-ordained principles. Solomon's investigation - if it tells us anything - tells us of the utter futility of pursuing truth apart from God. Qoheleth's father said it well: "The fool has said in his heart, 'There is no God'." (Ps. 14:1, NASB). To deliberately begin any pursuit from a position of foolishness is beyond madness.

Second, philosophy is not the tool God has designed to win people to Himself. It does not and cannot (by its own naturalistic animus) achieve that end. Paul warns believers to

> See to it that no one takes you captive through philosophy and empty deception, according to the tradition of men, according to the elementary principles of this world, rather than according to Christ. (Col. 2:8, NASB)

Believing that one can use these systems of thought, invented to promote the denial of God and man's accountability to Him as Creator, for the purposes of evangelism or apologetics is indeed a deception.

To what end, then, the study of philosophy? If initiated with an under the sun perspective – none. It is vanity of vanities of the highest order. However, if it is launched with a beyond the sun worldview from the start, such a study can be a joyous and productive labor, as God's ways will, time and time again, be proven to be infinitely higher than ours. The learner will be constantly reminded of the worthiness of God to be feared, and thoroughly filled with gratitude that the Glorious Almighty would choose to love such an unmeritorious worm as I.

To God be the glory!

Notes

[1] Adapted from Christopher Cone, *The Promises of God: A Synthetic Bible Survey* (Ft. Worth, TX: Exegetica, 2008), 97-99.
[2] Hume, *Treatise*, Section VII.
[3] Friedrich Nietzsche, *The Gay Science* (1882, 1887), ed. Walter Kaufmann (New York: Vintage, 1974), 181-182.
[4] Erwin Fahlbusch and Geoffrey William Bromiley, *The Encyclopedia of Christianity* (Grand Rapids, MI: Eerdmans, 2005), 198.
[5] Paul Tillich, Systematic Theology (Chicago: University of Chicago Press, 1963), 1:26.
[6] W.K.C. Guthrie, *The History of Greek Philosophy Vol. I: The Earlier Presocratics and the Pythagoreans* (Great Britain: Cambridge University Press, 1962), 38.
[7] Ibid., 1.
[8] Victor Davis Hanson, *The Other Greeks: The Family Farm and the Agrarian Roots of Western Civilization* (New York: Free Press, 1995), 3.
[9] Anthony Snodgrass, "Archeology and the study of the Greek city," in *City and Country in the Ancient World*, eds. Rich and Wallace-Hadrill (London: Routledge, 1992), 19.
[10] Ian Morris, "The early polis as city and state," in *City and Country in the Ancient World*, 26.
[11] Guthrie, *Vol. I*, 30.
[12] Aristotle, *Politics*, Jowett (trans.),1337a31.
[13] Ibid., 1338a1.
[14] Ibid., 1338a8.
[15] Seneca, *De Brevitate Vitae*, XIV, 1-2. J. W. Basore (trans.) Loeb Classical Library, Vol. 254, 333.
[16] Guthrie, 35.
[17] Ibid., 31.
[18] Ibid., 32.
[19] Ibid.
[20] Ibid., 33.
[21] Ibid.
[22] Plato, *Timaeus*, trans. Desmond Lee, 21-23.
[23] Andrew Ford, "From Letter to Literature: Reading the 'Song' of Ancient Greece," in W*ritten Texts and the Rise of Literate Culture in Ancient Greece*, ed. Harvey Yunis (Cambridge University Press, 2003), 24.
[24] James T. Chambers, "Review of *Literacy and Orality in Ancient Greece* by Rosalind Thomas, (New York: Cambridge, 1992)," in *History of Reading News*, XIX/1 (Fall, 1995).
[25] Guthrie, 36.
[26] Ibid., 38.
[27] shamelessly anachronistic reference to the Wizard of Oz.
[28] Guthrie, 7.
[29] Ibid., 26.

30 Ibid., 44.
31 E.g., Thales characterization of water or moisture as arche.
32 William S. Sahakian, *History of Philosophy: From the Earliest Times to the Present* (New York: Barnes and Noble, 1968), 1.
33 H.G. Wells, *The Outline of History* (Garden City, NY: Garden City Books, 1949), 1:331-332.
34 Paru dans A. Wiercinski (Dir.), *Between the Human and the Divine. Philosophical and Theological Hermeneutics* (Toronto, CA: The Hermeneutic Press, 2002), 97-101.
35 Thomas Aquinas, *On Nature and Grace*, ed. A.M. Fairweather (Philadelphia, PA: Westminster Press, 1954), 36.
36 Richard Lewontin, "Billions and Billions of Demons", *New York Review of Books*, January 9, 1997.
37 Adapted from Guthrie's comments in W.K.C. Guthrie, *The History of Greek Philosophy, Vol. I: The Earlier Presocratics and the Pythagoreans* (Great Britain: Cambridge University Press, 1962), 38.
38 from Christopher Cone, "Dualism, Ontology, and Pauline Authority" in *Journal of Dispensational Theology*, 12/36 (August, 2008).
39 The existence of this unknowable and alien God is not explained by Plato's causation statement, and is explained by some in an allegorical manner: "The introduction of a creative God in the Timaeus is, of course, purely allegorical. Nothing existed before Existence itself; and no external power was needed to combine the abstract elements into which it is decomposed by thought, as in reality they had never been separated. So much is now generally admitted." (Benn, 1902). Oakeley discusses a contrasting argument which presents the Timaeus as showing a kinship to Christianity: "Especially is the dualism of the Platonic conception emphasized – the picture of the Demiurges doing the best possible with a material only in part submissive to creative form – as essential to a truly religious view of the world...." (Oakeley, 1926). In short, the debate is whether or not Plato's presents a truly "religious" world view or simply uses a mythical mode to communicate a secular one. In either case, the dualism of Plato is inarguable as a grounding for his metaphysical and epistemological conceptions.
40 Bos, as an example, suggests that Plato was perhaps not as impactful as Aristotle on this development, but views Plato as foundational nonetheless.
41 Stewart defends such a statement in part based on, among other factors, Plato's apparent negativity regarding important aesthetic conditions of his time.
42 Vlastos, 66-80
43 Ibid., 79
44 from Plato, *Republic*, Book VII.
45 Descartes says, "I learned to believe nothing too certainly of which I had only been convinced by example and custom." The contrast here is between knowledge acquired via means other than reason, which is not certain, and knowledge from reason, which can be certain.

⁴⁶ Richard Kennington, *On Modern Origins: Essays in Early Modern Philosophy* (Lanham, MD: Lexington Books, 2004), 108.
⁴⁷ (1) to obey laws and customs - to conform to that which will allow for philosophizing, (2) to be resolute – having to do with an internal perseverance, (3) control oneself rather than nature – an apparent contradiction of Descartes elsewhere, Kennington sees satirical elements here, but also, as a provisional tenet, Descartes has not yet earned mastery of nature (that is to be done with the method, not with the provisional morality), and (4) to continue the pursuit of truth – continue examining opinions in order to find better ones (this includes the realm of morality, and provides a kind of self-destruct mechanism for the provisional morality).
⁴⁸ "Methodology and metaphysics are mutually exclusive." Kennington, 120.
⁴⁹ Ibid.
⁵⁰ This edition of "Why I Am Not a Christian" was first made available by Bruce MacLeod on his "Watchful Eye Russell Page." It was newly corrected (from Edwards, NY 1957) in July 1996 by John R. Lenz for the Bertrand Russell Society. accessible at http://users.drew.edu/~jlenz/whynot.html
⁵¹ Kevin Mooney and Josiah Ryan, "Atheists Infiltrate Events for Intelligent Design Film," cnsnews.com, April 2, 2008.
⁵² Harry Rimmer, *Modern Science and the Genesis Record* (Grand Rapids, MI: Eerdmans, 1937), 22.
⁵³ Steven Jay Gould, *Rocks of Ages: Science and Religion in the Fullness of Life* (New York: Ballantine, 1999), 4.
⁵⁴ Ibid., 6.
⁵⁵ Ibid., 127.
⁵⁶ Ibid., 125-126.
⁵⁷ Ibid., 127.
⁵⁸ Ibid., 148.
⁵⁹ Ibid.
⁶⁰ R. Hooykaas, *Religion and the Rise of Modern Science* (Grand Rapids, MI: Eerdmans, 1972), 13.
⁶¹ Ibid., 15.
⁶² Ibid., 16.
⁶³ Hans Jonas, *The Phenomenon of Life* (New York: Delta, 1966), 1.
⁶⁴ Ibid., 70.
⁶⁵ Ibid., 71.
⁶⁶ Plato, *Phaedo*, 96b. (trans. H. N. Fowler).
⁶⁷ Ibid., 99a-c.
⁶⁸ Aquinas' conclusion of a personal God – as well as other related conclusions would be later fodder for *Hume's stopper* – Hume's argument that natural theology has not proved enough to conclude that a *personal* God exists. Hume's critique represents another very important challenge to the sufficiency of natural theology, but will not be discussed in any length here as it considers a different thesis than the one with which this writer is here concerned: namely, the incompatibility of mechanistic evolutionism and an ordered universe.

⁶⁹ Anton C. Pegis, ed., *Introduction to St. Thomas Aquinas* (New York: Random House, 1948): Thomas Aquinas, *Summa Theologica*, Q. 2, Art. 3.
⁷⁰ William Paley, *Natural Theology* (Boston, MA: Gould and Lincoln, 1857), 12.
⁷¹ Ibid., 292.
⁷² Ibid.
⁷³ www.blavatsky.net/darwin/, viewed 4/08/2008.
⁷⁴ www.intelligentdesignnetwork.org/, viewed 4/18,2008.
⁷⁵ Ibid.
⁷⁶ Jonas, 38ff.
⁷⁷ Ibid., 39-40.
⁷⁸ Ibid., 40.
⁷⁹ Ibid., 40-41.
⁸⁰ Ibid., 45.
⁸¹ Ibid.
⁸² Ibid., 47.
⁸³ Ibid.
⁸⁴ Ibid., 48.
⁸⁵ Henry M. Morris, "Neocreationism: A More Accepted Creationism?" in *The Genesis Factor*, ed., Ron J. Bigalke Jr. (Green Forest, AR: Master Books, 2008), 221.
⁸⁶ Lucretius, *On The Nature of Things*, trans. Charles Bennett (New York: Walter J. Black, Inc., 1946), 207.
⁸⁷ All quotes from White are from the "The Historical Roots of our Ecological Crisis," *Science*, 155 (March 10, 1967).
⁸⁸ J. Baird Callicott, *In Defense of the Land Ethic* (New York: State University of New York Press, 1989), 137.
⁸⁹ R. Bruce Hull, *Infinite Nature* (Chicago, IL: University of Chicago Press, 2006), 126-127.
⁹⁰ Means *the preacher*, and references King Solomon, historically recognized as the author of the Biblical book of Ecclesiastes.
⁹¹ The author uses the phrase 28 times, making the hypothetical vantage point of his writing very clear. For his conclusions he steps away from the human centered perspective, but throughout his writing here he emphasizes the human perspective. This is a germane contextual element in deciphering the writer's meanings here.
⁹² Karl Feyerabend, *Langensheidt's Hebrew and English Dictionary to the Old Testament* (Berlin: Langensheidt, 1956), 5.
⁹³ Each of these elements are specifically dealt with in the text of Ecclesiastes.
⁹⁴ Susan Neiman, *Evil in Modern Thought* (Princeton, NJ: Princeton University Press, 2002), 7.
⁹⁵ W.K.C. Guthrie, *A History of Greek Philosophy Vol. II: The Presocratic tradition from Parmenides to Democritus* (Cambridge: Cambridge University Press, 1965), 34-46.
⁹⁶ Habakkuk questions God directly as to how He can tolerate sinfulness (the presence of evil) without bringing about immediate judgment, and then later how God can use the wicked as instruments of judgment against those who are seemingly far less wicked.

⁹⁷ Particularly in chapter 9, perhaps anticipating and offering resolution to Epicurus' riddle.
⁹⁸ Mian Mohammed Sharif, *A History of Muslim Philosophy* (Wiesbaden: Harrassowitz, 1966), 1658.
⁹⁹ Rem B. Edwards, *Reason and Religion: An Introduction to the Philosophy of Religion* (New York: Harcourt Brace Jovanovich, Inc., 1972), 28.
¹⁰⁰ (1) the existence of impermanence, (2) the cause of suffering is craving (3) cessation of suffering comes by cessation of craving, and (4) the means is the middle way, or eightfold path.
¹⁰¹ As translated by V.A. Gunasekara, in *The Buddhist Attitude to God*, viewed at http://www.buddhistinformation.com/buddhist_attitude_to_god.htm (10/16/07).
¹⁰² Lanctantius, *On the Anger of God*.
¹⁰³ Ibid.
¹⁰⁴ Plotinus, *Enneads*, 8:3.
¹⁰⁵ Irenaeus, *Against Heresies*, 5: 8:2.
¹⁰⁶ Augustine, *Enchiridion*, 10-12.
¹⁰⁷ Augustine, *Confessions*, 7:9:13.
¹⁰⁸ Augustine, *Enchiridion*, 10-12.
¹⁰⁹ Augustine, *City of God*, 12:3.
¹¹⁰ Anselm, *Proslogion*, ch. 2.
¹¹¹ From Thomas Aquinas, *Compendium theologiae* 114, 125-126, as quoted in Bill King, "Thomas Aquinas on the Metaphysical Problem of Evil" *Quodlibet Journal*, 4/2-3 (Summer 2002).
¹¹² John S. Feinberg, *The Many Faces of Evil: Theological Systems and the Problems of Evil* (Wheaton, IL: Crossway, 2004), 37.
¹¹³ Joe E. Barnhart, *The Billy Graham Religion* (Philadelphia, PA: Pilgrim Press, 1972), 135.
¹¹⁴ John Calvin, *Institutes of the Christian Religion*, Henry Beveridge, trans., 3:23:2.
¹¹⁵ Ibid.
¹¹⁶ Charles Nussbaum, "Aesthetics and the Problem of Evil," *Metaphilosophy*, 34/3 (April 2003).
¹¹⁷ Zbigniew Janowski, *Cartesian Theodicy: Descartes' Quest for Certitude* (Norwell, MA: Kluwer Academic Publishers,2000), 13.
¹¹⁸ Nussbaum.
¹¹⁹ Spinoza, *The Ethics*, Part I, Appendix.
¹²⁰ Ibid.
¹²¹ From *Sämtliche Schriften und Briefe*. (Darmstadt and Berlin: Berlin Academy, 1923), A6.3:151 as quoted in "Leibniz and the Problem of Evil," *Stanford Encyclopedia of Philosophy*.
¹²² Susan Neiman, *Evil in Modern Thought* (Princeton, NJ: Princeton University Press, 2004), 22.

[123] David Hume, *Dialogues Concerning Natural Religion: The Posthumous Essays on the Immortality of The Soul and Suicide*, ed. Richard Popkin, (Hackett Publishing, 1980), 63.
[124] Section 11, in particular.
[125] David Hume, *Dialogues Concerning Natural Religion*, Section 11:8.
[126] Ibid.
[127] Ibid., 11:9.
[128] Immanuel Kant, *Religion Within the Limits of Reason Alone*, Book 1, Section 15.
[129] Ibid.
[130] Ibid.
[131] Ibid., Book 3, Section 85.
[132] Formalizations and explanations adapted from Christopher Cone, Aesthetics as an Example of the Cross-Disciplinary Pervasiveness of the Problem of Evil, an unpublished paper.
[133] In terms of universal applicability.
[134] Raymond Geuss, "Nietzsche and Genealogy", in *Nietzsche*, ed. John Richardson and Brian Leiter (Oxford: Oxford University Press, 2006), 324.
[135] Philippa Foot, "Nietzsche's Revaluation of Value" in Richardson, John and Leiter, Brian (eds.). *Nietzsche* (New York: Oxford University Press, 2006), 211.
[136] Raymond Geuss, "Nietzsche and Genealogy" in Richardson, John and Leiter, Brian (eds.). *Nietzsche* (New York: Oxford University Press, 2006), 323ff.
[137] For Geuss, pedigree legitimizes authority as stemming directly from some authoritative origin. It is important in this context that the origin is authoritative, for that which receives the authority can only bear what it receives, and if that handed down was not originated in authority then at present it bears none of the same. Geuss calculates five important aspects of pedigree: (1) positive valorization, (2) stems from singular origin, (3) which is actual source of value, (4) traces an unbroken line, (5) which preserves the value intact. Geuss reckons Nietzsche's genealogy to differ with pedigree on all five counts: (1) there is no intent of valorization, (2) does not (necessarily) stem from singular origin, (3) is not the actual source of value, (4) won't exhibit unbroken lines (characteristically), but will instead be characterized by contingency – sometimes a break, a leap, a coercion, and (5) as the original did not fundamentally possess value, there is nothing to remain intact, but if it did, then it would be greatly altered by the transmission (particularly at the fourth step).
[138] It should be noted at this juncture that rather than utilize Geuss' pedigree in a traditional chronological sense, I will employ the pedigree to examine Nietzsche's flow of thought.
[139] Nietzsche describes three epochs in the evolution of morality. The first is pre-historic, with contemporary example in China (as per Nietzsche). This is a period in which there is little concern for the act itself or for its origin, rather the value of the action is determined by the consequences. This is the pre-moral stage. The second has been achieved little by little, as gravitation to the importance of origins (and intention) replaced emphasis on consequence. This is the moral period (characterized by intention morality). The third is an emerging period

that is extra-moral. An action's value is demonstrated by that which is not intentional. (BGE:32).
[140] (1) Primitive, (2) Slave, (3) Feudal, (4) Capitalism, (5) Communism.
[141] As quoted in Harry J. Ausmus "Nietzsche and Eschatology" *The Journal of Religion*, 58/4 (Oct., 1978).
[142] See Leiter's definition and discussion, Leiter, 2002, 74.
[143] Leiter expresses three options: (1) the noumenal world is unintelligible – reality itself is perspectival (Poellner); (2) the noumenal world is irrelevant (Clark) – all basis lost for regarding the empirical world as illusory; (3) the noumenal world is not useful (Johnston) – pragmatic theory. (Brian Leiter, Routledge *Philosophy Guidebook to Nietzsche on Morality* (New York: Routledge, 2002), 276ff).
[144] As quoted in William MacKintire Salter "Nietzsche's Attitude to Religion" *The Journal of Philosophy*, 20/4 (Feb. 15, 1923).
[145] Foot, 211.
[146] Ibid., 212.
[147] Ibid.
[148] As quoted from Nietzsche, *Werke XIII*, 125, in Salter, 1915.
[149] The English is one verse ahead of the Hebrew for the duration of ch. 5.
[150] Robin Usher and Richard Edwards, *Postmodernism and Education* (New York: Rutledge, 1994), 8.
[151] Kevin J. Vanhoozer, "One Rule to Rule Them All",in *Globalizing Theology*, ed. Craig Ott and Harold A. Netland (Grand Rapids, MI: Baker Books, 2006), 89.
[152] Usher and Edwards, 9.
[153] Thomas L. Friedman, *The World is Flat* (Updated and Expanded, New York: Farrar, Straus, and Giroux, 2006), 9-11.
[154] Zygmunt Bauman, *Globalization: The Human Consequences* (New York, Columbia University Press, 1998), 1.
[155] Arjun Appadurai, *Modernity at Large: Cultural Dimensions of Globalization* (Minneapolis, MN: University of Minnesota Press, 1996), 27.
[156] North America Free Trade Agreement.
[157] Free Trade Area of the Americas.
[158] Central America Free Trade Agreement.
[159] Arjun Appadurai, *Modernity at Large: Cultural Dimensions of Globalization* (Minneapolis, MN: University of Minnesota Press, 1996), 20.
[160] Bauman, 58.
[161] Ibid., 59.
[162] Ibid., 66.
[163] Ibid., 69.
[164] Ibid., 47.
[165] Giddens' term akin to *new world disorder.*
[166] Ott and Netland, 331.
[167] Karen Armstrong, *The Battle for God* (NY: Ballantine, 2000), xi.
[168] The teacher narrates, depositing information in the unquestioning and imaginatively unchallenged.

[169] Paulo Friere, *Pedagogy of the Oppressed* (New York: Continuum, 2002), 75.
[170] This approach makes the student a co-investigator, dialoguing with the educator.
[171] Usher and Edwards, 213.
[172] Ott and Netland., 324-326.
[173] Ibid., 325.
[174] Immanuel Kant, *Fundamental Principles of the Metaphysics of Morals*, Section I.
[175] John Calvin, *Institutes of the Christian Religion*, trans. Battles, ed. McNeill (Philadelphia, PA: Westminster Press, 1940), 35-39.
[176] Although he makes clear that reason is to be guided by holy writ.
[177] John Calvin, *Institutes of the Christian Religion*, trans. Battles, ed. McNeill (Philadelphia, PA: Westminster Press, 1940), 43.
[178] David Hume, *An Enquiry Concerning the Principles of Morals*, ed. J.B. Schneewind (Indianapolis, IN: Hackett Publishing, 1983), 5.
[179] David Hume, *The Natural History of Religion*, ed. John M. Robertson (London: A. and H. Bradlaugh Bonner, 1889), Section XV, Viewed at http://oll.libertyfund.org/Texts/Hume0129/HistoryReligion/0211_Bk.html.
[180] David Hume, *An Enquiry Concerning the Principles of Morals*, ed. Niditch, 3rd. ed. (Oxford: Oxford University Press, 1975), 172.
[181] David Hume, *An Enquiry Concerning the Principles of Morals*, ed. Niditch, 172.
[182] John Calvin, *Institutes of the Christian Religion*, trans. Battles, ed. McNeill (Philadelphia, PA: Westminster Press, 1940), 56.
[183] David Hume, *An Enquiry Concerning the Principles of Morals*, ed. J.B. Schneewind, 3.
[184] Ibid., 4.
[185] In Calvin's view, other religions [including Islam, although not here named by Calvin] borrow from this concept of divine law as an ethical base. The primary differences between the various religious systems in this context is (1) claimed basis of authority, (2) contents of the system of law, and (3) degree of focus on temporality vs. eternity.
[186] John Calvin, *Institutes of the Christian Religion*, 62.
[187] David Hume, *An Enquiry Concerning the Principles of Morals*, ed. J.B. Schneewind, 3.
[188] David Hume, *The Natural History of Religion*, ed. John M. Robertson, Viewed at http://oll.libertyfund.org/Texts/Hume0129/HistoryReligion/0211_Bk.html.
[189] Doxa – glory, logos – word, discourse - - the doxological purpose is that which speaks glory of God.
[190] David Hume, *An Enquiry Concerning the Principles of Morals*, ed. Niditch, 172.
[191] David Hume, *An Enquiry Concerning the Principles of Morals*, ed. Niditch, 181.
[192] David Hume, *An Enquiry Concerning the Principles of Morals*, ed. J.B. Schneewind, 6.
[193] John Calvin, *Institutes of the Christian Religion*, 44.
[194] David Hume, *The Natural History of Religion*, Viewed at http://oll.libertyfund.org/Texts/Hume0129/HistoryReligion/0211_Bk.html.

¹⁹⁵ i.e., Jesus Christ.
¹⁹⁶ David Hume, *An Enquiry Concerning the Principles of Morals*, ed. J.B. Schneewind, 9.
¹⁹⁷ See *The Natural History of Religion* – there is some debate as to whether or not Hume's views best supported atheism or whether he showed a leaning at times to a basic deistic approach.
¹⁹⁸ A deity is first cause, yet is transcendent and has absolutely no involvement in the day to day activities of the world.
¹⁹⁹ David Hume, *The Natural History of Religion*, introduction, Viewed at http://oll.libertyfund.org/Texts/Hume0129/HistoryReligion/0211_Bk.html.
²⁰⁰ David Hume, *An Enquiry Concerning the Principles of Morals*, ed. J.B. Schneewind, 9.
²⁰¹ There may be indeed a first cause, but as in his argument referred to as Hume's stopper, the argument from first cause does not logically prove the existence - or necessity of the existence - of God.
²⁰² David Hume, *The Natural History of Religion*, Section XIV, Viewed at http://oll.libertyfund.org/Texts/Hume0129/HistoryReligion/0211_Bk.html.
²⁰³ David Hume, *An Enquiry Concerning the Principles of Morals*, ed. Niditch, 289.
²⁰⁴ A faith informed by Scripture, see *Institutes*, 47.
²⁰⁵ Bertrand Russell, *Why I Am Not A Christian*, March 6, 1927, National Secular Society, South London Branch, at Battersea Town Hall.
²⁰⁶ By the use of the term "second level" I mean to imply an ethic which is simply an outworking of and built upon a more overarching and preexisting framework. In this case that overarching and preexistent framework is the holiness imperative.
²⁰⁷ It could be delayed (as it indeed was), but not eliminated.
²⁰⁸ As indicated by the Greek *dunamis*.
²⁰⁹ Notably of the more universal variety in Jn. 3:3 than the kingdom of heaven in the sense of Davidic fulfillment as emphasized in Matthew.
²¹⁰ Jesus was Himself the *petra* of Mt. 16:18, and was confirmed as such by Peter in 1 Pet. 2:6-8.
²¹¹ Fyodor Dostoevsky, *The Brothers Karamazov*, trans. Andrew R. McAndrew (New York: Bantam, 1981), 712.
²¹² Ibid., 80.
²¹³ This writer assumes divine mandate as the source of ethics.
²¹⁴ Joe Barnhart, "Can Ethics be Both Subjective and Objective?" unpublished essay. New Mexico/West Texas Philosophical Society. Santa Fe, NM. April 2003.
²¹⁵ Barnhart sees irreconcilable problems with divine-command as an ethical base, see ibid.
²¹⁶ R. Bruce Hull, *Infinite Nature* (Chicago, IL: University of Chicago Press, 2006), 126-127.
²¹⁷ Creation serves God's purpose, not man's: Ps. 24:1; Rom. 1:20; Col. 1:16; Rev. 4:11 – specifically no item in creation was made to serve man's purpose as its highest end.

[218] Anthropocentrism is not a reality to be sought after but is fully condemned: Is.2:22; 40:15-17, 26; Mt. 22:37-38; Jn. 3:30.

[219] Despite even Paul's later assertions that in the body of Christ there is no *ethnic* distinction, Israel's *national* identity as unrelated to the body of Christ still remains an important prophetic reality.

[220] J. W. Shepherd, *The Christ of the Gospels* (Grand Rapids, MI: Eerdmans, 1946), 452.

[221] J. Dwight Pentecost, *The Words and Works of Jesus* (Grand Rapids, MI: Zondervan, 1981), 356.

[222] Some would connect this forward looking statement as a categorical definitive describing conditions applicable to Gen. 6:4, etc.

[223] Again, as the angels in heaven do not marry (as indicated by the present tense of v. 30), this does not negate the possibility of angel involvement in Gen. 6:4, although angelic involvement is not an entirely necessary conclusion from the Genesis text.

[224] Joesph Fletcher, *Situation Ethics* (Philadelphia, PA: Westminster Press, 1966), 17.

[225] Ibid.

Bibliography

Anselm. *Proslogion.*

Appadurai, Arjun. *Modernity at Large: Cultural Dimensions of Globalization*, Minneapolis, MN: University of Minnesota Press, 1996.

Armstrong, Karen. *The Battle for God*, NY: Ballantine, 2000.

Aristotle, *Politics*, Jowett, trans.

Augustine. *Confessions.*

_____. *Enchiridion.*

_____. *City of God.*

Ausmus, Harry J. "Nietzsche and Eschatology" *The Journal of Religion*, 58/4 (Oct., 1978), 347-364..

Aquinas, Thomas. *On Nature and Grace*, ed. A.M. Fairweather. Philadelphia, PA: Westminster Press, 1954.

_____. Compendium theologiae 114, 125-126, as quoted in Bill King, "Thomas Aquinas on the Metaphysical Problem of Evil" *Quodlibet Journal*, 4/2-3, Summer 2002.

Bakewell, Charles M. "The Teachings of Friedrich Nietzsche" *International Journal of Ethics*, 9/3, (Apr., 1899).

Barnhart, Joe E. *The Billy Graham Religion*. Philadelphia, PA: Pilgrim Press, 1972.

_____. "Can Ethics be Both Subjective and Objective?" unpublished essay. New Mexico/West Texas Philosophical Society. Santa Fe, NM, April 2003.

Bauman. Zygmunt, *Globalization: The Human Consequences*. New York, Columbia University Press, 1998.

Benn, Alfred W. "The Morals of an Immoralist-Friedrich Nietzsche" *International Journal of Ethics*, 19/1, (Oct., 1908).

Boice, James. *The Parables of Jesus*. Chicago, IL: Moody Press, 1983.

Callicott, J. Baird. *In Defense of the Land Ethic*. New York: State University of New York Press, 1989.

Calvin, John. *Institutes of the Christian Religion*, trans. Battles, ed. McNeill. Philadelphia, PA: Westminster Press, 1940.

Chambers, James T. "Review of Literacy and Orality in Ancient Greece by Rosalind Thomas (New York: Cambridge, 1992)," in *History of Reading News*, XIX/1 (Fall, 1995).

Dostoevsky, Fyodor. *The Brothers Karamazov*, trans. Andrew R. McAndrew. New York: Bantam, 1981.

Edersheim, Alfred. *The Life and Times of Jesus the Messiah*. New York: Longmans, Green, and Co., 1883.

Edwards, Rem B. *Reason and Religion: An Introduction to the Philosophy of Religion*. New York: Harcourt Brace Jovanovich, Inc., 1972.

Fahlbusch, Erwin and Bromiley, Geoffrey William. *The Encyclopedia of Christianity*. Grand Rapids, MI: Eerdmans, 2005.

Feinberg, John S. *The Many Faces of Evil: Theological Systems and the Problems of Evil*. Wheaton, IL: Crossway, 2004.

Feyerabend, Karl. *Langensheidt's Hebrew and English Dictionary to the Old Testament*. Berlin: Langensheidt, 1956.

Fletcher, Joseph. *Situation Ethics*. Philadelphia, PA: Westminster Press, 1946.

Ford, Andrew. From Letter to Literature: Reading the 'Song' of Ancient Greece, in *Written Texts and the Rise of Literate Culture in Ancient Greece*, ed. Harvey Yunis. Cambridge University Press, 2003.

Friedman, Thomas L. *The World is Flat, Updated and Expanded*. New York: Farrar, Straus, and Giroux, 2006.

Friere, Paulo. *Pedagogy of the Oppressed*. New York: Continuum, 2002.

Gellner, Ernest. *Postmodernism, Reason and Religion*. London: Routledge, 1992.

Gemes, Ken. "Nietzsche's Critique of Truth" in *Philosophy and Phenomenological Research*, 52/1, (Mar., 1992).

Gould, Stephen Jay. *Rocks of Ages*. New York: Ballantine, 1999.

Guthrie, W.K.C. *The History of Greek Philosophy Vol. I: The Earlier Presocratics and the Pythagoreans*. Great Britain: Cambridge University Press, 1962.

——. *A History of Greek Philosophy Vol. II: The Presocratic tradition from Parmenides to Democritus*. Cambridge: Cambridge University Press, 1965.

Hales, Steven D. "Nietzsche on Logic" in *Philosophy and Phenomenological Research*, 56/4, (Dec., 1996).

Hanson, Victor Davis. *The Other Greeks: The Family Farm and the Agrarian Roots of Western Civilization*. New York: Free Press, 1995.

Hartford Institute For Religion Research (www.hartfordinstitute.org).

Hull, Bruce R. *Infinite Nature*. Chicago, IL: University of Chicago Press, 2006.

Hume, David. *An Enquiry Concerning the Principles of Morals*, ed. Niditch. 3rd. ed. Oxford: Oxford University Press, 1975.

——. *Dialogues Concerning Natural Religion: The Posthumous Essays on the Immortality of The Soul and Suicide*, ed. Richard Popkin. Hackett Publishing, 1980.

——. *An Enquiry Concerning the Principles of Morals*, ed. J.B. Schneewind. Indianapolis, IN: Hackett Publishing, 1983.

_____. *The Natural History of Religion*, ed. John M. Robertson. London: A. and H. Bradlaugh Bonner, 1889.

_____ *Dialogues Concerning Natural Religion*

Irenaeus. *Against Heresies.*

Janowski, Zbigniew. *Cartesian Theodicy: Descartes' Quest for Certitude.* Norwell, MA: Kluwer Academic Publishers, 2000.

Kant, Immanuel. *Religion Within the Limits of Reason Alone.*

Lackey, Michael. "Killing God, Liberating the "Subject"" in *Nietzsche and Post-God Freedom* Michael Lackey. Source: *Journal of the History of Ideas*, 60/4, (Oct., 1999).

Laing, Bertram M. "The Metaphysics of Nietzsche's Immoralism" *The Philosophical Review*, 24/4, (Jul., 1915).

Lanctantius. *On the Anger of God.*

Leiter, Brian. "Nietzsche and the Morality Critics" *Ethics*, 107/2 (Jan., 1997).

_____. "Review of *Nietzsche and Metaphysics* by Peter Poellner," in *Nietzsche's System* by John Richardson. Source: *Mind, New Series*, 107/427, (Jul., 1998).

_____. Routledge *Philosophy Guidebook to Nietzsche on Morality*. New York: Routledge, 2002.

Lewontin, Richard. "Billions and Billions of Demons," *New York Review of Books*, January 9, 1997.

Morris, Ian. "The early polis as city and state," in John Rich and Andrew Wallace-Hadrill eds., *City and Country in the Ancient World*. London: Routledge, 1991.

Nieman, Susan. *Evil in Modern Thought*. Princeton. NJ: Princeton University Press, 2002.

Nola, Robert. "Nietzsche's Theory of Truth and Belief" *Philosophy and Phenomenological Research*, 47/4 (Jun., 1987).

Nussbaum, Charles. "Aesthetics and the Problem of Evil," *Metaphilosophy*, 34/3 (April 2003).

Ott, Craig and Netland, Harold A. *Globalizing Theology*. Grand Rapids, MI: Baker Books, 2006.

Pearson, Keith Ansell and Large, Duncan, eds. *The Nietzsche Reader*. Malden, MA: Blackwell Publishing, 2006.

Pentecost, Dwight. *The Words and Works of Jesus Christ*. Grand Rapids, MI: Zondervan, 1981.

Peters, George. *The Theocratic Kingdom*. Grand Rapids, MI: Kregel, 1979, Vol. 1.

Plato, *Timaeus,* trans. Desmond Lee.

Plotinus. *Enneads*.

Richardson, John and Leiter, Brian, eds. *Nietzsche*. New York: Oxford University Press, 2006.

Rozzi, Ricardo; Hargrove, Eugene; Armesto, Juan J. Armesto; Pickett, Steward; Silander, John Jr. "Natural Drift as a Post-Modern evolutionary metaphor," *Revista Chilena de Historia Natural* 71 (1998) 5-17.

Russell, Bertrand. "Why I Am Not a Christian," March 6, 1927, National Secular Society, South London Branch, at Battersea Town Hall.

Sahakian, William S. *History of Philosophy: From the Earliest Times to the Present.* New York: Barnes and Noble, 1968.

Salter, William MacKintire. "Nietzsche on the Problem of Reality" *Mind, New Series*, 24/96 (Oct., 1915).

_____. "Nietzsche's Attitude to Religion" *The Journal of Philosophy*, 20/4 (Feb. 15, 1923).

Salter, William MacKintire. "Nietzsche's Moral Aim" *International Journal of Ethics*, 25/2 (Jan., 1915).

Scroggie, Graham. *The Gospel of Mark*. Grand Rapids, MI: Zondervan, 1979.

Seneca, *De Brevitate Vitae, XIV*, 1-2. trans. J. W. Basore. Loeb Classical Library, Vol. 254.

Sharif, Mian Mohammed. *A History of Muslim Philosophy*. Wiesbaden: Harrassowitz, 1966.

Shepherd, J. W. *The Christ of the Gospels*. Grand Rapids, MI: Eerdmans, 1946.

Snodgrass, Anthony. "Archeology and the study of the Greek city," in John Rich and Andrew Wallace-Hadrill eds., *City and Country in the Ancient World*. London: Routledge, 1991.

Spinoza, *The Ethics*.

Thomas, Robert and Gundry Stanley. *A Harmony of the Gospels*. Chicago, IL: Moody Press, 1978.

Tillich, Paul. *Systematic Theology*. Chicago: University of Chicago Press, 1963, Vol. 1.

Toussaint, Stanley. *Behold the King: A Study of Matthew*. Portland, OR: Multnomah Press, 1980.

Usher, Robin and Edwards, Richard. *Postmodernism and Education*. New York: Rutledge, 1994.

Van Til, Cornelius. *A Christian Theory of Knowledge*. Philipsburg, NJ: Presbyterian and Reformed, 1969.

Wells, H.G. *The Outline of History*. Garden City, NY: Garden City Books, 1949, Vol. 1.

White, Lynn. "The Historical Roots of Our Ecological Crisis," *Science,* 155 (March 10, 1967), 1203–1207.

Whitelaw, Thomas. *Commentary on John.* Grand Rapids, MI: Kregel, 1993.

Wiercinski, P.A., Dir. *Between the Human and the Divine. Philosophical and Theological Hermeneutics.* Toronto, CA: The Hermeneutic Press, 2002.

Williams, Bernard. *Ethics and the Limits of Philosophy.* Cambridge, MA: Harvard University Press, 1985.

www.ingramcontent.com/pod-product-compliance
Lightning Source LLC
Chambersburg PA
CBHW070934180426

43192CB00039B/2180